The Canadian Writer's World

ESSAYS

The Canadian Writer's World
ESSAYS

Lynne Gaetz
Lionel Groulx College

Suneeti Phadke
St. Jerome College

Toronto

Library and Archives Canada Cataloguing in Publication

Gaetz, Lynne, 1960–
    The Canadian writer's world : essays / Lynne Gaetz, Suneeti Phadke.

Includes index.
ISBN 978-0-13-188656-8

    1. English language—Rhetoric—Textbooks. 2. Editing—Textbooks. 3. Report writing—
Textbooks. I. Phadke, Suneeti, 1961– II. Title.

PE1408.G24 2009   808'.042   C2008-900026-9

ISBN-13: 978-0-13-188656-8
ISBN-10: 0-13-188656-8

Vice President, Editorial Director: Gary Bennett
Acquisitions Editor: Christopher Helsby
Signing Representative: Françoise Dykler
Marketing Manager: Sally Aspinall
Senior Developmental Editor: Joel Gladstone
Production Editor: Richard di Santo
Copy Editor: Ann McInnis
Proofreaders: Anne Holloway, Camille Isaacs
Production Coordinator: Janis Raisen
Composition: Christine Velakis, Susan MacGregor
Photo and Permissions Research: Lisa Brant
Art Director: Julia Hall
Interior Design: Gail Ferreira Ng-A-Kien
Cover Design: Kerrin Hands
Cover Image: istock

1 2 3 4 5   12 11 10 09 08

Printed and bound in the United States of America.

Brief Contents

Contents

Preface

About the First Edition of *The Canadian Writer's World*: *Essays*

The Canadian Writer's World can help students produce writing that is technically correct and rich in content. The book's unique features will appeal to both native and non-native English speakers with varying skill levels.

A Research-Based Approach

From the onset of the development process, we have comprehensively researched the needs and desires of current developmental writing instructors. We met with many instructors, asking for their opinions and insights regarding (1) the challenges posed by their courses, (2) the needs of today's ever-changing student population, and (3) the ideas and features we are proposing in order to provide them and you with a more effective teaching and learning tool. Pearson Education Canada also commissioned detailed manuscript reviews from instructors, asking them to analyze and evaluate the manuscript (they are individually acknowledged at the end of this preface). These reviewers identified numerous ways in which we could refine and enhance our key features. Their invaluable feedback was incorporated throughout *The Canadian Writer's World*. The text you are seeing is truly the product of a successful partnership between the authors, publisher, and well over 100 developmental writing instructors.

How We Organized *The Canadian Writer's World*

The Canadian Writer's World presents essay development in five parts.

Part I: The Writing Process teaches students (1) how to formulate ideas (Exploring), (2) how to expand, organize and present those ideas in a piece of writing (Developing), and (3) how to polish writing so that students convey their message as clearly as possible (Revising and Editing). Students will find the step-by-step approach clear and easy to follow.

Part II: Essay Patterns gives students a solid overview of the patterns of development. Using the same easy-to-understand process (Exploring, Developing, and Revising and Editing), each chapter explains how to convey ideas using specific writing patterns.

Part III: Other Writing Skills covers topics ranging from paraphrasing and summarizing to the research essay. This section also gives students tips on studying for and preparing essay exams.

Part IV: The Editing Handbook is a thematic grammar handbook. In each chapter, the examples correspond to a section theme, such as The Forces of Nature or Human Development. As students work through the chapters, they hone their grammar and editing skills while gaining knowledge about a variety of topics. In addition to helping retain interest in the grammar practices, the thematic material provides a spark that ignites new ideas that students can apply to their writing.

Part V: Reading Strategies and Selections offers tips, readings, and follow-up questions. Students learn how to write by observing and dissecting what they read. The readings contain themes that are found in Part IV: The Editing Handbook, thereby providing more fodder for generating writing ideas.

How *The Canadian Writer's World* Meets Students' Diverse Needs

The Canadian Writers World: Essays engages students in a systematic approach to the basics of essay writing (through the steps of exploring, developing, revising and editing). At the same time, it enhances cultural literacy by encouraging students to think about the world and their place in it through examples that expand the students' knowledge of history, literature, arts, science, and workplace issues. In addition to this, the content, form, structure, and pedagogy of the text are designed with the recognition and understanding that the Canadian classroom is made up of many different cultural communities that include native English speakers, non-standard English speakers, and non-native speakers. The various needs of these communities are addressed inherently in this text without marginalization.

Seamless Coverage for Non-native Speakers

Instructors in our focus groups noted the growing number of non-native/ESL speakers enrolling in developmental writing courses. Although some of these students have special needs relating to the writing process, many of you still have a large portion of native speakers in your course whose more traditional needs must also be satisfied. In order to meet the challenge of this rapidly changing dynamic, we have carefully implemented and integrated content throughout to assist both native and non-native speakers.

The Canadian Writer's World does not have separate ESL boxes, ESL chapters, or tacked-on ESL appendices. Instead, information that traditionally poses a challenge to non-native speakers is woven seamlessly throughout the book. In our extensive experience teaching writing to both native and non-native speakers of English, we have learned that both groups learn best when they are not distracted by ESL labels. With the seamless approach, non-native speakers do not feel self-conscious and segregated, and native speakers do not tune out to detailed explanations that may also benefit them. Many of these traditional problem areas receive more coverage than you would find in other developmental writing textbooks, arming the instructor with the material to effectively meet the needs of non-native speakers.

Issue-Focused Thematic Grammar

In our survey of the marketplace, many of you indicated that one of your primary challenges is finding materials that are engaging to students in a contemporary context. This is especially true in grammar instruction. **Students come to the course with varying skill levels**, and many students are simply not interested in grammar. To address this challenge, we have introduced **issue-focused thematic grammar** into *The Canadian Writer's World*.

Each section in Part IV revolves around a common theme. These themes include Conflict, Urban Development, International Trade, Forces of Nature, Flora and Fauna, and Human Development

and Creativity. Each chapter, within the sections, includes issues related to the theme. The thematic approach enables students to broaden their awareness of important subjects, allowing them to infuse their writing with reflection and insight. Also, we believe and our reviewers concur that the themes make grammar more engaging. And the more engaging grammar is, the more likely students will retain key concepts.

It is important to teach grammar in the context of the writing process. Students should not think that grammar is an isolated exercise. Therefore, **each grammar chapter includes a Grammar Snapshot activity**, and the end of each grammar chapter contains writing prompts and readings links that relate to the chapter's theme.

What Tools Can Help Students Get the Most from *The Canadian Writer's World*?

Overwhelmingly, reviewers asked that both a larger number and a greater diversity of exercises and activities be incorporated into a new text. In response to this feedback, we have developed and tested the following items in *The Canadian Writer's World*. These tools form the pedagogical backbone to the book, and we are confident they will help your students become better writers.

Hints

In each chapter, **Hint** boxes highlight important writing and grammar points. Hints are useful for all students, but many will be particularly helpful for non-native speakers. For example, in Chapter 8: Description, there is a hint about how to create a dominant impression, and in Chapter 19: Sentence Combining, there is one about how to recognize Compound Sentences.

Writer's Desk

Parts I, II, and III include **Writer's Desk** exercises that help students to practise all stages and steps of the writing process. Students begin with prewriting and then progress to developing, organizing (using essay plans), drafting, and finally, revising and editing to create a final draft.

Essay Patterns "At Work"

To help students appreciate the relevance of their writing tasks, Chapters 6–14 begin with an authentic writing sample. Titled **Illustration at Work**, **Narration at Work**, and so on, this feature offers a glimpse of the writing patterns people use in different types of workplace writing.

Vocabulary Boost

In Chapters 6–14, the Vocabulary Boost is a collaborative activity that helps students to broaden their vocabulary.

Checklist

Major points are reviewed in the Checklist box, which appears at the end of each chapter.

Chat Rooms

Students who learn best by collaborating and sharing ideas will appreciate the discussion and group work activities in the Chat Room in each chapter of Part II: Essay Patterns. Each activity introduces the students to the writing pattern in a fun and non-intimidating way.

Writer's Room

Writer's Room boxes contain writing activities that correspond to general, academic, and workplace topics. Some prompts are brief to allow students to freely form ideas while others are expanded to give students more direction.

In Part II: Essay Patterns, students can respond to thought-provoking quotations. To help students see how grammar is not isolated from the writing process, there are also **Writer's Room** activities in each chapter in Part IV: The Editing Handbook.

Acknowledgments

Many people have helped us produce *The Canadian Writer's World*. First and foremost, we would like to thank our students for inspiring us and providing us with invaluable feedback. Their words and insights pervade this book.

We also benefited greatly from the insightful comments and suggestions from the many reviewers who provided feedback and suggestions during the development of this edition. Our colleagues' feedback was invaluable and helped shape *The Canadian Writer's World* content, focus, and organization. They include the following:

Justina Abenina, George Brown College

Sue Adams, Sheridan College

Wendy Chan, Centennial College

Mary Gelinas, St. Lawrence College

John Hampton, Camosun College

Chandra Hodgson, Humber College

Paul Hutchinson, Niagara College of Applied Arts and Technology

Marlene Lecompte, Seneca College

Peter Miller, Seneca College

Jean Mills, Conestoga College

Patricia Morgan, Humber College

Melanie Rabishaw, Loyalist College

Lara Sauer, George Brown College

Trisha Yeo, George Brown College

Katherine Yuk, Seneca College

We are indebted to the team of dedicated professionals at Pearson Education Canada who have helped make this project a reality. They have boosted our spirits and have believed in us every step of the way. Special thanks to Joel Gladstone for his magnificent job in polishing this book and to Patty Riediger for encouraging us to write this textbook for Canadian students, trusting our instincts and enthusiastically propelling us forward. We would also like to thank the following members of the Pearson team who helped complete this book: Chris Helsby, Sally Aspinall, Richard di Santo, Janis Raisen, and Ann McInnis.

Finally, we would like to dedicate this book to our husbands and children who supported us and who patiently put up with our long hours on the computer. Manu, Octavio, and Natalia continually encouraged us. We especially appreciate the help and sacrifices of Diego, Becky, Kiran, and Meghana.

Lynne Gaetz and Suneeti Phadke
January 2008

A Note to Students

Your knowledge, ideas, and opinions are important. The ability to clearly communicate those ideas is invaluable in your personal, academic, and professional life. When your writing is error-free, readers will focus on your message, and you will be able to persuade, inform, entertain, or inspire them. *The Canadian Writer's World* includes strategies that will help you improve your written communication. Quite simply, when you become a better writer, you become a better communicator. It is our greatest wish for *The Canadian Writer's World* to make you excited about writing, communicating, and learning.

Enjoy!

Lynne Gaetz and Suneeti Phadke

The Canadian
Writer's World
ESSAYS

The Writing Process

EXPLORING

Step 1 : Think about your topic.

Step 2 : Think about your audience.

Step 3 : Think about your purpose.

Step 4 : Try exploring strategies.

DEVELOPING

Step 1 : Express your main idea.

Step 2 : Develop your supporting ideas.

Step 3 : Make a plan or an outline.

Step 4 : Write your first draft.

REVISING AND EDITING

Step 1 : Revise for unity.

Step 2 : Revise for adequate support.

Step 3 : Revise for coherence.

Step 4 : Revise for style.

Step 5 : Edit for technical errors.

The writing process is a series of steps that most writers follow to advance from thinking about a topic to preparing the final draft. Generally, you should follow the process step by step. However, sometimes you may find that your steps overlap. For example, you might do some editing before you revise, or you might think about your main idea while you are prewriting. The important thing is to make sure that you have done all the steps of the process before preparing your final draft.

Before you begin the next chapters, review the steps in the writing process.

Exploring

*How much has to be explored and discarded before
reaching the naked flesh of feeling.*

—CLAUDE DEBUSSY, *French composer*

Visualizing the Paragraph and the Essay

A **paragraph** is a series of sentences that are about one central idea. Paragraphs can stand alone, or they can be part of a longer work such as an essay, a letter, or a report. A paragraph contains a **topic sentence** that expresses the main idea and **body sentences** that develop that idea. Most paragraphs end with a **concluding sentence** that brings the paragraph to a satisfactory close.

> The **topic sentence** ➤
> *introduces the subject of
> the paragraph and shows
> the writer's attitude
> towards the subject.*
>
> *The **body** of the ➤
> paragraph contains
> details that support the
> topic sentence.*
>
> *The paragraph ends with ➤
> a **concluding sentence.***

People learn negotiation skills through sports. Children playing informally at recess must decide what game to play and what rules to follow. They must negotiate with the other children about game boundaries. Every day, my daughter comes home from school telling me that she and her friends have invented a new game. The children make up the rules of the new game by bargaining with each other. In team sports, athletes must make choices about who will play a certain position or which player will play for how much time. Such decisions require negotiation skills, which help people in other areas of their lives.

An **essay** contains several paragraphs that revolve around one central idea. The introductory paragraph includes a **thesis statement** expressing the main idea of the essay. **Body paragraphs** support the thesis statement. Finally, the essay closes with a **concluding paragraph** that wraps up the main ideas the writer has presented throughout the paper.

Sports: A Vital Necessity

1   Humans have been playing sports since the beginning of civilization. Cave art in France and Africa depicts people playing archery, wrestling, and horse racing. Indigenous North Americans engaged in team sports such as lacrosse or running. The ancient Greeks, Romans, Chinese, and Egyptians enjoyed many physical activities. Similarly, most people enjoy sports today. Young girls and boys play in soccer leagues, or they may play a baseball game during recess. Adults also play or watch sports. Athletic activities are very necessary to people's well-being. In fact, sports help people to develop good character because they learn many skills.

2   First, when people play games, they learn how to make friends. In Canada, according to the Canadian Heritage Sport Canada website, 34 percent of all Canadians engage in some form of physical activity three or more times a week and approximately 69 percent of youth participate in some type of exercise program. Whether it is exercising informally or playing a team sport, people interact with strangers. Going to the gym, participating in a hiking club, and playing a team sport bring different people into close personal contact with each other. These strangers all have something in common. They like to engage in the same activity, so most people end up developing friendships.

3   People learn negotiation skills through sports. Children playing informally at recess must decide what game to play and what rules to follow. They must negotiate with the other children about game boundaries. Every day, my daughter comes home from school telling me that she and her friends have invented a new game. The children make up the rules of the new game by bargaining with each other. In team sports, athletes must make choices about who will play a certain position or which player will play for how much time. Such decisions require negotiation skills, which help people in other areas of their lives.

4   Players learn how to deal with disappointments and pressure. Disappointment about the level of play or an important loss is common for most people involved in sports. For example, many Olympic athletes are very discouraged when they lose, but most continue training to become even better. Players on high school and college teams also learn to win and lose. For example, my neighbour's son plays on the volleyball team. His team had a winning streak, but the team lost in the semifinals. All the players on the team were extremely disappointed, but they vowed to play better in the next season. Sports teach people how to win and lose gracefully. Such a lesson is invaluable in life.

5   People build character through sports. In fact, they learn many valuable life lessons, including social skills. They learn practical skills such as how to negotiate. As Jeff Kemp, in his article "A Lesson in Humility," says, "In fact, sports teach important moral lessons that athletes can apply on and off the playing field." So don't just sit around at home; go and participate in a sport.

Essay-length prose is the backbone of written communication in and out of college. Throughout your life, you will use principles of essay writing in various formats, including research papers, emails, reports, formal letters, newsletters, and webpages. Essays help you explore ideas and share those thoughts with others. By reading through this text and completing the many helpful writing practices in it, you will significantly improve your chances of getting more out of your courses and jobs. Enjoy the journey!

The title gives a hint about the essay's topic.

The introductory paragraph introduces the essay's topic and contains its thesis statement.

The thesis statement contains the essay's topic and its controlling idea.

Each body paragraph begins with a topic sentence that supports the thesis statement.

Each body paragraph contains details that support the topic sentence.

The concluding paragraph brings the essay to a satisfactory close.

Key Steps in Exploring

Perhaps you have been given a writing assignment and then stared at the blank page, thinking, "I don't know what to write?" Well, it is not necessary to write a good essay immediately. There are certain things that you can do to help you focus on your topic.

Understand Your Assignment

As soon as you are given an assignment, make sure that you understand what your task is. Answer the following questions about the assignment.

- How many words or pages does the assignment require?
- What is the due date for the assignment?
- Are there any special qualities my writing should include? For example, should my writing be double-spaced? Should I include a list of works cited?

After you have considered your assignment, then think about your topic, audience, and purpose.

There are four steps in the exploring stage of the writing process.

EXPLORING

STEP 1 ——➤ **Think about your topic.** Determine what you will write about.

STEP 2 ——➤ **Think about your audience.** Consider your intended readers and what interests them.

STEP 3 ——➤ **Think about your purpose.** Ask yourself why you want to write.

STEP 4 ——➤ **Try exploring strategies.** Experiment with different ways to generate ideas.

Topic

Sometimes your topic has been assigned and is already very specific. At other times, it may be very general. For example, if your assigned topic is "food," narrow it so that you can focus on something specific about food. You might write about the dangers of diets or how to cook a certain type of cuisine. You might describe the symbolism of food in a literary work or try to explain the chemical makeup of a specific food. When you are given a general topic, find an angle that interests you and make it more specific.

To find a focus for your topic, ask yourself the following questions.

- What is it about the topic that interests me? Will it interest other readers?
- Do I have special knowledge about the topic?
- Does anything about the topic arouse my emotions?

Audience

Your **audience** is your intended reader. In your personal, academic, and professional life, you will often write for a specific audience; therefore, you can keep your readers interested by adapting your tone and vocabulary to suit them.

Tone is your general attitude or feeling towards a topic. You might write in a tone that is humorous, sarcastic, serious, friendly, or casual. For example, imagine you are preparing an invitation to an event. To determine the design, phrasing, and format, you need to know some important information about your recipients. What are their ages and lifestyles? Are they mostly males or females? Would they prefer printed invitations or email invitations? Questions like these can help you connect with your audience.

Knowing your readers is especially important when preparing academic or workplace documents. When you consider your audience, ask yourself the following questions:

- Who will read my assignment—an instructor, other students, or people outside the college?
- Do the readers have a lot of knowledge about my topic?
- How will I need to adjust my vocabulary, writing style, or tone to appeal to my readers?

In academic writing, your audience is generally your instructor or other students, unless your instructor specifically asks you to write for another audience, such as the general public, your employer, or a family member.

> **HINT** **Instructor as the Audience**
>
> Your instructor represents a general audience. Such an audience of educated readers will expect you to reveal what you have learned or what you have understood about the topic. Your ideas should be presented in a clear and organized manner. Do not leave out information because you assume that your instructor is an expert in the field. Also, you should write in standard English. In other words, try to use correct grammar, sentence structure, and vocabulary.

PRACTICE I

As you read the following messages, consider the differences in both the tone and the vocabulary the writer uses. Then answer the questions that follow.

A

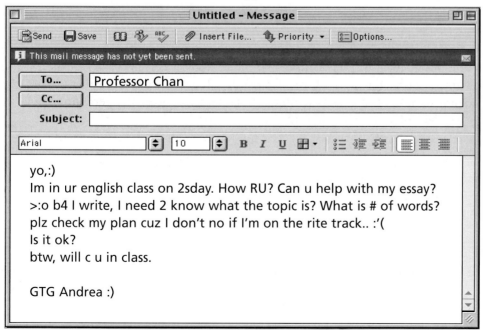

yo,:)
Im in ur english class on 2sday. How RU? Can u help with my essay?
>:o b4 I write, I need 2 know what the topic is? What is # of words?
plz check my plan cuz I don't no if I'm on the rite track.. :'(
Is it ok?
btw, will c u in class.

GTG Andrea :)

B

```
┌──────────────────────────────────────────────────────────────────┐
│ ▢         ═══════════════ Untitled – Message ═══════════════   ▣▤ │
├──────────────────────────────────────────────────────────────────┤
│  📨Send  💾Save  ▦  ⬧  ᴬᴮᶜ⬧   📎 Insert File...  ⬆Priority ▾  ▤Options... │
├──────────────────────────────────────────────────────────────────┤
│ ℹ This mail message has not yet been sent.                     ✉  │
├──────────────────────────────────────────────────────────────────┤
│  ┌───────┐  ┌─────────────────────────────────────────────────┐   │
│  │  To...│  │ Professor Chan                                  │   │
│  └───────┘  └─────────────────────────────────────────────────┘   │
│  ┌───────┐  ┌─────────────────────────────────────────────────┐   │
│  │  Cc...│  │                                                 │   │
│  └───────┘  └─────────────────────────────────────────────────┘   │
│  Subject: │  ┌─────────────────────────────────────────────────┐  │
│           └──┤                                                 │  │
│              └─────────────────────────────────────────────────┘  │
├──────────────────────────────────────────────────────────────────┤
│ Arial             ⬆⬇ │ 10 ⬆⬇ │ B I U ▦▾ │ ⣿⣿ ⬧ ⬧ │ ▤ ▤ ▤       │
├──────────────────────────────────────────────────────────────────┤
```

Dear Professor Chan

I am in your Tuesday morning English class. I have started working on my essay and have prepared an essay plan, but I am not sure if my thesis statement is appropriate and focused enough. Could you please look at my plan and let me know if I am on the right track? Also, could you please remind me of the length of the assignment?

Thank you,

Reginald Harper

1. Why is the language inappropriate in the first instant message?

   _____

   _____

2. What judgments might the instructor make about the two students based on the messages?

   _____

   _____

   _____

Purpose

Your **purpose** is your reason for writing. Keeping your purpose in mind will help you focus your writing.

When you consider your purpose, ask yourself the following questions.

- Is my goal to **entertain**? Do I want to tell a story?
- Is my goal to **persuade**? Do I want to convince readers that my point of view is the correct one?
- Is my goal to **inform**? Do I want to explain something or give information about a topic?

It is possible to write for a combination of reasons. In fact, most essays have more than one purpose. For example, an essay describing a personal experience with fraud could also inform readers about protecting themselves from identity theft, or an essay describing how the heart pumps blood could simultaneously persuade readers to reconsider smoking.

> **HINT General and Specific Purposes**
>
> Your **general purpose** is to entertain, to inform, or to persuade. Your **specific purpose** is your more precise reason for writing. For example, imagine that you have to write about an election. You can have the following general and specific purposes.
>
> **General purpose:**   to inform
>
> **Specific purpose:**   to compare platforms of two different candidates

PRACTICE 2

The following selections are all about food; however, each excerpt has a different purpose, has been written for a different audience, and has been taken from a different source. Read each selection carefully. Then underline any language clues (words or phrases) that help you identify its source, audience, and purpose. Finally, answer the questions that follow each selection.

EXAMPLE:

I just made my very first dessert. It looks <u>awesome</u>. I hope it tastes alright. I   ◄ *slang*
almost <u>freaked out</u> when I realized I forgot to turn the oven on. My instructor   ◄ *slang*
is <u>super</u>, and he's <u>got a great sense of humour</u> with me and the other students.   ◄ *slang, informal tone*
Next, I am going to try to make a more complicated dessert.

What is the most likely source of this paragraph?

    a. website article   (b.) personal letter   c. textbook   d. memoir

What is its primary purpose? _____ *To inform* _____

Who is the audience? _____ *Friend or family member* _____

1. I went out with my old friends Nuzhat Ahmad and Ayla, as the three of us often did, in a comradeship of girlhood. We went driving to Bagh-e-Jinnah, formerly known as Lawrence Gardens, located opposite the Governor's House along the Mall in Lahore. We were trying to locate the best *gol guppa* vendor in town and stopped by to test the new stand in Lawrence Gardens. Gol guppas are a strange food: I have never located an equivalent to them or their culinary situation. They are an outdoor food, a passing whim, and no one would dream of recreating their frivolity inside his or her own kitchen. A gol guppa is a small hollow oval of the lightest pastry that is dipped into a fiery liquid sauce made of tamarind and cayenne and lemon and cold water. It is evidently a food invented as a joke, in a moment of good humour.

What is the most likely source of this paragraph?

    a. website article   b. personal letter   c. textbook   d. memoir

What is its primary purpose? _____

Who is the audience? _____

2. Eat regularly. Eating is one of life's great pleasures, and it is important to take time to stop, relax, and enjoy mealtimes and snacks. Scheduling eating times also ensures that meals are not missed, resulting in missed nutrients that are often not compensated for by subsequent meals. This is especially important for schoolchildren, adolescents, and the elderly.

What is the most likely source of this paragraph?

    a. website article   b. personal letter   c. textbook   d. memoir

What is its primary purpose? _____

Who is the audience? _____

3. About 5,000 years ago, another revolution in technology was taking place in the Middle East, one that would end up changing the entire world. This was the discovery of agriculture, large-scale cultivation using ploughs harnessed to animals or more powerful energy sources. So important was the invention of the animal-drawn plough, along with other breakthroughs of the period—including irrigation, the wheel, writing, numbers, and the use of various metals—that this moment in history is often called "the dawn of civilization."

What is the most likely source of this paragraph?

    a. website article   b. personal letter   c. textbook   d. memoir

What is its primary purpose? _____

Who is the audience? _____

Exploring Strategies

After you determine your topic, audience, and purpose, try some **exploring strategies**—also known as **prewriting strategies**—to help get your ideas flowing. Four common strategies are *freewriting*, *brainstorming*, *questioning*, and *clustering*. It is not necessary to do all of the strategies explained in this chapter. Find the strategy that works best for you.

You can do both general and focused prewriting. If you have writer's block, and do not know what to write about, use **general prewriting** to come up with possible writing topics. Then, after you have chosen a topic, use **focused prewriting** to find an angle of the topic that is interesting and which could be developed in your essay.

HINT **When to Use Exploring Strategies**

You can use the exploring strategies at any stage of the writing process.

- To find a topic
- To narrow a broad topic
- To generate ideas about your topic
- To generate supporting details

Narrow Your Topic

An essay has one main idea. If your topic is too broad, you might find it difficult to write a focused essay about it. For example, imagine that you are given the topic "mistakes." If the topic is not narrowed, it will lead to a meandering and unfocused essay. To narrow the topic, think about types of errors, examples of errors, or people who make errors. A more focused topic could be "mistakes newlyweds make" or "mistakes first-year college students make." Find one angle of the topic that you know a lot about and that you personally find interesting. If you have a lot to say, and you think the topic is compelling, chances are that your reader will also like your topic.

Review the following examples of general and narrowed topics.

Topic	Narrowed Topic
jobs	preparing for a job interview
music	protest songs from the past and present

To help narrow and develop your topic, you can use the following exploring strategies.

Freewriting

Freewriting gives you the freedom to write without stopping for a set period of time. The goal of this exercise is to record the first thoughts that come to mind. If you run out of ideas, don't stop writing. Simply fill in the pause with phrases like "blah blah blah" or "What else can I write?" As you write, do not be concerned with word choice, grammar, or spelling. If you use a computer, let your ideas flow and do not worry about typing mistakes. You could try typing without looking at the screen.

Alicia's Freewriting College student Alicia Parera thought about mistakes college students make. During her freewriting, she wrote down everything that came to mind.

> Mistakes students make? Not doing the homework. Not asking for help when they need it? I sometimes feel shy to speak up when I don't understand something. What else? Some college students leave college early. Why do they leave? Tim. He only stayed for one semester. I don't think he was ready for college life. He treated college like high school and always came late. Goofed off. Cut class. What else? What about Amanda who had that family crisis? She had to leave when her mother was sick. Of course, finances. It's tough. Sometimes I go crazy trying to keep up with my job, friends, schoolwork. It's really hard.

Brainstorming

Brainstorming is like freewriting, except that you create a list of ideas, and you can take the time to stop and think when you create your list. As you think about the topic, write down words or phrases that come to mind. Do not worry about grammar or spelling; the point is to generate ideas.

Alicia's Example of Brainstorming

Topic: Mistakes that college students make
- party too much
- not doing homework
- feeling too shy to speak with instructors when they have problems
- getting too stressed
- choosing the wrong career path
- some students don't know what they want to do
- feeling intimidated in class

Questioning

Another way to generate ideas about a topic is to ask yourself a series of questions and write responses to them. The questions can help you define and narrow your topic. One common way to do this is to ask yourself *who, what, when, where, why,* and *how* questions.

Alicia's Example of Questioning

Who makes the most mistakes?	first-year students because they aren't always prepared for college life
Why do some students miss classes?	feel like there are no consequences, don't feel interested in their program
When do most students drop out?	administrators say that November is the most common month that students drop out
How should colleges encourage students who are at risk of dropping out?	give more financial aid offer career counselling
Where can students get help?	guidance counsellors, professors, friends, family, professionals doing student's dream job
Why is it an important topic?	new students can learn about pitfalls to avoid, administrators can develop strategies for helping students

Clustering

Clustering is like drawing a word map; ideas are arranged in a visual image. To begin, write your topic in the middle of the page and draw a box or a circle around it. That idea will lead to another, so write the second idea and draw a line connecting it to your topic. Keep writing, circling, and connecting ideas until you have groups or "clusters" of them on your page.

Alicia's Example of Clustering

Writer's Desk **Exploring**

Explore the next three topics. Use a different exploring strategy for each topic. You can choose to do freewriting, brainstorming, questioning, or clustering.

stereotypes   mistakes   volunteer work

Journal and Portfolio Writing

Keeping a Journal

You may write for work or school, but you can also practise writing for pleasure. One way to practise your writing is to keep a journal. A **journal** can be a book, computer file, or even a blog where you record your thoughts, opinions, ideas, and impressions. Journal writing gives you a chance to practise your writing without worrying about the audience and what they might think about it. It also gives you a source of material when you want to write about a topic of your choice.

In your journal, you can write about any topic that appeals to you. Here are some possible topics for journal writing.

- Anything related to your personal life, such as your feelings about your career goals, personal problems and solutions, opinions about your courses, your reflections about past and future decisions, or feelings about your job
- Your reactions to controversies in your family, neighbourhood, college, city, country, or world
- Your reflections on the opinions and philosophies of others, including your friends or people whom you read about in your courses

Keeping a Portfolio

A **writing portfolio** is a place (a binder or an electronic file folder) where you keep samples of all of your writing. The purpose of keeping a portfolio is to have a record of your writing progress. In your portfolio, keep all drafts of your writing assignments. When you work on new assignments, review your previous work in your portfolio. Identify your main problems and try not to repeat the same errors.

 Writer's Room Topics to Explore

Writing Activity

Choose one of the following topics, or choose your own topic. Then generate ideas about the topic. You may want to try the suggested exploring strategy.

General Topics

1. Try freewriting about people who have helped you succeed.

2. Brainstorm a list of thoughts about different types of fear.

3. Ask and answer questions about voting.

4. Create a cluster diagram about a useful invention.

Academic and Work-Related Topics

5. Try freewriting about an unforgettable day at work or college. Include any emotions, or details that come to mind.

6. Brainstorm a list of ideas about career goals.

7. Ask and answer questions about bosses.

8. Create a cluster diagram about pressures students face.

CHECKLIST: EXPLORING

When you explore a topic, ask yourself these questions.

- What is my **topic**? Consider what you will write about.
- Who is my **audience**? Think about your intended reader.
- What is my **purpose**? Determine your reason for writing.
- Which exploring strategy will I use? You could try one of these strategies, or a combination of strategies.
  - **Freewriting** is writing without stopping for a limited period of time.
  - **Brainstorming** is making a list.
  - **Questioning** is asking and answering a series of questions.
  - **Clustering** is drawing a word map.

CHAPTER

2

Developing the Main Idea

*The skill of writing is to create a context in which
other people can think.*

—EDWIN SCHLOSSBERG, *cultural historian*

Key Steps in Developing the Main Idea

In Chapter 1, you learned how to consider your reading audience and your purposes for writing. You also practised using exploring strategies to formulate ideas. In this chapter, you will focus on developing a main idea that can be expanded into a complete essay. There are two key steps in this process.

DEVELOPING THE MAIN IDEA

STEP 1 ────▶ Write a thesis statement. Write a statement that expresses the main idea of the piece of writing.

STEP 2 ────▶ Develop the supporting ideas. Find facts, examples, or anecdotes that best support your main idea. Choose the best ideas, and place them in a logical order.

Writing a Thesis Statement

The **thesis** is your main idea that you want to express. A good thesis statement presents the topic of the essay, and it includes a **controlling idea** that expresses the writer's opinion, attitude, or feeling about the topic. The controlling idea can appear at the beginning or end of the thesis statement.

       topic   controlling idea

Art courses <u>should be compulsory in all high schools.</u>

             controlling idea   topic

<u>School districts should stop funding</u> **art courses.**

PRACTICE 1

Circle the topic and underline the controlling idea in each thesis statement.

EXAMPLE:

(Insomnia) is caused by several factors.

1. Three strategies can help you become a better public speaker.

2. Moving to a new country was a traumatic experience for me.

3. There should not be racial profiling at borders.

4. School uniforms should be compulsory in public schools.

5. There are several reasons for Australia's compulsory voting system.

6. Phishing is a dangerous Internet scam.

7. My office is an obstacle course.

8. There are three types of annoying office workers.

Writing an Effective Thesis Statement

When you develop your thesis statement, ask yourself the following questions to help you avoid thesis statement errors.

1. Is my thesis a complete statement?

Ensure that your thesis does not express an incomplete idea or more than one idea. A thesis statement should reveal one complete thought.

Incomplete:	Allergies: so annoying.
	(This is not a complete statement.)
More than one idea:	There are many types of allergens, and allergies affect people in different ways.
	(This statement contains two distinct ideas. Each idea could become an essay.)
Thesis statement:	Doctors suggest several steps you can take to relieve symptoms related to pet allergies.

2. Does my thesis statement have a controlling idea?

Rather than announcing the topic, your thesis statement should make a point about the topic. It should have a controlling idea that expresses your attitude or feeling about the topic. Avoid phrases such as *My topic is* or *I will write about*.

Announces:	I will write about computers.
	(This sentence says nothing relevant about the topic. The reader does not know what the point of the essay is.)
Thesis statement:	When Microsoft develops a new operating system, there are political, financial, and environmental consequences.

3. Can I support my thesis statement in an essay?

Your thesis statement should express an idea that you can support in an essay. If it is too narrow, you will find yourself with nothing to say. If it is too broad, you will have an endless composition.

Too broad:	There are many childless couples in our world.
	(This topic needs a more specific and narrow focus.)
Too narrow:	The average age of first-time mothers is approximately twenty-six years old.
	(It would be difficult to write an entire essay about this fact.)
Thesis statement:	Many couples are choosing to remain childless for several reasons.

4. **Does my thesis statement make a valid and interesting point?**
   Your thesis statement should make a valid point. It should not be a vaguely worded statement or an obvious and uninteresting comment.

Vague:	Censorship is a big problem.
	(For whom is it a big problem?)
Obvious:	The Internet is important.
	(So what? Everyone knows this.)
Invalid:	The Internet controls our lives.
	(This statement is difficult to believe or prove.)
Thesis statement:	The Internet has become a powerful presence in our personal, social, and working lives.

PRACTICE 2

Examine each statement.

- Write **TS** if it is an effective thesis statement.
- Write **I** if it is an incomplete idea.
- Write **M** if it contains more than one complete idea.
- Write **A** if it is an announcement.

EXAMPLE: This essay is about spousal abuse.   _A_

1. The high price of oil.   ____

2. My hometown has a great sports stadium, but it needs to give more help to female athletes.   ____

3. Nursing is physically demanding.

                                                                   ____

4. In this paper, I will discuss global warming.   ____

5. My subject is the torture of war prisoners.   ____

6. There are many excellent commercials on television, but some are too violent.   ____

7. A job loss can actually have positive effects on a person's life.   ____

8. The problem of negative election advertisements.   ____

PRACTICE 3

Examine each statement.

- Write **TS** if it is a complete thesis statement.
- Write **V** if it is too vague.
- Write **O** if it is statement is too obvious.

EXAMPLE: Canadians are less nationalistic.   _V_

1. Mexico City has a large population.   _____

2. We had a major problem.   _____

3. Some adult children have legitimate reasons for moving back into their parents' homes.   _____

4. The roads are very crowded during holiday periods.   _____

5. There are several ways to do this.   _____

6. Children in our culture are changing.   _____

PRACTICE 4

Examine each pair of sentences.

- Write **B** if the sentence is too broad.
- Write **TS** if the sentence is an effective thesis statement.

EXAMPLE:

Plants can help people.   _B_

Learning to care for plants gave me unexpected pleasure.   _TS_

1. Music is important around the world.   _____

   Some simple steps can help musicians successfully promote their music.   _____

2. My neighbourhood is being transformed by youth gangs.   _____

   Violence is a big problem in our world.   _____

3. My life has been filled with mistakes.   _____

   My jealousy, insecurity, and anger ruined my first relationship.   _____

4. The car accident transformed my life.   _____

   Everybody's life has dramatic moments.   _____

5. Good email manners are important in the business world.   _____

   Good manners are important.   _____

PRACTICE 5

Examine each pair of sentences.

- Write **N** if the sentence is too narrow.
- Write **TS** if the sentence is an effective thesis statement.

EXAMPLE:

I grow coriander in my garden.   N

Learning to care for plants gave me unexpected pleasure.   TS

1. My poodle's name is Short Stop.   _____

   Owning a pet taught me how to be more responsible.   _____

2. Our roads are very icy.   _____

   Driving in the winter requires particular skills.   _____

3. The carjacking rates are increasing in our city.   _____

   There are several ways to prevent yourself from being a
   victim of a carjacking.   _____

4. I hurt myself in various ways during my three days on the beach. _____

   There are many sharp pieces of shell on the local beach.   _____

5. Identical twins who are raised together have distinct personalities. _____

   My twin sisters have similar birthmarks on their necks.   _____

HINT   Writing a Guided Thesis Statement

Give enough details to make your thesis statement interesting. Your instructor may want you to guide the reader through your main points. To do this, mention both your main point and your supporting points in your thesis statement. In other words, your thesis statement provides a map for the readers to follow.

Weak:	My first job taught me many things.
Better:	My first job taught me about the importance of responsibility, organization, and team work.

Revise Your Thesis Statement

A thesis statement is like the foundation that holds up a house. If the thesis statement is weak, it is difficult to construct a solid and compelling essay. Most writers must revise their thesis statements to make them strong and interesting.

When you plan your thesis, ask yourself if you can support it with at least three ideas. If not, you have to modify your thesis statement. To enliven a dead-end statement, ensure that your thesis can answer the questions *why, what,* or *how?* Sometimes, just by adding a few words, a dead-end statement becomes a supportable thesis.

Poor thesis:	Many students drop out of college.
	(How could you develop this into an essay? It is a dead-end statement.)

Better thesis: Students drop out of college for several reasons.
(You could support this thesis with at least three ideas.
This thesis statement answers the question "Why?")

PRACTICE 6

The next thesis statements are weak. First, identify the problem with the
statement (write vague, incomplete, and so on) and ask yourself questions to
determine how you might be able to revise it. Then revise each statement to
make it more forceful and focused.

EXAMPLE:

Spousal abuse is a big problem.

Comments: _Obvious. Vague. For whom is it a problem?_
How is it a problem?

Revision: _Our provincial government should provide better support_
for victims of spousal abuse.

1. I will explain how the family is falling apart.

   Comments: _____

   Revision: _____

   _____

2. I made a difficult decision.

   Comments: _____

   Revision: _____

   _____

3. The media is essential in our lives.

   Comments: _____

   Revision: _____

   _____

4. I am an environmentalist.

   Comments: _____

   Revision: _____

   _____

5. Fashions are too impractical.

   Comments: _____

   Revision: _____

   _____

Overview: Writing a Thesis Statement

To create a forceful thesis statement, you can follow these steps.

Step 1	Step 2	Step 3
Find your topic. You can use exploring strategies to get ideas.	Narrow your topic. Decide what point you want to make.	Develop a thesis statement that you can support with specific evidence. You may need to revise your statement several times.
General topic: Traditions	**Narrowed topic:** Initiation ceremonies	**Initial thesis statement:** Initiation ceremonies serve a valuable function.
Brainstorming: • Commercialization of holidays • My family traditions • Important ceremonies • Why do we celebrate? • Benefits of traditions	**Point I want to make:** Initiation ceremonies can help people make the transition from childhood to adulthood.	**Revised thesis statement:** Meaningful initiation ceremonies benefit individuals, families, and communities.

Writer's Desk **Write Thesis Statements**

Write a thesis statement for each of the following topics. If you explored these topics in Chapter 1, you can use those ideas to help you write your thesis statement. If you have not explored these topics yet, then spend a few minutes exploring them. Use an exploring strategy such as brainstorming to help you define and narrow each topic. Then develop a thesis statement that makes a point and is not too broad or too narrow.

    stereotypes   mistakes   volunteer work

EXAMPLE:

Topic: *mistakes students make*

Narrowed topic: *reasons students drop out*

Thesis statement: *Students may drop out of college because they are unprepared, have financial problems, or experience an emotional crisis.*

Developing the Supporting Ideas

The next step in essay writing is to plan your supporting ideas. Support is not simply a restatement of the thesis. The body paragraphs must develop and prove the validity of the thesis statement.

Each body paragraph has a **topic sentence** that expresses the main idea of the paragraph. Like a thesis statement, a topic sentence must have a controlling idea. Details and examples support the topic sentence. In the following illustration, you can see how the ideas flow in an essay. Topic sentences support the thesis statement, and details bolster the topic sentences. Every idea in the essay is unified and helps to strengthen the essay's thesis.

PRACTICE 7

Write a thesis statement for each group of supporting ideas. Ensure that your thesis statement is clear, makes a point, and is not too broad or too narrow.

EXAMPLE:

Thesis statement: *When you buy a car, make an informed decision.*

    a. Ask family members what type of car they would prefer.

    b. Research on the Internet or in car guides to find information about specific models that interest you.

    c. Keeping your budget in mind, compare new and used cars.

1. Thesis statement: _____

    _____

    a. First, internalize and believe in your sales pitch.

    b. Speak softly, and do not scare the customer with a commanding voice or aggressive mannerisms.

    c. Finally, involve the customer in your sales presentation.

2. Thesis statement: _____

    _____

    a. When boys are in all-male classrooms, teachers can modify their activities to keep the boys' attention.

    b. All-female classrooms permit the female students to focus on the material and show their intelligence.

   c. Unlike co-education classrooms, same-gender classrooms are easier for teachers to control.

3. Thesis statement: _____

_____

   a. Most people under twenty-five years of age simply mimic how their parents or friends vote.

   b. To make an informed choice during an election, people need to have life experiences, which include paying rent and bills.

   c. Twenty-five-year-olds are also less likely to be manipulated by politicians because they have a stronger sense of what they want.

PRACTICE 8

Read the full essay in this practice and then do the following.

1. Determine the topic of each body paragraph. Then write a topic sentence for each body paragraph.

2. Ask yourself what this essay is about. Then compose a thesis statement that sums up the main point of the essay. You might look in the concluding paragraph to get some ideas.

(Introduction) When I was a child, we had a daily routine. My parents both worked, but they got home about 5 p.m. They spent about half an hour unwinding over a cup of coffee. Then they worked together to cook the meal, and by 6:30 they called us children to dinner. We ate and talked together. The same thing cannot be said about many families today.

Thesis statement: _____

_____

(Body 1) Topic sentence: _____

_____

Overtime was not so common in the past, but today many employers expect their workers to spend an extra hour or two in the workplace, so employees don't get home until 7 or 8 p.m. Also, children's lives are filled with more activities than they were in past decades. For example, my daughter takes dance class at 7 p.m., and my son gets together with friends for band practice every evening. They dash through the door at different times, throw a frozen pizza in the microwave, and eat alone.

(Body 2) Topic sentence: _____

_____

The little box certainly is entertaining, but people won't talk about their daily experiences when the television is on. According to Statistics Canada, a growing number of families have placed televisions in the kitchen. "It keeps the sofas and carpets much cleaner if everybody just watches TV in the kitchen," says Sylvie Labelle, a mother of four. Thirteen-year-old Jeremy Labelle mentions, outside his mother's hearing, that he doesn't really talk to anybody in the family. Daily communication, which is an important staple for healthy family life, is disappearing and being replaced by a television set.

(Body 3) Topic sentence: _____

_____

Even a seven-year-old child can heat up his own dinner. Most parents don't want to cook from scratch after a long workday. Our grocery stores and specialty markets understand this need and provide families with a wide variety of frozen meals. Brigitte Lofgren says that the microwave oven is the most useful appliance in her house: "We all heat up our own meals. Nobody has to cook." When family members heat up their own meals, one after another, it is less likely that they will bother to eat together.

(Conclusion) Most families recognize that they are losing communication time. They watch in frustration as the family dinner disappears. They assure themselves that because of hectic lifestyles, they have no choice but to stagger eating times. A television on the kitchen counter provides something to focus on during meals. And the quality of prepackaged and frozen meals is improving, so who really needs to cook? Yet it is tragic that the family meal, a simple and effective way to keep family members linked together, is no longer a priority for most families.

Generating Supporting Ideas

When you develop supporting ideas, ensure that they all focus on the central point that you are making in the thesis statement. To generate ideas for body paragraphs, you could use the exploring strategies (freewriting, brainstorming, questioning, or clustering) that you learned in Chapter 1.

Overview: Generating Supporting Ideas

Review the process that student Alicia Parera went through. First, she created a list to support her thesis statement. Then she reread her supporting ideas and removed ideas that she did not want to develop in her essay. She also grouped together related ideas.

Initial Ideas

Draft thesis statement: Students drop out of college for many reasons.

Supporting ideas:
- Can't adapt to college life
- Feel confused about career goals
- Don't have study skills
- Can't afford tuition
- Part-time job takes time away from school work
- Financial problems
- Lose a family member
- Undergo emotional crisis such as a breakup
- ~~Want to start their own business~~

After critically examining her supporting ideas, Alicia chose three that could become body paragraphs. She evaluated each set of linked ideas and summarized the connection between them. These sentence summaries then became her topic sentences. Alicia also reworked her thesis statement.

Revised Thesis and Supporting Points

Thesis statement: *Students may drop out of college because they are unprepared, have financial problems, or experience an emotional crisis.*

Topic sentence: *Some students face overwhelming financial burdens.*

Topic sentence: *Furthermore, they may undergo an emotional crisis.*

Topic sentence: *Many students are unable to adapt to college life.*

HINT **Look Critically at Your Supporting Ideas**

After you have made a list of supporting ideas, look at it carefully and ask yourself these questions.

- **Which ideas could I develop into complete paragraphs?**
  Look for connections between supporting ideas. Group together ideas that have a common thread. Then create a topic sentence for each group of related ideas. In Alicia's example, three of her ideas became topic sentences.

- **Does each idea support my thesis?**
  Choose ideas that directly support the thesis statement and drop any ideas that might go off topic. In Alicia's example, the last idea, "Want to start their own businesses" didn't support her thesis, so she crossed it out.

PRACTICE 9

Brainstorm three supporting ideas for the next thesis statements. Find ideas that do not overlap, and ensure that your ideas support the thesis. (You can brainstorm a list of ideas on a separate sheet of paper, and then add the three best ideas here.)

EXAMPLE:

Growing numbers of people blatantly disregard rules of the road.

- *Pedestrians engage in careless practices.*

- *Many cyclists refuse to take safety precautions and ignore road signs.*

- *Drivers endanger others with their tailgating, speeding, and aggressive lane changes.*

1. Losing a job can have some positive consequences.

_____

_____

_____

2. There are several concrete steps that you can take to help preserve the environment.

_____

_____

_____

3. When young people move away from home, they quickly learn the next lessons.

_____

_____

_____

Writer's Desk Generate Supporting Ideas

Brainstorm supporting ideas for two or three of your thesis statements from the previous Writer's Desk. Look critically at your lists of supporting ideas. Ask yourself which supporting ideas you could expand into complete essays, then drop unrelated ideas.

Writer's Room   **Develop the Main Idea**

Writing Activity 1

Choose one of the Writer's Room topics from Chapter 1 and write a thesis statement. Using an exploring strategy, develop supporting ideas for your thesis.

Writing Activity 2

Narrow one of the following topics. Then develop a thesis statement and some supporting ideas.

General Topics	Academic and Work-Related Topics
1. good hygiene	6. pressures students face
2. annoying rules	7. credit cards
3. delaying childbirth	8. creative teaching
4. traditions	9. improving services
5. allergies	10. benefit of extracurricular activities

 CHECKLIST: THESIS STATEMENT

Each time you write a thesis statement, ask yourself these questions.

☐ Is my thesis a complete sentence?

☐ Does it contain a narrowed topic and a controlling idea?

☐ Is my main point clear and interesting?

☐ Can the thesis be supported with several body paragraphs? (Ensure that the topic is not too narrow, or you will hit a dead end with it. Also ensure that the topic is not too broad. Your essay requires a clear focus.)

☐ Can I think of details, examples, and other ideas to support the thesis?

☐ Is my thesis forceful and direct, and not too vague or obvious?

☐ Does my thesis make a valid point?

Developing the Essay Plan

3
CHAPTER

Good plans shape good decisions.

—LESTER R. BIDDLE, *management consultant*

Key Steps in Developing the Essay Plan

In the previous chapters, you learned how to narrow topics and how to use exploring strategies to formulate ideas. You also learned to develop main ideas. In this chapter, you will focus on the third stage of the writing process: Developing the Essay Plan. There are two key steps in this process.

DEVELOPING THE ESSAY PLAN

STEP 1 ──────▶ Organize your ideas. Choose an appropriate method of organization.

STEP 2 ──────▶ Make an essay plan. Place your main and supporting ideas in an essay plan.

Organizing Supporting Ideas

In Chapter 2, you practised developing a list of supporting ideas. The next step in the writing process is to organize your supporting ideas using time, space, or emphatic order.

Time Order

To organize an essay using **time order (chronological order)**, arrange the details according to the sequence in which they have occurred. Time order can be effective for narrating a story, explaining how to do something, or describing an event.

When you write essays using time order, you can use the following transitional expressions to help your readers understand when certain events happened. (There is a more extensive list of transitions on pages 57 and 58 in Chapter 5.)

after that	last
eventually	meanwhile
finally	months afterward
first	next
in the beginning	suddenly
later	then

PRACTICE I

The supporting ideas for the following thesis statement are organized using time order.

Thesis statement: My one and only ferry ride was a disaster.

1. To begin with, the only available seat was in a horrible location near the back of the boat.

2. Next, the rain began, and the passengers on deck rushed inside.

3. After that, the ferry began to rock, and some passengers became ill.

One paragraph from the essay also uses time order. Underline any words or phrases that help show time order.

> Next, the rain began, and the passengers on deck rushed inside. Suddenly, a sprinkle became a downpour. I was in the middle of the crowd, and water was running in rivulets down my face and down the back of my collar. Then, those behind me got impatient and began to shove. The doorway was narrow, and many people were jostling for position. I was pushed to the right and left. Meanwhile, I was soaked, tired, and cranky. The crowd squeezed me more and more. Finally, I was pushed through the door; I stumbled and tried not to fall. The inner seating room was so crowded that I had to stand in the aisle holding on to the back of one of the seats.

Emphatic Order

To organize the supporting details of an essay using **emphatic order**, arrange them in a logical sequence. For example, you can arrange details from least to most important, from general to specific, from least appealing to most appealing, and so on.

Here are some transitional expressions that help readers understand which ideas you want to emphasize the most or the least in the body paragraphs of an essay.

above all	most importantly
clearly	of course
especially	principally
first	the least important
in particular	the most important
moreover	

PRACTICE 2

The supporting ideas for the following thesis statement are organized using emphatic order.

Thesis statement: In our city, some types of public transportation are more dependable and pleasant than others.

1. First, subways are uncomfortable and even frightening.
2. Bus trips have certain drawbacks.
3. The most pleasant and reliable way to travel is the suburban train.

One paragraph from the essay also uses emphatic order. Underline any words or phrases that help show emphatic order.

Subways are uncomfortable and even frightening. First, subway riders must deal with crowds. In front of the tracks, there is very little seating room, so people line the walls. Of course, the lighting is usually terrible, so ordinary people look sad and even sinister under the fluorescent tubes. Feeling uncomfortable and unattractive, they avoid eye contact. Moreover, for those who feel claustrophobic, being in a subway can feel like being in a grave. There is no sunlight, no sky, and no outdoors for the entire duration of the journey. Passengers can only stare at the sullen faces of the other travellers. Thus, the entire subway experience can be unpleasant and disturbing.

HINT Using Emphatic Order

When you organize details using emphatic order, use your own values and opinions to determine what is most or least important, upsetting, remarkable, and so on. Another writer may organize the same ideas in a different way.

Space Order

Organizing ideas using **space order** helps the reader to visualize what you are describing in a specific space. For example, you can describe someone or something from top to bottom or bottom to top, from left to right or right to left, or from far to near or near to far.

Help readers find their way through your essay by using the following transitional expressions.

above	nearby
behind	on the bottom
below	on the left
beneath	on top
closer in	toward
farther out	under

PRACTICE 3

The supporting ideas for the following thesis statement are organized using space order.

Thesis statement: With very little money, local students helped turn a tiny old house into a vibrant youth centre.

1. Working outdoors, two students cleared the yard.
2. Focusing on the exterior surfaces of the building, a second team of students painted and made minor repairs.
3. Inside the house, some students turned the living room into a recreation and meeting place.

One paragraph from the essay also uses space order. Underline any words or phrases that indicate space order.

Inside the house, some students turned the living room into a recreation and meeting place. First, they washed and then painted the walls. At the far end of the room, next to the fireplace, there was an old bar with an orange counter and frayed, yellow bar stools. The students stripped and varnished the counter of the bar and cleaned the sink. They turned the space into an art corner. Local teenagers who love to paint and sculpt now have a nice workspace. In the centre of the room, there was a rope area rug that had seen better days. They removed the rug and replaced it with woven straw matting. Beside the rug was a stained and smelly pink and green sofa. The students discarded the sofa. Rather than purchase a new one, which would have cost hundreds of dollars, they used the centre's funds to buy large blue cushions at a discount department store. When the renovations were finished, the room looked like a new and fresh space.

> **HINT Combining Time, Emphatic, or Space Order**
>
> You will likely use more than one type of organizational method in an essay. For example, in a time order essay about a journey, one paragraph might be devoted to a particular place that you visited, and in that paragraph, you might use space order to describe the scene.

PRACTICE 4

Read each list of supporting ideas, and number the items in a logical order. Then write **time**, **emphatic**, or **space** to indicate the organization method.

EXAMPLE:

Thesis statement: Painting a basic picture can be a rewarding experience.

___1___ Choose a location that you find particularly peaceful.

___3___ Add colours to your sketch that best represent the mood you are feeling.

___2___ Settle in and make a preliminary sketch of the place.

Order: _Time_____

1. Thesis statement: Overexposure to the sun can have terrible consequences.

_____ The skin cells lose elasticity and wrinkles set in earlier.

_____ Some people develop cancers that can lead to premature death.

_____ Brown spots can develop in parts of the face.

Order: _____

2. Thesis statement: We encountered many problems during our trip from Mexico City to Guadalajara.

_____ We arrived late at night and had a lot of trouble finding our friend's house.

_____ We didn't have enough money for the first tollbooth, so we took the side roads.

_____ On a small road halfway there, an accident completely blocked our route.

Order: _____

3. Thesis statement: For an important interview, dress conservatively.

_____ Employers may notice every detail, so pay attention to your footwear.

_____ If possible, invest in a good haircut a few days before the interview.

_____ Wear a suit jacket and matching pants or a skirt.

Order: _____

4. Thesis statement: Harold Roos should win the Citizen's Award for three reasons.

_____ Every Sunday, Mr. Roos does volunteer work at the hospital.

_____ Last September, Mr. Roos saved Eduardo Borsellino's life when he pulled the young man out of a submerged car.

_____ Mr. Roos employs many local citizens in his downtown clothing store.

Order: _____

Writer's Desk **Organize Your Ideas**

Brainstorm ideas for an essay topic. You can choose ideas that you developed in Chapter 2. Then do the following.

1. Highlight at least three ideas from your list that you think are most compelling and most clearly illustrate the point you are making in your thesis statement.

2. Group together any related ideas with the three supporting ideas.

3. Organize your ideas using time, emphatic, or space order.

Developing an Essay Plan

A contractor would never build a house without making a drawing or plan of it first. In the same way, an **essay plan** or an **outline** can help you to organize your thesis statement and supporting ideas before writing your first draft. Planning your essay actually saves you time because you have already figured out your supporting ideas and how to organize them so your readers can easily follow them. To create an essay plan, follow the next steps.

- Looking at your list of ideas that you created while prewriting, identify the ones that most effectively support your thesis statement.
- Next, write topic sentences that express the main supporting ideas.
- Finally, add details under each topic sentence.

A formal essay plan uses Roman numerals and letters to identify main and supporting ideas. A formal plan also contains complete sentences. The basic structure looks like this.

Thesis statement: _____

I. _____

    A. _____

    B. _____

II. _____

    A. _____

    B. _____

III. _____

    A. _____

    B. _____

Concluding idea: _____

In the planning stage, you do not have to develop your introduction and conclusion. It is sufficient to simply write your thesis statement and an idea for your conclusion. Later, when you write your essay, you can develop the introduction and conclusion.

Alicia's Essay Plan

Alicia Parera wrote topic sentences and supporting examples and organized her ideas into a plan. Notice that she begins with her thesis statement, and she indents her supporting ideas.

Thesis statement: Students may drop out of college because they have financial problems, experience an emotional crisis, or are unprepared for college life.

I. Some students face overwhelming financial burdens.

    A. They may have a part-time job to pay for such things as tuition and rent.

    B. Moreover, a part-time job leaves no time for studying and homework.

    C. Also, transportation may be expensive and beyond a student's means.

II. Furthermore, some students face life-changing events and must leave college to cope.

    A. A pregnancy and childbirth consume energy and attention.

    B. Also, a serious illness or death in the family can cause a student to miss classes, and it becomes too difficult to catch up.

    C. Of course, a broken relationship can cause a student to feel emotionally fragile and unable to concentrate.

III. They may be unprepared for college life.

    A. They might have poor study skills.

    B. Furthermore, some students cannot respect schedules.

    C. The increased freedom in college causes some students to skip too many classes.

    D. Additionally, many students feel confused about career goals and decide to leave college.

PRACTICE 5

Read the thesis statement and the list of supporting ideas and details. First, highlight three supporting ideas (topic sentences) and number them 1, 2, and 3. Then, using numbers such as *1a, 1b, 1c, 2a, 2b,* etc., organize the details that could follow each topic sentence. On a separate paper, place the ideas in an essay plan.

Thesis statement: Men have disadvantages at home and in the workplace.

_____ High tower construction work, which is mainly done by males, is very risky.

_____ In family court, men do not get custody of children as often as women.

_____ According to journalist Ian McArthur, most boys are told to "take it like a man" so they learn to rein in their emotions.

_____ More men do work that puts their lives at risk than women.

_____ Sheila Siskel, a Toronto lawyer, acknowledges that many judges still consider women as the primary caregivers of children.

_____ Men are more likely to repair roofs, scale electrical poles, and operate heavy machinery.

_____ Greg Chu says, "It unsatisfying and heartbreaking when I am reduced to visiting my own children twice a month!"

_____ Over ninety percent of workplace deaths happen to men, according to Statistics Canada.

_____ Some men are ridiculed when they show emotion.

_____ Manuel Figuera, a graphic designer from Winnipeg, says, "Some believe a crying man is an emotional weakling or a wimp."

_____ Men's groups, including Divorced Dads, protest the attitudes of the courts toward fathers in their fight for parental rights.

_____ Movies such as *Saving Private Ryan* reinforce the stereotype that men must be stoic and control their emotions.

PRACTICE 6

On a separate sheet of paper, create an essay plan for the following thesis statement.

Thesis statement: Women have disadvantages at home and in the workplace.

PRACTICE 7

Read the following essay plan. Brainstorm and develop three supporting ideas for each topic sentence.

Thesis: Common fairy tales follow a certain model.

Topic Sentence: Fairy tales never mention a real date or place.

Supporting ideas: _____

_____

_____

Topic Sentence: The main character must overcome great obstacles to achieve his or her goal.

Supporting ideas: _____

_____

_____

Topic sentence: The main character accomplishes his or her goals with the help of magic or some other supernatural phenomenon.

Supporting ideas: _____

_____

_____

PRACTICE 8

Read the following essay plan. Brainstorm and develop three supporting ideas for each topic sentence.

Thesis: I learned valuable lessons during my years in elementary school and high school.

Topic sentence: First, I learned how to get along with others.

Supporting ideas: _____

_____

_____

Topic Sentence: I learned to organize my time.

Supporting ideas: _____

_____

_____

Topic Sentence: Most importantly, I learned about respect and compassion.

Supporting ideas: _____

_____

_____

Writer's Desk **Write an Essay Plan**

Brainstorm ideas for an essay on a separate piece of paper. You can choose ideas that you developed in Chapter 2. Then do the following.

1. Highlight at least three ideas from your list that you think are most compelling and most clearly illustrate the point you are making in your thesis statement. These three ideas will make up your body paragraphs.

2. Group together any related ideas with the three supporting ideas.

3. Organize your ideas for the body paragraphs using time, emphatic, or space order.

Writer's Room   **Develop an Essay Plan**

Writing Activity 1

Choose one of the Writer's Room topics from Chapter 2, and create an essay plan. Using an exploring strategy, develop supporting ideas for your thesis.

Writing Activity 2

Create a list of supporting ideas for one of the next thesis statements. Then develop an essay plan.

General Topics

1. Single people should (or should not) have the right to adopt children.
2. The three talents I would most like to have are . . .
3. Noise pollution is increasing in our homes and neighbourhoods.
4. There are good reasons to postpone marriage.

Academic and Work-Related Topics

5. New employees make three types of common mistakes.
6. An elected official should have the following characteristics.
7. I do (or do not) vote for these reasons.
8. The novel has important lessons for all of us.

 CHECKLIST: ESSAY PLAN

When you develop an essay plan, ask yourself these questions.

☐ Does my thesis statement express the main idea of the essay?

☐ In my plan, does each body paragraph contain a topic sentence?

☐ Does each topic sentence support the thesis statement?

☐ In each body paragraph, do the sentences support the topic sentence?

☐ Are my ideas well organized?

Developing the First Draft

CHAPTER 4

Detail makes the difference between boring and perfect writing. It's the difference between a pencil sketch and a lush oil painting. As a writer, words are your paint. Use all the colours.

—RHYS ALEXANDER, *author*

CHAPTER CONTENTS

Key Steps in Developing the First Draft

In previous chapters, you learned how to develop a thesis statement, support it with ideas, and create an essay plan. The next stage in the writing process is developing the first draft.

DEVELOPING THE FIRST DRAFT

STEP 1 → Write an introduction. Try to attract the reader's attention in the first paragraph of your essay.

STEP 2 → Write complete body paragraphs. Expand each supporting idea with specific details.

STEP 3 → Write a conclusion. Bring your essay to a satisfactory close.

STEP 4 → Title your essay. Sum up your essay topic in a few words.

STEP 5 → Write the first draft. Tie the introduction, body paragraphs, and conclusion into a cohesive essay.

Writing an Introduction

The **introductory paragraph** introduces the subject of your essay and contains the thesis statement. A strong introduction will capture the reader's attention and make him or her want to read on. Introductions may have a lead-in, and they can be developed in several different ways.

The Lead-In

The point of writing an essay is to have people read it and to entertain, inform, or persuade them. So, try to grab your readers' attention in the first sentence. There are three common lead-ins that you can try.

- a quotation
- a surprising or provocative statement
- a question

Introduction Styles

You can develop the introduction in several different ways. Experiment with any of the following introduction styles.

- **Give general or historical background information** that gradually leads to your thesis. For example, in an essay about movie violence, you might begin by discussing some classic films.

- **Tell an interesting anecdote** or a story that leads to your thesis statement. For example, you might begin your essay about film violence by describing how aggressive your younger brother and his friends became after they watched the movie *Fight Club*.

- **Describe something in vivid detail** and then state your thesis. For example, you might begin your essay about movie violence by describing a particularly gory film scene.

- **Define a term**, and then state your thesis. For example, in an essay about ways to avoid marital conflicts, you can begin by defining a happy marriage.

- **Present a contrasting position**, which is an idea that is the opposite of the one you will later develop, and then offer your thesis. Your readers will not expect you to present one side and then to argue for the other side. For example, in an essay about a woman's right to an abortion, you might begin by presenting the arguments of anti-abortion activists.

- **Pose several questions**, and end with a thesis statement. The purpose may be to engage your readers by inviting them to think about the topic. You might also ask questions that you will answer in your essay. For instance, in an essay about lotteries, you might ask, *Have you ever bought a lottery ticket? Why do so many people play lotteries?*

The next example presents the structure of a typical introduction.

> **Have good manners disappeared?** In past centuries, a gentleman would spread his cloak over a muddy road so that his lady wouldn't dirty her feet. Twenty years ago, an elderly man or woman would never have to stand in a bus because other passengers would offer up their seats. Times have certainly changed. Today, many people have a lack of consideration for others. **In contemporary society, parents and schools should teach children basic good manners.**

◄ *Lead-in*

◄ *Historical background information*

◄ *Thesis statement*

PRACTICE 1

Read the following introductions. Underline each thesis statement and determine what introduction style the writer used.

1. I got out of bed as usual. I shaved, showered and put on a clean shirt. Trotting out to the kitchen where my wife, Nadine, was standing, I looked at her and asked, "Now what?" The day before, I had accepted a generous buyout offer at Verizon Corp., effectively ending my 30-year career there as a midlevel manager. I was 51. With the papers in front of me, I listened patiently as my financial adviser cautioned me that some people in my position are not mentally prepared to retire, but I never dreamed that his advice would apply to me. I was wrong. Retirement left a void in my life that I filled in some odd ways.

   —Peter Borghesi, "I Was Out of a Job and an Identity," *Newsweek*

   a. Underline the thesis statement.
   b. What is the introduction style? Indicate the best answer.

   ___ general background
   ___ anecdote
   ___ definition
   ___ questions

2. Adolescent males are dangerous. They join gangs, and they are responsible for most of the crime in our society. They drive too fast, causing accidents on our highways. They all experiment with drugs, and they annoy others with their loud music. But is such a portrayal of our nation's young men really fair? In fact, most stereotypes about adolescent males are incorrect and misleading.

   —Abeer Hamad, student

   a. Underline the thesis statement.
   b. What type of lead-in did the writer use?

   ___ quotation
   ___ question
   ___ surprising statement

   c. What is the introduction style? Indicate the best answer.

   ___ historical background
   ___ anecdote
   ___ definition
   ___ contrasting position

3. Where did you buy that blouse? I heard the question every time I wore it. It was a truly lovely designer model that had been marked down to $40. It was pale blue with swirling tiny flower buds running down each front panel. The little buttons were topped with imitation pearls. Unfortunately, the middle button kept coming undone. People at a certain angle to my left could peek in and view the lace eyelets on my brassiere. When I wore the blouse, my head kept bobbing down, looking to see if I was exposing myself. Over the years, I have had several humorous and embarrassing wardrobe and makeup malfunctions.

   —Catalina Ortega, student

a. Underline the thesis statement.
b. What type of lead-in was used?

___ quotation
___ question
___ surprising statement

c. What is the introduction style? Indicate the best answer.

___ general background
___ anecdote
___ definition
___ description

4. Nationalism is the sometimes angry belief in the independence of one's people. It often includes resentment or even hatred of alien rulers or threatening foreigners: "No foreigners will push us around!" It is the strongest and most emotional of the world's ideologies. Most of the world's people—including Americans—are nationalistic.

—Michael G. Roskin and Nicholas O. Berry, *The New World of International Relations*

a. Underline the thesis statement.
b. What is the introduction style? Indicate the best answer.

___ historical background
___ anecdote
___ definition
___ contrasting position

5. "Men only." A century ago, the campuses of colleges and universities across the United States might as well have hung out that sign. Almost all of the students and faculty were male. There were a small number of women's colleges, but many more schools—including some of the best-known American universities, such as Yale, Harvard, and Princeton— barred women outright. Since then, women have won greater social equality. By 1980, the number of women enrolled at American colleges finally matched the number of men. In a surprising turn of events, women now outnumber men on college campuses for several reasons.

—Adapted from John J. Macionis, "The Twenty-First-Century Campus: Where Are the Men?" *Sociology*

a. Underline the thesis statement.
b. What type of lead-in was used?

___ quotation
___ question
___ surprising statement

c. What is the introduction style? Indicate the best answer.

___ historical background
___ anecdote
___ definition
___ questions

6. Why do some hip-hop artists embed jewels and gold in their teeth? Are the grills meant to impress others, or do the grills fit some deep need on the part of the artists to show that they matter? Is the hip-hop artist who shows off his "bling" any different than the accountant who buys a BMW to show that she has succeeded or the corporate executive who marries a beautiful trophy wife? Showing off one's wealth is not new. In fact, throughout history, people have found extravagant ways to flaunt their wealth.

—Jamal Evans, student

a. Underline the thesis statement.
b. What is the introduction style? Indicate the best answer.

    ___ general background
    ___ anecdote
    ___ definition
    ___ questions

PRACTICE 2

Write interesting lead-ins (opening sentences) for the next topics. Use the type of lead-in that is indicated in parentheses.

EXAMPLE:

Bicycle helmet laws (a question)

How many cyclists have needlessly died this year from head injuries?

1. dangerous dogs (a surprising or controversial statement)

    _____

    _____

2. ridiculous fashions (a question)

    _____

    _____

3. the junk food nation (a surprising fact or idea)

    _____

    _____

PRACTICE 3

Choose one of the next thesis statements. Then write three introductions using three different introduction styles. Use the same thesis statement in each introduction.

It's important to know more than one language.

Famous musicians generally make poor (or good) role models

There are several reasons that nations have wars.

You can choose any three of the following introduction styles:

- anecdote
- definition
- description
- contrasting position
- series of questions
- general or historical background

Writer's Desk   **Write Two Introductions**

In Chapter 3, you prepared an essay plan. Now, on a separate piece of paper, write two different styles of introductions for your essay. Use the same thesis statement in both introductions. Later, you can choose the best introduction for your essay.

Writing Complete Body Paragraphs

In your essay plan, you developed supporting ideas for your topic. When you prepare the first draft, you must flesh out those ideas. As you write each body paragraph, ensure that it is complete. Do not offer vague generalizations, and do not simply repeat your ideas. Provide evidence for each topic sentence by inserting specific details. You might include examples, facts, statistics, anecdotes, or quotations.

Examples are people, places, things, or events that illustrate your point. To support the view that some local buildings are eyesores, the writer could give the following examples.

> The car dealership on Labelle Boulevard is rundown.
> The grey block apartment buildings that line Main Street are monotonous.
> The Allen Drive mini-mall has tacky signs and cracked store windows.

Facts are objective details that can be verified by others. **Statistics** are facts that are expressed in percentages. (Make sure that your statistics are from reliable sources.) To support the view that transportation costs are too high for students, the following facts and statistic could be given as evidence.

A one-way bus ticket now costs $3.50 for students.

The monthly subway pass just increased to $260 for students.

In a survey of four hundred students, 70 percent expressed concern about the recent rate increases in public transportation.

Anecdotes are true experiences that you or someone else went through. An anecdote expresses what happened. **Quotations** are somebody's exact words, and they are set off in quotation marks. To support the view that lack of sleep can have dangerous consequences, the following anecdote and quotation could be included as evidence.

When Alan Turner finished his nightshift, he got into his car and headed home. On Forest Drive, he started to nod off. Luckily, a truck driver in another lane noticed that Turner's car was weaving and honked. Turner said, "My eyes snapped open and I saw a wall growing larger in front of me. I slammed on my brakes just before smashing into it."

Essay with Sample Body Paragraphs

The following body paragraphs are excerpts from a larger essay. Read the paragraphs and notice how they are fleshed out with specific evidence.

Thesis statement: Young people in the 1920s were very much like young people today.

Body Paragraphs

fact ➤   Today, young people want to be popular, and they go to great lengths to fit in with their friends, yet this was also true in the past. In the 1920s, F. Scott Fitzgerald wrote stories and novels about peer pressure. In his short story, "Bernice Bobs Her Hair," the main character is a shy,

quotation ➤ socially awkward girl who feels a "vague pain" that she is "not at present engaged in being popular." In a desperate effort to make friends, Bernice changes her style and modifies her personality in order to be accepted by her peers. Today's youths also worry about popularity.

statistic ➤ Over 70 percent of high school students are anxious about their social status, according to a report published by *Maclean's*.

            Throughout history, teens have tried to distinguish themselves from previous generations. In the 1920s, young "flapper" women stopped

example ➤ wearing corsets, they wore skirts that showed their legs, and in an act of extreme rebellion, they cut their long hair short. In Fitzgerald's story,

quotation ➤ Bernice calls bobbed hair on women "immoral" but then notes that "you've either got to amuse people or feed 'em or shock 'em." Today, teenagers also differentiate themselves from their elders in an attempt to forge their own identities and create a sense of independence. College student Ariane Lebel has several tattoos, and she recently

quotation ➤ shaved a pattern into her hair. "My mother hates my new look but I don't care. I want to make a statement and be noticed," she says.

HINT Using Research to Support Your Point

Your instructor might ask you to back up your ideas with research. You can look in books and magazines or on the Internet for relevant quotations, statistics, and factual evidence. For more information about doing research, see Chapter 16: The Research Essay.

PRACTICE 4

Make the next body paragraphs more complete by adding specific examples. You can include the following:

- examples
- anecdotes from your own life or from the lives of others
- quotations (for this exercise, you can make up punchy quotations)
- facts, statistics, or descriptions of events that you have read about or seen

Do not add general statements. Ensure that the details you add are very specific.

Thesis statement: Prospective pet owners should become informed before buying an animal.

Body Paragraph 1 First, when families choose a dog, they should consider the inconvenience and possible dangers. Some breeds of dogs can become extremely aggressive. _____

_____

_____

_____ Moreover, dog owners must accept that dogs require

a lot of time and attention. _____

_____

_____

_____ Furthermore, it is very expensive to own a dog.

_____

_____

Body Paragraph 2 Some new pet owners decide to buy exotic pets. However, such pets come with very specific problems and require very particular environments. _____

_____

_____

_____ Also, some exotic pets seem interesting when they are young, but they can become distinctly annoying or dangerous when they reach maturity. _____

_____

_____

> **HINT** **Making Detailed Essay Plans**
>
> You can shorten the time you spend developing the first draft if you make a very detailed essay plan. In addition to writing main ideas, your plan can include details for each supporting idea. Notice the detailed evidence in the following excerpt from an essay plan.
>
> **Thesis statement:** For personal and financial reasons, a growing number of adult children are choosing to live with their parents.
>
> **I. Topic sentence:** The cost of education and housing is very high.
>   A: Rents have increased dramatically in the past ten years. ⟶ fact
>   Evidence: *The Daily Journal* states that rents tripled in the past ten years.
>   B: Student wages have not risen as much as the rents.
>   Evidence: The minimum wage is still $6.15 an hour. ⟶ fact
>   C: Tuition fees are very high.
>   Evidence: Tuition and fees at both universities and colleges rose by an average of $344, or 6.3 percent this year, to an average of $5,836, according to the Education Board's annual "Trends in Tuition Pricing" report. ⟶ statistic

Writer's Desk **Make Complete Body Paragraphs**

In Chapter 3, you prepared an essay plan. Now write complete body paragraphs for your essay. Ensure that each body paragraph contains specific details.

Writing a Conclusion

The **concluding paragraph** gives you one last chance to impress the reader and to make your point clear. A good conclusion makes the essay seem complete. One common and effective way to conclude a composition is to summarize the main ideas. The essay then comes full circle, and you remind the reader of your strongest points.

To make your conclusion more interesting and original, you could also close with a prediction, a suggestion, a quotation, or a call to action.

> **HINT** **Linking the Conclusion to the Introduction**
>
> One effective way to conclude an essay is to continue an idea that was introduced in the introduction.
>
> ■ If you began an anecdote in the introduction, you can finish it in the conclusion.
> ■ If you posed some questions in the introduction, you can answer them in the conclusion.
> ■ If you highlighted a problem in the introduction, you might suggest a solution in the conclusion.

Look at the concluding paragraph of an essay about etiquette in our technological age.

Do not hide behind technology as your excuse for having rude or annoying behaviour. Your cell phone has a button that turns it off when you are with someone you care about. If someone is writing an email, do not read over his or her shoulder. Also, never send nor accept chain emails that promise wealth, happiness, or cures for cancer.

The last sentence in the essay could be one of the following.

Prediction: If you follow the basic rules of etiquette, you will ensure that your friends and colleagues maintain their respect for you.

Suggestion: The next time someone forwards you a nasty chain letter asking you to send it to at least ten people or else, return it to the sender ten times.

Quotation: As the French author Collette once said, "It is wise to apply the oils of refined politeness to the mechanism of friendship."

Call to action: To help the next generation learn good manners, offer to teach a class to local high school students about etiquette in the technological age.

PRACTICE 5

Read the following conclusions and answer the questions.

1. Laws designed to spook such scammers may be on the way, in the same way legislators tried to wipe out spam a few years ago. California Governor Arnold Schwarzenegger has approved legislation specifically outlawing such scams, giving prosecutors another tool to pursue the fraudulent. But it's still too early to measure whether such laws will be effective at curbing phishing attacks. Until then, consumers should continue to click carefully and be cautious about how and where they hand over personal information.

—Mike Musgrove, "Phishing," *Washington Post*

What method does the author use to end the conclusion? _____

2. Just as a peacock spreads its tail feathers to attract the opposite sex, human beings flaunt their wealth to impress their mates and to establish their power over others. The grills on the teeth of hip-hop artists are simply modern versions of the Taj Mahal, the pyramids, or the elaborate castles of kings and queens. As Mel Brooks said in *The Producers*, "When you've got it, baby, flaunt it."

—Jamal Evans, student

What method does the author use to end the conclusion? _____

3. In this new millennium, let's put the concept of IQ to rest, once and for all. Stop giving IQ tests. Stop all the studies on IQ and birth order, IQ and nutrition, or IQ and Mozart. Let's find newer, more fluid, and more fair ways to debate and enable human potential. Let's use our heads for a change.

—Dorothy Nixon, "Let's Stop Being Stupid About IQ"

What method does the author use to end the conclusion? _____

HINT **Avoiding Conclusion Problems**

In your conclusion, do not contradict your main point, and do not introduce new or irrelevant information. Also, avoid ending your essay with a rhetorical question, which is a question that cannot be answered, such as "When will humans stop having wars?"

Writer's Desk **Write a Conclusion**

Write a conclusion for the essay you've been preparing in the previous Writer's Desk exercises.

Choosing an Essay Title

Think of a title *after* you have written your essay because you will have a more complete impression of your essay's main point. The most effective titles are brief, depict the topic and purpose of the essay, and attract the reader's attention.

Descriptive Titles

Descriptive titles are the most common titles in academic essays. They depict the topic of the essay clearly and concisely. Sometimes, the writer takes key words from the thesis statement and uses them in the title. Here are some descriptive titles.

> Etiquette in the Technological Age
> Avoiding Mistakes in the First Year of University

Titles Related to the Writing Pattern

You can also relate your title directly to the writing pattern of your essay. Here are examples of titles for different writing patterns.

Illustration:	Problems with Internet Dating
Narration:	My Worst Nightmare
Description:	The Anniversary Party
Process:	How to Handle a Workplace Bully
Definition:	The Meaning of Tolerance
Classification:	Three Types of Fathers
Comparison and contrast:	Fads Versus Timeless Fashions
Cause and effect:	The Reasons People Pollute
Argument:	Why Writing Matters

> HINT **Grammar Link**
>
> Place your title at the top centre of your page. Capitalize the first word of your title, and capitalize the main words except for prepositions (*in, at, for, to*, etc.) and articles (*a, an, the*). Leave about 2.5 cm (one inch) of space between the title and the introductory paragraph.

> HINT **Avoiding Title Pitfalls**
>
> When you write your title, watch out for problems.
>
> ■ Do not view your title as a substitute for a thesis statement.
> ■ Do not write a really long title because it can confuse readers.
> ■ Do not put quotation marks around the title of your essay.

PRACTICE 6

Read the following introductions and underline the thesis statements. Then write titles for each essay.

1. Some people fear mistakes more than others fear snakes. Perfectionism refers to self-defeating thoughts and behaviours aimed at reaching excessively high unrealistic goals. Unfortunately, nobody is perfect. In fact, there are many problems associated with the desire to be perfect.

   Title:_____

2. Gang life, once associated with large urban centres, has become a common part of adolescent experience in towns and rural areas across Canada. Many of the gang members have no strong role models at home, and their gang affiliation makes them feel like part of a powerful group. To combat the problems associated with youth gangs, adolescents need to be given more responsibilities in our society.

   Title:_____

3. "A person who is not initiated is still a child," says Malidoma Somé. Somé is from the Dagara tribe in West Africa, and he underwent a six-week initiation ceremony. Left alone in the bush with no food or clothing, he developed a profound appreciation of nature and of magic. When he returned to his village, everyone welcomed him and other initiates with food and dancing. Somé had passed from childhood into adulthood and was expected to assume adult responsibilities. The ceremony helped Somé and the other initiates feel like valued participants in village life. Our culture should have formal initiation ceremonies for adolescents.

   Title:_____

PRACTICE 7

Read the following body paragraphs of a short essay. First, highlight the topic sentence in each body paragraph. Then, on a separate sheet of paper, develop a title, a compelling introduction, and a conclusion.

Add a Title

Add an Introduction

Body 1 First, family communication suffers when a television is present. The TV is turned on from morning to night. Families install televisions in the kitchen, living room, and bedrooms. Thus, in locations where families traditionally congregated to talk, they now sit mutely—sometimes next to each other—staring at the screen. Instead of reading a bedtime story together, families deposit children in front of the television to watch a bedtime video. Fourteen-year-old Annie Wong says, "When I get home from school, I head straight for my bedroom. I watch my shows in my room, and my brother watches the TV in the living room. I never have to talk to him."

Body 2 Too often, when people do communicate, their discussions revolve around television shows. It is common to hear people quoting Rick Mercer or Oprah, and water cooler conversations often revolve around the latest hot series. Thirty-year-old William and his friend Jay love nothing more than to reminisce about their favourite programs. When *Lost* was at its peak, they discussed each episode in detail. They also love theme songs. "I know the songs for about fifteen television shows," William says, as he proceeds to do the *Fresh Prince of Belair* rap. Jay admits that his conversations with William rarely stray beyond the lightness of the television world.

Body 3 Most importantly, the health of children has changed since the introduction of television. Before televisions existed, children played outdoors and spent most of their free time doing physical activities. Today, most children pass hours sitting or lying down as they stare at the television screen. According to Anna Franklin, a researcher at Montreal's Children's Hospital, such inactivity is contributing to the obesity epidemic in our nation. Ben Tyler, a 10-year-old from Winnipeg, admits that he watches between six and eight hours of television each day. "I can watch whatever I want," he says proudly. But Ben is also overweight and suffers from asthma.

Add a Conclusion

Writing the First Draft

After creating an introduction and conclusion, and after arranging the supporting ideas in a logical order, you are ready to write your first draft. The first draft includes your introduction, several body paragraphs, and your concluding paragraph.

Writer's Desk **Write the First Draft**

In previous Writer's Desks, you wrote an introduction, a conclusion, and an essay plan. Now write the first draft of your essay.

Writer's Room **Develop the First Draft**

Writing Activity 1

Choose an essay plan that you developed for Chapter 3, and write the first draft of your essay.

Writing Activity 2

Write the first draft of an essay about one of the following topics.

General Topics

1. In divorce cases, grandparents should receive visitation rights.
2. Movies and television shows glorify crime and criminals.
3. Lying is appropriate in certain situations.
4. I would like to improve three of my traits.

Academic and Work-Related Topics

5. People go to college for the following reasons.
6. Getting fired can be a liberating experience.
7. Compare learning from experience versus learning from books.
8. I do (or do not) have the skills to be a salesperson.

CHECKLIST: FIRST DRAFT

When you develop the first draft, ask yourself these questions.

☐ Do I have a compelling introduction?

☐ Does my introduction lead into a clear thesis statement?

☐ Do my body paragraphs contain interesting and sufficient details?

☐ Do the body paragraphs support the idea presented in the thesis statement?

☐ Do I have an interesting title that sums up the essay topic?

☐ Does my conclusion bring my essay to a satisfactory close?

CHAPTER

5 Revising and Editing

Mistakes obviously show us what needs improving. Without mistakes, how would we know what we had to work on?

—PETER MCWILLIAMS, *American author*

Key Steps in Revising and Editing

Revising and editing is the final step in the writing process. When you **revise**, you modify your writing to make it stronger and more convincing. To revise, read your first draft critically, and look for faulty logic, poor organization, or poor sentence style. Then reorganize and rewrite it, making any necessary changes. When you **edit**, you proofread your final draft for errors in grammar, spelling, punctuation, and mechanics.

There are five key steps to follow during the revising and editing stage.

REVISING AND EDITING

STEP 1 ——➤ Revise for unity. Ensure that all parts of your work relate to the main idea.

STEP 2 ——➤ Revise for adequate support. Determine that your details effectively support the main idea.

STEP 3 ——➤ Revise for coherence. Verify that your ideas flow smoothly and logically.

STEP 4 ——➤ Revise for style. Ensure that your sentences are varied and interesting.

STEP 5 ——➤ Edit for technical errors. Proofread your work and correct errors in grammar, spelling, mechanics, and punctuation.

Revising for Unity

Unity means that the ideas in an essay clearly support the focus of the essay. All information heads in the same direction, and there are no forks in the road. If an essay lacks unity, then some ideas drift away from the main idea a writer has expressed in the essay. To check for unity in an essay, consider the following:

- Ensure that all topic sentences in the body paragraphs support the thesis statement of the essay.
- Ensure that all sentences within a body paragraph support the topic sentence of that paragraph.

Essay Without Unity

The next essay plan looks at the reasons for deforestation. The third topic sentence veers away from the writer's central focus that deforestation has implications for the quality of life.

> **Thesis statement:** Deforestation in the Amazon has tremendous implications for people's quality of life.
>
> **Topic sentence 1:** First, logging, mining, and agriculture displace indigenous peoples in the Amazon.
>
> **Topic sentence 2:** Also, scientists believe that deforestation in the Amazon will lead to a rapid increase in global climate change.
>
> **Topic sentence 3:** Many development experts are trying to find methods to have sustainable development in the Amazon.

PRACTICE I

The following thesis statements have three supporting points that can be developed into body paragraphs. Circle the point that does not support the thesis statement.

1. Thesis statement: North America is developing a culture of victimization.

   a. First, many people blame their personal and professional problems on addiction.

   b. Furthermore, the increase in personal injury lawsuits suggests that more people see themselves as victims.

   c. In addition, lobbyists are petitioning on behalf of special interest groups.

2. Thesis statement: International adoptions should be banned.

   a. An internationally adopted child will often lose contact with his or her culture.

   b. Too many celebrities have adopted internationally.

   c. By adopting from poor countries, westerners are complicit in the exploitation of poor people forced to give up their babies due to poverty.

Paragraph Without Unity

Not only must your essay have unity, but each body paragraph must have unity. The details in the paragraph must support the paragraph's topic sentence. The next paragraph is part of a larger work. In it, the writer drifted away from his main idea. Some sentences do not relate to the topic sentence. If the highlighted sentences are removed, then the paragraph has unity.

The writer took a ➤ detour here.

Canadians should not fear the practice of outsourcing by businesses. First, outsourcing is the same practice as subcontracting. In the past, many companies subcontracted work to companies within the same country. Now businesses simply subcontract to other nations. Furthermore, outsourcing usually leads to higher profits because the product or service is produced more cost effectively. Therefore, the head company's profit margin increases, allowing it to reinvest in domestic markets. In addition, when a company increases its profit, not only do the stockholders benefit, but so also do the employees of the company. The stockholders receive more value for their stock, and the employees receive more salaries and benefits. <u>My sister worked in computers and her job became obsolete when her company outsourced the work to India. Now my sister is devastated. She has lost her house and car, and she cannot find another job in her field.</u> Thus, with more disposable incomes, people can help the domestic economy by buying more products.

PRACTICE 2

Paragraphs A and B contain problems with unity. In each paragraph, underline the topic sentence and cross out any sentences that do not support the controlling idea.

A. The gated community is an attempt to create a modern utopia. First, many people are buying property in gated communities because they want to feel more secure. Gated communities are surrounded by fences and guarded entrances. Therefore, tenants feel that crime will stop at the gate. People also buy homes in gated communities because they do not want to spend time maintaining the yard. Most gated communities have lawn-mowing or snow-clearing services available. In fact, home maintenance services are becoming very popular in all types of neighbourhoods. Such services are not meant only for the elderly. They are also meant for busy young families. For some people, gated communities give them a lifestyle choice. Since there are rules to follow in a gated community, some homeowners feel that they will be able to live in a community with likeminded neighbours. For example, people with similar religious values may want to live in one community. Thus, gated communities seem to be an attempt at creating utopian living conditions.

B. The electric car is not as good for the environment as many people think. First, many people buy electric cars thinking that such vehicles produce no carbon dioxide emissions. Consumers forget how electricity is produced. Most electricity plants generate power by burning coal, oil, or diesel fuel. In fact, burning coal releases many contaminants into the air, which create a great deal of air pollution. Moreover, electric car batteries contain toxic ingredients. If these are not properly recycled, they could contaminate landfill sites. My friend is in the market for a car, and we are going to test drive a few on the weekend. He is considering both new and used cars. So think carefully about environmental concerns before buying your next car.

Revising for Adequate Support

An essay has **adequate support** when there are enough supporting ideas to make it strong, convincing, and interesting.

When revising an essay for adequate support, consider the following:

- Ensure that your thesis statement is broad enough to develop several supporting points. It may be necessary to revise the thesis statement to meet the length requirements of the essay.

- When you write the body paragraphs of the essay, insert specific details and try to include vivid descriptions, anecdotes, examples, facts, or quotations.

Avoiding Circular Reasoning

Circular reasoning means that a paragraph restates its main point in various ways but does not provide supporting details. The main idea goes around and around in circles and never progresses. Avoid using circular reasoning by providing a clear, concise topic sentence and by supporting the topic sentence with facts, examples, statistics, or anecdotes.

Paragraph with Circular Reasoning The following paragraph contains circular reasoning. The main point is repeated over and over. The writer does not provide any evidence to support the topic sentence.

> Travelling is a necessary educational tool. Students can learn a lot by visiting other countries. Many schools offer educational trips to other places for their students. Students may benefit from such cultural introductions. Clearly, travelling offers students an important educational opportunity.

◄ This writer leads the reader in circles.

In the second version of this paragraph, the paragraph contains specific examples that help to illustrate the main point.

Revised Paragraph

> Travelling is a necessary educational tool. Students can learn a lot by visiting other places. Many schools and colleges offer educational trips. On such trips, students visit museums, art galleries, and historical sites. For example, the art department of our college sponsored a trip to Ottawa, and the students visited the Canadian Museum of Civilization. Other travel programs are work programs. Students may travel to another region or country to be involved in a community project. Students in the local high school, for example, helped build a community centre for children in a small town in Nicaragua. The students who participated in this project all said that they learned some very practical lessons, including organizational and construction skills. Clearly, travelling offers students an important educational opportunity.

◄ Anecdotes and examples provide supporting evidence.

PRACTICE 3

Read the following paragraphs and write OK next to the ones that have adequate support. Underline the specific details in those paragraphs. Then, to the paragraphs that lack adequate support, add details such as descriptions, examples, quotations, or anecdotes. Use arrows to indicate where you should place specific details.

This example is from an essay. In the first paragraph, the writer was repetitive and vague. After the writer added specific examples and vivid details, the paragraph was much more interesting.

Weak Support	Better Support with Details
To become a better dresser, follow the next steps. First, ask friends or family members what colours suit you. Also, don't be a slave to the latest fashion. Finally, spend money on a few good items rather than filling your closet with cheap outfits. My closet is half-full, but the clothing I have is of good quality.	**To become a better dresser, follow the next steps.** First, ask friends or colours suit you. *I love green, for instance, but when I wore an olive-green shirt, a close friend said it brought out the green in my skin and made me look ill.* Also, don't be a slave to the latest fashion. *Although tank tops and low-waist jeans were popular for several years, I didn't have the right body type for that fashion because my belly spilled over the top of my jeans. Instead, I wore longer shirts with my jeans, so I looked stylish but not ridiculous.* Finally, spend money on a few good items rather than filling your closet with cheap outfits. My closet is half full, but the clothing I have is of good quality.

1. **Many cyclists are inconsiderate.** Some think that they don't have to obey traffic rules and that traffic signs are just for car drivers. Also, some cyclists are pretty crazy and do dangerous things and risk their lives or the lives of others. People have ended up in the hospital after a run-in with these two-wheeled rebels. Cyclists should take safety courses before they ride on public roads.	Write OK or add details
2. **During my first job interview, I managed to overcome my fright.** I sat in a small, brightly lit room in front of four interviewers. A stern woman stared at me intently and curtly asked me why I wanted the job. Perspiration dripped into my eyes as I stammered that I had seen an advertisement. She smirked and asked me to be more specific. Feeling that I didn't have a chance anyway, I relaxed and stopped worrying about the faces gazing at me. I spoke about my first experience in a hospital, and I described the nurses who took care of me and the respectful way the orderlies treated me. I expressed my heartfelt desire to work as an orderly, and I got the job.	Write OK or add details

3. **Hollywood producers should stop making movies based on old television shows.** Many of the original series were on television in the 1960s or 1970s, and younger audiences cannot relate to movies based on those television shows. Even when those programs were first on the air, they were mediocre. The remakes are boring for young people even when studios hire stellar actors and spend fortunes on special effects. Then the studio bosses are surprised when the remakes are not successful. Hollywood studios should realize that the public doesn't want any more remakes of old television shows.	Write OK or add details

Revising for Coherence

Make your writing as smooth as possible by using expressions that logically guide the reader from one idea to the next. When revising an essay for **coherence**, consider the following:

- Ensure that sentences within each body paragraph flow smoothly by using transitional expressions.
- Ensure the supporting ideas of an essay are connected to each other and to the thesis statement by using paragraph links.

Transitional Expressions

Just as stepping stones make for a smooth crossing, **transitional expressions** are linking words or phrases, and they ensure that ideas are connected.

Here are some common transitional expressions.

Function	Transitional Word or Expression
Addition	again, also, besides, finally, first (second, third), for one thing, furthermore, in addition, in fact, last, moreover, next, then
Concession of a point	certainly, even so, indeed, of course, no doubt, to be sure
Comparison and contrast	as well, equally, even so, however, in contrast, instead, likewise, nevertheless, on the contrary, on the other hand, similarly
Effect or result	accordingly, as a result, consequently, hence, otherwise, then, therefore, thus
Example	for example, for instance, in other words, in particular, namely, specifically, to illustrate
Emphasis	above all, clearly, first, especially, in fact, in particular, indeed, least of all, most important, most of all, of course, particularly, principally
Reason or purpose	for this purpose, for this reason, the most important reason
Space	above, behind, below, beneath, beside, beyond, closer in, farther out, inside, near, nearby, on one side/on the other side, on the bottom, on the left/right, on top, outside, to the north/east/south/west, under

continued

Summary or conclusion	in conclusion, in other words, in short, generally, on the whole, therefore, thus, to conclude, to summarize, ultimately
Time	after that, afterward, at that time, at the moment, currently, earlier, eventually, first (second, etc.), gradually, immediately, in the beginning, in the future, in the past, later, meanwhile, months afterward, now, one day, presently, so far, subsequently, suddenly, then, these days

---

HINT   Use Transitional Expressions with Complete Sentences

When you add a transitional expression to a sentence, ensure that your sentence is complete. Your sentence must have a subject and a verb, and it must express a complete thought.

Incomplete: For example, violence on television.

Complete: For example, violence on television is very graphic.

Adding Transitional Words Within a Paragraph

The next paragraph shows transitional words linking sentences within the same paragraph.

> Learning a new language provides invaluable benefits to a person's life. **First**, researchers have found that learning a foreign language is a kind of exercise for the brain. It improves the area in the brain that processes information. Such people display better problem-solving abilities. **Furthermore**, people who speak a second language can communicate with more people. **Therefore**, they can use this skill to acquire greater understanding of different cultures. **For example**, knowing a foreign language may give them more personal satisfaction when they are travelling because it allows them more opportunities to communicate with other people. **In addition**, bilingual people are more competitive in the job market. Because they know another language, they may be more mobile in their careers. They may **also** be able to take advantage of more job opportunities. In their spare time, people should learn a second language. They won't regret it.

PRACTICE 4

Add appropriate transitional expressions to the following paragraph. Choose from the following list, and use each transitional word once. There may be more than one correct answer.

in addition	in fact
first	for example
therefore	for instance
then	moreover

> Counterculture is a pattern of beliefs and actions that oppose the cultural norms of a society. _____ , hippies are the most well-known counterculture group in the recent past, and they are known for rebelling against authority. _____ , they rejected the consumer-

based capitalist society of their parents in favour of communal living arrangements. _____ , the hippie generation migrated to Toronto's Yorkville and Vancouver's Kitsilano neighbourhoods, where they meditated and experimented with drugs. They also listened to music about love, peace, and social concerns. _____ Joni Mitchell's music was very popular because it summarized the values of her generation. _____ , small religious groups such as the Hutterites or the Amish belong to the counterculture current. These groups live with other likeminded people and turn away from widely accepted ideas on lifestyle. _____ , some counterculture members, like the Mennonites, are pacifists, or they reject modern technology. _____ , militant groups and anarchist groups reject conventional laws. Some of these groups want to eliminate legal, political, and social institutions. Counterculture social patterns will always remain part of the mainstream society.

PRACTICE 5

The next paragraph lacks transitional expressions. Add appropriate transitional expressions wherever you think they are necessary.

People in our culture tend to idolize notorious gangsters. Al Capone operated during Prohibition, selling alcohol and building a criminal empire. He became infamous and his name is instantly recognizable. The Gotti patriarch was the head of a large and vicious crime family in New Jersey. The family members are celebrities, and one of the daughters, Victoria Gotti, had her own reality television show. Filmmakers contribute to the idealization of criminals. Movies, such as *The Godfather* and *Live Free or Die Trying*, celebrate gangsters and criminals. Gangsters appear to have exciting and glamorous lives. It is unfortunate that our culture elevates criminals to heroic status.

Adding Links Between Paragraphs

To achieve coherence in an essay, use transitions to connect body paragraphs. Here are three methods for using transitions.

1. Repeat words or phrases from the thesis statement in the topic sentence of each body paragraph. In this example, *gifted* and *ambiguity* are repeated words.

    Thesis statement: Although many schools offer a program for **gifted** children, there continues to be **ambiguity** concerning the definition of **gifted**.

    Body paragraph 1: One **ambiguity** is choosing the criteria for assessing the **gifted**.

    Body paragraph 2: Another **ambiguity** pertains to defining the fields or areas of those who are **gifted**.

2. Refer to the main idea in the previous paragraph, and link it to your current topic sentence. In the topic sentence for the second body paragraph, the writer reminds the reader of the first point (insomnia) and then introduces the next point.

> **Thesis statement:** Sleeping disorders cause severe disruption to many people's lives.
>
> **Body paragraph 1: Insomnia**, a common **sleep disorder**, severely limits **people's quality of life**.
>
> **Body paragraph 2:** The **opposite condition of insomnia**, narcolepsy also causes **mayhem in people's lives**.

3. Use a transitional word or phrase to lead the reader to your next idea.

> **Body paragraph 3: Moreover**, when sufferers go untreated for their sleep disorders, they pose risks to the people around them.

Revising for Style

When you revise for sentence **style**, you ensure that your essay has concise and appropriate language and sentence variety. You can ask yourself the following questions.

- Have I used a variety of sentence patterns? (To practise using sentence variety, see Chapter 20.)
- Are my sentences parallel in structure? (To practise revising for parallel structure, see Chapter 23.)
- Have I used exact language? (To learn about slang, wordiness, and overused expressions, see Chapter 31.)

Alicia's Revision   In Chapter 3, you read Alicia's essay plan about college dropouts. After writing her first draft, she revised her essay. Look at her revisions for unity, support, coherence, and style.

Why Students Drop Out

≺ *Add title*

I live in a small costal town in Nova Scotia. The town attracts

tourists from all over the country. Because of its beautiful beach. My

college roommate, Farrad, works as a cook at the local pizza stand.

Last year, Farrad started working a few hours per week, but then,

because of his efficiency, his boss increased Farrad's hours. My

roommate then joined a growing group of people. He became a

college dropout. **Students may drop out of college because they lack**

≺ *Thesis statement*

financial support, experience an emotional crisis, or are unprepared.

First, s

~~S~~ome students drop out because they may face overwhelming

≺ *Add transition*

According to a report, "The Price of Knowledge 2006" by Joseph Berger, fifty-nine percent of Canadian post-secondary students borrowed money for their studies, which means that a majority of students are in debt.

≺ *Add detail*

financial burdens. Like Farrad, they may have a part-time job

to help pay for tuition and rent. If the job requires students to work for

many hours, they might not have time to study or to do homework.

Nadia, for example, works in the computer lab four nights a week.

The number of hours is overwhelming and she may drop out of college.
Some students

≺ *Add detail*

~~They~~ may also drop out because they are too far from campus,

≺ *Clarify pronoun*

transportation may be too expensive or inconvenient.

, and they

Furthermore, some students undergo life-changing events. ~~They~~

≺ *Combine sentences*

In an interview with the <u>McGill Reporter</u>, Donal Sedgewick, an advisor for student affairs, offers a further explanation why students drop out: "Often it will have to do with something that happened outside their academic life."

must leave college. A student may get married or a female student

≺ *Unify problem*

may become pregnant and taking care of a baby may consume all

of her time and energy. ~~There are public and private daycare~~

Add transition ➤   ~~centers. But parents must choose very carefully.~~ _{Also, an} An illness in the

family may cause a student to miss too many classes. A student

may also feel emotionally fragile because the student may not be

able to cope with their feelings and wanted to leave college.

Better word ➤   Moreover, some students may be unable to _{adapt to} ~~get into~~ college life.

Accordingly, some students may experience homesickness if they

are away for the first time in their lives.

Add detail ➤   In the article "Retention Efforts Take Hold," Julia Matusky researches programs
that help students stay in colleges and universities. "Those students who leave their
home and community for the first time tend to have a more difficult time," explains
Vera Pezer, associate vice-president of student affairs at the University of
Saskatchewan, explains to Matusky.

Add transition ➤   _{In addition, s} ~~S~~ome students have poor study skills and fall behind in

homework assignments. Students may not be able to organize there

time, or a student might be unused to freedom in college and skip

too many classes. Not every student has clear career goals. Those

who are unsure about their academic futur may drop out rather

than continue to study in a field they do not enjoy.

Add detail ➤   For instance, my cousin realized she did not want to be an engineer, so she left
school until she could figure out what she really wanted to do.

Add transition ➤   Even though students drop out of school for many good reasons,

_{For example,}
some decide to return to college life. Farrad hopes to finish his

studies next year.

Improve conclusion ➤   He knows he would have to find a better balance between work and school to
succeed, but he is motivated to complete his education.

Editing for Errors

When you **edit**, you reread your writing and make sure that it is free of errors. You focus on the language, and you look for mistakes in grammar, punctuation, mechanics, and spelling.

There is an editing guide on the inside back cover of this book. It contains some common error codes that your instructor may use. It also provides you with a list of errors to check for when you proofread your text.

Editing Tips

The following tips will help you to proofread your work more effectively.

- Put your text aside for a day or two before you do the editing. Sometimes when you have been working closely with a text, you might not see the errors.

- Begin your proofreading at any stage of the writing process. For example, if you are not sure of the spelling of a word while writing the first draft, you could either highlight the word to remind yourself to verify it later, or you could immediately look up the word in the dictionary.

- Use the grammar and spelling checker that comes with your word processor. However, be vigilant when accepting the suggestions. Do not always choose the first suggestion for a correction. For example, a grammar checker cannot distinguish between when to use *which* and *that*. Make sure that suggestions are valid before you accept them.

- Keep a list of your common errors in a separate grammar log. When you finish a writing assignment, consult your error list and make sure that you have not repeated any of those errors. After you have received each corrected assignment from your instructor, you could add new errors to your list. For more information about a grammar and spelling log, see Appendix 5.

Alicia's Edited Essay Alicia edited her essay about college dropouts. She corrected errors in spelling, punctuation, and grammar.

GRAMMAR LINK

To practise your editing skills, try the practices in Chapter 39.

Why Students Drop Out

coastal ➤ I live in a small ~~costal~~ town in Nova Scotia. The town attracts

because ➤ tourists from all over the country. ~~Because~~ of its beautiful beach. My

college roommate, Farrad, works as a cook at the local pizza stand.

Last year, Farrad started working a few hours per week, but then

because of his efficiency, his boss increased Farrad's hours. My

roommate then joined a growing group of people, and he became a

college dropout. **Students may drop out of college because they lack**

financial support, experience an emotional crisis, or are unprepared.

First, some students drop out because they face overwhelming

financial burdens. According to a report, "The Price of Knowledge

2006" by Joseph Berger, fifty-nine percent of Canadian post-

secondary students have borrowed money for their studies, which

means that a majority of students are in debt. Like Farrad, they may

have a part-time job to help pay for tuition and rent. Nadia, for

example ➤ ~~exemple~~ , works in the computer lab four nights a week. The

number of hours is overwhelming, and she may drop out of college.

If the job requires students to work for many hours, they might not

have time to study or to do homework. Students may also drop out

because they live too far from campus, and transportation may be

too expensive or inconvenient.

Furthermore, some students undergo life-changing events, and

they must leave college. In an interview with the <u>McGill Reporter</u>,

Donal Sedgewick, an advisor for student affairs, offers a further

explanation why students drop out: "Often it will have to do with

something that happened outside their academic life." A student

may get married, or a female student may become pregnant and

taking care of a baby may consume all of her time and energy. In

addition, a death in the family may cause a student to miss too

emotionally ➤ many classes. A student may also feel ~~emotionaly~~ fragile because

of a broken relationship. The student may not be able to cope with

his or her ➤ ~~their~~ feelings and ~~wanted~~ to leave college.

want ➤

Moreover, some students may be unable to adapt to college life.

Accordingly, some students may experience homesickness if they are away for the first time in their lives. In the article "Retention Efforts Take Hold," Julia Matusky researches programs that help students stay in colleges and universities. "Those students who leave their home and community for the first time tend to have a more difficult time," Vera Pezer, associate vice-president of student affairs at the University of Saskatchewan, explains to Matusky. In addition, some students may have poor study skills and fall behind in homework assignments. Also, students may not be able to organize ~~there~~ time, or a student might not be used to freedom in ◁*their* college and skip too many classes. For instance, my lab partner has missed about six classes this semester. In addition, not every student has clear career goals. Those who are unsure about their academic ~~futur~~ may drop out rather than continue to study in a field ◁*future* they do not enjoy. For instance, my cousin realized she did not want to be an engineer, so she left school until she could figure out what she really wanted to do.

   Even though students drop out of college for many good reasons, some decide to return to college life. Farrad, for example, hopes to finish his studies next year. He knows he ~~would~~ have to ◁*will* find a better balance between work and school to succeed, but he is motivated to complete his education.

Writer's Desk **Revise and Edit Your Essay**

Choose an essay that you have written for Chapter 4, or choose one that you have written for another assignment. Carefully revise and edit the essay. You can refer to the revising and editing checklists at the end of this chapter and on the inside covers of this book.

Peer Feedback

After you write an essay, it is useful to get peer feedback. Ask a friend, family member, or fellow student to read your work and give you comments and suggestions on its strengths and weaknesses.

HINT   Offer Constructive Criticism

When you peer edit someone else's writing, try to make your comments useful. Phrase your comments in a positive way. Look at the examples.

Instead of saying...	You could say...
You repeat the same words.	Maybe you could find synonyms for some words.
Your paragraphs are too short.	You could add more details here.

You can use the peer feedback form on the next page to evaluate written work.

Writing the Final Draft

When you have finished making revisions on the first draft of your essay, write the final draft. Include all the changes that you have made during the revising and editing phases. Before you submit your final draft, proofread it one last time to ensure that you have caught any errors.

Writer's Desk **Write Your Final Draft**

You have developed, revised, and edited your essay. Now write the final draft.

HINT   Spelling, Grammar, and Vocabulary Logs

- **Keep a Spelling and Grammar Log.** You probably repeat, over and over, the same types of grammar and spelling errors. You will find it very useful to record your repeated grammar mistakes in a Spelling and Grammar Log. You can refer to your list of spelling and grammar mistakes when you revise and edit your writing.
- **Keep a Vocabulary Log.** Expanding your vocabulary will be of enormous benefit to you as a writer. In a vocabulary log, you can make a list of unfamiliar words and their definitions.

    See Appendix 5 for more information about spelling, grammar, and vocabulary logs.

Peer Feedback Form

Written by _____ Feedback by _____

Date: _____

1. What is the main point of the written work?

   _____

   _____

   _____

2. Which details effectively support the thesis statement?

   _____

   _____

   _____

3. What, if anything, is unclear or unnecessary?

   _____

   _____

   _____

4. Give some suggestions about how the work could be improved.

   _____

   _____

   _____

5. What are the most interesting or unique features of this written work?

   _____

   _____

   _____

Writer's Room **Essay Topics**

Writing Activity 1

Choose an essay that you have written for this course or for another course. Revise and edit that essay, and then write a final draft.

Writing Activity 2

Choose any of the following topics, or choose your own topic, and then write an essay. Remember to follow the writing process.

General Topics

1. online shopping
2. heroes in sports
3. a problem in politics
4. unfair gender roles
5. making the world better

Academic and Work-Related Topics

6. something you learned in college
7. bad work habits
8. reasons to accept a job
9. unpleasant jobs
10. a funny co-worker

 CHECKLIST: REVISING AND EDITING

When you revise and edit your essay, ask yourself these questions.

☐ Does my essay have unity? Ensure that every paragraph relates to the main idea.

☐ Does my essay have adequate support? Verify that there are enough details and examples to support your main point.

☐ Is my essay coherent? Try to use transitional expressions to link ideas.

☐ Does my essay have good style? Check for varied sentence patterns and exact language.

☐ Does my essay have any errors? Edit for errors in grammar, punctuation, spelling, and mechanics.

☐ Is my final draft error-free?

Essay Patterns

Paragraph Patterns

Illustration

To illustrate or prove a point using specific examples

Narration

To narrate or tell a story about a sequence of events that happened

Description

To describe using vivid details and images that appeal to the reader's senses

Process

To inform the reader about how to do something, how something works, or how something happened

Definition

To explain what a term or concept means by providing relevant examples

Classification

To classify or sort a topic to help readers understand different qualities about that topic

Comparison and contrast

To present information about similarities (compare) or differences (contrast)

Cause and effect

To explain why an event happened (the cause) or what the consequences of the event were (the effects)

Argument *

To argue or to take a position on an issue and offer reasons for your position

* Argument is included as one of the nine patterns, but it is also a purpose in writing.

What Is an Essay Pattern?

A **pattern** or **mode** is a method used to express one of the three purposes: to inform, to persuade, or to entertain. Once you know your purpose, you will be able to choose which writing pattern to use.

6

CHAPTER

Illustration

Sports serve society by providing vivid examples of excellence.

—GEORGE F. WILL, *editor and columnist*

HINT **Patterns May Overlap**

You can combine writing patterns. You may use one predominant pattern, but you can also introduce other patterns as supporting material.

 CHAT ROOM

Work with a partner. You have three minutes to list as many words as you can that are examples of the following.

For example, *bungee jumping* is a dangerous sport.

dangerous sports   bad fashion fads   sticky food

EXPLORING

WHAT IS ILLUSTRATION?

Illustration writing includes specific examples that help readers acquire a clearer, deeper understanding of an essay's subject. You illustrate or give examples each time you explain, analyze, narrate, or express an opinion. Examples might include something that you have experienced or observed, or they may include factual information, such as a statistic.

Here are some examples people give every day to explain or clarify what they mean.

Audience: Family or roommates	Audience: Classmate	Audience: Co-worker
The house is becoming a pigsty.	**Our instructors give us too much homework.**	**Financial cutbacks are hurting productivity.**
• There are piles of shoes and boots in the entrance. • Newspapers and letters are on the kitchen table. • Dishes are piled in the sink.	• Our science lab is due tomorrow. • We must submit a five-page research essay on Monday. • We must also study for our history exam, which is also on Monday.	• Each employee must do the work of several people. • Jobs are not completed properly. • Employees are stressed and suffering from burn-out.

LIFE SNAPSHOT **Illustration at Work**

Portland Bolt and Manufacturing Company requires a large sales force. In the following excerpt from a job announcement on their website, there is a list of examples showing what a sales associate must do.

Sales Associate Duties

■ Estimating the costs associated with manufacturing bolts.

■ Assigning appropriate profit margins to estimates.

■ Selling bolts and fasteners primarily via the telephone to an established customer base made up of contractors, steel fabricators, and other construction-related companies.

■ Tracking and following up of a small quantity of specific construction projects.

■ Making sales order entries.

■ Doing a limited amount of prospecting.

■ (Optional) Limited selling in both local and regional marketplace.

The Illustration Essay

There are two effective ways to exemplify your main point and support your body paragraphs in an illustration essay.

1. Use a **series of examples**. When writing an essay about innovative commercials, you might list things that some directors do, such as using bizarre camera angles, introducing hilarious scenarios, adding fun jingles, or creating catchy slogans.
2. Use an **extended example** such as an anecdote or a description of an event. When writing about problems faced by first-year college students, you might tell a story about a specific student's chronic lateness.

A Student Essay

Read the student essay and answer the questions that follow.

Priceless Euphoria

By Lisa Monique

1   The Beatles recorded a song satirically titled *Money*, in which they sing, "The best things in life are free." Undoubtedly, the best things in life are free. Although costs might be associated, these "things" are not purchased items. The best things are a common thread among all people regardless of sex, race, religion, or nationality. In fact, the best things in life are not things but

are precious segments in time involving and engaging us in experiences, emotions, and various states of being.

2   Nature provides us with many priceless treasures of breathtaking scenery. We might view a cascading waterfall, a brilliant sunset casting a serene, pink glow on the mountain jags and peaks, or the glistening beauty of a fresh, undisturbed snowfall. Each location we visit stimulates the senses. A day at the beach allows us to listen to crashing waves, watch a school of dolphins play, splash in the shallow water, or bury our feet in the gushy wet sand. The desert is also a smorgasbord of sensations. Marvels include the mighty Saguaro cacti, the ethereal haze of the Palo Verde trees, and the grace and gentleness of a passing butterfly.

3   Emotional experiences, as well, are often the best "things" in life. Falling in love, viewing the birth of a child, having the first kiss, laughing and conversing with an old friend, and watching the klutzy steps of a puppy are some simple delights in life. Emotional experiences can occur with loved ones, but they can also be kindled in natural environments. A day at the beach is renewing and refreshing. Hiking and observing the desert help us to feel wild, free, and reckless. The purity of a fresh snowfall makes us feel childlike and innocent.

4   Similarly, states of being bring great satisfaction, which is, yet again, a great thing. Good health after a prolonged illness or even after a short bout of the flu is a greatly appreciated state of being. Invaluable gratification is derived from meeting a deadline, winning a race, nurturing a garden, sculpting a creation, giving a gift, receiving a gift, dispensing good advice, accepting good advice, planning a successful event, helping someone in need, and achieving a well-earned goal.

5   Money does directly buy cars, jewellery, furs, vacations, large homes, designer clothing, or French perfume. Purchases are not the best "things" in life. It is true that crayons and paper are purchased, but colouring is free. Writing, dancing, laughing, loving, and learning are all beneficial activities with peripheral costs. The value is found in each experience. Consequently, "The best things in life are free" is not just a simple song lyric, but also a rather complex and admirable human philosophy.

PRACTICE I

1. Who is the intended audience?_____

   _____

2. Highlight the essay's thesis statement.

3. Underline the topic sentence in each body paragraph.

4. In body paragraphs 2, 3, and 4, what does the author use?

   a. series of examples   b. extended examples

5. In paragraph 4, what does the author mean by *states of being*? Using your own words, explain her point. _____

   _____

6. What organizational strategy does the author use?

   a. time order   b. space order   c. emphatic order

7. Add one more example to each body paragraph.

nature _____

_____

emotional experiences _____

_____

states of being _____

_____

Explore Topics

In the following Writer's Desk, you will try an exploring strategy to generate ideas about different topics.

Writer's Desk **Warm Up**

Read the following questions, and write the first ideas that come to your mind. Think of two to three ideas for each topic.

EXAMPLE:
What can go wrong when you rent an apartment?

– hard to find a landlord who will rent to a student

– can't find a good apartment in a decent area on a student budget

– roommate problems

1. What are some things you would like to accomplish in the near future?

_____

_____

_____

2. What are some professions that make useful or worthwhile contributions to society?

_____

_____

_____

3. What are some status symbols in today's society?

_____

_____

_____

THE THESIS STATEMENT

The thesis statement of the illustration essay is a general statement that expresses both your topic and your controlling idea. To determine your controlling idea, think about what point you want to make. Remember to express an attitude or point of view about the topic.

topic   controlling idea
Newlyweds often have misconceptions about married life.

controlling idea   topic
I am unable to control **the mess in my work space.**

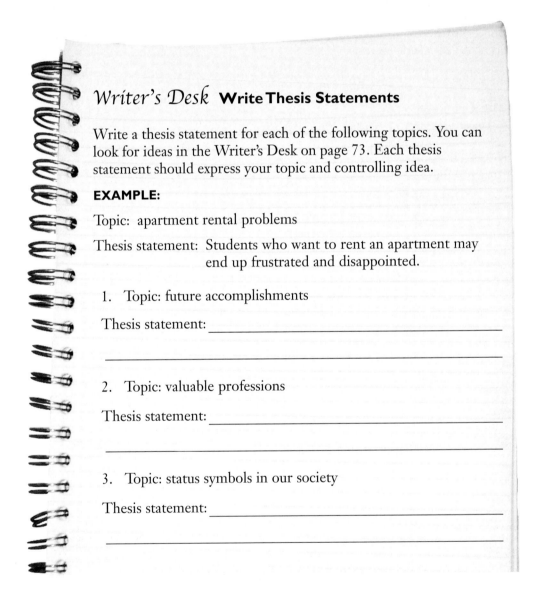

Writer's Desk **Write Thesis Statements**

Write a thesis statement for each of the following topics. You can look for ideas in the Writer's Desk on page 73. Each thesis statement should express your topic and controlling idea.

EXAMPLE:

Topic: apartment rental problems

Thesis statement: Students who want to rent an apartment may end up frustrated and disappointed.

1. Topic: future accomplishments

    Thesis statement: _____

    _____

2. Topic: valuable professions

    Thesis statement: _____

    _____

3. Topic: status symbols in our society

    Thesis statement: _____

    _____

THE SUPPORTING IDEAS

After you have developed an effective thesis statement, generate supporting ideas.

- Use prewriting strategies to generate a list of examples. Brainstorm a series of examples and extended examples that will best illustrate your main point.
- Choose the best ideas.
- Organize your ideas. Choose the best organizational method for this essay pattern.

Writer's Desk **Generate Supporting Ideas**

Choose one of your thesis statements from the previous Writer's Desk. List three or four examples that support the thesis statement.

EXAMPLE:
Thesis statement: Students who want to rent an apartment may end up frustrated and disappointed.

Supports:

– can't find an affordable place

– landlords might be hesitant to rent to them

– roommates may be immature

– not enough housing for students

– only available housing is in dangerous neighbourhood

Thesis statement: _____

_____

_____

Supports: _____

_____

_____

The Essay Plan

When writing an outline for an illustration essay, ensure that your examples are valid and relate to the thesis statement. Also, include details that will help clarify your supporting examples and organize your ideas in a logical order.

Thesis statement: Students who want to rent an apartment may end up frustrated and disappointed.

I. Landlords often hesitate to rent to students.
   A. Young people might be irresponsible.
   B. They don't have credit ratings.

II. Students have money problems.
  A. They have limited choices.
  B. They cannot apply for nicer apartments because many are too expensive.
  C. They must settle for dives and dumps.

III. Sharing a place with another student can end badly.
  A. The roommate might be very messy.
  B. The roommate might be a party guy or girl.
  C. There could be financial disputes over unpaid rent and bills.

IV. Some students choose to rent alone but have other problems.
  A. They may feel lonely.
  B. Girls living alone may feel unsafe.
  C. They may be unable to pay all of the bills.

Writer's Desk **Write an Essay Plan**

Refer to the information you generated in previous Writer's Desks, and prepare a detailed essay plan. Consider the order in which you list details.

The First Draft

After outlining your ideas in a plan, write the first draft using complete sentences. Also, include transitional words or expressions to help your ideas flow smoothly. Here are some transitional expressions that can help you introduce an example or show an additional example.

To Introduce an Example		To Show an Additional Example	
for example	namely	also	in addition
for instance	specifically	first (second)	in another case
in other words	to illustrate	furthermore	moreover

VOCABULARY BOOST

Here are some ways to vary sentences, which will help you avoid boring readers with repeated phrases.

1. Underline the opening word of every sentence in your first draft. Check to see if some are repeated.

2. Replace repeated opening words with adverbs, such as *Usually*, *Generally*, or *Luckily*, or a prepositional phrase such as *With his help* or *Under the circumstances* instead of beginning every sentence with a noun.

Repeated First Words: People make many mistakes with their finances. They want luxuries that they cannot afford. They buy items on credit. They do not consider the high interest rates that credit card companies charge.

Variety: People make many mistakes with their finances. Desiring luxuries that they cannot afford, consumers buy items on credit. Sadly, many do not consider the high interest rates that credit card companies charge.

Writer's Desk **Write the First Draft**

In the previous Writer's Desk, you developed an essay plan. Now write the first draft of your illustration essay. Remember to include details such as specific names, places, facts, or statistics to flesh out each body paragraph.

REVISING AND EDITING

REVISE AND EDIT AN ILLUSTRATION ESSAY

When you finish writing an illustration essay, review your work and revise it to make the examples as clear as possible to your readers. Ensure that the order of ideas is logical, and remove any irrelevant details. Before you work on your own essay, practise revising and editing a student essay.

A Student Essay

A student from Montreal, Quebec, wrote the next essay. Read the essay, and then answer the questions that follow. As you read, correct any errors that you find and make comments in the margins.

Finding an Apartment

By Shannon Nolan

1   Renting an apartment for the first time is one of the defining rites of passage that marks the transition from adolescence to young adulthood. Many young people have a dream of what their first apartment will be like, whether it is the boho chic flat in a trendy neighbourhood, the immaculate penthouse in the heart of downtown, or the ultimate party pad with a gang of best friends for roommates. Unfortunately, it is often harder to find that perfect apartment than it is to daydream about it. Students who want to rent an apartment may end up frustrated and disappointed.

2   Finding an apartment—any apartment—can be hard enough. Landlords are often hesitant to rent to students for the very reasons students want an apartment. Young renters do not have credit ratings with banks, and they haven't proved that they're capable of handling responsability. They throw parties, make noise, and never stay in one place very long. Landlords usually require a reference from a former landlord and a security deposit, if not the co-signature of a parent or relative. However, landlords are far from the sainted beings their high standards might indicate. The ones who don't ask for references are usually equally lax about fixing blocked drains or leaking ceilings, and the ones who do demand references aren't necessarily any better.

3   Money is another common issue when renting a place. A student budget in most cases is fairly limited. Rent, bills, and tuition must be paid, on a part-time salary at best. The cost of renting an apartment larger than a refrigerator box is usually too much for one person alone. Often after one weekend of apartment hunting, the dream of the perfect apartment goes up in smoke. The place advertised as a "spacious studio" turns out to be a sort of basement mausoleum with grime-covered slats for windows, more appropriate as the setting for a horror movie than a romantic year of independence. "One bedroom" means "walk-in closet." A trend emerges—if the price is right, everything else is wrong.

4   To reduce expenses, many people opt to share a place, but the joys of shared housekeeping can turn overnight into a disaster. Students quickly wonder why did they want a roommate in the first place. A certain amount of messiness can be expected from first-time renters, but some people take this to an extreme. No one wants to end up rooming with the guy who starts a biology lab in the kitchen—studying the growth patterns of breakfast cereal mould (especially when he is a sociology major). Similarly, no one who is serious about their studies wants to live with a party-guy or -girl who is out all night, every night, and who seems to come home only for about five minutes at a time to puke in the sink.

5   Some students, unhappy with their experiences sharing a closet-sized bedroom in a dorm decide to rent a bachelor or studio apartment, prefering to pay a little more in exchange for peace of mind. Sandra, a second-year student, took this route and found that a whole new problem confronted her. "I couldn't believe how lonely I was the first few months," she said. "Even though I hated my roommate, I actually missed her. I spent so much time studying in coffee shops that I might as well have stayed in res." Besides loneliness, safety is another problem for those living alone. Many students, especially girls, are worried about the risks of walking home alone.

6   The first year or so of independence can be a vulnerable time, and not just emotionally. Finding apartments is tough, and renting can be expensive. Sharing can be a solution—unless roommates become a nightmare. Then there is the dangers of being lonely and depressed or of having something bad happen with no one there to offer support. It might seem like the pitfalls of apartment renting outweigh the benefits. But the first step into true independence has its rewards too, and after all, it's a step everyone must take.

PRACTICE 2

Revising

1. Highlight the thesis statement.

2. Highlight the topic sentence in paragraphs 2 and 4.

3. In paragraph 2, the writer veers off course. Cross out the sentences that do not support the topic sentence.

4. Paragraph 3 is missing a topic sentence. Which sentence best sums up the main point of paragraph 3?

   a. Many apartments are small and ugly.

   b. Landlords do not rent to students easily.

   c. Because students have limited budgets, they must settle for small rundown apartments.

   d. Apartments are often not as nice as they are described in the advertisements.

5. Paragraph 5 is also missing a topic sentence. Which sentence best sums up the main point of paragraph 5?

   a. Furthermore, students who can afford to live alone might have problems.

   b. There are safety issues when renting an apartment.

   c. Sandra had her own studio apartment.

   d. Sometimes students who live alone feel lonely.

6. Which paragraph contains an extended example? _____

Editing

7. Paragraph 4 contains an embedded question error. (For information about embedded questions, see the Grammar Hint below this practice.) Underline and correct the error.

   Correction: _____

8. Paragraph 5 contains a missing comma. Underline and correct the error.

   Correction: _____

9. This essay contains misspelled words in paragraphs 2 and 5. Underline and correct them.

   Corrections: _____

GRAMMAR LINK

See the following chapters for more information about these grammar topics:
Embedded Questions, Chapter 20
Commas, Chapter 33
Spelling, Chapter 32
Subject–Verb Agreement, Chapter 25

10. Underline and correct a subject–verb agreement error in paragraph 6.

Correction: _____

GRAMMAR HINT **Writing Embedded Questions**

When a question is part of a larger sentence, do not use the question word order. View the next examples.

Error: I wondered how would I pay the rent.

Correction: I wondered how I would pay the rent.

See Chapter 20 for more information about writing embedded questions.

Writer's Desk **Revise and Edit Your Essay**

Revise and edit the essay that you wrote for the previous Writer's Desk. You can refer to the checklist for illustration essays at the end of this chapter and the revising and editing checklists on the inside covers of this book.

A Professional Essay

Eric Gall is a freelance writer based in Toronto. His articles have appeared in the *National Post*, the *Queen's Journal*, and various other publications. In the next essay, he examines the power of intrusive technology.

Little Brother Is Watching

By Eric Gall

killer app: a very useful computer application as program.

1   In late 2006, Michael Richards, Seinfeld's shock-haired neighbour Kramer, found out the hard way that messing up in public is now a whole lot messier. Thanks to the cell phone video camera and the Internet's latest **killer app**— YouTube.com—Richards' racist meltdown at a heckler during a standup routine in L.A. was viewed by millions. As Richards discovered, Little Brother is watching, again and again, and he is emailing the link to all his friends.

2   Back in 2005, when Chad Hurley, Steve Chen, and Jawed Karim founded YouTube, they thought they were building a place where ordinary people could share their favourite camcorder movies, TV moments and, yes, cell phone clips. And share they did. One would have to have been living on one of the more desolate craters on Pluto not to have seen the Backstreet Boys' "I Want It That Way" as lip-synched by two Chinese pranksters. Arguably the site's tipping point, their dorm-made video spawned a million imitations and clicked YouTube to the top of every browser bookmark list.

3   What Chad, Steve, and Jawed couldn't have predicted was that they were bringing George Orwell's dystopic *1984* to life in a way no one saw coming.

While Orwell's protagonist, Winston Smith, lived a miserable existence, at least he knew he was being watched as he carried out life's mundane tasks. It was not the same case with University of Missouri quarterback Chase Daniel, whose moment of fame came during a game on November 4, 2006. He didn't anticipate being filmed as he sat on the bench performing his own digital download—from nose to mouth—and having his little picnic uploaded onto the World Wide Web. Students worldwide have also happily uploaded cell phone videos of teachers "losing it" in class—some actually hitting their students. Many of these educators, it is alleged, were pushed to the brink by their pupils for the very purpose of being **surreptitiously** filmed.

surreptitiously: secretly

4   Beyond the facility to humiliate, there is a positive side to the power of YouTube. Two Los Angeles cops were caught on a cell phone camera "subduing" an alleged **perp** (another of the site's recent top hits). While their YouTube moment now has them slapping their own foreheads, it demonstrates that "the whole world is in fact watching." So what better way to blow the whistle than to use the powers of online video blogs, especially if you've tried and failed by every other means? That's what Michael DeKort, former Lockheed Martin engineer on the U.S. Coast Guard's "Deepwater" project, did when nobody would listen to his concerns about serious security flaws the company and the coastguard were determined to ignore. His ten-minute "kitchen confidential" shot on grainy home video finally caught the eye of the navy, Congress and, crucially, other Lockheed and Coast Guard personnel eager to corroborate his story—not to mention the media and two dozen lawyers eager to help him advance and defend his case.

perp: perpetrator

5   Other "good" causes are also getting their fifteen minutes of infamy via the site. Take the Canadian-made Dove commercial that shows an ordinary woman being transformed through the magic of technology into an impossibly beautiful billboard model in just ninety seconds. Within hours of its arrival on the site, the ad was on its way to becoming a global phenomenon—selling soap and reinforcing the idea that images, especially digitally produced ones, can't be trusted.

6   Orwell's Big Brother and YouTube's Little Brother both have potent methods of exerting thought control over those who mess up in public. For his crimes against the Party, *1984*'s protagonist Winston Smith faced compulsory re-education (also known as torture and brainwashing) courtesy of the Thought Police. For Michael Richards, the L.A. police, and anyone else caught in an embarrassing scenario, there is "voluntary" cultural sensitivity training, along with anger management classes and public apologies, which ironically are also available on—you guessed it—YouTube.

7   But if we're smart, we won't wait until our "Kramer moment" is being endlessly replayed by sniggering surfers from Moose Jaw to Mogadishu. We'll just make sure we never do anything embarrassing, illegal, or stupid ever again. Right?

9   Yeah, sure. See you on YouTube.

PRACTICE 3

1. Highlight the thesis statement.

2. Highlight the topic sentence in body paragraphs 4, 5, and 6.

3. Which of the following would make a good topic sentence for paragraph 3?

a. Chase Daniel was humiliated by an online video blog.

b. There are many Internet sites that contain video blogs.

c. Today, people are caught off guard when their embarrassing moments are uploaded and viewed by millions.

d. The World Wide Web has images of teachers who have abused their students.

4. How many examples does Gall use to show the positive power of YouTube?

a. one

b. two

c. three

d. four

5. How is the "Little Brother is watching" phenomenon positive? Provide your own examples to show that it benefits society. _____

_____

_____

_____

 Writer's Room   **Topics for Illustration Essays**

Writing Activity 1

Write an illustration essay about one of the following topics, or choose your own topic.

General Topics

1. mistakes that parents make
2. annoying holidays
3. mistakes that newlyweds make
4. great or horrible films
5. bad habits

Academic and Work-Related Topics

6. things people should know about my school
7. examples of successful financial planning
8. qualities of an ineffective manager
9. mistakes students make
10. examples of obsolete jobs

Writing Activity 2

Choose a quotation you agree or disagree with, and then write an illustration essay based on it.

> If the only tool you have is a hammer, you tend to see every problem as a nail.
>
> —Abraham Maslow, psychologist

> A photograph is a secret about a secret.
>
> —Diane Arbus, photographer

> The squeaky wheel gets the grease.
>
> —Proverb

> Obstacles are those frightful things you see when you take your eyes off your goal.
>
> —Henry Ford, businessman

READING LINK

More Illustration Readings

"Songs of Insects" by Sy Montgomery (page 490) "Guilt-Free Goofing Off" by Brian Bergman (page 497) For a more complete list of readings by rhetorical mode, see Appendix 6.

 CHECKLIST: ILLUSTRATION ESSAY

After you write your illustration essay, review the essay checklist on the inside front cover. Also ask yourself these questions.

- Does my thesis statement include a controlling idea that I can support with examples?

- Do I use a series of examples or an extended example in each body paragraph?

- Does each body paragraph support the thesis statement?

- Does each body paragraph focus on one idea?

- Do I have sufficient examples to support my thesis statement?

- Do I logically and smoothly connect paragraphs and supporting examples?

WRITING LINK

More Illustration Writing Topics

Chapter 18, Writer's Room topic 1 (page 264) Chapter 22, Writer's Room topic 1 (page 303) Chapter 32, Writer's Room topic 1 (page 406) Chapter 35, Writer's Room topic 1 (page 437)

Submit your best essays for possible publication to **thewritersworld@prenhall.com**.

7 CHAPTER

Narration

Everyone is necessarily the hero of his or her own life story.

—JOHN BARTH, *author*

CHAT ROOM

Try some non-stop talking. First, sit with a partner and come up with a television show or movie that you have both seen. Then, starting at the beginning, describe what happened in that episode or film. Remember that you must speak without stopping. If one of you stops talking, the other must jump in and continue describing the story.

EXPLORING

WHAT IS NARRATION?

Narrating is telling a story about what happened. You generally explain events in the order in which they occurred, and you include information about when they happened and who was involved in the incidents.

The next examples show how you might use narration in everyday situations.

Audience: Neighbour	Audience: Instructor	Audience: Clients
The car accident was really my fault.	**My homework isn't ready because of events beyond my control.**	**Our marketing campaign will work like a puzzle to pique consumers' interest.**
• When I left the house, I was late for work, so I was driving too fast.	• My binder containing the instructions was in my basement when it flooded.	• The first billboard will not have any words—just a stunning

- My cell phone, which was in my purse, rang.
- I leaned over to get the phone out of the purse when I crashed into the stop sign.
- Luckily, I wasn't hurt, but my car needed major repairs.

- I called a classmate to give me the instructions, but he gave me the incorrect information.
- I then tried to contact you, but you were not available during your office hours.

photograph of the product with a question mark where the name should be.
- Two weeks later, we will include variations of the brand name with the letters mixed up and a giant question mark.
- In four weeks, consumers will view the completed image with the brand name.

LIFE SNAPSHOT   Narration at Work

After real-estate agent Francine Martin has shown a home to a client, she records the client's reactions. Here is an excerpt from one of her client records.

Clients: The Nguyens

Needs: The Nguyens have twin sons, and Mrs. Nguyen works at home. They would like a three bedroom and prefer two bathrooms or a full bath and powder room. A garage is unnecessary. They will accept townhouses, but cannot spend more than $150 000, which limits their possibilities in this region. They are not willing to view other municipalities.

March 14: We visited 114 Philippe Street. Their first impressions were not favourable. The master bedroom was too small. Cracks in the wall near the ceiling worried them. (Discuss repair of cracks with owner.) However, they appreciated the view. They like the main floor and especially appreciate the kitchen, which may sell the house. The price is in their range. Suggest a second visit.

The Narrative Essay

When you write a narrative essay, consider your point of view.

- Use **first-person narration** to describe a personal experience. To show that you are directly involved in the story, use *I* (first-person singular) or *we* (first-person plural). This is an example of first-person narration: "When I got on the tiny plane, I tried to calm myself. I strapped myself in beside the pilot. As the plane lurched down the runway, I screamed."

- Use **third-person narration** to describe what happened to somebody else. Show that you are simply an observer or story-teller by using *he*, *she*, *it* (third-person singular) or *they* (third-person plural). This is an example of third-person narration: "Every morning, Joe cut out pieces of cardboard and placed them in his shoes. Then Joe buttoned up his only good shirt and smoothed down his hair. He was going to look for a job, and he had to look his best."

Narration is not only useful on its own; it also enhances other types of writing. For example, student writer Omar Hakim had to write an essay about the effects of gambling. His essay was more compelling than it might otherwise have been because he included an anecdote about his uncle's gambling addiction.

A Student Essay

A student from New Brunswick's Mount Allison wrote the next essay. Read the essay and answer the questions that follow.

My Journey Down the Grand Canyon
By Andrew Wells

1   Twenty years old, on a break from studies, I decided to set out backpacking to see where it would take me. Having found myself in a youth hostel in Flagstaff, Arizona, I spontaneously decided to see the Grand Canyon. My plan was to hike right from the top of the canyon, down to the Colorado River, and then back up. What I didn't realize was that this sort of hiking is not a simple test of aerobic fitness or personal desire. No, it's a type of brutal self-destruction. The next two days hiking in the canyon left me dazed and depleted.

2   On the first day, I walked and hitchhiked from Flagstaff and descended eight kilometres before nightfall. I set out the next morning toward the river, and my physical condition rapidly deteriorated. First, the soles of my boots gave out, partially tearing from the seams and flapping against the pads of my feet with every step I took. My blisters ached continuously. The straps from my backpack tore into my shoulder blades and pain ran down my spine. But the dull pounding of my boots against the rocky terrain drowned out my thoughts. My focus remained on the path in front of me. I knew that if I lost concentration, at any point I could trip and fall over the edge. At least the awe-inspiring surroundings made it easier to forget the pain.

3   In the canyon, my surroundings were ever changing. At one moment, I was following a winding dirt path under light tree cover, with deer roaming, birds chirping, and small mammals scurrying about. Then suddenly I was on a sandy ledge following a stream that cut between towering walls of red rock. I could see nothing but the metre in front of me where the wall curved with the stream. Then when I turned a corner, the walls opened up into a majestic gorge two kilometres across; it was green, lush, and lightly snow-covered. A little farther, as I looked down below me, I could trace the trail winding down the gorge and gradually disappearing.

4   Eventually I reached Phantom Ranch at the bottom of the canyon. It serves as a rest stop for die-hard hikers and is so popular that people have to reserve years ahead of time. At the ranch I encountered two types of people. There are retired couples who are passionate hikers and who wait a year and a half for reservations. Some that I met had scaled Mount Everest. And then there are those who work at the ranch. Most of them don't leave the canyon for months on end because the only way out is a gruelling twenty-five-kilometre trek or a rather expensive ride on the back of a mule. To further their isolation,

the media are virtually non-existent. The ranger has a radio, and there's one emergency telephone.

5   I spoke with the man working the canteen desk. He was a calm slow talker in his early thirties, tall and thin, with ear-length tangled hair and a dull, emotionless expression. While poking at a block of wood with a steel pick, he droned on and on about all the people he knew about who had died in the canyon. "Once, some parents let their three-year-old girl walk alone, and she just walked right off the edge. Another time a couple tried to hike in from the far west, ran out of water, and expired." He kept tapping the wood with his pick. "Then there was the guy who was knocked off the edge by one of the sheep." In my head I begged him to stop.

6   If a hiker is tired at the bottom of the canyon, he's in serious trouble. Trouble was what I came face to face with. Climbing back up, I encountered a big-horned sheep on a narrow ledge. It wanted to go where I was, and I wanted to go where it was, but there was no room to pass. For minutes on end the sheep and I engaged in a stare-down. Then all of a sudden it got bored with me and climbed up an 85-degree sheer rock face! I was dumbfounded. It was so smart, and as soon as I passed, it climbed back down, turned and looked at me, and walked on. It understood perfectly what was going on.

7   After several hours of non-stop hiking, I had absolutely no drive left. The rock face kept getting steeper and the air significantly thinner. Each layer of the canyon above me was hidden behind the nearest sheet of towering sandstone. So when I thought I had gotten to the top, to my great dismay, a whole new area opened up above me. Then a woman in at least her late seventies ploughed past me on her way uphill out of the canyon. She was a small woman with short grey hair and a hunched back. I was honestly in pretty good hiking shape from all the heavy walking I had done. I passed just about everyone else, but this woman was unbelievable. (I was carrying a ten-kilogram-pack though, so I call it a no-contest and want a rematch.)

8   At certain points, I felt like saying, "That's it. I'm living the rest of my life on this ledge. I'm not moving." And then I started making deals with myself, planning what I was going to do with my life once I got out, just to motivate myself to keep going. When I reached the top, I looked down into the bowels of the canyon and felt relieved that I had done it. It's something that does not need to be done more than once. I can retain the knowledge of what I have accomplished. I have come out believing that there's nothing that can stop me, and there's no greater feeling.

PRACTICE I

1. Highlight the thesis statement.

2. Highlight the topic sentence in paragraphs 2 and 3. Remember, the topic sentence is not necessarily the first sentence in the paragraph.

3. Using your own words, sum up what happened in each body paragraph. Begin with paragraph 4.

   Paragraph 4: _____

   _____

Paragraph 5: _____

_____

_____

Paragraph 6: _____

_____

_____

Paragraph 7: _____

_____

_____

4.   In paragraph 5, Wells describes a man he met. Which images help you
     visualize the man? _____

_____

_____

5.   Why did the author write about his experience? You will need to make a
     guess based on the information in the essay. _____

_____

_____

Explore Topics

In the following Writer's Desk, you will try an exploring strategy to generate
ideas about different topics.

Writer's Desk **Warm Up**

Read the following questions, and write the first ideas that come to
your mind. Think of two to three ideas for each topic.

EXAMPLE:

What difficult realizations have you made?

My choice to stay in college was hard. Leaving home

was difficult. When I broke up with my girlfriend. What

else? My friend told me that I interrupt others too

much. When I let my brother take the blame for

something I did, I realized that I have a dark side.

1. What are some disagreements or misunderstandings that you have had with someone you love?

_____

_____

_____

2. What were some significant moments in your childhood?

_____

_____

_____

3. Think about some stressful situations that brought out the best or worst in you. List some ideas.

_____

_____

_____

DEVELOPING

THE THESIS STATEMENT

When you write a narrative essay, choose a topic that you personally find very interesting, and then share it with your readers. For example, very few people would be interested if you simply list what you did during your recent vacation. However, if you write about a particularly moving experience during your vacation, you could create an entertaining narrative essay.

Ensure that your narrative essay expresses a main point. Your thesis statement should have a controlling idea.

topic   controlling idea
When I got hired for my job, my life took a dramatic turn.

controlling idea   topic
Sadie's problems began **as soon as she drove her new car home.**

> **HINT** **How to Make a Point**
>
> In a narrative essay, the thesis statement should make a point. To help you find the controlling idea, you can ask yourself the following questions:
>
> - What did I learn?
> - How did it make me feel?
> - How did I change?
> - What is important about it?
>
> **Example:**
>
> Topic: *ran away from home*
>
> Possible controlling idea: *learned the importance of family*
>
>   topic   controlling idea
> **When I ran away from home at the age of fifteen,** <u>I discovered the importance of my family.</u>

PRACTICE 2

Practise writing thesis statements. Complete the following sentences by adding a controlling idea.

1. During my sister's wedding, she realized _____

    _____

    _____

2. Because my family is large, I know _____

    _____

    _____

3. When I graduated, I _____

    _____

    _____

Writer's Desk **Write Thesis Statements**

Write a thesis statement for each of the following topics. You can look for ideas in the Writer's Desk on pages 85–89. Each thesis statement should mention the topic and express a controlling idea.

EXAMPLE:

Topic: A difficult realization

Thesis statement: *When I betrayed my brother, I made an unpleasant discovery about myself.*

1. Topic: A disagreement with a loved one
    Thesis statement: _____

    _____

2. Topic: A significant moment in childhood
    Thesis statement: _____

    _____

3. Topic: A stressful situation
    Thesis statement: _____

    _____

The Supporting Ideas

A narrative essay should contain specific details so that the reader understands what happened. To come up with the details, ask yourself a series of questions. Your essay should provide answers to those questions.

- **Who** is the essay about?
- **What** happened?
- **When** did it happen?
- **Where** did it happen?
- **Why** did it happen?
- **How** did it happen?

When you orally recount a story to a friend, you may go back and add details, saying, "Oh, I forgot to mention something." However, you do not have this luxury when writing narrative essays. When you write, organize the sequence of events clearly so that your reader can follow your story easily.

HINT   Narrative Essay Tips

Here are some tips to remember as you develop a narrative essay.

- Do not simply recount what happened. Try to indicate why the events are important.
- Organize the events in chronological order (the order in which they occurred). You could also reverse the order of events by beginning your essay with the outcome of the events, and then explaining what happened that led to the outcome.
- Use some descriptive language. For example, you could use images that appeal to the senses. For more information on using descriptive imagery, see page 103 in Chapter 8.

Writer's Desk **Develop Supporting Ideas**

Choose one of your topics from the previous Writer's Desk on page 90. Then generate supporting ideas. List what happened.

EXAMPLE:

A difficult realization

- about four years old
- broke sister's glass ornaments
- blamed brother
- Mark was scolded
- didn't admit the truth, kept denying it
- felt extremely guilty

Topic: _____

_____

_____

_____

_____

_____

_____

The Essay Plan

Before you write a narrative essay, make a detailed essay plan. Write down main events in the order in which they occurred. To make your narration more complete, include details about each event.

Thesis statement: When I betrayed my brother, I made an unpleasant discovery about myself.

    I. I wanted to touch my sister's glass ornaments.
       A. I snuck into her room.
       B. I climbed her dresser.
       C. My brother watched me climb.

   II. The dresser fell forward.
       A. I jumped off.
       B. A glass deer crashed to the floor and broke.

III. Our mother asked who did it, and I blamed my brother.
   A. My brother was scolded.
   B. He was confined to his bedroom.
   C. I heard him crying.

IV. I never admitted that I had done it.
   A. My brother was sad more than angry.
   B. I felt really guilty, but I still couldn't confess.
   C. I realized that my actions made me a liar and a coward.

Writer's Desk **Write an Essay Plan**

Refer to the information you generated in previous Writer's Desks, and prepare a detailed essay plan. Include details for each supporting idea.

The First Draft

After you outline your ideas in a plan, you are ready to write the first draft. Remember to write complete sentences and to use transitions to help readers understand the order in which events occur or occurred. Here are some transitions that are useful in narrative essays.

To Show a Sequence of Events			
afterward	finally	in the end	meanwhile
after that	first	last	next
eventually	in the beginning	later	then

Enhancing Your Essay

One effective way to enhance your narrative essay is to use dialogue. A **direct quotation** contains the exact words of an author, and the quotation is set off with quotation marks. When you include the exact words of more than one person in a text, then you must make a new paragraph each time the speaker changes.

"Who did this?" my mom shrieked, as my brother and I stood frozen with fear.

"Mark did it," I assured her shamelessly, as my finger pointed at my quivering brother.

An **indirect quotation** keeps the author's meaning but is not set off by quotation marks.

> As Mark and I stood frozen with fear, our shrieking mother asked who did it. I assured her shamelessly that Mark did it, as my finger pointed at my quivering brother.

GRAMMAR HINT **Using Quotations**

When you insert a direct quotation into your writing, capitalize the first word of the quotation, and put the final punctuation inside the closing quotation marks.

- Place a comma after an introductory phrase.

    Manuel Figuera said, "Everyone was terrified."

- Place a colon after an introductory sentence.

    Manuel Figuera described the atmosphere: "Everyone was terrified."

See Chapter 35 for more information about using quotations.

Writer's Desk **Write the First Draft**

In the previous Writer's Desk, you developed an essay plan. Carefully review your essay plan, make any necessary changes to the details or chronology, and then write the first draft of your narrative essay.

REVISING AND EDITING

Revise and Edit a Narrative Essay

When you finish writing a narrative essay, carefully review your work and revise it to make the events as clear as possible to your readers. Check that you have organized events chronologically, and remove any irrelevant details. Before you revise and edit your own essay, practise revising and editing a student essay.

A Student Essay

A student from Calgary, Alberta, wrote the next essay. Read the essay, and then answer the questions that follow. Correct any errors that you find, and make comments in the margins.

Crashing Glass Deer

By Adele Berridge

1   My brother and I grew up in a suburban bungalow near a freeway. Built in the 1950s, my house boasted a living room with a picture window, three

bedrooms, and a bathroom. My older sister and I shared the middle bedroom, and my brother Mark, as the only boy, was given his own room next to ours. He was my fraternal twin and my best friend. On the day that I betrayed Mark, I made an unpleasant discovery about myself.

2   Sherry, my sister, had just turned eight, and my brother and I were both four. We had celebrated my sister's birthday a few days before, and some of her prized possessions were on display in our shared bedroom. Most impressive of all was a set of glass deer. My sister placed the three fragile deer on top of her dresser, well out of reach of my grubby little hands. Those deer fascinated me, and I thought they represented Bambi's family. I longed to hold them, but I can't reach them.

3   That morning, my sister had gone to school, and my mother was doing laundry at the opposite end of the house. I brought my brother into my room and told him that we would play with Sherry's deer. We would be carefull, I assured him. He didn't want to proceed, but he watched me as I pulled out each drawer on my sister's dresser, starting with the bottom drawer, then the middle, and then the top, until I made a series of steps.

4   I had my slippers on, and I climbed up, carefully stepping on the edge of each drawer. I reached the second drawer from the top, and was just reaching for the deer when the dresser started to tip toward me. I leapt off the drawer to safety just as the large piece of furniture crashed to the ground. The glass ornaments smashed on the hardwood floor. My brother and I stared in stunned silence as hard footsteps clomped down the hall.

5   "Who did this?" my mom shrieked, as my brother and I stood frozen with fear. "He did it," I assured her shamelessly, as my finger pointed at my quivering brother. My brother denied it, of course.

6   Peering closely at us both, my mother's eyes rested on her son. The next minutes were a torrent of shouting and loud wailing as my brother was punished for the act. I remained perfectly still, numb. Noises and colours swirled around me, the occasional image registering like a snapshot. Then, as I backed out of the room and slunk down the hall to the living room, I heard the distant sound of my brother's muffled sobs. At the time, I knew that I was being *really, really bad*, but there was no turning back.

7   That incident haunted me for years to come. As a child, I thought that the human soul was a round white pie plate and that sins were like black specks of dirt on it. In my mind's eye, my soul was stained with the mud of sin. I knew what I was: a liar and a coward. My brother's tear-streaked face burned into my brain, I saw his disappointed eyes staring at me not with anger but with bewilderment. I was his sister and best friend, and I had betrayed him in order to save myself. The guilt wouldn't go away, nor would my sense that I was inherently bad. Occasionaly my brother would remind me of the incident, and I pretended that I couldn't remember that time, yet I *couldn't forget* it. Denying it only intensified the guilt, of course.

8   I wish I could say I changed overnight, but I'm a slow learner. I lied again and again. However, that incident planted a seed in me that budded and grew with time. I would have to overcome my own inherent cowardice and learn to take responsibility for my actions. It had to feel better than lying and living with horrible guilt.

9   Today, I get it. On that day all those years ago, if I had simply told the truth and taken the punishment, most likely I would'nt even remember the incident today. Because I lied, I've never forgotten it.

PRACTICE 3

Revising

1. Write down the two parts of the thesis statement.

   topic   +   controlling idea

   _____

2. What type of order do the specific details follow? Circle your response.

   a. space   b. time   c. emphatic

3. What type of narration is this?

   a. first person   b. third person

4. Paragraph 4 lacks a topic sentence. An appropriate topic sentence for paragraph 4 could be

   a. The glass deer was on top of the dresser.
   b. I concentrated on my goal of getting my hands on those glass deer.
   c. My brother didn't move.
   d. The glass deer were fragile.

5. Underline a dialogue problem in paragraph 5, and then write a rule regarding quotations and dialogue.

   _____

Editing

GRAMMAR LINK

See the following chapters for more information about these grammar topics:

Verb Consistency: Chapter 27
Spelling: Chapter 32
Run-Ons: Chapter 22
Apostrophes: Chapter 34

6. Underline a tense consistency error in paragraph 2. The tense shifts for no apparent reason. Write the correction on the line below.

   Correction: _____

7. This essay contains misspelled words in paragraphs 3 and 7. Underline and correct them.

   Corrections: _____

8. Paragraph 7 contains a run-on sentence. Underline the error, and show three ways to correct the sentence

   Corrections: _____

   _____

9. Underline an apostrophe error in paragraph 9. Write the correct word on the line below.

   Correction: _____

Writer's Desk **Revise and Edit Your Essay**

Revise and edit the essay that you wrote for the previous Writer's Desk. You can refer to the revising and editing checklists at the end of this chapter and on the inside covers of this book.

A Professional Essay

Ryan Knighton, a university professor, lives in North Vancouver. Several years ago, Knighton realized that he was slowly losing his vision. He describes his descent into blindness in his memoir *Cockeyed*. In the following excerpt from an article, he narrates what happened. Read the essay and answer the questions that follow.

Out of Sight

By Ryan Knighton

1   On my 18th birthday, my first retina specialist, a man who delivered his bedside manner like napalm, informed me that I would be blind within a few years. "No cure," he said. "Sorry." The specialist told me the name of the condition, retinitis pigmentosa. He described how it would soon eradicate my remaining night vision, limit me to tunnel vision, and eventually blinker me altogether. The whole scene took less than ten minutes.

2   For four years, I had exhibited clumsy behaviour nobody could account for. As a warehouse worker during summer vacations, I drove a forklift and ran over nearly everything possible, including one of my co-workers. True, I hated him and his insistence that we play nothing but Iron Maiden on the shipping area stereo, but it wasn't in my character to crush him.

3   But the real giveaway came when I drove my father's Pontiac into a ditch. Lots of friends crashed their parents' cars, but my accident stood out. I did my teenaged duty at roughly five miles per hour. How do you miss a turn at that speed unless your eyes are closed? After sundown, mine might as well have been.

4   When I reported to my mother that, as a new driver, I was having trouble on rainy nights, she said they gave everybody trouble and told me not to worry. I was on my way out the door, about to drive to work. "But do you use the cat's eyes sometimes?" I asked.

5   "Sure," she said. "That's what they're for, reflecting light when it's hard to see the yellow line."

6   "No, I mean do you use them? Do you drive on them?"

7   When I couldn't see the yellow line, I had taken to steering onto the cat's eyes. This, I found, helped position me on the road. I was a little close to the middle, maybe, but better than anything I could determine on my own. The *clunk clunk clunk* of the reflectors under my tires let me know where I was. I suppose I drove Braille.

8   "You drive on the cat's eyes?" my mother asked.

9   "Well, only at night." I would wager my mother called for my first ophthalmological appointment by the time I had shut the front door behind me.

10   Retinitis pigmentosa is the loss of photoreceptors associated with pigmentary changes in the retina. Another way to put it is that my retina is scarring itself to death. I've enjoyed the slow loss of all peripheral and night vision. By my own estimate, I have a year to go until that tiny pinhole of clarity in which I live will consume itself, and the lights will go out. To know what's filling up my little tunnel, I rely mostly on context.

11   Once I asked a red-headed waitress for directions to the washroom. I didn't know she was a waitress by the colour of her hair, of course—the bit of it I saw—but by the smell of coffee, which was quickly overwhelmed by a perfumy fog.

12   "Would you like more coffee?"

13   "I'd love coffee," I said, "but I'd love to be in the men's room even more."

14   "Um, okay, the men's room is over that way."

15   I stared vacantly ahead while she, I imagine, continued to point "that way." Then I heard the pleasant sound of coffee being poured.

16   "I'm sorry," I said, "but I don't know what *that way* means." I plucked my white cane from the bag beside me. "I guess it wasn't obvious, and I forgot to—"

17   "Oh my God, I'm sorry, I didn't know you're blind! You didn't look—you don't look—not at all—I mean really."

18   I smiled with that warm sensation you get when you are sixteen and someone says you look like you're in your twenties. "Thanks. That is very kind. Where did you say the washroom is?"

19   "At the back."

20   "Which way is back?"

21   "It's over there," she said, and walked away.

22   All I wanted were specific directions. Instead, my waitress gave me a demonstration of the fact that, along with vision, parts of language disappear into blindness. The capacity of language to guide me has atrophied. Not even Braille can substitute for some words. *This way. Right here, in front of you. No, there. Right there, under your nose.* Such directional cues have lost their meaning. Who would have guessed that a disease can alter language as it alters the body, disabling parts of speech—that language is, in this way, an extension of the body and subject to the same pathologies.

23   "EXCUSE ME."

24   My waitress was back, not a second too soon. I really did need to use the facilities.

25   "I don't mean to intrude," she said, "but didn't you go to Langley Secondary School?"

26   "Yes, I did."

27   "It's Ryan, right? I'm Danielle! We were in drama class together. God, I didn't recognize you at all. You look so different now," she said.

28   I braced myself. "I'm not sure what it is. Maybe it's—" *The fierce squint? The white cane? The expression of perpetual disorientation?*

29   "It's—well. I know!" She put a hand on my head with daring compassion. "You shaved your hair off. When did you do that?"

30   Now I was free to burn with embarrassment at my self-centredness. Just because it's a sighted world doesn't mean blindness is the first thing people notice about me, nor the first thing that comes to mind. Along with mutant celebrity and meaningless words, I suppose paranoia is another side effect. "A couple of years ago, I guess," I replied.

31   "Looks cool."

32   "Thanks."

33   "I remember in high school your hair used to be long," she said. "Really long. It was down to here, right?"

PRACTICE 4

1. What type of narration is this text?

    a. first person   b. third person

2. The thesis of this essay is not stated directly, but it is implied. Using your own words, write the thesis of this essay.

    _____

3. Describe how Knighton introduces his topic. What introduction style does he use? Circle the letter of the best answer.

    a. definition   c. anecdote
    b. general   d. historical

4. Knighton divides his essay into two time periods. What are they?

    _____

5. How does Knighton realize that he is losing his sight? In two or three sentences, explain what happens.

    _____

    _____

6. In which paragraph is there a definition of a term? _____

7. Describe what happens during Knighton's encounter with the waitress. Use your own words.

    _____

    _____

    _____

8. Write down one example of an indirect quotation from the essay.

    _____

    _____

9. Write down one example of a direct quotation from the essay.

    _____

    _____

10. Narrative writers do more than simply list a series of events. Knighton explains why the events were meaningful. What did he learn?

    _____

    _____

WRITING LINK

More Narrative Writing Topics
Chapter 19, Writer's Room topic 1 (page 275)
Chapter 29, Writer's Room topic 1 (page 377)
Chapter 33, Writer's Room topic 2 (page 416)

 Writer's Room   Topics for Narrative Essays

Writing Activity 1

Choose any of the following topics, or choose your own topic, and write a narrative essay.

General Topics

1. a break-up
2. a risky adventure
3. a personal ritual
4. a thrilling or frightening moment
5. a news event that affected you

Academic and Work-Related Topics

6. an interesting encounter
7. a sudden realization at school or work
8. a uncomfortable incident at work
9. a positive or negative job interview
10. a difficult lesson at work or school

Writing Activity 2

Choose a quotation you agree or disagree with, and then write a narrative essay based on it.

Youth would be an ideal state if it came a little later in life.

—Herbert Henry Asquith, politician

Always do what you are afraid to do.

—Ralph Waldo Emerson, essayist

There's always one who loves and one who lets himself be loved.

—W. Somerset Maugham, author

Blind belief is dangerous.

—Kenyan proverb

CHECKLIST: NARRATION ESSAY

After you write your narration essay, review the checklist on the inside front cover. Also ask yourself these questions.

- Does my thesis statement clearly express the topic of the narration?

- Does my thesis statement contain a controlling idea that is meaningful and interesting?

- Does my essay answer most of the following questions: *who*, *what*, *when*, *where*, *why*, *how*?

- Do I use transitional expressions that help clarify the order of events?

- Do I include details to make my narration more interesting?

Submit your best essays for possible publication to **thewritersworld@prenhall.com**.

READING LINK

More Narrative Readings

"My Head Rolled in Syria" by Josh Freed (page 479)
"I, Telemarketer" by Eugene Henry (page 470)
For a more complete list of readings by rhetorical mode, see Appendix 6.

8 Description

CHAPTER

The greatest honour that can be paid to the work of art, on its pedestal of ritual display, is to describe it with sensory completeness. We need a science of description.
—CAMILLE PAGLIA, *writer*

CHAPTER CONTENTS

Exploring
- What Is Description?
- The Descriptive Essay
- Explore Topics

Developing
- The Thesis Statement
- The Supporting Ideas

- The Essay Plan
- The First Draft

Revising and Editing
- Revise and Edit a Descriptive Essay
- A Professional Essay: "Living Among the Bees" by Lucie L. Snodgrass

---

CHAT ROOM

Choose one of the objects from the following list. Then, brainstorm a list of descriptive words about the object. Think about the shape, texture, smell, taste, colour, and so on. List the first words that come to your mind.

Example

cake → *gooey, sweet, chocolate, smooth, pink icing, layered*

panther	old car	sweater	baby	apple

EXPLORING

WHAT IS DESCRIPTION?

Description creates vivid images in the reader's mind by portraying people, places, or moments in detail. Here are some everyday situations that might call for description.

Audience: Roommate	Audience: Classmate	Audience: Intern
The apartment we will rent is close to the campus.	**The experiment in chemistry class went well.**	**Our company has renovated the front lobby.**
• The north side of the campus has student housing.	• We dissolved Epsom salts on construction paper.	• The walls are painted in warm browns and beiges.
• Our apartment is in the middle of Grove Street, which is still a dusty unpaved road.	• Crystals of many different shapes formed as the paper dried.	• There are two overstuffed chairs and a soft leather couch.

- The building is next to the wooded lot.

- The crystals were mainly bright coral and sunny yellow.

- There are oil paintings on the walls and dried flowers in ceramic vases on the tables.

LIFE SNAPSHOT   **Description at Work**

To help hikers plan camping trips effectively, the Parks Canada website describes Quttinirpaaq National Park in Nunavut.

During the brief arctic summer on Quttinirpaaq, the sun remains high in the sky, bathing the land in continuous daylight. There is no darkness to mark the passage of time, telling you when to sleep and when to wake.

There are no trees to remind you of lands further south. The scale of the land is both immense and intimate at the same time. Intricate patterns of rock, frost-cracked ground, willows, and wildflowers at your feet extend out from where you stand into endless vistas in the clear, dry air. Glaciers on a mountainside 15 km away seem to be details in a landscape within reach.

The Descriptive Essay

When you write a descriptive essay, focus on three main points.

1. **Create a dominant impression.** The dominant impression is the overall atmosphere that you wish to convey. It can be a strong feeling, mood, or image. For example, if you are describing a casual Sunday afternoon party, you can emphasize the relaxed ambience in the room.

2. **Express your attitude toward the subject.** Do you feel positive or negative toward the subject? For instance, if you feel pleased about your last vacation, then the details of your essay will convey the good feelings you have about it. If you feel tense during a business meeting, then your details can express how uncomfortable the situation makes you feel.

3. **Include concrete details.** Details will enable a reader to visualize the person, place, or situation that you are describing. You can use active verbs and adjectives so that the reader imagines the scene more clearly. You can also use **imagery**, which is description using the five senses. Review the following examples of imagery.

Sight: A Western Tiger Swallowtail dipped by my face. About three inches across, its lemon-yellow wings were striped improbably and fluted in black. They filliped into a long forked tail with spots of red and blue.

—Sherman Apt Russell, "Beauty on the Wing"

Sound: The tree outside is full of crows and white cranes who gurgle and screech.

—Michael Ondaatje, *Running in the Family*

Smell: I think it was the smell that so intoxicated us after those dreary months of nostril-scorching heat, the smell of dust hissing at the touch of rain and then settling down, damply placid on the ground.

—Sara Suleri, *Meatless Days*

Touch: The straps from my backpack tore into my shoulder blades and pain ran down my spine.

—Andrew Wells, "My Journey Down the Grand Canyon"

Taste: Entirely and blessedly absent are the cloying sweetness, chalky texture and oily, gummy aftertaste that afflict many mass-manufactured ice creams.

—R. W. Apple Jr., "Making Texas Cows Proud," *New York Times*

A Student Essay

Read the following student essay and answer the questions that follow.

The Wake-Up Call
By Jennifer Alvira

1   My hands were covered in flavoured syrup, and my hair sat in a messy bun on the top of my head. I cringed at the sight of last-minute customers. I had had enough of people for one day and was ready to close the shop for the night.

2   I picked up the dingy mop from an old pail and started mopping the chocolate-encrusted tiles. Our milkshake machine splattered the checkerboard walls in a vanilla mess while the eight glass jars of candies spilled out over the marble countertop. After five long minutes of hard scrubbing, the black and white of the wall started to shine through. I swept up the broken candies from the floor. When the stressful day finally came to an end, I grabbed my purse and headed for the door. Little did I know that, in the next hour, I was about to destroy my car and my self-confidence as a driver.

3   The air grew heavy with storm clouds, and I noticed that a thin layer of car oil residue coated the road. If driving in the dark was not terrifying enough, it was pouring rain. I climbed into my silver '92 Dodge Spirit, the car given to me on my sixteenth birthday. The interior was a deep burgundy red and emanated a distinct aroma of wet tennis shoes and old carpet. The exterior had its own collection of dents and scratches but remained beautiful to me. It was my personal dream car despite what anyone else said; it always started and never gave me any real problems.

4   Night blanketed the roads, and my nerves started to twist in knots—I hated driving at night. I arrived about a kilometre from the intersection at Eber and Dairy Road. An abandoned white chapel sat peacefully to the right, and a humble section of mysterious houses thrived in a community called Little Oak Creek further up the road. It appeared to me that I was the only car on the road at this hour. As I neared the intersection, I pressed on the gas pedal to make sure I would fly through before the light turned yellow.

5   I had just made it past the light when the glare of a pair of headlights caught the corner of my left eye. I slammed on the brakes only to feel my tires lose traction and slide across pavement. The abrupt impact barely gave me enough time to close my eyes. I gripped the steering wheel so tightly that my palms stung when I finally let go. The two-ton weight of my car shoved the other completely off the road into a patch of trees in front of Little Oak Creek.

6   My air bag deployed with a loud bang and burst with white powder. I pushed open the door and stumbled out. The smell of burnt tires and exhaust smoke permeated the night. The accident seemed like a nightmare.

7   By then, I couldn't force myself to hold back fear anymore. Tears smeared my stunned face, while cars passed by with none stopping to assist me. I hyperventilated, and my entire body shook. Everything happened so quickly; I didn't have a chance to feel the throbbing in my wrist from the sprain or the enormous bruise from where my knee had slammed into the dashboard.

8   Finally, a young woman and her son appeared in the warm rays of the streetlamp. The woman clutched a small blue jacket, with her son closely behind.

9   "Darling, are you okay?"

10   She draped a light jacket over my frail shoulders and proceeded to cup my trembling hands within hers. I noticed a metallic taste in my mouth, and I could barely form a coherent sentence. "I'm alive and can feel all my limbs. I'm okay."

11   The young lady rubbed my shoulders, and made sure to stand next to me in case my body gave way to the shock. "What's your mom's phone number so that I can tell her you're fine?" Her sweet voice eased my terror, and I could finally take a deep breath. I looked over at her son, who stood quietly beside his mother. His eyes widened as he stared at my now non-existent source of transportation.

12   The police showed up after two hours of waiting for their arrival. I found out that the sixteen-year-old girl driving the other vehicle jumped out of her car in a bout of panic. Her knees bled from the rough impact of asphalt. Her boyfriend and mother were at the scene and stayed close to her side. The police ticketed the girl with failure to yield to passing cars while making a left turn. The accident was not my fault, and I welcomed the flood of relief.

PRACTICE 1

1. Look in the opening paragraphs and highlight the thesis statement.

2. The writer describes in detail the events of the fateful night. Find direct examples from the essay of imagery using the five senses.

    a. Sight _____

    _____

    b. Sound _____

    _____

    c. Taste _____

    _____

    d. Touch _____

    _____

    e. Smell _____

    _____

3. What dominant impression does the writer create in this essay? Underline examples in the essay to support your answer.

    _____

Explore Topics

In the following Writer's Desk, you will try an exploring strategy to generate ideas about different topics.

Writer's Desk **Warm Up**

Read the following questions, and write the first ideas that come to your mind. Think of two or three ideas for each topic.

EXAMPLE:

List some memorable trips you have taken.

- my trip to Africa

- the time I stayed with my grandmother in Saskatoon

- a field trip to the Natural History Museum

1. Who are your best friends?

_____

_____

_____

2. What are some unattractive fashion trends?

_____

_____

_____

3. List some memorable trips that you have taken.

_____

_____

_____

DEVELOPING

When you write a descriptive essay, choose a subject that lends itself to description. You should be able to describe images or objects using some of the five senses. To get in the frame of mind, try thinking about the sounds, sights, tastes, smells, and feelings you would experience in certain places, such as a busy restaurant, a hospital room, a subway car, a zoo, and so on.

The Thesis Statement

In the thesis statement of a descriptive essay, you should convey a dominant impression about the subject. The dominant impression is the overall impression or feeling that the topic inspires.

       topic   controlling idea

The photograph of me as a ten-year-old has an embarrassing story behind it.

       controlling idea   topic

Feeling self-satisfied, **Odysseus Ramsey started his first day in public office.**

HINT   **How to Create a Dominant Impression**

To create a dominant impression, ask yourself how or why the topic is important.

Poor: Land developers have built homes on parkland.

           (Why should readers care about this statement?)

                        topic   controlling idea

Better: **The once pristine national park** <u>has been converted into giant estate homes that average families cannot afford.</u>

Writer's Desk   **Write Thesis Statements**

Write a thesis statement for each of the following topics. You can look for ideas in the Writer's Desk on page 106. Each thesis statement should state what you are describing and contain a controlling idea.

EXAMPLE:

Topic: a memorable trip

Thesis statement: *My first day in Ghana left me enthralled but exhausted.*

1. Topic: a close friend

   Thesis statement: _____

   _____

2. Topic: unattractive fashion trends

   Thesis statement: _____

   _____

3. Topic: a memorable trip

   Thesis statement: _____

The Supporting Ideas

After you have developed an effective thesis statement, generate supporting details.

- Use prewriting strategies such as freewriting and brainstorming to generate ideas.
- Choose the best ideas. Most descriptive essays use imagery that best describes the person or scene.
- Organize your ideas. Choose the best organizational method for this essay pattern.

Show, Don't Tell

Your audience will find it more interesting to read your written work if you show a quality or an action of a place or person rather than just state it. For example, if you want to describe a person who is kind, write about the person's kindly actions.

Example of Telling:	Mr. Leon was a very kind man.
Example of Showing:	Our neighbour, Mr. Leon, a retired seventy-year-old grandfather, always told the neighbourhood children not to play street hockey, not to make so much noise, and not to throw the ball near his roses. When it came to important matters, however, he was always supportive of us. Mr. Leon taught all the local youths to ride bikes. He used to walk along beside us holding on to the cycle as we wobbled down the sidewalk. One day, we learned that Mr. Leon had been donating fifty bicycles to the local children's charity annually for many years.

PRACTICE 2

Choose one of the following sentences, and write a short description that shows—not tells—the quality of the person or place.

1. Today was a perfect day.
2. I was frightened as I walked down the street.
3. The weather did not cooperate with our plans.

Use Different Figurative Devices

When writing a descriptive essay, you can use other figurative devices (besides **imagery**) to add vivid details to your writing.

- A **simile** is a comparison using *like* or *as*.

  My thoughts ran as fast as a cheetah.

  Let us go then you and I,
  When the evening is spread out against the sky
  Like a patient etherised upon a table;

  —from "The Love Song of J. Alfred Prufrock" by T. S. Eliot.

- A **metaphor** is a comparison that does not use *like* or *as*.

  Life is sweet-and-sour soup.

  You need a blue sky holiday.

  —from "Bad Day" by Daniel Powter

- **Personification** is the act of attributing human qualities to an inanimate object or animal.

  The chocolate cake winked invitingly at us.

  Life has a funny way of helping you out.

  —from "Ironic" by Alanis Morrissette

PRACTICE 3

Practise using figurative language. Use one of the following to describe each item: simile, metaphor, or personification. If you are comparing two things, try to use an unusual comparison.

EXAMPLE:

  toddler: *The toddler climbed like a monkey out of his crib. (simile)*

1. mountain _____

2. hair   _____

3. generous _____

VOCABULARY BOOST

Use Vivid Language

When you write a descriptive essay, try to use **vivid language**. Use specific action verbs and adjectives to create a clear picture of what you are describing.

  livid
My boss was ~~angry~~.
(Use a more vivid, specific adjective.)

  whimpered
The child ~~cried~~.
(Use a more vivid, specific verb or image.)

  Think about other words or expressions that more effectively describe these words: *laugh, talk, nice, walk.*

Writer's Desk List Sensory Details

Choose one your thesis statements from the previous Writer's Desk and make a list of sensory details. Think about images, impressions, and feelings that the topic inspires in you.

EXAMPLE: a memorable trip

- colourful clothes
- bright warm sand
- appetizing smell of food
- putrid odour of sewers
- a cool breeze
- powerful drumbeat of music
- bodies moving to a beat

Your list of sensory details: _____

_____

_____

_____

_____

The Essay Plan

An essay plan helps you organize your thesis statement, topic sentences, and supporting details before writing a first draft. When you make an essay plan, remember to include concrete details and to organize your ideas in a logical order. If you want to emphasize some descriptive details more than others, arrange them from least affecting to most affecting. If you want your readers to envision a space (a room, a park, and so on), arrange details using spatial order.

Thesis: My first day in Ghana left me enthralled but exhausted.

    I. I was overwhelmed by my surroundings.
       A. People wore traditional African clothing.
       B. Some walked balancing objects on their heads.
       C. Mothers carried babies tied to their backs.
       D. I could smell different types of food.

II. The beach was unlike any other beach I'd seen.
   A. I felt a cool breeze and saw orange sand.
   B. I sat in the shade and had a cold beverage.
   C. People were swimming and dancing.

III. The scenery of the countryside was breathtaking.
   A. There were mud huts with straw roofs.
   B. People were cooking on open fires.
   C. Many animals roamed, including dogs and goats.
   D. I saw immense anthills.

Writer's Desk **Write an Essay Plan**

Choose one of the ideas that you have developed in previous Writer's Desks and prepare an essay plan. Remember to use vivid details and figurative language to help create a dominant overall impression.

The First Draft

After you outline your ideas in a plan, you are ready to write the first draft. Remember to write complete sentences. Also, as you write, think about which transitions can effectively help you lead your readers from one idea to the next. Descriptive writing often uses space order. Here is a list of transitions that are useful for describing the details of a person, place, or thing.

To Show Place or Position			
above	beyond	in a distance	outside
behind	closer in	nearby	over there
below	farther out	on the left / right	over there
beside	in front	on top	underneath

Writer's Desk **Write the First Draft**

In the previous Writer's Desk, you developed an essay plan. Now write the first draft of your descriptive essay. Before you write, carefully review your essay plan and make any necessary changes.

REVISING AND EDITING

REVISE AND EDIT A DESCRIPTIVE ESSAY

When you finish writing a descriptive essay, review your work and revise it to make the description as vivid as possible to your readers. Check that you have organized your ideas, and remove any irrelevant details. Before you work on your own essay, practise revising and editing a student essay.

GRAMMAR HINT   Using Adjectives and Adverbs

When you revise your descriptive essay, check that you have used adjectives and adverbs correctly. For example, many people use *real* when the proper adverb is *really*.

Incorrect: My brother, Magnus, is real tall and powerful.

Correct: My brother, Magnus, is real**ly** tall and powerful.

See Chapter 30 for more information about adjectives and adverbs.

A Student Essay

Natalia MacDonald lives in Toronto. She recently went on a trip of a lifetime to Ghana. Read the essay, and then answer the questions that follow. As you read, correct any errors that you find, and make comments in the margins.

African Adventure

By Natalia MacDonald

1   My trip to Africa began with a twenty-hour journey filled with boring flights and long layovers. When I finaly arrived in Ghana, it was 9:00 p.m. local time, and I was exhausted. I went straight to my hotel to get some rest for the long day I had ahead of me. My first day in Ghana left me enthralled but exhausted.

2   On waking, Kwame, the coordinator of my volunteer program picked me up to accompany me for the day. As we left the hotel I was overwhelmed by the heat and my surroundings. Although many people dressed in Western-style clothing, the majority wore traditional African dress. The colours were incredibly vibrant: bright blues, purples, and yellows. Men, women, and children alike walked by carrying incredible amounts of things balanced on their heads with such an amazing grace and poise. Mothers also carried their babies in a way you had never seen before, tied to their backs with colourful scarves in almost a piggyback position with their little feet sticking out at either side. As we hurried through the centre, I noticed the strong smells of food being cooked by street vendors, fruit being sold in baskets, and of course the not-so-pleasant smell of the open sewers lining the roads. After getting to the bank and cashing my travellers' cheques, it was off to the beach.

3   Everything from the sand to the activities people were doing was unique. The first thing I noticed was the much-needed cool breeze from the ocean brushing against my face as I approached. After being in the hustle and bustle of the capital, feeling the rich dark orange sand between my toes felt very relaxing. I then took a seat in the shade to enjoy a cold beverage and observe

my surroundings. Some people were swimming and sun bathing, and others were dancing. There was a particular group of young boys dressed in colourful loincloths dancing to traditional music. The powerful drumbeat of the music was moving. The boys moved their bodies with such a natural fluidity along with the music that it was hard not to be completely captivated. I was thoroughly enjoying myself, but it was time to catch my bus.

4   The bus was a large white van that left from a station not too far from the beach. As we drove out of the city and onto the dirt road, the scenery was breathtaking. We drove past many different types of villages along the way. Some of the villages were large and had schools, stores, and houses while others were much smaller and more basic and consisted of a circle of around twenty little mud huts with straw roofs with people cooking over an open fire in the middle. Along the road there were many animals walking around such as dogs and mules, but mostly there were small goats. Next month, I am going to visit a national park to see wild animals. The road itself was the same rich dark orange colour that the sand had been at the beach. One of the most incredible sights were the numerous huge anthills that were formed from the dark orange dirt. They stood about a metre high! After driving through some rain, we finally arrived in Manya Krobo, my new home.

5   My first full day in Ghana was one filled with new discoveries and adventure. In a mere matter of hours, I saw things that I had only read about in books and seen in movies. In one day, I had gone from the snowy minus 28-degree weather of Toronto to the humid 32 degrees of Ghana. My long-planned and awaited adventure in Africa was finally a reality.

PRACTICE 4

Revising

1. Highlight the thesis statement.
2. Highlight the topic sentences for paragraphs 2 and 4.
3. Paragraph 3 lacks a topic sentence. One possible topic sentence could be

   a. I went to the beach that evening.
   b. La Pleasure beach was unlike any other beach I had ever seen.
   c. There were many people at La Pleasure beach.
   d. Everyone goes to La Pleasure beach in Ghana.

4. What overall dominant impression does the writer convey in the essay? Underline examples in the essay to support your answer. _____

   _____

5. In paragraph 4, cross out the sentence that does not support the topic sentence.

Editing

6. Paragraph 1 contains a spelling mistake. Underline and correct the mistake

   Correction: _____

   _____

GRAMMAR LINK

See the following chapters for more information about these grammar topics:
Commas, Chapter 33
Sentence Fragments, Chapter 21
Spelling, Chapter 32

7. Underline and correct a comma error in paragraph 2. _____

_____

_____

8. Paragraph 2 contains a sentence with a pronoun shift. Underline and correct the error.

Correction: _____

_____

9. Underline and correct one subject–verb agreement error in paragraph 4.

Correction: _____

_____

Writer's Desk **Revise and Edit Your Essay**

Revise and edit the essay that you wrote for the previous Writer's Desk. You can refer to the checklists at the end of this chapter and on the inside covers of this book.

A Professional Essay

Lucie L. Snodgrass, a regular contributor to *Vegetarian Times*, is a passionate gardener and a college teacher. She is also the author of *Green Roof Plants: A Resource and Planting Guide*. In the following essay, she reflects on the importance of bees.

Living Among the Bees
By Lucie L. Snodgrass

1   Scattered along a gently sloping hill on our farm is a series of white wooden boxes that resemble fallen tiles from a game of giant dominoes. The boxes arrived one spring six years ago in an old pickup truck driven by Ed Yoder, a longtime neighbor and beekeeper who sells his honey at local supermarkets. Always searching for open land in this county of dwindling farms, Ed approached my husband and me, asking whether we would mind having some hives on our property. Since we didn't, twenty of them—home to about a million bees—came to share our 135 acres. At least that's how we described it initially. In reality, we've come to understand, it is the bees who have consented to share their workspace with us, and we, clumsy and often inadvertently destructive humans, are the better for it.

2   Our coexistence did not get off to an auspicious start. Shortly after the bees moved in, I began, as I always do in spring, spending most of my free time in the vegetable garden—tilling the raised beds, pulling early weeds, and carrying out flats of plants started in the greenhouse some fifty feet away. The bees, I quickly learned, disapproved of my activity. They had claimed this formerly quiet area as their own. They had chosen well, packed as the garden was with nectar-dripping flowers and fruit trees in brilliant bloom, a veritable juice bar that they frequented from early to late.

3   Each of my trips into the garden brought an angry protest as dozens of them dive-bombed my head, just as barn swallows do to cats when their territory is encroached upon. I had always found that funny, but being the victim myself was eminently less amusing. I tried varying the hours that I gardened; I tried apologizing to the bees each time I walked in; I even tried singing to them—all to no avail. Whether I was early or late, contrite or in song, the bees were piqued to see me, a fact made clear by the number of welts on various parts of my body. After six stings, I'd had enough.

4   "Ed," I complained on the beekeeper's next visit, "every time I go into the vegetable garden, your bees sting me. Something's got to give." He returned my gaze, his sympathy evident. "Of course they sting you," he said after a long silence. "You're walking right into their flight path."

5   And so my real experience began of living with the bees and their fiercely protective keeper. I quickly learned that Ed's devotion was complete, his concern solely for them. Implicit in his reply was the suggestion that I, and not the bees, was at fault for getting stung. Only after I pointed out that the garden had been there longer than the hives and that it wasn't feasible to move the orchard did he agree to move the hives that were closest to the garden—a concession I'm sure he secretly regrets even today.

6   That was the only disagreement we've ever had, and perhaps if I had avoided the garden for a while, as Ed bluntly suggested, the problem would have resolved itself. In retrospect, perhaps the bees, like people moving into a new neighborhood, needed some time to settle in without the threat of interference. In any event, they have long since accepted my presence, whether I am picking raspberries, walking on the road back to our nursery—a trip that takes me within ten feet of some of the hives—or simply sitting beside a hive for long stretches, watching the bees come and go. I've never again been stung, not when I've scooped some into my hand to rescue them from drowning in the birdbath or when I've picked them up, so covered with pollen they couldn't fly, to avoid someone trampling them. Ed says that the bees have come to trust me, and I believe that I, in turn, have given them my trust.

7   As wonderful as watching the bees is watching Ed, who is an old-fashioned suitor. He visits the bees almost every day, wooing them with presents, fixing things, delighting in the offerings they give back to him. When he has to disturb the bees, he calms them first, moving among them with his smoker like a priest with incense burners. **Loquacious** by nature, Ed can spend   **loquacious:** talkative the day talking about his charges: waxing on about their cleanliness, their loyalty to their queen, and their industriousness. Ed's love is infectious. We felt no small amount of pride when he told us after the first year's harvest that their honey production increased dramatically after the bees moved to our farm, certain that our unsprayed fields and flower gardens were responsible. We mourned with him when he lost many of his colonies to mites several years ago and others to a harsh winter. And we have done things that we would

never have contemplated, like ploughing up a few acres to plant clover because Ed told us that the bees would love it.

8   As with any good teachers, the bees have made me see things in a new light. About a half a mile from the hives is a small, perpetually muddy bog with a boardwalk of old heart pine running through it. In early spring, when the skunk cabbage blooms, I find bees there by the thousands, humming happily and drinking greedily. It is, I now know, their first source of nectar in spring. I am glad, and wiser, to know that the skunk cabbages, which always make my nose wrinkle, are to bees what poached strawberries are to me: both a delectable perfume and a welcome harbinger of spring.

9   The bees' contributions to the farm are everywhere. Berry bushes that bore modestly before the bees' arrival now hang heavy with fruit; my vegetable plants produce an embarrassing abundance of heirloom squash, cucumbers, and runner beans. Even seemingly barren fruit trees, far from the house and orchard in what were once cow pastures, have suddenly begun producing again. And, of course, there is the honey itself, velvety brown and perfectly sweet, dissolving in my tea and rippling across my bread. None of this is my work; it is all the bees' doing, and in their labor I have found wonder, gratitude and a welcome sense of my own very modest place in the world.

PRACTICE 5

1. What is the writer's attitude towards the subject?

    a. positive   b. negative   c. neutral

2. Highlight the thesis statement.

3. How has the relationship between the writer and the bees changed? Explain, using your own words._____

    _____

4. The writer describes her life with the bees. Highlight some of the most effective examples of imagery.

5. A simile is a comparison using *like* or *as*. Highlight one simile in paragraph 6 and another in paragraph 7.

6. Circle some examples where the writer personifies or attributes human qualities to the bees.

7. Throughout the essay, the writer shows how the bees have had a positive influence on her life. In your own words, give some examples of how the bees have helped the writer._____

    _____

    _____

    _____

    _____

Writer's Room   Topics for Descriptive Essays

Writing Activity 1

Write a descriptive essay about one of the following topics, or choose your own topic.

General Topics

1. a music concert
2. the day _____ went to the_____
3. a family meal
4. a night out
5. an exciting sports event

Academic and Work-Related Topics

6. a beautiful building or area on campus
7. a frustrating day
8. an eccentric professor
9. a new person I have met
10. an exciting event

Writing Activity 2

Choose a quotation that you agree or disagree with, and then write a descriptive essay based on it.

Everything has its wonders, even darkness and silence, and I learn whatever state I am in to be content.

—Helen Keller, blind and deaf educator

Every artist dips his brush in his own soul and paints his own nature into his pictures.

—Henry Ward Beecher, abolitionist and clergyman

A few days ago I walked along the edge of the lake and was treated to the crunch and rustle of leaves with each step I made. The acoustics of this season are different, and all sounds, no matter how hushed, are as crisp as autumn air.

—Eric Sloane, artist

Train up a fig tree in the way it should go, and when you are old sit under the shade of it.

—Charles Dickens, novelist

WRITING LINK

More Descriptive Writing Topics
Chapter 19, Writer's Room topic 1 (page 275)
Chapter 21, Writer's Room topic 1 (page 294)
Chapter 23, Writer's Room topic 1 (page 309)
Chapter 26, Writer's Room topic 1 (page 344)
Chapter 27, Writer's Room topic 1 (page 356)
Chapter 29, Writer's Room topic 1 (page 377)
Chapter 36, Writer's Room topic 1 (page 444)

READING LINK

More Descriptive Readings
"Into Thin Air" by Jon Krakauer, page 485
"Monsoon Time" by Rahul Goswami, page 488
For a more complete list of readings by rhetorical mode, see Appendix 6.

✓ CHECKLIST: DESCRIPTIVE ESSAY

After you write your descriptive essay, review the essay checklist on the inside front cover. Also ask yourself these questions.

- Does my thesis statement clearly show what I will describe in the essay?

- Does my thesis statement have a controlling idea that makes a point about the topic?

- Does my essay have a dominant impression?

- Does each body paragraph contain supporting details that appeal to the reader's senses?

- Do I use vivid language?

Submit your best essays for possible publication to **thewritersworld@prenhall.com**.

Process

I am always doing that which I cannot do, in order that I may learn how to do it.

—PABLO PICASSO, *Cubist painter*

CHAPTER CONTENTS

CHAT ROOM

Choose one of the following topics and have a group or class discussion. Describe the steps you would take to do that process.

- How to become an annoying neighbour
- How to write an essay
- How to get rich quickly
- How to parallel park

EXPLORING

WHAT IS PROCESS?

A **process** is a series of steps usually done in chronological order. In process writing, you explain how to do something, how an incident took place, or how something works. Take a look at the following examples of processes that people discuss in everyday life.

Audience: Family member	Audience: Classmate	Audience: Intern
Cook pasta in the following way.	**Follow these steps to become a tutor.**	**Take the customer's order by following these procedures.**
• Boil a pot of water.	• Decide what subject you want to tutor.	• First, check to see the order form is filled out correctly.

- Add a pinch of salt.

- Put pasta into boiling water.

- See the person responsible for hiring a tutor.

- Find out the number of hours you need to tutor.

- Next, call our warehouse to verify stock.

- Then, send the order form to the warehouse

LIFE SNAPSHOT Process at Work

Frank Morelli is a mechanic who specializes in repairing Toyotas and Volvos. In this pamphlet excerpt, he advises customers on how to buy a car.

First, decide if you want a new or used car. There are some advantages and disadvantages for both. A new car will be more expensive, but you can buy an extended warranty, and a new car will likely not incur expensive repairs. A used car is, of course, more economical. However, if the previous owner has not properly maintained the car, you may have to pay for costly repairs, and the car may not last for very long.

Next, research the safety record of the car that you want to buy. Some types of cars offer extensive safety features such as dual airbags and a reinforced frame. To find information about the safety statistics of the car you want to buy, consult the car insurance Web sites or read some consumer magazines that deal with cars.

The Process Essay

Before planning a process essay, you need to determine your purpose. Do you want to tell readers how to complete a process or how to understand a process?

1. **Complete a process.** This type of essay contains directions for completing a particular task. For example, a writer might explain how to change a flat tire, how to decorate a room, or how to use a particular computer program.
2. **Understand a process.** This type of essay explains how something works or how something happens. For example, a writer might explain how the admissions process at a college works or how food goes from the farm to the table.

A Student Essay

Read the essay and answer the questions that follow.

Learning Good Finances

By Tony Ruiz

1   Every year, when you apply for more student aid, it takes a toll on your fiscal confidence. If you are anything like I am, no matter how well you think you have curbed your spending, you always find yourself staring at your T4 tax slip return form in disbelief. Your humble living standards do not reflect the overwhelming discrepancy between your alleged total earnings and your most recent bank statement. Students can begin making smart financial decisions today and help reduce the financial burden they are likely to experience after graduation.

2   Students should avoid spending money on unnecessary gadgets. For example, the iPod is a terrible investment for students who are trying to save money. Besides paying at least $199 for the iPod nano or $269 for the iPod

Video, consumers end up buying crucial trendy accessories. An FM transmitter that will let listeners wire their iPod through a car's sound system costs $29.95. For those who want to listen to FM radio while walking to class, the FM Radio Remote costs another $49.95. And before long, the iPod's dead battery will have to be replaced for $59 (plus shipping and handling). Some students might even be tempted to buy a newer model of iPod. Meanwhile, an impressive iTunes library costs $.99 for every song and $1.99 for every episode of *Lost* that could be watched Wednesday nights at no cost.

3   Another common mistake students make is adopting expensive daily regimens. They should reduce "treat" spending by half. For the sluggish, a $4.50 personalized Starbucks coffee is the only way to function. Jamba Juice is the formidable, health-conscious counterpart. Replacing the designer drink every day with generic coffee or fruit juice would amount to substantial savings. Skipping the Chai Latte or the Mocha Cappuccino Delight three days out of five is painless, but effective.

4   Students can earn more money by investing carefully. Setting aside even as little as $500 every year toward student debt means that after a four-year period, one will have $2000 less to worry about paying off. The elimination of interest charges will generate pocket change in the long term as well. Furthermore, student loans also offer a unique advantage since the cost to students will not be felt until graduation, so they should make that money work for them. Those who are absolutely sure that they will not need a certain amount of money until graduation can lock up the money with a certificate of deposit and let it earn interest yields typically higher than those of savings and money market accounts.

5   Nobody expects students to invest all of their time and money in scholarly endeavours. Everybody needs to have some leisure activities. But they should be reasonable. New gadgets and expensive habits are unnecessary indulgences.

PRACTICE 1

1. Highlight the thesis statement.

2. Highlight the topic sentence in each body paragraph.

3. Who is the audience for this essay?

4. For each of the body paragraphs, list some supporting details the writer gives.

    Paragraph 2: _____

    _____

    Paragraph 3: _____

    _____

    Paragraph 4: _____

    _____

Explore Topics

In the following Writer's Desk, you will try an exploring strategy to generate ideas about different topics.

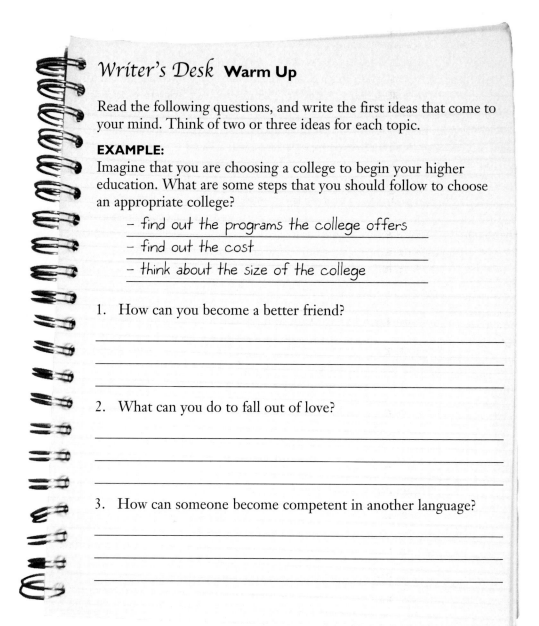

Writer's Desk **Warm Up**

Read the following questions, and write the first ideas that come to your mind. Think of two or three ideas for each topic.

EXAMPLE:

Imagine that you are choosing a college to begin your higher education. What are some steps that you should follow to choose an appropriate college?

– find out the programs the college offers

– find out the cost

– think about the size of the college

1. How can you become a better friend?

_____

_____

2. What can you do to fall out of love?

_____

_____

3. How can someone become competent in another language?

_____

_____

_____

DEVELOPING

When you write a process essay, choose a process that you know something about. For example, you might be able to explain how to become more environmentally conscious; however, you might not know how to reduce nuclear waste.

The Thesis Statement

In a process essay, the thesis statement states what process you will be explaining and what readers will be able to do after they have read the paragraph.

topic   controlling idea

Remaining attractive to your spouse can help keep a relationship exciting.

              controlling idea   topic

Consistency, patience, and time are essential **to becoming a good parent.**

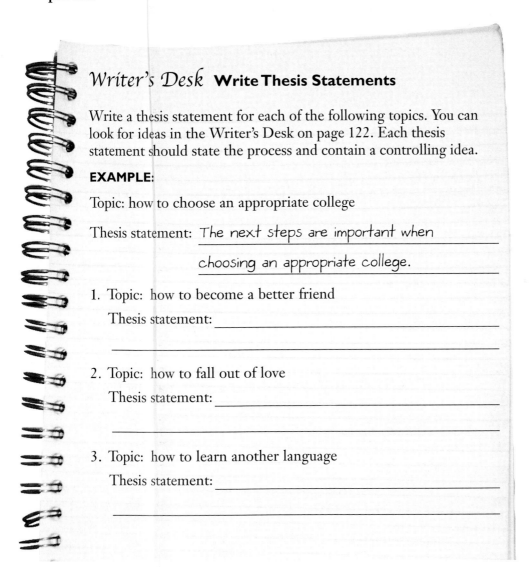

Writer's Desk **Write Thesis Statements**

Write a thesis statement for each of the following topics. You can look for ideas in the Writer's Desk on page 122. Each thesis statement should state the process and contain a controlling idea.

EXAMPLE:

Topic: how to choose an appropriate college

Thesis statement: The next steps are important when choosing an appropriate college.

1. Topic: how to become a better friend

   Thesis statement: _____

   _____

2. Topic: how to fall out of love

   Thesis statement: _____

   _____

3. Topic: how to learn another language

   Thesis statement: _____

   _____

The Supporting Ideas

A process essay contains a series of steps. When you develop supporting ideas for a process essay, think about the main steps that are necessary to complete the process.

- Use prewriting strategies such as freewriting and brainstorming to generate ideas.

- Choose the best ideas. Clearly explain the steps of the process.
- Organize your ideas. Choose the best organizational method for this essay pattern. Process essays generally use chronological or time order.

HINT   **Give Steps, Not Examples**

When you explain how to complete a process, describe each step. Do not simply list examples of the process.

Topic: How to Plan an Interesting Vacation

List of Examples	Steps in the Process
• go to a tropical island	• decide what your goal is
• ride a hot air balloon	• research possible locations
• swim with the sharks	• find out the cost
• tour an exotic city	• plan the itinerary according to budget

---

Writer's Desk   **List the Main Steps**

Choose one thesis statement from the previous Writer's Desk. List the main steps to complete the process.

EXAMPLE:

Thesis statement: These steps are important when choosing an appropriate college.

1. Ask about programs.
2. Find out the cost.
3. Consider the size of the college.
4. Ask about student housing.

Thesis statement: _____

_____

Steps to complete the process:

_____

_____

_____

_____

_____

The Essay Plan

An essay plan helps you organize your thesis statement, topic sentences, and supporting details before writing a first draft. Decide which steps and which details your reader will really need to complete the process or understand it.

Thesis statement: The next steps are important for choosing an appropriate college.

I. Find out which programs the college offers.
   A. Look for different options like majors and minors.
   B. Make note of the number of years to complete the program.
   C. Figure out the prerequisites necessary to get accepted.

II. Determine what you can afford to spend on your education.
   A. Ask the administration for details on tuition and other expenses.
   B. Research the available student loans and grants.
   C. Find out about scholarships.

III. Consider the size of the college.
   A. A smaller college may have smaller class sizes and more individualized attention.
   B. It may be easier to make friends in smaller classes.
   C. A bigger college may have more programs, a more heterogeneous student population, and more student services.

Writer's Desk   **Write an Essay Plan**

Refer to the information you generated in previous Writer's Desks, and prepare a detailed essay plan. Add details and examples that will help to explain each step.

The First Draft

As you write your first draft, explain the process in a way that would be clear for your audience. Address the reader directly. For example, instead of writing, "You should scan the newspaper for used cars," simply write, "Scan the newspaper for used cars." Also, remember to use complete sentences and transitions to smoothly string together the ideas from your essay plan. Here are some time order transitions that are useful for explaining processes.

To Begin a Process	To Continue a Process		To End a Process
(at) first	after that	later	eventually
initially	afterward	meanwhile	finally
the first step	also	second	in the end
	furthermore	then	ultimately
	in addition	third	

GRAMMAR HINT **Avoid Sentence Fragments**

Ensure that you do not use sentence fragments to list the steps of the process. A sentence must have a subject and a verb to express a complete idea.

Consider your airline's carry-on luggage requirements. First, the weight of your
check
suitcase.
^

See Chapter 21 for more information about sentence fragments.

Writer's Desk **Write the First Draft**

In the previous Writer's Desk, you developed an essay plan. Now, carefully review your essay plan, make any necessary changes, and write the first draft of your process essay.

REVISING AND EDITING

REVISE AND EDIT A PROCESS ESSAY

When you finish writing a process essay, carefully review your work and revise it to make the process as clear as possible to your readers. Check to make sure that you have organized your steps, and remove any irrelevant details. Before you revise and edit your own essay, practise revising and editing a student essay.

A Student Essay

Dilip Dharmaratna is a graduate of New Brunswick Community College. Read the essay, and then answer the questions that follow. As you read, correct any errors that you find, and make comments in the margins.

The Right College

By Dilip Dharmaratna

1   When I first thought about a college to attend, I really did not know what to do. It was very lucky that Dave Hunt, my good friend, was more organized than me and could help me make such an important decision. One Sunday afternoon, very close to the deadline, we sat in a café, and he proceeded to explain exactly what I should think about when choosing a college. The next steps are crucial for finding an appropriate college.

2   Learn about the programs different colleges offer. Some important factors to consider are the number of years to complete the program that interests you. You need to know about different program options like major and minor subjects. It is necessary to know the prerequisite courses or experience necessary to get accepted into a program. If you want to pursue social work, perhaps you need some experience working with people. If you are interested in bookkeeping, maybe you need a particular high school math course to get

accepted into the program. For instance, when I applied to our college's nursing program, I needed my Grade 12 science credit.

3   First, the cost. Education is very expensive. When determining which college to go to, find one where you can afford to spend several years studying. For example, a college in the next city with a great reputation might cost a lot for tuition, housing, and transportation. I live far from the campus. The traffic is incredibly heavy, and it takes me a long time to get there. The local college might not be as well known or respected, but perhaps you will be able to afford the tuition, or you may be able to live at home, and your transportation costs might be much lower. For example, my neighbour Trang Hoang, a mechanical engineering student, saved money by going to our local college. "My decision to study locally has never hurt my career prospects," she says.

4   You may not know what you want to study. In such a case, it is advisable to take a variety of courses to see where your interests lie. When Dave Hunt was eighteen, he started out majoring in art, but after one term, he worried about earning a good living, and he switched to administration. He realized that he loves working with numbers, so he is very happy about his decision. Keep your mind open to different subjects.

5   A smaller college will have smaller class sizes and more individualized attention. It is easier to make friends in smaller classes. But a larger college may have more programs. It may also have a more heterogeneous student population, which would enable you to meet students with different backgrounds. A larger college may also provide more student services, clubs, and other activities, you may find such experiences enriching.

6   So think very carefully when choosing a college. The right college will provide you with innumerable advantages such as a good education, the right career opportunity, and long-lasting friendships. Take advantage of different sources and become informed. You will never regret it.

PRACTICE 2

Revising

1. Highlight the thesis statement.
2. Highlight the topic sentences for paragraphs 2 and 3.
3. A possible topic sentence for paragraph 5 could be
   a. It is easy to make friends at college.
   b. Participate in different activities at a bigger college.
   c. Small colleges are not as interesting as big colleges.
   d. Keep the size of the college in mind when making your decision.

4. Which paragraph is unnecessary for the development of ideas? Explain why. _____

   _____

   _____

5. In paragraph 3, cross out the sentence that does not support the topic sentence.

6. Paragraph 5 lacks adequate support. Think of a detailed example that would help flesh out the paragraph. _____

_____

_____

_____

7. Paragraph 2 lacks transitions. Add at least three transitions to link the sentences.

Editing

8. Underline a pronoun problem in the introductory paragraph. Write the correction in the following space.

   Correction: _____

9. Underline the sentence fragment in paragraph 3. Then correct it in the following space.

   Correction: _____

10. Underline the run-on sentence in paragraph 5. Then correct it in the following space.

    Correction: _____

GRAMMAR LINK

See the following chapters for more information about these grammar topics:
Pronouns, Chapter 29
Run-Ons, Chapter 22
Fragments, Chapter 21

ABC VOCABULARY BOOST

Look at the first draft of your process essay. Underline the verb that you used in each step of the process. Then, when possible, come up with a more evocative verb. Use your thesaurus for this activity.

Writer's Desk **Revise and Edit Your Process Essay**

Revise and edit the essay that you wrote for the previous Writer's Desk. You can refer to the checklists at the end of this chapter and on the inside covers of this book.

A Professional Essay

Journalist Stacey Colino specializes in health, psychological, and family issues and has written for the *Washington Post*, *Parenting*, and *Shape*. In the next essay, she writes about how to become a happier person.

Do You Have What It Takes to Be Happy?
By Stacey Colino

1   If you add up money, beauty, fame, and admiration, you've got the formula for a lifetime of bliss, right? Wrong. The truth is, your financial status, external circumstances, and life events account for no more than 15 percent of your happiness quotient, studies show. What elements do make a difference? Surprisingly simple internal factors such as having healthy self-esteem, a sense of optimism and hope, gratifying relationships, and meaning and purpose in your life have the most influence, according to recent studies on what researchers call "subjective well-being."

2   If that sounds like a tall order, here's the good news: Even if they don't come naturally, many of the attitudes and thought patterns that influence happiness can be cultivated, which means you can boost your capacity for happiness today—and in the future. "Studies with twins reveal that happiness is somewhat like a person's cholesterol level—it's genetically influenced, but it's also influenced by some factors that are under our control," explains David Myers, Ph.D., a social psychologist at Hope College in Holland, Michigan, and author of *The Pursuit of Happiness* (HarperCollins, 1993). In other words, while your genetically determined temperament has a fairly strong influence on your happiness quotient, you can nudge it upward with the attitudes and approaches you bring to your life. To develop a sunnier disposition, use the simple strategies outlined in this essay, and you'll be on your way to a richer, more satisfying life, starting now!

3   Develop an upbeat attitude. No, you don't want to become a Pollyanna who overlooks problems and thinks everything is peachy even when it isn't. But you do want to consciously focus on what's positive in your life because this can engender a sense of optimism and hope. And research has found that happy people are brimming with these key ingredients. In one study at Southern Methodist University in Dallas, happy subjects were more hopeful about their wishes than their less **sanguine** peers. It's not that their wishes came true more often, but the happy people expected them to come true. How? They do it by expecting to have a joyful summer every day, not just when they're on vacation, by identifying negative thoughts and countering them with positive or neutral ones, and by embracing challenges (such as parasailing or public speaking) instead of fearing them. Such people realize that challenges will help them grow.

sanguine: optimistic

4   Hang out with your favourite people. It's as simple as this: Carving out as much time as you can to spend with people you value gives you a sense of connection, as well as a support system for when your luck heads south. Research at the University of Illinois at Urbana-Champaign found that people who are consistently very happy have stronger romantic and social relationships than unhappy people. "We're social creatures by nature," says Louis H. Janda, an associate professor of psychology at Old Dominion University in Norfolk, Virginia. "When you're involved with others, it gives you a sense of belonging and lets you engage in mutually enjoyable activities, all of which can buffer you from stress."

5   Infuse your life with a sense of purpose. If you want to be happy, it is important to give your life meaning: Research at Middle Tennessee State University in Murfreesboro found that having a sense of purpose is a significant predictor of happiness and life satisfaction. To create a vision of what's meaningful to you, ask yourself, "What activities make me feel excited

or enthusiastic? What do I want to be remembered for? What matters most to me?" If you can articulate these desires to yourself, you can set specific goals to help you fulfill them. If you realize that your strongest desire is to become an influential teacher and role model, for example, you might set a goal of volunteering to help disadvantaged kids or of going back to school to get your teaching degree.

6   Count your blessings, not your burdens. When people keep a gratitude journal, in which they jot down a daily list of what they appreciate in their lives, they experience a heightened sense of well-being, according to research at the University of California, Davis, and the University of Miami in Florida. "There's a natural tendency to take things for granted, but if you stop and think of all the ways you are blessed, it doesn't take long for the mind to use that as the new baseline for perceiving how happy you are," explains study co-author Michael E. McCullough, Ph.D., an associate professor of psychology and religious studies at the University of Miami.

R&R: rest and relaxation

7   Recharge your energy and your spirits. Sure, exercise can work wonders in keeping your mood buoyant, but so can getting some simple **R&R**. "Happy people lead active, vigorous lives yet reserve time for restorative sleep and solitude," Myers says. Short-change yourself of the shut-eye you need, and it's hard to enjoy much of anything when you're exhausted. In a recent study involving more than nine hundred women, researchers assessed how happy women were based on their daily activities and found that sleep quality had a substantial influence over how much the women enjoyed life, even when they engaged in plenty of pleasurable activities like sex and socializing.

8   Put on a happy face! If you act as if you're on cloud nine—by smiling with your mouth and eyes, speaking in a cheerful voice and walking confidently—going through the motions can trigger the actual emotion. There's even science to prove it: A study at Fairleigh Dickinson University in Teaneck, New Jersey, found that when people forced themselves to smile or laugh, they experienced a substantial boost in mood afterward.

9   So start off by acting as if you're walking on the sunny side of the street—even if it's cloudy. Chances are, you'll begin to feel a little happier after just a few steps!

PRACTICE 3

1. What is the writer's specific purpose?_____

    _____

2. Highlight the thesis statement. It may not be in the first paragraph.
3. Read the topic sentence of each body paragraph. Highlight the verbs in each topic sentence.
4. In each topic sentence, the subject is implied but not stated. What is the subject?_____

    _____

5. List the examples the writer gives to support the topic sentence of each paragraph.

    _____

    _____

6. The writer supported her main ideas with many specific examples. Identify and underline six research studies that the writer refers to.

7. Circle the names of three experts that the writer quotes.

8. The writer uses no transitional words or phrases to link the steps of the process. Add a transitional word or expression to the beginning of at least four body paragraphs.

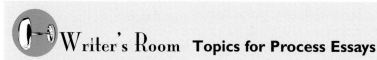 **Writer's Room** **Topics for Process Essays**

Writing Activity 1

Write a process essay about one of the following topics or choose your own topic.

General Topics

How to . . .

1. buy a used car
2. become a good driver
3. communicate more effectively with family members
4. win a _____
5. live on a budget

Academic and Work-Related Topics

How to . . .

6. look for a new job
7. assemble a _____
8. become a better manager or supervisor
9. change a law
10. make a good impression at an interview

Writing Activity 2

Choose a quotation that you agree or disagree with, and then write a process essay based on it.

> The first step to getting the things you want out of life is this: Decide what you want.
>
> —Ben Stein, writer

> We now accept the fact that learning is a lifelong process of keeping abreast of change. And the most pressing task is to teach people how to learn.
>
> —Peter Drucker, writer

> There was a definite process by which one made people into friends, and it involved talking to them and listening to them for hours at a time.
>
> —Rebecca West, journalist

> Civilization is a slow process of adopting the ideas of minorities.
>
> —Anonymous

WRITING LINK

More Process Writing Topics
Chapter 19, on page 275, see Writer's Room Topic 2.
Chapter 23, on page 309 see Writer's Room Topic 2.
Chapter 24, on page 316, see Writer's Room Topic 1.
Chapter 28, on page 365, see Writer's Room Topic 1.

READING LINK

More Process Readings

"The Rich Resonance of Small Talk" by Roxanne Roberts (page 473)
"The Rules of Survival" by Laurence Gonzales (page 482)
For a more complete list of readings by rhetorical mode, see Appendix 6.

CHECKLIST: PROCESS ESSAY

As you write your process essay, review the checklist on the inside front cover. Also ask yourself these questions.

- Does my thesis statement make a point about the process?

- Do I include all of the steps in the process?

- Do I clearly explain each step so my reader can accomplish the process?

- Do I mention all of the supplies that my reader needs to complete the process?

- Do I use transitions to connect all of the steps in the process?

Submit your best essays for possible publication to **thewritersworld@prenhall.com**.

Definition

Freedom's just another word for nothing left to lose.

—Kris Kristofferson, *actor and singer*

CHAT ROOM

Brainstorm some common slang expressions. Think about words you use to express pleasure or disgust. You can also consider words describing a specific type of person. Choose one expression and define it without using a dictionary. Make your definition clear so that a non-native speaker will understand the word.

EXPLORING

WHAT IS DEFINITION?

When you define, you explain the meaning of a word. Some terms have concrete meanings, and you can define them in a few words. For example, a *town* is "a small city." Other words, such as *values*, *faith*, or *human rights*, are more abstract and require more detailed definitions. It is possible to write a paragraph, an essay, or even an entire book about such concepts. Here are some examples of terms people regularly define in different situations.

Audience: Children	Audience: Classmate	Audience: Colleague
I expect you to be *reliable*.	**In my sociology class we are discussing the term** *poverty*.	**My supervisor said my presentation "needs improvement."**
• Phone if you are going to be late.	• Poverty means different things to different cultures.	• I spoke too quickly.

- Do your chores to help out.

- Do your homework every night.

- In this country, the government always talks about low income.

- Some countries, like China, define poverty by the minimum caloric intake of an individual.

- I relied too heavily on my PowerPoint slides.

- My presentation was too long.

LIFE SNAPSHOT **Definition at Work**

In the following excerpt, Teacher of the Year, Heidi Capraro, defines what makes a great teacher.

We have a passion for teaching. We care about our students, parents, and the communities in which we work and teach. We celebrate the positive accomplishments in the field of teaching and look for brighter possibilities for the future.

I think teachers have to be sensitive to each student's tolerance for frustration and recognize that each one handles this kind of stress differently. We want to engage and motivate students, not force them to shut down and quit. This applies to students at every age. I think people assume that as children grow up, they don't need the same support and understanding. In reality, they have more difficulties to face as they reach their teenage years. Kindness, empathy, opportunities for success, modifications, and adults with a personal interest in them—these are what every child needs.

The Definition Essay

When you write a definition essay, try to explain what a term means to you. For example, if someone asks you to define *overachiever*, you might tell stories to illustrate the meaning of the word. You may give examples of overachievers and what you think those people do that goes beyond the limits. You may also explain what an overachiever is not. Also, remember the next two points.

1. **Choose a term that you know something about.** You need to understand a term to say something relevant and interesting about it.
2. **Give a clear definition.** Write a definition that is understandable to your reader, and support your definition with examples.

HINT **Consider Your Audience**

Consider your audience when you write a definition essay. You may have to adjust your tone and vocabulary, depending on who reads the essay. For example, if you write a definition essay about cloning for your political science class, you may have to explain concepts using basic, non-technical terms. If you write the same essay for your biology class, you may be able to use more technical terms.

A Student Essay

Read the student essay and answer the questions that follow.

Journalists Are History's Record Keepers

By Lindsey Davis

1   When you want to find research for that paper on World War II for class, you hit the books in the library, looking for the historian who summed up the events or the political scientist who offered critical insight as to why it happened. But when you want to find out what is happening in the world right now, you pick up the *Globe and Mail* or log onto your computer and browse the **plethora** of news sites. Journalists play multiple roles in society. From the **Fourth Estate** as the check on government and business to the responsibility of creating a forum for debate and free speech, the job of journalists is crucial to society's progress. But beyond this role, journalists are historians. They are the note takers and storytellers who document today's activities and events to safeguard their accuracy and preserve the record of history.

plethora: a large amount

Fourth Estate: the entire press including newspapers, television news programs, magazines, etc.

2   First, different types of media are crucial for preserving historical records. Newspapers, news websites, and television news programs are the only place you can turn to find the latest breaking developments of what is happening in Ottawa, what reforms the Prime Minister is planning, the status of the war in Iraq, and the crucial stats of the last CFL playoff game. Before it goes in the history books, it goes in the newspaper. Before you can find it in the library, you can find it in the news.

3   Moreover, journalists are the record keepers for the community. They will give you the plain and simple facts. They will find out how much those tickets were selling for at the SkyDome. They will tell you who won the basketball games and what the upcoming baseball season looks like. But beyond simple facts, they will record the emotions of a Stanley Cup defeat. How about those new movies and CDs that are coming out next week? They will give you the scoop of what's good and what's bad. They will tell you what you can't miss in Montreal. You can find the thoughts and analyses of a vast array of differing voices.

4   Furthermore, journalists are also crucial to preserving the spirit of the times. It is within the media that you'll find the record of the year's events. But this history won't be complete unless it includes your voice, your opinion, and your perspective on events. Tell the journalists what's going on and what you would like to see covered. Send them an email. Talk to reporters and tell them what you think. The media will never be able to create an accurate record of history unless you help gather all the facts by saying what you know or what you saw. Do you think something was wrongly covered? Let the media know. Do you disagree with a column you have read? Send a letter to the editor and make sure your viewpoint is printed and recorded as well.

5   Journalists are committed to ensuring that whatever happens is recorded forever. Some people say that journalists write the rough draft of history. But they strive to report accurately enough that it will be the final draft. Their dedication ensures that you get the news and ensures that history is recorded. All they ask is that you read to keep the history alive.

PRACTICE I

1. What is the specific purpose of this essay? _____

_____

2. Highlight the thesis statement.

3. Highlight the topic sentence of each body paragraph.

4. What introductory style is used?

   a. anecdote   b. historical

   c. contrasting position   d. general background

5. In your own words, list some of the specific examples in each body paragraph.

   Paragraph 1 _____

   Paragraph 2 _____

   Paragraph 3 _____

6. Circle the transitional links in this essay.

Explore Topics

In the following Writer's Desk, you will try an exploring strategy to generate ideas about different topics.

Writer's Desk **Warm Up**

Read the following questions, and write the first ideas that come to your mind. Think of two or three ideas for each topic.

EXAMPLE:
What is a volunteer? Think of some characteristics of a volunteer.

– is involved in charitable causes

– wants to help people

– has love for humankind

1. What is a home?

   _____

   _____

   _____

2. What is a Canadian?

   _____

   _____

   _____

3. What is a religion?

   _____

   _____

   _____

DEVELOPING

THE THESIS STATEMENT

A clear thesis statement for a definition essay introduces the term and provides a definition. There are three basic ways to define a term.

Definition by Synonym

Providing a definition by synonym is useful if the original term is difficult to understand, and the synonym is a more familiar word.

term   +   synonym
He is a neophyte, which means he is a beginner or novice.

Definition by Category

When you define by category, you determine the larger group to which the term belongs. Then you determine what unique characteristics set the term apart from others in that category.

term   +   category   +   detail
A forest ranger is a worker who is trained to protect wildlife in national parks.

Definition by Negation

When you define by negation, you explain what a term does not mean. You can then include a sentence explaining what it does mean.

term   +   what it is not   +   what it is
Obsession is not an eccentricity; it is a mental illness.

GRAMMAR HINT Using Semicolons

You can join two related and complete ideas with a semicolon.

Example: Marriage is not the end of your freedom; it is the beginning
of a shared journey.

See Chapter 19 for more information about using semicolons.

Making a Point

Defining terms by synonym, category, and negation are only guidelines for writing thesis statements for a definition essay. Keep in mind that your essay will be more interesting if you express your attitude or point of view in your thesis statement.

No point: Avarice means greed.

Point: Human avarice, or greed, invariably leads to tragedy.

PRACTICE 2

Write thesis statements by defining the following terms using your own words. Try to make definitions by synonym, category, and negation. Remember to indicate your controlling idea in the thesis statements.

EXAMPLE:

Road rage <u>is not a momentary lapse of judgment; it is serious</u>
<u>criminal behaviour.</u>

1. A misfit _____

_____

2. A jock _____

_____

3. B-list actors _____

_____

4. Rush-hour traffic _____

_____

5. A mentor _____

_____

HINT **Be Precise!**

When you write a definition essay, it is important to use the precise words to define the term. Moreover, when you define a term by category, make sure that the category for your term is correct.

Anorexia nervosa is the <u>inability</u> to eat.
(Anorexia is not an ability or an inability.)

Anorexia nervosa is <u>when</u> you want to be thin.
(*When* refers to a time, but anorexia is not a time.)

Anorexia nervosa is <u>where</u> it is hard to eat properly.
(*Where* refers to a place, but anorexia is not a place.)

Now look at a better definition of anorexia.

Anorexia nervosa is a tragic **eating disorder** characterized by the desire to become thin.

PRACTICE 3

Revise each sentence using precise language.

EXAMPLE:

Multitasking is when you do many activities at once.

<u>Multitasking is doing many activities at once.</u>

1. A blacklist is when a list of people comes under suspicion.

   _____

2. A poor loser is the inability to accept defeat graciously.

   _____

3. A twixter is overdependence on parents by adult children.

   _____

4. Feedback is when you get constructive criticism.

   _____

5. Networking is where you keep in contact with people to help your career.

   _____

ABC
ABC
AB
VOCABULARY BOOST

Some words have neutral, positive, or negative associations. Look at each set of words, and categorize each as neutral, positive, or negative. Do this with a partner.

1. thin, cadaverous, lean, emaciated, wiry, skinny, slender
2. home, shack, cottage, slum, stomping ground, dump, sanctuary
3. dainty, delicate, finicky, fussy, prissy, fragile, elegant, frail
4. honest, coarse, crude, open, gross, straightforward
5. brat, child, sweetheart, cutie, munchkin, delinquent, heir, mama's boy

---

Writer's Desk Write Thesis Statements

Write a thesis statement in which you define each of the following topics. You can look for ideas in the previous Writer's Desk. Remember to make a point in your thesis statement.

EXAMPLE:

Topic: a volunteer

Thesis statement: A volunteer is a necessary and generous person who is emotionally involved in the betterment of humankind.

1. Topic: home

    Thesis statement: _____

    _____

2. Topic: a Canadian
    Thesis statement: _____

    _____

3. Topic: a religion
    Thesis statement: _____

    _____

The Supporting Ideas

After you have developed an effective thesis statement, generate supporting ideas. In a definition essay, you can give examples that clarify your definition. To develop supporting ideas follow these three steps.

- Use prewriting strategies to generate ideas. Think about facts, anecdotes, and examples that will help define your term.
- Choose the best ideas. Use examples that clearly reveal the definition of the term.
- Organize your ideas. Choose the best organizational method for this essay pattern.

Writer's Desk **Generate Supporting Ideas**

Choose one of your thesis statements from the previous Writer's Desk. List three or four ideas that most effectively illustrate the definition.

EXAMPLE:
Thesis statement: A volunteer is a necessary and generous person who is emotionally involved in the betterment of humankind.

- offers to help others
- brings attention to charitable causes
- selfless
- is important for society

Thesis statement:

_____

_____

Supports:

_____

_____

_____

_____

The Essay Plan

An essay plan helps you organize your thesis statement and supporting details before writing the first draft. A definition essay includes a complete definition of the term and provides adequate examples to support the central definition. When creating a definition essay plan, ensure that your examples provide varied evidence and do not just repeat the definition. Organize your ideas in a logical sequence.

Thesis statement: A volunteer is a necessary and generous person who is involved in the betterment of humankind.

I. Volunteers do not earn money; they gain a sense of personal satisfaction.
   A. Donne wrote "Meditation XVII: No man is an island."
   B. He believed that people are not isolated, but interconnected.
   C. Donne's philosophy influenced people such as Martin Luther King, Jr.

II. Many people of all types are volunteers.
   A. Extremely rich people contribute to charity.
   B. Ordinary people donate their time.

III. By giving their time and money, volunteers are crucial for charities to function.
   A. Non-profit organizations help develop public awareness of different issues and problems.
   B. International organizations rely on volunteers.
   C. Volunteers also work at local community churches and schools.

Writer's Desk   **Write an Essay Plan**

Refer to the information you generated in previous Writer's Desks and prepare a detailed essay plan.

The First Draft

Your essay plan is the backbone around which you can craft your first draft. Use it to write your first draft. As you write, remember to vary your sentence structure and to write complete sentences. Also include transitional words or expressions to help your ideas flow smoothly. Here are some transitional expressions that can help you show different levels of importance in a definition essay.

To Show the Level of Importance	
clearly	next
first	one quality…another quality
most important	second
most of all	undoubtedly

Writer's Desk   Write the First Draft

Carefully review the essay plan you prepared in the previous Writer's Desk. Make any necessary changes to the definition or its supporting details, and then write your first draft.

REVISING AND EDITING

REVISE AND EDIT A DEFINITION ESSAY

When you finish writing a definition essay, carefully review your work and revise it to make the definition as clear as possible to your readers. You might have to adjust your definition and supporting ideas to suit their knowledge. Also keep in mind the tone of your essay. Certain words have either negative or positive connotations. Finally, check that you have organized your ideas logically and remove any irrelevant details. Before you revise and edit your own essay, practise revising and editing a student essay.

A Student Essay

Read the essay, and then answer the questions that follow. As you read, correct any errors that you find, and make comments in the margins.

Volunteers

By Michael Newberg

1   "What do we live for, if it is not to make life less difficult for each other"? wrote the English writer, George Eliot. This question has been discussed throughout history during times of prosperity and poverty. Human beings need to be kind and giving to each other. Volunteers are the backbone of a kind world, and we desperately need their acts of charity. A volunteer is a necessary and generous person who is involved in the betterment of humankind.

2   Volunteers do not earn money; they gain a sense of personal satisfaction. One of the English poets, John Donne, believed that humanity has a collective responsibility. In a powerful poem, *Meditation XVII*, Donne wrote, "No man is an island, entire of itself . . . any man's death diminishes me, because I am involved in mankind." According to Donne, people must care for each other. His philosophy has influenced many people such as Martin Luther King, Jr. Volunteers want to help people because they want to make the world a more just society.

3   Some very wealthy people donate tremendous amounts of time and money to help others. Oprah, for example. She spends a lot of time and money with her girls' school in South Africa. Many middle class and poor people also volunteer and help those in need. Soup kitchens, for instance, could not function without the service of many unpaid workers. Bae Kim is a cook in our college cafeteria, but he also volunteers once a week for the Meals on Wheels program in our district.

4   By giving their time and money, volunteers are crucial for charities to function. Non-profit organizations, such as Doctors Without Borders or the Red cross help raise public awareness about different issues, including the AIDS epidemic, war, political injustices, and so on. Most of these organizations rely on large numbers of volunteers from all walks of life. Doctors Without Borders won the Nobel Peace Prize several years ago. Volunteers not only work in large international organizations, but they also donate their time and money to local churches, schools, and youth centres. Our community refugee help centre could not function without the local high school students who regularly volunteer there.

5   Volunteers are increasingly necessary to create a kinder world. With powerfull communication technology, we see tragedy every day in our living rooms. Those volunteers from all walks of life who give their time and skills help to alleviate the suffering of others. As Martin Luther King, Jr. said, "Life's most persistent and urgent question is, what are you doing for others?" So get involved because the other people need you.

PRACTICE 4

Revising

1. Highlight the thesis statement.

2. What type of definition does the thesis statement have? Circle the best answer.

   a. synonym   b. category   c. negation

3. Highlight the topic sentences in paragraphs 2 and 4.

4. What type of definition is in the topic sentence for paragraph 2? Circle your answer.

   a. synonym   b. category   c. negation

5. Paragraph 3 does not have a topic sentence. Which sentence would be an effective topic sentence for that paragraph? Circle the best answer.

   a. Oprah Winfrey is one of the most generous people in America.

   b. Many people reflect on the act of giving.

c. Many poor people donate their time to charitable organizations.

d. Volunteers are found in all social classes.

6. Cross out the sentence in paragraph 4 that does not support the topic sentence.

GRAMMAR LINK

See the following chapters for more information about these grammar topics:

Quotations, Chapter 35
Fragments, Chapter 21
Capitalization, Chapter 35
Spelling, Chapter 32

Editing

7. The quotation in the introductory paragraph is incorrectly punctuated. Underline and correct the error.

   Correction: _____

   _____

8. Paragraph 3 has a fragment. Underline and correct the error.

   Correction: _____

   _____

9. There is an error in capitalization in paragraph 4. Underline and correct the error.

   Correction: _____

   _____

10. There is one spelling mistake in paragraph 5. Underline and correct the mistake.

    Correction: _____

    _____

Writer's Desk   **Revise and Edit Your Essay**

Revise and edit the essay that you wrote for the previous Writer's Desk. You can refer to the revising and editing checklists at the end of this chapter and on the inside covers of this book.

A Professional Essay

Dorothy Nixon, a freelance writer from Montreal, has written for Salon.com, *Chatelaine*, and *Today's Parent* magazine. In the following article, Nixon ponders the meaning of genius.

On Genius
By Dorothy Nixon

1   When Albert Einstein was chosen as *Time* magazine's Man of the Century, I was not surprised. Our society is simply obsessed with the idea of genius, and no man embodies that concept in this scientific age better than

Albert Einstein, with his godlike grasp of mathematics and his messy mad-scientist hair.

2   Around the same time, a group of Canadian researchers were grabbing headlines. The researchers, while analyzing Einstein's brain, had discovered some extra connections in the famous physicist's grey matter. They theorized that Einstein's brain held the secret to the man's genius. "I held Einstein's brain, and I was in awe," said a researcher, revealing the fact that the research was not entirely objective on his part. After all, *awe* is usually a feeling reserved for religious experiences.

3   Rationally speaking, holding Einstein's brain cannot feel too differently from holding a chimp's brain or a Vegas chorus girl's brain. Still, everyone understood what he meant: he was moved by the idea of Einstein's genius, which seems almost mystical in nature and therefore something to be "in awe of." The question remains, why were the scientists trying to quantify Einstein's genius by locating it somewhere in his brain in the first place? Genius is not quantifiable. Genius cannot be captured in a butterfly net or put in a bottle. Genius is not even that that mysterious, really: it exists all around us, almost always in unrecognized form.

4   Societies tend to value some forms of genius over others. In the Renaissance, artists, sculptors, and architects were esteemed above all; in sixteenth century Vienna, musicians were revered; today, mathematicians and scientists are lauded. Da Vinci, Mozart, and Einstein arose from these environments.

5   Genius has to be given a chance; it has to be nurtured. It has to be rigorously trained, too. (Remember, genius is one percent inspiration and ninety-nine percent perspiration, according to Thomas Edison.) Genius has to have good timing, or it is liable to be labelled lunacy. Above all, it has to be recognized for what it is.

6   A while back, I was sitting on the Montreal–Toronto train. To my dismay, the grandmotherly woman beside me wanted to talk. I don't normally like talking on trains, but within minutes I was truly mesmerized by the old woman's story. In broken English, the old woman told me about her life; how she had grown up in a poor country and spent only a few years in school; how she had eloped to Canada with a hardworking young man from her village; how she had helped out her husband with his landscaping business "doing the money part" until they had enough cash scraped together to buy a small apartment building. She told me how her husband had died soon thereafter and left her with three young boys, and how, with good business "luck" (for she had never remarried), she made enough money to put all her boys through graduate school. Indeed, she was on her way this minute to visit her youngest son and his wife, both law school professors.

7   She felt sorry for young people these days, she said. They were all so busy juggling careers and kids that they found it so hard to cope. That is why she often visited her sons' homes to help out. While there, she cooked all the meals, mostly Italian specialties (as she described them my mouth watered uncontrollably), and even whipped up some outfits for the kids.

8   By modern definitions, this woman was not a genius: she did not discover a new element or the reason the stars stay up in heaven. She had not even been to high school. But as I got off the train, I felt that I had been in the presence of someone very special; someone with extraordinary gifts who had lived and was continuing to live a full and balanced life.

9   If that is not pure genius, what is?

PRACTICE 5

1. Highlight the thesis statement of the essay.
2. According to the writer, what four things does genius need to flourish?

   _____

   _____

3. According to the writer, how has the definition of genius changed over time?

   _____

   _____

4. Highlight the topic sentence of paragraph. Remember that it may not always be the first sentence of the paragraph.

5. The old woman tells the writer her life story. What can you infer (conclude) about the old woman's personality from this tale?

   _____

   _____

6. The writer acknowledges that society recognizes Einstein as a genius. But why does the writer think that the old woman is also a good example of genius?

   _____

   _____

   _____

   _____

WRITING LINK

More Definition Writing Topics
Chapter 27, Writer's Room topic 2 (page 356)
Chapter 31, Writer's Room topic 1 (page 394)
Chapter 34, Writer's Room topic 2 (page 424)

 Writer's Room **Topics for Definition Essays**

Writing Activity 1

Write a definition essay about any of the following topics, or choose your own topic.

General Topics

1. a soulmate
2. meltdown
3. a fairweather friend
4. family
5. a good sport

Academic and Work-Related Topics

6. teamwork
7. poor workplace communication
8. equal opportunity
9. good education
10. healthy competition

Writing Activity 2

Choose a quotation that you agree or disagree with, and then write a definition essay based on it.

The deepest definition of youth is life as yet untouched by tragedy.

—Alfred North Whitehead, mathematician

The absence of flaw in beauty is itself a flaw.

—Havelock Ellis, psychologist

The fearless are merely fearless. People who act in spite of their fear are truly brave.

—James A. LaFond-Lewis, restaurateur

Leadership is a combination of strategy and character. If you must be without one, be without strategy.

—General H. Norman Schwarzkopf

READING LINK

More Definition Readings

"Twixters" by Betsy Hart (page 495)
"Seeing Red Over Myths" by Drew Hayden Taylor (page 462)
For a more complete list of readings by rhetorical mode, see Appendix 6.

 CHECKLIST: DEFINITION ESSAY

As you write your definition essay, review the checklist on the inside front cover. Also ask yourself these questions.

☐ Does my thesis statement contain a definition by synonym, category, or negation?

☐ Do I use concise language in my definition?

☐ Do I make a point in my thesis statement?

☐ Do all of my supporting paragraphs relate to the thesis statement?

☐ Do the body paragraphs contain enough supporting details that help define the term?

11 Classification

Seeing much, suffering much, and studying much are the three pillars of learning.

—BENJAMIN DISRAELI, *British politician*

CHAPTER CONTENTS

 CHAT ROOM

Work with a partner or group. Divide the following words into three or four different categories. What are the categories? Why did you choose those categories?

art	stethoscope	workshop
construction	paintbrush	hospital
doctor	sculptor	hammer
studio	medicine	welder

EXPLORING

WHAT IS CLASSIFICATON?

When you classify, you sort a subject into more understandable categories. For instance, if a bookstore simply put books randomly on shelves, you would have a hard time finding the book that you need. Instead, the bookstore classifies books according to subject area.

In classification writing, each of the categories must be part of a larger group, yet they must also be distinct. For example, you might write an essay about the most common types of hobbies and sort those into board games, sports, and crafts. Take a look at some ways people use classification in common situations.

Audience: Family Member	Audience: Classmate	Audience: Customer
Your dirty laundry should be sorted in the following way.	**Our different labs on campus are high-tech, quaint, and outdated.**	**Our beds come in three categories.**
• Put the coloured clothing in the red basket. • Put your whites in the beige basket. • Put all bath towels in the green bin by the door.	• Our science lab has the latest technology. • The music lab is old, but quite beautiful and quaint. • The language lab is outdated, and the audio needs to be upgraded to digital.	• Innerspring mattresses have a variety of coil gauges and numbers of springs. • Air mattresses can be pumped for a softer or firmer feel. • Foam beds may be made from polyurethane foam, memory foam, or latex.

LIFE SNAPSHOT **Classification at Work**

Ahmad Bishr is a Web-design consultant based in Halifax, Nova Scotia. In the next excerpt from an email to a client, he makes suggestions about classifying a website.

The second thing you need to do is decide how to divide your site. The opening page should only contain the most pertinent information about the cottage you are renting. For instance, include the number of rooms, the location, the most spectacular traits of the cottage, and so on. Each subcategory will become a link. Because you are trying to rent your cottage, I suggest that one link contain photos of the interior, with details about each room. You will also need a link that includes a rental calendar and rates. A fourth section might contain information about local attractions. Remember that too many categories will confuse the viewer. You'll want a simple, uncluttered site. Keep the divisions down to four or five pages at most.

The Classification Essay

To find a topic for a classification essay, think of something that you can sort or divide into different groups. Also, determine a reason for classifying the items. When you are planning your ideas for a classification essay, remember the following points.

1. **Use a common classification principle.**

   A **classification principle** is the overall method that you use to sort the subject into categories. To find the classification principle, think about one common characteristic that unites the different categories. For example, if your subject is "jobs," your classification principle might be any of the following:

   – jobs in which people work with their hands

   – dangerous jobs

   – outsourced jobs

2. **Sort the subject into distinct categories.** A classification essay should have two or more categories.

Topic: Jobs

Classification principle: **Dangerous jobs**

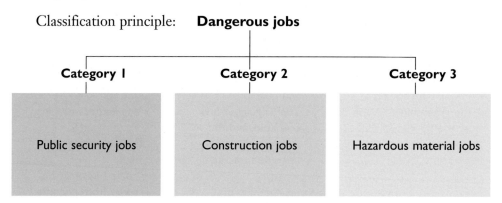

HINT **Categories Should Not Overlap**

When sorting a topic into categories, make sure that the categories do not overlap. For example, you would not classify roommates into aloof, friendly, and messy, because a messy roommate could also be aloof or friendly. Although the categories share something in common, each category should be distinct.

A Student Essay

Diego Pelaez is a student at Montreal's Dawson College. Read the student essay and answer the questions that follow.

Heroes

By Diego Pelaez

1   The word "hero" comes from the Greek word *heros*, which means a person of superhuman ability. *Webster's Dictionary* defines a hero as a person "admired for courage, fortitude, prowess, nobility, and so on." Certainly, heroes come in many forms throughout a person's life. Somewhere out there, there is always a model, real or fictional, that drives people to better themselves and gives them the dream of being heroic. The three general ideas of a hero that most embrace are the fictional superhero, the sports or media hero, and, finally, the practical hero.

2   The dominant heroes of childhood are fictional superheroes. Action figures represent these titans and are the absolute blueprint for the average young person. Be they on television, in comic books, or in children's movies, characters such as Batman, Superman, and Spiderman usually dominate the imaginations of youngsters. It is common to see children blazing down the street wearing the capes of their idols. Thankfully, the female crowd has gotten away from Barbie; female action heroes such as Buffy the Vampire Slayer and Sydney Bristow from *Alias* are models of strength for young girls. These heroes defy the laws of physics and are capable of superhuman feats that any child dreams of.

3   However, as time wears on, children outgrow the superhero phase and idolize another form of superior humans: celebrities. With the information age,

celebrities are **ubiquitous**. The Internet, television, newspapers, and magazines feature images of athletes, singers, and movie stars, providing them with more exposure than they could have ever possibly wanted. Thus, the superhero stage is followed by the "I want to be famous" stage, where adolescents start trying to shoot like Michael Jordan, act like Al Pacino, or sing like Mariah Carey. A good example is the unbelievable amount of worldwide acclaim for soccer player David Beckham; some nations have even erected statues in his image. These people are superheroes who make the game-winning shot on a basketball court, kill the bad guy on film, or perform on stage in front of thousands of screaming fans.

ubiquitous: everywhere

4   Alas, for the vast majority of people, there will come a day when fantasies of fame must give way to more realistic goals. Along with these goals come more practical, real-life heroes. Teachers, although they sometimes get a bad reputation, are heroes to far more people than they realize. Many teachers become mentors to their pupils, providing guidance and inspiration. Young adults also look to inspirational figures in their field; thus, an aspiring journalist might idolize a writer from the local paper. Of course, most people, as they grow older, realize that the most potent figures in their lives are those family members—parents, grandparents, siblings, aunts, or uncles—who have guided them and been compelling role models.

5   Heroes fill people with a sense of their own possibilities. Children think they are indestructible, and this attitude is reflected in larger-than-life heroes who always seem to achieve the impossible. However, with the passage of time, goals become more realistic and so do definitions of heroes. Heroes drive children to dream of the impossible, and heroes encourage young adults to strive toward an ideal.

PRACTICE 1

1. Highlight the thesis statement.

2. Highlight the topic sentence in each body paragraph.

3. State the three categories that the author discusses and list some details about each category.

    a. _____

        Details: _____

    b. _____

        Details: _____

    c. _____

        Details: _____

4. Which introductory style does this essay use?

    a. anecdote   b. definition

    c. historical   d. opposing position

Explore Topics

In the next Writer's Desk, you will try an exploring strategy to generate ideas about different topics.

Writer's Desk **Warm Up**

Read the following questions, and write the first ideas that come to your mind. Think of two to three ideas for each topic.

EXAMPLE:

What are some types of lawbreakers?

– petty thieves (pickpockets, scam artists)

– people who break traffic laws

– violent criminals like carjackers and terrorists

1. What are some different categories of families?

    _____

    _____

2. What are some different types of shoppers?

    _____

    _____

    _____

3. When an election comes around, people act in different ways. What are some categories of political responses?

    _____

    _____

    _____

Making a Classification Chart

A **classification chart** is a visual representation of a main topic and its categories. Making a classification chart can help you to identify the categories more clearly so that you will be able to write more exact thesis statements.

When you classify items, remember to use a single method of classification and a common classification principle to sort the items. For example, you could classify friends according to the length of time you have known them. You could also classify friends according to the activities you do with them or the places you met them.

Classification principle:

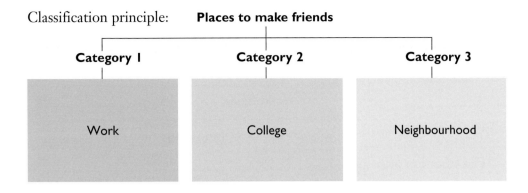

HINT   Categories Versus Examples

When you are trying to find a topic for a classification essay, don't simply list examples. Each category of items should have subcategories. The following lists are for an essay about the physical and psychological benefits of playing certain sports. In the list of examples, the sports are all active team sports, so the advantages in each sport would be similar. In the second list of categories, each type of sport has particular benefits.

Topic:	Sports
Classification principle:	Physical and psychological benefits

List of Examples	**Categories**
football	solo sports
baseball	pair sports
hockey	team sports

PRACTICE 2

In the following classification charts, a subject has been broken down into distinct categories. The items in the group should have the same classification principle. Cross out one item in each group that does not belong. Then write down the classification principle that unites the group.

EXAMPLE:

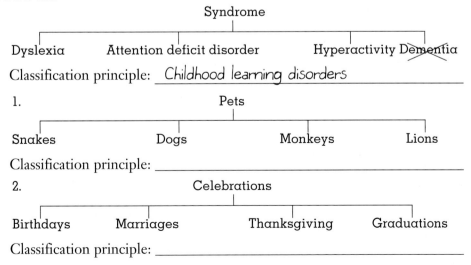

Syndrome

Dyslexia   Attention deficit disorder   Hyperactivity ~~Dementia~~

Classification principle: *Childhood learning disorders*

1.   Pets

Snakes   Dogs   Monkeys   Lions

Classification principle: _____

2.   Celebrations

Birthdays   Marriages   Thanksgiving   Graduations

Classification principle: _____

3.   Co-workers

| Friendly | Lazy | Know-it-all | Nosy |

Classification principle: _____

4.   Workplaces

| Cockpit | Garden | Toll booth | Cubicle |

Classification principle: _____

5.   Relationships

| Husband–wife | Parent–child | Brother–sister | Boss–employee |

Classification principle: _____

HINT Make a Point

To make interesting classification essays, try to express an attitude, opinion, or feeling about the topic. For example, in an essay about discipline, your classification principle might be types of discipline methods; however, the essay needs to inform readers of something specific about those methods. For example, you could write about discipline methods that are most effective, least effective, ethical, unethical, violent, non-violent, and so on.

Writer's Desk **Find Distinct Categories**

Break down the following topics into three distinct categories. Remember to find categories that do not overlap. You can look for ideas in the previous Writer's Desk on page 152.

EXAMPLE:

                          Lawbreakers

| Pedestrians | Cyclists | Drivers |

Classification principle: *People who break traffic laws*

1.   Families

_____   _____   _____

Classification principle: _____

2. Shoppers

_____ _____ _____

Classification principle: _____

3. Political responses

_____ _____ _____

Classification principle: _____

DEVELOPING

THE THESIS STATEMENT

The thesis statement in a classification essay clearly indicates what you will classify. It also includes the controlling idea, which is the classification principle that you will use.

> Several types of co-workers can completely destroy a workplace environment.

You can also mention the types of categories in your thesis statement.

> Nosy, lazy, and know-it-all coworkers can completely destroy a workplace environment.

GRAMMAR HINT **Parallel Structure**

Use parallel structure when words or phrases are joined in a series.

Some annoying sales methods include <u>calling customers on the phone</u>, <u>putting

leaving
pop-up ads on the Internet</u>, and ~~when people leave~~ <u>flyers on car windows.</u>

See Chapter 23 for more information about parallel structure.

Writer's Desk **Write Thesis Statements**

Write clear thesis statements. You can refer to your ideas in previous Writer's Desks. Remember that your thesis statement can include the different categories you will be discussing.

EXAMPLE:

Topic: lawbreakers

<u>Thesis statement:</u> Pedestrians, cyclists, and drivers regularly break the rules of the road.

1. Topic: Family

<u>Thesis statement:</u> _____

_____

_____

2. Topic: Shoppers

<u>Thesis statement:</u> _____

_____

_____

3. Topic: Political responses

<u>Thesis statement:</u> _____

_____

_____

The Supporting Ideas

After you have developed an effective thesis statement, generate supporting ideas. In a classification essay, you can list details about each of your categories.

- Use prewriting strategies to generate examples for each category.
- Choose the best ideas.
- Organize your ideas. Choose the best organizational method for this essay pattern.

One way to visualize your categories and your supporting ideas is to make a detailed classification chart. Break down the main topic into several categories, and then list supporting ideas for each category.

The public should be grateful to those who do dangerous jobs in three particular areas.

Public security	Construction	Hazardous materials
– border guards – police officers – security guards – air marshals	– high tower workers – electricians – roofers	– nuclear power plant workers – farmers handling pesticides – chemical plant workers

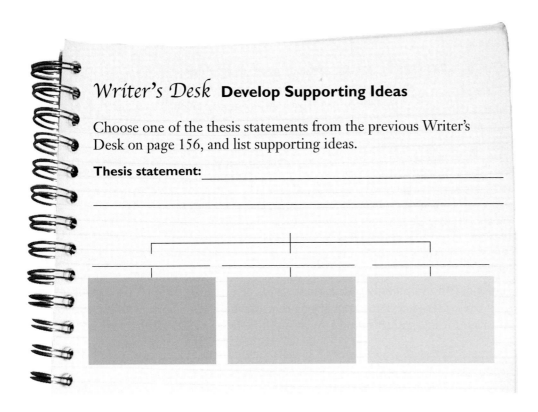

Writer's Desk **Develop Supporting Ideas**

Choose one of the thesis statements from the previous Writer's Desk on page 156, and list supporting ideas.

Thesis statement:

The Essay Plan

Before you write a classification essay, make a detailed essay plan. Add supporting details for each category.

Thesis Statement: Pedestrians, cyclists, and drivers regularly break the rules of the road.

I. Pedestrians are supposed to obey traffic rules, but most do not.
   A. Many cross between intersections instead of at corners.
   B. A lot of pedestrians walk on the road.
   C. Some people disobey walking signals.

II. Cyclists regularly break traffic laws.
   A. Many cyclists don't wear bicycle helmets.
   B. Some don't put proper reflectors on their bikes.

   C. It is common to see cyclists going through lights and stop signs.

III. Drivers are the most dangerous lawbreakers.
   A. Speeding is common on roads and highways.
   B. Some people drive on the shoulders of roads.
   C. Many drivers disobey traffic signs.
   D. There are even drivers who go the wrong way on one-way streets.

Writer's Desk **Make an Essay Plan**

Refer to the information you generated in previous Writer's Desks, and prepare a detailed essay plan. Arrange the supporting details in a logical order.

The First Draft

After you outline your ideas in a plan, you are ready to write the first draft. Weave together the ideas you have in your essay plan. Remember to write complete sentences and to include transitional words or expressions to help your ideas flow smoothly. Here are some transitions that can help you express which category is most important and to signal a movement from one category to the next.

To Show Importance	To Show Types of Categories
above all	one kind . . . another kind
clearly	the first / second kind
most of all	the first / second type
the most important	the last category
particularly	

Writer's Desk **Write the First Draft**

Carefully review the classification essay plan you prepared in the previous Writer's Desk and make any necessary changes. Then write the first draft of your classification essay.

REVISE AND EDIT A CLASSIFICATION ESSAY

When you finish writing a classification essay, carefully review your work and revise it to make sure that the categories do not overlap. Check to make sure that you have organized your essay logically, and remove any irrelevant details. Before you work on your own essay, practise revising and editing a student essay.

A STUDENT ESSAY

A student from Toronto, Ontario, wrote the next essay. As you read, correct any errors that you find, and make comments in the margins.

Breaking Traffic Laws
By Lonzell Courtney

1   Ask most people, and they will insist they are law-abiding. Dig a little deeper, though, and the hidden criminal emerges. Stand on any street corner for a few hours, and you probably will observe all types of people breaking traffic laws. Pedestrians, cyclists, and drivers regularly break the rules of the road.

2   There are many traffic laws that pedestrians ignore. For example, jaywalking. When people arrive at a crossing with traffic lights, they are supposed to wait for the walk signal. They should also cross the street at corners and proper crossings, and they should not walk on the road. Yet most people be breaking these rules. Armando Guzman, an exterminator from Sudbury, is an unapologetic jaywalker. When him and I go for a walk, he crosses between intersections rather than make the long walk to the corner. Kate Shapiro, a hairdresser, admits that she always crosses when the "Don't Walk" signal is blinking if there is no traffic. "It is ridiculous to wait when I know I can cross safely," she argues. Some pedestrians are also very rude. They push through crowds, knock people over, and are basically very unpleasant.

3   Cyclists also disrespect traffic laws. For example, many municipalities have bicycle helmet laws, but citizens regularly flout the law and drive with bare heads. In some provinces, bicycles must be equipped with reflectors, but many cyclists do not bother getting them. Other rules of the road apply to cyclists, yet they regularly plough past stop signs or zoom through red lights. Most unpleasant are the cyclists who speed along busy sidewalks even though that is illegal. Thus, most cyclists are lawbreakers, too.

4   Drivers, of course, are the worse offenders. They can harm or even kill others, yet virtually every driver has occasionally broken a traffic law. Who hasn't gone over the speed limit, for example? Many people believe that the maximum speed limit sign generally means, "I can go fifteen or twenty kilometres per hour over that limit." Drivers also change lanes without signalling, they drive on the shoulder to pass slow traffic, and they allow children to ride without seatbelts. In 2006, Britney Spears famously placed her infant on her lap while driving. Of course, if she would have known about the subsequent scandal, she might have acted differently.

5   Most lawbreakers are unrepentant, and some of them have original excuses for ignoring traffic rules. They claim that everyone else does it. Some people condemn seatbelt and helmet laws as infringements on their rights.

PRACTICE 3

Revising

1. Highlight the thesis statement.

2. In paragraph 2, one of the examples is not a valid support. Cross it out.

Explain why it is not valid. _____

_____

3. This essay does not have a concluding sentence. Write a concluding
   sentence in the space. _____

_____

Editing

4. A fragment lacks a subject or a verb and is an incomplete sentence.
   Underline one fragment in paragraph 2. Then write a correct sentence
   in the space.

   Correction: _____

5. Paragraph 2 contains a verb-tense error. Underline the error and
   correct it.

   Correction: _____

6. The writer uses a pronoun incorrectly in paragraph 2. Underline and
   correct the error.

   Correction: _____

7. In paragraph 4, there is an error with the superlative form of an
   adjective. Underline the error and correct it.

   Correction: _____

8. In paragraph 4, there is an error with conditional forms (*if . . . would*).
   Underline the error and correct it.

   Correction: _____

GRAMMAR LINK

**See the following
chapters for more
information about these
grammar topics:**

Fragments: Chapter 21
Verb Tenses: Chapter 26
Pronouns: Chapter 29
Adjectives: Chapter 30
Conditionals: Chapter 26

**ABC
ABC
AB** **VOCABULARY BOOST**

Writers commonly overuse the same vocabulary. To make your writing
more vivid and interesting, look at your first draft and underline at least ten
repeated nouns and verbs. (Remember that a noun is a person, place, or thing.) Then add
details or specific descriptions to five of the nouns and make some of the verbs more
evocative. Here is a brief example of how you might avoid repetition of nouns and verbs.

Dull, repetitive: Patrice likes cycling. Patrice often cycles to work at his
bookstore. Often, Patrice is reckless and cycles without a helmet.

Detailed, uses synonyms: **Patrice** likes **cycling** and **commutes** to work
on his **bike**. Although **the 30-year-old bookstore owner** knows better, **he**
often **recklessly rides** without a helmet.

Writer's Desk **Revise and Edit Your Essay**

Revise and edit the essay that you wrote for the previous Writer's Desk. You can refer to the revising and editing checklists at the end of this chapter and on the inside covers of this book.

A Professional Essay

Frank Schmalleger is director of the Justice Research Association, a private consulting firm that focuses on issues relating to crime and justice. The following excerpt is from his book *Criminal Justice Today*.

Types of Correctional Officers
By Frank Schmalleger

1   Prison staff culture, in combination with naturally occurring personality types, gives rise to a diversity of officer types. Correction staff can be classified according to certain distinguishing characteristics. Among the most prevalent types are the dictator, the friend, the merchant, the turnkey, the climber, and the reformer.

The Dictator

2   Some officers go by the book; others go beyond it, using prison rules to reinforce their own brand of discipline. The guard who demands signs of inmate subservience, from constant use of the word *sir* or *ma'am* to frequent free shoeshines, is one type of dictator. Another goes beyond legality, beating or "macing" inmates even for minor infractions or perceived insults. Dictator guards are bullies.

3   Dictator guards may have sadistic personalities and gain ego satisfaction through feelings of near omnipotence, which come from the total control of others. Some may be fundamentally insecure and employ a false bravado to hide their fear of inmates. Officers who fit the dictator category are the most likely to be targeted for vengeance should control of the institution temporarily fall into the hands of the inmates.

The Friend

4   Friendly officers try to fraternize with inmates. They approach the issue of control by trying to be "one of the guys." They seem to believe that they can win inmate cooperation by being nice. Unfortunately, such guards do not recognize that fraternization quickly leads to unending requests for special favours—from delivering mail to bending "minor" prison rules. Once a few rules have been bent, the officer may find that inmates have the upper hand through the potential for blackmail.

5   Many officers have amiable relationships with inmates. In most cases, however, affability is only a convenience that both sides recognize can quickly evaporate. "Friendly officers," as the term is being used here, are *overly*

friendly. They may be young and inexperienced. On the other hand, they may simply be possessed of kind and idealistic personalities built on successful friendships in free society.

The Merchant

6   Contraband could not exist in any correctional facility without the merchant officer. The merchant participates in the inmate economy, supplying drugs, pornography, alcohol, and sometimes even weapons to inmates who can afford to pay for them.

7   Probably only a very few officers consistently perform the role of merchant, although a far larger proportion may occasionally turn a few dollars by smuggling some item through the gate. Low salaries create the potential for mercantile corruption among many otherwise "straight-arrow" officers. Until salaries rise substantially, the merchant will remain an institutionalized feature of most prisons.

The Turnkey

8   The turnkey officer cares little for what goes on in the prison setting. Officers who fit this category may be close to retirement, or they may be alienated from their jobs for various reasons. Low pay, the view that inmates are basically "worthless" and incapable of changing, and the monotonous ethic of "doing time" all combine to numb the professional consciousness of even young officers.

9   The term *turnkey* comes from prison argot where it means a guard who is there just to open and shut doors and who cares about nothing other than getting through his or her shift. Inmates do not see the turnkey as a threat, nor is such an officer likely to challenge the status quo in institutions where merchant guards operate.

The Climber

10   The climber is apt to be a young officer with an eye for promotion. Nothing seems impossible to the climber, who probably hopes eventually to be warden or program director or to hold some high-status position within the institutional hierarchy. Climbers are likely to be involved in schooling, correspondence courses, and professional organizations. They may lead a movement toward unionization for correctional personnel and tend to see the guard's role as a profession that should receive greater social recognition.

11   Climbers have many ideas. They may be heavily involved in reading about the latest confinement or administrative technology. If so, they will suggest many ways to improve prison routine, often to the consternation of complacent staff members. Like the turnkey, climbers turn a blind eye toward inmates and their problems. They are more concerned with improving institutional procedures and with their own careers than they are with the treatment or day-to-day control of inmates.

The Reformer

12   The reformer is the "do-gooder" among officers, the person who believes that prison should offer opportunities for personal change. The reformer tends to lend a sympathetic ear to the personal needs of inmates and is apt to offer armchair counselling and suggestions. Many reformers are motivated by personal ideals, and some of them are highly religious. Inmates tend to see the reformer guard as naive but harmless. Because the reformer actually tries to help, even when help is unsolicited, he or she is the most

likely of all the guard types to be accepted by prisoners.

13   Correctional officers have generally been accorded low occupational status. Historically, the role of prison guard required minimal formal education and held few opportunities for professional growth and career advancement. Such jobs were typically low paying, frustrating, and often boring. Growing problems in our nation's prisons, including emerging issues of legal liability, however, increasingly require a well-trained and adequately equipped force of professionals. As correctional personnel have become better trained and more proficient, the old concept of guard has been supplanted by that of correctional officer. Thus, many states and a growing number of large-city correctional systems make efforts to eliminate individuals with potentially harmful personality characteristics from correctional officer applicant pools.

PRACTICE 3

1. What is the topic of this essay?_____

     _____

2. What are the main characteristics of the following types of guards?

    a. the dictator

    _____

    _____

    b. the friend

    _____

    _____

    c. the merchant

    _____

    _____

    d. the turnkey

    _____

    _____

    e. the climber

    _____

    _____

    f. the reformer

    _____

    _____

3. What is the author's purpose?

    a. to entertain   b. to persuade   c. to inform

4. Consider the order in which the guards are listed. Think of another effective way to organize the guards, and list them in order here.

    Organizational method: _____

    a. _____
    b. _____
    c. _____
    d. _____
    e. _____
    f. _____

WRITING LINK

More Classification Writing Topics

Chapter 20, Writer's Room topic 1 (page 285)
Chapter 24, Writer's Room topic 2 (page 316)
Chapter 28, Writer's Room topic 2 (page 365)
Chapter 35, Writer's Room topic 2 (page 437)

Writer's Room Topics for Classification Essays

Writing Activity 1

Choose any of the following topics, or choose your own topic, and write a classification essay. Determine your classification principle and ensure that your categories do not overlap.

General Topics

Types of . . .

1. computer games
2. politicians
3. living arrangements
4. siblings
5. punishment

Academic and Work-Related Topics

Types of . . .

6. electronic modes of communication
7. procrastination techniques
8. success
9. risks
10. work spaces

Writing Activity 2

Choose a quotation that you agree or disagree with, or one that inspires you, and then write a classification essay based on it.

> The four stages of life are infancy, childhood, adolescence, and obsolescence.
>
> —Art Linkletter, entertainer

> There are really only three types of people: those who make things happen, those who watch things happen, and those who say, "What happened?"
>
> —Ann Landers, advice columnist

The wit makes fun of other persons; the satirist makes fun of the world; the humorist makes fun of himself.

—James Thurber, author

I'll keep it short and sweet—family, religion, and friendship. These are the three demons you must slay if you wish to succeed in business.

—Matt Groening, creator of *The Simpsons*

READING LINK

More Classification Readings

"Living Environments" by Avi Friedman (page 465)
"Fads" by David A. Locher (page 500)
 For a more complete list of readings by rhetorical mode, see Appendix 6.

✔ CHECKLIST: CLASSIFICATION ESSAY

After you write your classification essay, review the checklist on the inside front cover. Also, ask yourself these questions.

  Does my thesis statement explain the categories that I will discuss?

  Do I use a common classification principle to unite the various items?

  Do I offer sufficient details to explain each category?

  Do I arrange the categories in a logical manner?

  Does all of the supporting information relate to the categories that I am discussing?

  Do I include categories that do not overlap?

Submit your best essays for possible publication to **thewritersworld@prenhall.com**.

12 CHAPTER

Comparison and Contrast

I know not anything more pleasant, or more instructive, than to compare experience with expectation, or to register from time to time the difference between idea and reality. It is by this kind of observation that we grow daily.
—SAMUEL JOHNSON, *writer*

CHAT ROOM

What were your goals as a child? What are your goals as an adult? Think about work, money, and family. Compare your answers with a partner, and discuss how childhood goals are different from adult goals.

EXPLORING

WHAT IS COMPARISON AND CONTRAST?

When you want to decide between options, you compare and contrast. You **compare** to find similarities and **contrast** to find differences. The exercise of comparing and contrasting can help you make judgments about things. It can also help you to better understand familiar things. The following examples show comparisons and contrasts people might use in everyday situations.

Audience: Family Member	Audience: Another Student	Audience: Customer
A laptop is more sensible than a desktop computer.	**The summer course is easier than the fall course.**	**Our product is better than the competitor's product.**
• The desk is small and a laptop takes less space than a desktop computer.	• The summer course lasts only for three weeks and the material is condensed, so there is less homework.	• Our product is less expensive than the competitor's. • Our product is smaller and easier to use.

- Modern laptops have screens that are just as large and clear as many desktop monitors.
- Unlike a clunky desktop computer, we can easily transport a laptop to other rooms or to school or work.

- The fall course has more reading and writing homework.
- The summer course has fewer students, so you can get more help if you need it.
- The fall course has large groups, so if you don't understand something, it is difficult to get help.

- The competition does not offer a rebate.
- The competition does not offer a variety of colours and sizes.

LIFE SNAPSHOT   **Comparison and Contrast at Work**

Eric Hollymead works in a public relations company in Toronto. In this memo, he compares two job candidates. To respect each person's privacy, he has numbered the candidates.

Although both candidates have the required education, I suggest that we go with Candidate 1. Her experience is more relevant to this industry. I also believe she will be a better fit for the sales department because her energy level is high, and she seems like a real team player. Candidate 2, although highly competent, is less experienced in sales. He was quite nervous in the interview, and I sense he may be less at ease with clients. On the other hand, his questions were thoughtful, and he seemed interested in the business. I also appreciated his sense of humour. Perhaps we should keep his résumé on file should we have future positions that are more suitable to his skills.

The Comparison and Contrast Essay

In a comparison and contrast essay, you can compare and contrast two different subjects, or you can compare and contrast different aspects of a single subject. When you write using this essay pattern, remember to think about your specific purpose.

- Your purpose could be to make judgments about two things. For example, you might compare and contrast two cars to convince your readers that one is preferable.
- Your purpose could be to describe or understand two familiar things. For example, you might compare two movies to help your readers understand their thematic similarities.

Comparison and Contrast Patterns

Comparison and contrast essays follow two common patterns.

Point by Point   Present one point about Topic A and then one point about Topic B. Keep following this pattern until you have a few points for each topic. Go back and forth from one side to the other like tennis players hitting a ball back and forth across a net.

Topic by Topic   Present all of your points about one topic, and then present all of your points about the second topic. Offer one side and then the other side, just as opposing lawyers would do in the closing arguments of a court case.

Marina's Example   Marina is trying to decide whether she would prefer a part-time job in clothing store or in a restaurant. Marina can organize her information using a topic-by-topic pattern or a point-by-point method.

Thesis statement: The clothing store is a better place to work than the restaurant.

Point-by-Point Comparison	**Topic-by-Topic Comparison**
Topic sentence: Salaries	Topic sentence: Job A
Job A	– salary
Job B	– hours
	– working environment
Topic sentence: Working hours	Topic sentence: Job B
Job A	– salary
Job B	– hours
	– working environment
Topic sentence: Working environments	
Job A	
Job B	

A Student Essay

Alfonso Castillo Zavas lives in Scarborough, Ontario. Read his essay and answer the questions that follow.

Working Life

By Alfonso Castillo Zavas

1   My uncle Cayetano spent the first thirty years of his life in Mexico City. When he moved to Canada, he rented a room in our house, and he tried to get used to life in Toronto. Many evenings, my uncle told stories about his workplace, and he reminisced about his younger days when he was an office worker in Mexico City. We realized that the workplace culture is more relaxed in Canada than it is in Mexico.

2   One noticeable difference between the two nations is the attitude about arrivals and departures of employees. In the early 1980s, my uncle Cayetano worked as an accountant for a company in Mexico City. He was supposed to arrive at 8:00 a.m. each morning, but he was often late. He ran from the subway station to the door of the office building, hoping to arrive before 8:30 a.m., which was the time that the doors were locked for the day. Guards at the door ensured that employees arrived and left at the proper time. Local street vendors encouraged my uncle, yelling "Correle" when they saw him sprinting past. Every three months, his pay was docked because three late days counted for an absence. When my uncle came to Toronto in 1992, he found a job with a computer company. The first thing he noticed was that there were no guards at the doors of his workplace. Attendance at work depended on an honour system. Employees were only accountable to their immediate superiors. My uncle learned to be punctual not because of a guard locking a door, but because he wanted to complete his work in the amount of time allotted to him.

3   Another major difference in work cultures is the mealtime. In Mexico, there is no concept of lunch. Instead, most people eat the main meal, the

"comida," at around 3 p.m. When my uncle worked for a Mexican company, he took a two-hour break for his main meal. In the cafeteria, he often had a plate filled with meat, rice, beans, avocados, and chilli peppers, and a side dish filled with warm tortillas. After his meal, he returned to work from 5 to 7 p.m. Later, when he arrived home, he ate a small snack. In his Toronto job, he became acquainted with the lunch hour, which was earlier than he was used to. He learned that lunch is not the time to have a large meal; instead, most employees just have a bland sandwich or soup. He also learned that Canadians finish work by 4 or 5 p.m. and then eat their main meal between 6 and 8 p.m. So Canadians have a longer and more relaxed evening. In Mexico, my uncle had to work much later in the day and was quite tired when he finally got home from the office.

4   The most visible distinction between Mexican and Canadian workplaces is the level of formal dress in the workplace. Although Mexican dress codes are becoming slightly more relaxed, men in most offices and banks wear suits and ties, and women wear suit jackets, skirts, pantyhose, and heels. My aunt Lucia, who lives in Mexico City, never goes to work without manicured nails, makeup, and a very nice outfit. When my uncle Cayetano received his job in Toronto, he starched his shirt collar, put on a tie, and ensured that his shoes were shiny. He was surprised to see that some of his co-workers wore baggy casual trousers and even sneakers. Very few co-workers wore dress shirts, with most wearing polo shirts. He quickly learned that people dress nicely at his office in Canada, but much less formally than workers at his Mexican workplace.

5   When immigrants come to a new country, they must get used to food, eating times, dress codes, and workplace rules that may be very different from those they encountered in their native countries. While they adjust to the differences, they are sometimes judged. My uncle said that co-workers didn't understand why he always shined his shoes, and for a while his nickname was "Shiny." When a new immigrant arrives in your workplace, show tolerance and respect for cultural differences.

PRACTICE I

1. Highlight the thesis statement.

2. Highlight the topic sentence in each body paragraph.

3. What pattern of comparison does the writer follow in the entire essay?

    a. point by point

    b. topic by topic

4. What pattern of comparison does the writer follow in body paragraphs 2, 3, and 4?

    a. point by point

    b. topic by topic

5. Using your own words, sum up the main subjects in this essay.

    Paragraph 2:_____

    Paragraph 3:_____

    Paragraph 4:_____

6. What does this essay mainly focus on? Circle the correct answer.

   a. similarities

   b. differences

7. Underline transitional words or phrases that link ideas between body paragraphs.

8. How does the writer organize his arguments?

   a. time order

   b. emphatic order

   c. space order

ABC
VOCABULARY BOOST

In the student essay "Working Life," the writer uses the terms *accountable* and *accountant* in paragraph 2. The root word—or base word—for those terms is *count*. Prefixes and suffixes alter a word's meaning and are added to the root word. Prefixes appear at the beginning of a root word; suffixes appear at the end. Here are some examples.

Prefix	Example	Suffix	Example
anti = against	antiwar	*able* = ability	understandable
bi = two	bilingual	*al* = pertaining to	physical
hyper = excessive	hypersensitive	*dom* = a quality or state	freedom
il = not	illegal	*ful* = filled with	respectful
inter = between	interfaith	*ism* = belief	communism
mis = wrong	misspell	*ist* = practitioner	scientist
multi = many	multifunctional	*ive* = tends toward	regressive
pre = before	prenatal	*less* = without	helpless
re = again	rebirth	*ment* = condition	argument
un = not	unfaithful	*ness* = state of being	happiness

Brainstorm at least three variations of the following root words by using various prefixes and suffixes. Keep in mind that the previous list is not complete. There may be other prefixes or suffixes that you can think of.

1. use _____

2. act _____

3. social _____

Explore Topics

In the next Writer's Desk, you will try an exploring strategy to generate ideas about different topics.

Writer's Desk Warm Up

Read the following questions, and write the first ideas that come to your mind. Think of two to three ideas for each topic.

EXAMPLE: What are some key differences between girls' and boys' toys?

Girls' toys	Boys' toys
– pastel colours	– noisy
– animals, horses	– toy cars, trucks, and fire engines
– dolls with clothes	– action figures

1. What were your fears when you were a child? What are your current fears?

Childhood fears	Current fears
_____	_____
_____	_____
_____	_____

   Will you focus on ___ similarities or ___ differences?

2. What are the key features of your generation and your parents' generation?

Your generation	Your parents' generation
_____	_____
_____	_____
_____	_____

   Will you focus on ___ similarities or ___ differences?

3. How are your actions and appearance different in your public and private life?

Public life	Private life
_____	_____
_____	_____
_____	_____

   Will you focus on ___ similarities or ___ differences?

DEVELOPING

THE THESIS STATEMENT

In a comparison and contrast essay, the thesis statement indicates what you are comparing and contrasting, and it expresses a controlling idea. For example, the following thesis statement indicates that the essay will compare the myths and reality of mould to prove that it does not seriously threaten human health.

Common household mould is not as dangerous as many people believe.

PRACTICE 2

Read each thesis statement, and then answer the questions that follow. State whether the essay would focus on similarities or differences.

1. The weather in our region is more extreme than it was in the past.

   a. What is being compared?_____

   b. What is the controlling idea?_____

   c. What will the essay focus on? ___ similarities   ___ differences

2. Students need technical courses as well as academic courses for a well-rounded education.

   a. What is being compared?_____

   b. What is the controlling idea?_____

   c. What will the essay focus on? ___ similarities   ___ differences

3. Before marriage, people expect to feel eternally lustful towards their "soul mate," but the reality of married life is quite different.

   a. What is being compared?_____

   b. What is the controlling idea?_____

   c. What will the essay focus on? ___ similarities   ___ differences

---

GRAMMAR HINT   **Comparing Adjectives and Adverbs**

When comparing or contrasting two items, ensure that you have correctly written your comparative forms. For instance, never put *more* with an adjective ending in *–er*.

City life is ~~more~~ better than country life.

If you are comparing two actions, remember to use an adverb instead of an adjective.

more easily
Children learn lessons ~~easier~~ when they are treated with respect.

See Chapter 30 for more information about making comparisons with adjectives and adverbs.

Writer's Desk **Write Thesis Statements**

For each topic, write a thesis statement that includes what you are comparing and contrasting and a controlling idea.

EXAMPLE:

Topic: Girls' and boys' toys

Thesis statement: Both girls' and boys' toys reinforce gender stereotypes.

1. Topic: Childhood fears and adult fears

Thesis statement: _____

_____

_____

2. Topic: Two generations

Thesis statement: _____

_____

_____

3. Topic: Public versus private life

Thesis statement: _____

_____

_____

The Supporting Ideas

After you have developed an effective thesis statement, generate supporting ideas. In a comparison and contrast essay, think of examples that help to clarify the similarities or differences, and then incorporate some ideas in your final essay plan.

To generate supporting ideas, you might try using a Venn diagram. In this example, you can see how the writer draws two circles to compare traditional boys' and girls' toys and how some ideas fall into both categories.

Example:

Boys	Both	Girls
Bold red and black	Human figure toys	Pastel colours
Fighting figures	Active toys such as	Baby-like dolls
Uniforms, weapons	balls, hacky sacks,	Doll fashions
Hard plastic animals	skateboards	Stuffed animals
Toy guns	Video games	Bake ovens
	Blocks	

Writer's Desk **Develop Supporting Ideas**

Choose one of your thesis statements from the previous Writer's Desk. List some similarities and differences.

Similarities _____

_____

Differences _____

_____

The Essay Plan

Before you write a comparison and contrast essay, make a detailed essay plan. Decide which pattern you will follow: point by point or topic by topic. Then add supporting details. Make sure that each detail supports the thesis statement. Also think about the best way to organize your ideas.

Point by Point

Thesis statement: Both girls' and boys' toys reinforce gender stereotypes.

A/B Girls' toys focus on activities in the home, whereas boys' toys focus on outside activities.
Details: Girls have dollhouses and baking ovens whereas boys have carpenter sets and racecars.

A/B Colours are different in girls' and boys' toys.
Details: Girls' toys are pastel colours and boys' toys are bold colours.

A/B Girls' toys focus on nurturing, and boys' toys on heroic fighters.
Details: Girls have baby dolls and boys have GI Joes and guns.

Topic by Topic

A Girls' toys reinforce the importance of looks, body image, and fashion.
Details: They receive fashion dolls with clothing, shoes, and other accessories.

A Girls' toys are soft pastel colours
Details: They play with pink ponies and hug pale blue stuffed animals.

A Girls' toys encourage nurturing by focusing on home and the family.
Details: They have dolls with baby bottles, ovens, toy vacuums, and shopping carts.

B Boys' toys are more violent
Details: Boys have toy guns, violent video games, and soldier toys.

B Boys' toys are in bold colour
Details: They play with red toy cars and bright green soldiers.

B Boys' toys focus on activities and heroic fighters.
Details: Boys are given carpenter's tools, car racing, and service station play sets.

Writer's Desk **Write an Essay Plan**

Refer to the information you generated in previous Writer's Desks and prepare a detailed essay plan using a point-by-point or topic-by-topic pattern. You can use the letters A and B to indicate which side you are discussing in your plan. Include details about each supporting idea.

The First Draft

After you outline your ideas in an essay plan, you are ready to write the first draft. Remember to follow the topic-by-topic or the point-by-point pattern you used in your plan. Write complete sentences and use transitions to help your ideas flow smoothly. The following transitions can be helpful for guiding readers through a comparison and contrast essay.

To Show Similarities		To Show Differences	
additionally	in addition	conversely	nevertheless
at the same time	in the same way	however	on the contrary
equally	similarly	in contrast	then again

Writer's Desk **Write the First Draft**

Write the first draft of your comparison and contrast essay. Before you write, carefully review your essay plan to see if you have enough support for your points and topics. Flesh out each body paragraph with specific details.

REVISING AND EDITING

REVISE AND EDIT A COMPARISON AND CONTRAST ESSAY

When you finish writing a comparison and contrast essay, carefully review your work and revise it to make sure that the comparison or contrast as clear as possible to your readers. Check that you have organized your essay logically, and remove any irrelevant details. Before you work on your own essay, practise revising and editing a student essay.

A Student Essay

The next essay was written by a student from Victoria, British Columbia. Read the essay, and then answer the questions that follow. As you read, correct any errors that you find, and make comments in the margins.

Gender and Toys

By Ashley Lincoln

1   As a young mother, I am trying to avoid the pitfalls that parents so easily fall into. I try not to call my daughter cute and my son strong, thus reinforcing any cultural notions about their self-worth. I encourage my five-year-old daughter to play sports, and I bought my son a baby doll when he asked for one. My friends been saying they have the same concerns about gender roles. But insulating children against male or female role expectations is almost impossible. Most parents, in spite of their best efforts, reinforce gender stereotypes every time they shop for toys.

2   Girls' toys reinforce the importance of looks, body image, and fashion. Parents can buy their daughters makeup sets that include child-friendly lipstick, blush, and eye shadow. Fashion dolls of all shapes and sizes abound. Barbies, Bratz, and other teenage dolls stare at the buyer. Hanging next to the dolls are rows of clothing, shoes, hats, and tiny doll necklaces and bracelets. Girls can also play with a large doll head, changing and curling the hair and adding makeup. Of course, none of the dolls are pudgy, pimply, large-boned, or just plain unattractive. When girls play with these toys, they quickly learn that beauty and the right clothes and makeup are very important.

3   If a little girl does not like fashion toys, they will surely enjoy baby dolls with their fake bottles of milk, soft little blankets, and prams. Girls' toys encourage nurturing by focusing on the home and the family. At a very young age, girls learn to be competent mothers when they change the little diapers of their dolls. Girls can learn to cook with their Easy-Bake ovens, and they learn to shop with tiny shopping carts and cash registers. My daughter and her friends love playing "house" with one child acting as the mother. They shop, pull the "cry" strings on their dolls, and feed their "babies."

4   Boys' toys, on the other hand, stress jobs and activities outside the home. My son begged for, and received, a miniature workshop complete with a plastic saw, drill, screwdriver, and wrench. Lego sets prepare boys for creative occupations such as architecture and auto design. Computer and video games prepare boys for jobs in the high-tech industries. Finally, there is a lot of toy cars, trucks, and racetracks to remind boys that cars are very important to their identities.

5   Toys aimed at young males also permit boys to be the heroes in their fantasy games. In the boys' aisle of the toy store, there are rows of action figures. The GI Joes fight soldiers from other armies. Batman, Superman, and the X-Men fight fantasy villains. Curiously, the X-Men figures include female characters such as Storm, but the toys are not call "X-People." Aimed predominantly at boys, fighting action figures bolster ideas boys have about rescuing others. In their fantasy lives, boys learn early on that they are the heroes and the saviours.

6   Some suggest that it is useless to fight against the male and female roles. They point out that girls in previous centuries made their own dolls out of straw and rags, and boys made cars out of tin cans and wood. While that is

true, toy stores take the stereotyping to extremes. One solution is to try to buy gender-neutral toys such as modelling clay, painting supplies, or balls and other sporting equipment.

PRACTICE 3

Revising

1. Highlight the thesis statement.

2. Highlight the topic sentence in each body paragraph.

3. Circle a transitional word or phrase in the topic sentence of paragraph 4. Then add transitional words or phrases to the other topic sentences.

4. What pattern does the writer use to organize this essay? Circle your response.

   a.   point by point   b.   topic by topic

5. The student writer uses the word "reinforce" at the end of the introduction and in the first sentence of the second paragraph. To avoid repeating the same word, what synonym could the student use?

   _____

Editing

6. Underline the verb error in the introduction. Write the correction on the line.

   Correction: _____

7. Underline and correct the pronoun shift in paragraph 3.

   Correction: _____

8. Underline and correct the subject–verb agreement error in paragraph 4.

   Correction: _____

9. Underline and correct the passive verb that has been incorrectly formed in paragraph 5.

   Correction: _____

> **GRAMMAR LINK**
>
> **See the following chapters for more information about these grammar topics:**
>
> Verbs: Chapter 27
> Pronouns: Chapter 29
> Subject-Verb Agreement: Chapter 25
> Passive Voice: Chapter 26

Writer's Desk   Revise and Edit Your Essay

Revise and edit the essay that you wrote for the previous Writer's Desk. You can refer to the revising and editing checklists at the end of this chapter and on the inside covers of this book.

A Professional Essay

Montreal-based writer and translator Naomi Louder has published poetry in the *Fiddlehead Review* and the *New Quarterly*, among others. In the following essay, she uses the comparison and contrast pattern. Read the essay and answer the questions that follow.

The Dating World

By Naomi Louder

1   Dating has changed a lot over the years. Many people, post millennium, can't help associating the word "date" with a more innocent time and scenarios involving ice-cream sodas, varsity jackets, and drive-in movies. In smaller and more traditional communities, vestiges of this remain, and high school sweethearts who paired up early on wind up getting married straight out of school. Compared to previous generations, today's singles have a new dating ethic that involves flying straight into a whirlwind affair.

2   The most obvious difference between the past and the present is in dating methods. In the fifties and sixties, potential sweethearts met at school dances, the lunch-line at the school cafeteria, or at school sports events. There were certain formal rules of etiquette to be followed, down to the "base" system, dictating when, where, and how the relationship was to progress to its logical conclusion. People were concerned, after a date, with whether "first base"—a kiss—was attained. Nowadays, it is more common to obsess over the other party's sexual history, his or her expectations, and whether a relationship might be a possibility. The "base" system has been supplanted, in junior high or even elementary school, by the "gummy" trend, where cheap rubber bracelets, coded by colour, announce the sexual experience or willingness of the wearer.

3   In a traditional dating context, couples worried primarily about pregnancy, and—mainly in the case of the girls—about losing their reputations. An ill-timed boast on the part of a boy could jeopardize a girl's dating career, while a pregnancy could result in the ultimate shame to the girl and her family or a rushed and gossiped-over wedding. In a contemporary urban centre, these worries seem naïve. Early sexual relationships are more the norm than before, and the concerns are sexually transmitted infections, date rape, and abortion or adoption versus single parenthood. Certainly, some young people have reacted to these threats by rejecting the ethic of sexual freedom popularized in the 1960s. The revival of traditional religious values has influenced many young Canadians, and chastity rings and church events make even the dating system of a more innocent era seem fraught. However, the majority of teens and young adults are more determined than ever to fulfill their sexual and emotional needs, sometimes before they are clearly aware of the consequences.

4   Both the traditional and the new dating methods have downsides. The new generation, with all its scorn of traditional and prudish dating etiquette, finds itself lost and lonelier than ever. The old-fashioned courtship ritual has been condensed to a witty remark, a compliment or two, and an animal assault on a balcony, on a street corner, or in a taxi. Once the deed is done, people often find that they have no idea who they're dating. On the other hand, some would argue that when a mutual attraction is felt, holding back from intimacy is counter-productive. For instance, using the traditional

method, people may try to represent themselves dishonestly, behaving with courtesy, unselfishness, or generosity that they would never bother with if they weren't trying to impress. The person's true personality—perhaps that of a slob or a diva—may only be unveiled when a commitment has been made. Advocates of casual encounters argue that when the formalities are dispensed with, people show themselves as they truly are.

5   There are pitfalls to both of these ways of dating, but the fact is, most people are looking for a partner in life, and the only way to find one is to trust somebody. Whether it's a high school sweetheart, a knight in shining armour, or the best-looking person at a party, things don't necessarily work out the way people want them to. For the most part, relationships succeed because there is a sounder basis to them than passion or romance. If a true friendship is possible between two people, when passion and excitement fade, there will still be a reason to stay together.

PRACTICE 4

1. Highlight the thesis statement.

2. Highlight the topic sentence in paragraphs 2 and 4.

3. Paragraph 3 does not have a topic sentence. Which sentence best expresses the implied point?

    a. In the past, women worried about losing their reputations.

    b. Courtship rituals have changed.

    c. Dating concerns have also transformed since the 1950s.

    d. Today, there is a revival of religious values among young people.

4. In this essay, what pattern of comparison does the writer follow? Circle the correct answer.

    a. point by point

    b. topic by topic

5. Using your own words, sum up the main subjects in this essay.

    Paragraph 2:_____

    Paragraph 3:_____

    Paragraph 4:_____

6. Does this essay mainly focus on similarities or differences? Circle the correct answer.

    a. similarities

    b. differences

7. What is the author's purpose?

    a. to make a judgment

    b. to understand two things

WRITING LINK

More Comparison and Contrast Writing Topics

Chapter 18, Writer's Room topic 2 (page 264)

Chapter 21, Writer's Room topic 2 (page 294)

Chapter 25, Writer's Room topic 1 (page 327)

Chapter 30, Writer's Room topic 1 (page 385)

Chapter 36, Writer's Room topic 2 (page 444)

Writer's Room   Topics for Comparison and Contrast Essays

Writing Activity 1

Choose any of the following topics, or choose your own topic, and write a comparison and contrast essay.

General Topics

Compare or contrast . . .

1. team sports versus solo sports
2. an early bird versus a night owl
3. a true friend versus an acquaintance
4. a watcher versus a doer
5. living near family versus living away from family

Academic and Work-Related Topics

Compare or contrast . . .

6. courage versus recklessness
7. living on campus versus living off campus
8. being self-employed versus working for others
9. work versus drudgery
10. expectations about a job versus the reality of the job

Writing Activity 2

Choose a quotation that you agree or disagree with, or one that inspires you, and then write a comparison and contrast essay based on it.

A wise man can see more from the bottom of a well than a fool can from a mountaintop.

—Unknown

It seemed the world was divided into good and bad people. The good ones slept better . . . while the bad ones seemed to enjoy the waking hours much more.

—Woody Allen, filmmaker

Imagination is more important than knowledge.

—Albert Einstein, physicist

People who work sitting down get paid more than people who work standing up.

—Ogden Nash, poet

CHECKLIST: COMPARISON AND CONTRAST

After you write your comparison and contrast essay, review the checklist on the inside front cover. Also, ask yourself these questions.

- Does my thesis statement explain what I am comparing and contrasting?

- Does my thesis statement make a point about the comparison?

- Does my essay have a point-by-point or topic-by-topic pattern?

- Does my essay focus on either similarities or differences?

- Do all of my supporting examples clearly relate to the topics that I am comparing or contrasting?

READING LINK

More Comparison and Contrast Readings
"Religious Faith versus Spirituality" by Neil Bissoondath (page 502)
"The Zoo Life" by Yann Martel (page 493)
For a more complete list of readings by rhetorical mode, see Appendix 6.

Submit your best essays for possible publication to **thewritersworld@prenhall.com**.

CHAPTER 13

Cause and Effect

We cannot live only for ourselves. A thousand fibres connect us with our fellow men; and among those fibres, as sympathetic threads, our actions run as causes, and they come back to us as effects.

—HERMAN MELVILLE, *novelist*

CHAT ROOM

Work with a group of students. Each group has two minutes to brainstorm as many reasons as possible to explain why people eat fast food. Then each team will have two minutes to explain the effects of eating fast food. The team with the most causes and effects wins.

EXPLORING

WHAT IS CAUSE AND EFFECT?

Cause and effect writing explains why an event happened or what the consequences of such an event were. A cause and effect essay can focus on causes, on effects, or on both.

You often analyze the causes or effects of something. The next examples show you causes and effects of situations in your home, school, and work.

Audience: Family member	Audience: College administrator	Audience: Colleague
My accident happened for the following reasons.	**Several events have caused a lack of student housing.**	**My company is downsizing for the following reasons.**
• The fog had reduced visibility. • The driver behind me was following too closely.	• There has been an increase in enrolment in our college.	• There is too much competition.

- There was a sudden traffic jam, and I had to stop quickly.

- One student residence burned down during the summer.
- Another student residence was converted into condominiums.

- We rely more on machines than on manpower.
- The owners want to retire soon.

LIFE SNAPSHOT   **Cause and Effect at Work**

In this Canada Safety Council community newsletter, the writer explains the causes and effects of computer-related injuries.

Musculoskeletal disorders (MSDs) are a family of painful disorders affecting tendons, muscles, nerves, and joints in the neck, upper and lower back, chest, shoulders, arms, and hands. They include repetitive strain injuries (RSIs), which may take years to develop.

Recovery can be difficult and may even require surgery in extreme cases.

MSDs are the scourge of the computerized workplace. Workers can develop chronic pain if their workstations are set up without proper attention to ergonomics. A small change, such as re-positioning the screen or keyboard, or using an adjustable chair, can often eliminate the problem.

The Cause and Effect Essay

When you write a cause and effect essay, focus on two main tasks.

1. **Indicate whether you are focusing on causes, effects, or both.** If you do decide to focus on both causes and effects, make sure that your thesis statement indicates your purpose to the reader.

2. **Ensure that your causes and effects are valid.** You should determine real causes and effects and not simply list things that happened before or after the event. Also, verify that your assumptions are logical.

Illogical: Our furnace stopped working because the weather was too cold.

(This is illogical; cold weather cannot stop a furnace from working.)

Better: Our furnace stopped working because the filters needed replacing and the gas burners needed adjusting.

A Student Essay

Catherine Belisle Prevost studies at Collège Lionel Groulx in Quebec. Read the student essay and answer the questions that follow.

The Causes of Aggressiveness in Ordinary People
By Catherine Belisle Prevost

1   During World War II, many German citizens behaved in an inhuman manner toward the people who were put in concentration camps. In 1961, in an effort to understand how people could behave so callously, Stanley Milgram conducted a series of experiments. He wondered how ordinary people could be led to commit aggressive and horrible acts. A few years later, another

researcher named Philip Zimbardo conducted his own tests to determine how social roles influence behaviour. The experiments led to some astounding conclusions. Ordinary people can be persuaded to commit cruel acts when they are in submissive or dominant positions.

2   Many idealistic young men and women join the military. These ordinary soldiers and marines, who are in a submissive relationship with superior officers, sometimes have no choice but to act violently. During previous wars, soldiers have shot others, set fire to villages, and terrorized civilians because they had to do what their commanders asked. Thomas Brinson and Vince Treanor, in an article for *Veteran*, wrote, "In military training, soldiers are taught to react when threatened with aggressive, even violent behaviour. In Vietnam there were no rules. Violence was sanctioned, rewarded, and reinforced as crucial to survival." Furthermore, soldiers feel powerless because those who refuse orders can be charged with desertion. During the American Civil War and during previous world wars, many soldiers who deserted were imprisoned or sent before firing squads. Richard Norton Taylor, in an article for *The Guardian*, says that more than three hundred British soldiers were executed for desertion during World War I. Thus, many ordinary people who join the military may feel compelled to act in cruel and inhuman ways.

3   Even when people have the option of disobeying orders, they can still be persuaded to act cruelly. In Stanley Milgram's experiment, a professor asked ordinary volunteers to give electric shocks to another human. Although no shocks were actually given, the subjects in the experiment believed that they were hurting someone. In that case, the participants could easily have disobeyed and left the room with no consequences. Yet, as Joseph Dimow, the author of "Resisting Authority," says, "Of forty participants in Milgram's first experiment, fifteen refused to continue at some point, while twenty-five went all the way to 450-volt shocks." In a more recent case, managers of fast-food restaurant chains were telephoned by someone pretending to be a police officer. The "officer" said that a female employee was guilty of theft, and he convinced several restaurant managers in different locations across the nation to strip-search young employees. Donna Jean Summers, an assistant manager at McDonald's, received one of those calls on April 9, 2004. She obeyed the caller and strip-searched eighteen-year-old employee Louise Ogborn. Summers could easily have disobeyed the person on the phone, yet she did as she was told. Therefore, dominated people can commit cruel acts even when they simply think they are obeying orders.

4   People in submissive positions are not the only ones who can be persuaded to act aggressively. A lot of people in dominant positions also act in horrible ways. The news is filled with stories of prison guards, police officers, and others in roles of authority who abuse their power. When some people are in powerful positions, they can become filled with a sense of superiority and strength, and they may end up seeing those under their authority as objects. In Philip Zimbardo's Stanford Prison Experiment, students were randomly selected to be guards or prisoners. According to Kathleen O'Toole, in her article "The Stanford Prison Experiment," guards "increased their coercive aggression tactics, humiliation, and dehumanization of the prisoners. For example, the student guards forced prisoners to clean out toilet bowls with their bare hands." Christina Maslach, the woman credited with stopping the experiment, describes the change in one of the participants. When she first spoke with the student who was nicknamed "John Wayne," she thought that he

was charming. Later, she saw him in the experiment; she was shocked by his transformation into a sadistic and cruel guard: "He was talking in a different accent, a Southern accent, which I hadn't recalled at all. He moved differently. [. . .] It was like Jekyll and Hyde," said Maslach. The experiment demonstrated that some ordinary people in positions of authority can become cruel and aggressive toward those under their command.

5   Ordinary people in controlling or submissive positions have the capacity to become tyrants. Perhaps those in positions of power should get leadership training, and those who are dominated should be taught that there are logical and legal limits they must not cross. As George Eliot, the English novelist, once wrote, "Cruelty, like every other vice, requires no motive outside of itself; it only requires opportunity."

PRACTICE I

1. Highlight the thesis statement.

2. Does the thesis statement express causes, effects, or both? _____

    _____

3. What introductory style does the writer use?

    a. anecdote

    b. contrasting position

    c. historical background

4. Highlight the topic sentences in paragraphs 2, 3, and 4.

5. Using your own words, sum up the causes that contribute to tyrannical behaviour.

    _____

    _____

    _____

    _____

6. The writer closes her essay with which of the following?

    a. suggestion

    b. call to action

    c. prediction

    d. quotation

Explore Topics

In the next Writer's Desk, you will try an exploring strategy to generate ideas about different topics.

Writer's Desk Warm Up

Read the following questions, and write the first ideas that come to your mind. Think of two or three ideas for each topic.

EXAMPLE: Why are reality television shows so popular?

- voyeurism
- people are bored with sitcoms and other regular television programs
- a large variety for every taste

1. Why do people get into debt?

_____

_____

_____

2. What are some causes and effects of addictions? Specify the type of addiction.

_____

_____

_____

3. Why do some people want to become famous? What are the effects of fame?

_____

_____

_____

DEVELOPING

THE THESIS STATEMENT

When writing a thesis statement for a cause and effect essay, clearly demonstrate whether the focus is on causes, effects, or both. Also, make sure that you state a controlling idea that expresses your point of view or attitude.

controlling idea (causes)   topic
There are many reasons for **global warming.**

topic   controlling idea (effects)
Global warming may have a profound influence on our lifestyles.

topic   controlling idea (causes and effects)
Global warming, which has developed for many reasons, may have a profound influence on our lifestyles.

PRACTICE 2

Look carefully at the following thesis statements. Decide if the sentence focuses on the causes, effects, or both. Look at the key words that give you the clues and circle the best answer.

1. Poverty persists in developing countries because of lack of education, scarcity of jobs, and political corruption.

   a. causes   b. effects   c. both

2. In our college, the high student drop out rate, which is triggered by the tourist industry, results in long-term problems for the community.

   a. causes   b. effects   c. both

3. The Asian tsunami has created many problems for the environment, as well as in people's mental and physical health.

   a. causes   b. effects   c. both

GRAMMAR HINT Affect and Effect

Use *affect* as a verb and *effect* as a noun. *Affect* means "to influence or change" and *effect* means "the result."

                                                    verb
How does the ban on fast food in public schools <u>affect</u> children's health?

      noun
What <u>effects</u> will the ban on fast food in public schools have on children's health?

You can also use *effect* as a verb that means "to cause or to bring about a change or implement a plan."

Health care professionals lobbied to <u>effect</u> changes in public school lunch menus.

See Chapter 32 for more information about commonly confused words.

Writer's Desk **Write Thesis Statements**

Write a thesis statement for each of the following topics. You can look for ideas in the previous Writer's Desk. Determine if you will focus on the causes, effects, or both in your essay.

EXAMPLE: Popularity of reality shows

Thesis statement: *Reality television shows have become*

increasingly popular for several reasons.

1. Topic: Getting into personal debt

Thesis statement:

_____

_____

2. Topic: Having an addiction

Thesis statement:

_____

_____

3. Topic: Having fame

Thesis statement:

_____

_____

The Supporting Ideas

After you have developed an effective thesis statement, generate supporting ideas. In a cause and effect essay, think of examples that clearly show the causes or effects. To develop supporting ideas follow these three steps.

- Use prewriting strategies such as freewriting and brainstorming to generate ideas.
- Choose the best ideas. Use examples that clearly reveal the causes and effects.
- Organize your ideas. Choose the best organizational method for this essay pattern.

HINT Do Not Oversimplify

Avoid attributing a simple or general cause to a very complex issue. When you use expressions such as *it appears that* or *a possible cause is*, it shows that you are aware of the complex factors involved in the situation.

Oversimplification:	Global warming is caused by cars.
Better:	One possible cause of global warming is the CO_2 emissions from cars.

Identifying Causes and Effects

Imagine that you had to write a cause and effect essay on gambling. You could brainstorm and think of as many causes and effects as possible.

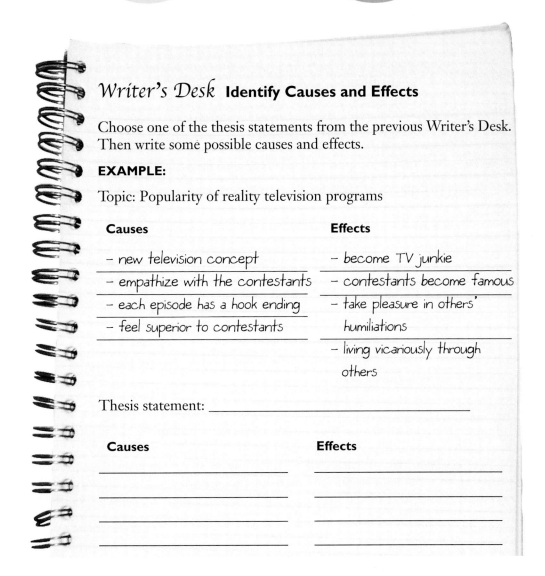

Causes
- need money quickly
- advertisements entice people to buy lottery tickets
- think winning is possible
- availability of gambling establishments

Gambling

Effects
- bankruptcy
- may cause problems in marriage or at work
- depression
- criminal behaviour such as forging checks

Writer's Desk **Identify Causes and Effects**

Choose one of the thesis statements from the previous Writer's Desk. Then write some possible causes and effects.

EXAMPLE:

Topic: Popularity of reality television programs

Causes	Effects
– new television concept	– become TV junkie
– empathize with the contestants	– contestants become famous
– each episode has a hook ending	– take pleasure in others' humiliations
– feel superior to contestants	– living vicariously through others

Thesis statement: _____

Causes	Effects
_____	_____
_____	_____
_____	_____
_____	_____

The Essay Plan

In many courses, instructors ask students to write about the causes or effects of a particular subject. Take the time to plan your essay before you write your first draft. Also, think about how you would logically arrange the order of ideas. As you make your plan, ensure that you focus on causes, effects, or both.

Thesis statement: Reality television shows have become increasingly popular for several reasons.

I.   Many situation comedies and movies of the week are no longer innovative, so people turn to reality shows.
     A. Some television comedies retell old jokes.
     B. Characters are often stereotypical.
     C. Many shows have predictable endings.

II: Reality television programs cater to a variety of tastes.
     A. Some shows focus on family dynamics.
     B. Some shows focus on romance.
     C. Other shows focus on extreme situations.

III: Home audiences live vicariously through contestants.
     A. Audiences may feel superior to contestant.
     B. An audience member can empathize with a contestant.
     C. Audience members think they can become famous like the contestants.

Writer's Desk Write an Essay Plan

Choose one of the ideas that you have developed in previous Writer's Desks and prepare an essay plan. If you think of new details that will explain your point more effectively, include them here.

The First Draft

After you have developed and organized your ideas in your essay plan, write the first draft. Remember to write complete sentences and to use transitional words or expressions to help your ideas flow smoothly. Most writers arrange cause and effect essays using emphatic order, which means that they place examples from the most to the least important or from the least to the most important. The transitional expressions shown below are useful for showing causes and effects.

To Show Causes	To Show Effects
for this reason	accordingly
the first cause	as a result
the most important cause	consequently

Writer's Desk **Write the First Draft**

Carefully review and, if necessary, revise your essay plan from the previous Writer's Desk, and then write the first draft of your cause and effect essay.

ABC ABC AB **VOCABULARY BOOST**

Using your thesaurus, come up with three synonyms for *cause* and three synonyms for *effect*.

REVISING AND EDITING

REVISE AND EDIT A CAUSE AND EFFECT ESSAY

When you finish writing a cause and effect essay, review your work and revise it to make the examples as clear as possible to your readers. Check that you have organized your ideas logically and remove any irrelevant details. Before you work on your own essay, practise revising and editing a student essay.

A Student Essay

Read the essay, and then answer the questions that follow. As you read, correct any errors that you find, and make comments in the margins.

Reality Television Is Here to Stay

By Ivan Pogrebkov

1   Matt is a twenty-one-year-old college student. Each Thursday evening, he and his friends get together to watch television. They are hooked on reality shows, which have changed the television landscape since they first arrived on the screen a few years ago. These television shows have become increasingly popular for several reasons.

2   First, the traditional situation comedies have become repetitive; therefore, bored viewers are looking for more innovative programming that will hold their attention. For example, many weekly comedy programs have the same mind-numbing plot in which the parents have to deal with their children getting into superficial trouble. The jokes are the same and the endings are predictable. The parents help the children solve the problem, and everybody learn a valuable life lesson. Most viewers are tired of this format where family problems can be solved in thirty minutes. Some comedies in the past were very good, though. *Seinfeld* was a great situation comedy that was very popular and ran for a decade. Reality television is more interesting than run-of-the mill television shows because ordinary people can react in unexpected ways.

3   There are reality shows that focus on family dynamics, shows concentrating on romance, and on extreme situations. Although reality shows are scripted to some degree, they do provide viewers with a degree of suspense and unpredictability. One never knows who is going to loose the competition. This factor attracts audiences to keep watching to find out the outcome for each participant.

4   Finally, reality shows are all the rage because audiences can relate to the situations and participants on some level. Most of the people appearing on reality shows are ordinary citizens as opposed to glamorous stars with expensive hairdos and clothes. Spectators' emotions may range from empathy for the participants to feeling superior to them. Because they are just like the participants, viewers enjoy envisioning themselves doing the same things and achieving fifteen minutes of fame. And, if the reality show is a contest, the winner usually wins money, prizes, and some amount of recognition.

5   People are loyal to reality shows because they offer variety, humour, and suspense. In fact, these programs are today's new soap operas. Although many critics find reality shows uninspiring, those programs are probably going to continue to be popular for a long time.

PRACTICE 3

Revising

1. Does the essay focus on causes, effects, or both?

2. Each body paragraph lacks adequate details. List some examples that could support the main idea of each body paragraph.

    Paragraph 2 _____

    _____

    Paragraph 3 _____

    _____

    Paragraph 4 _____

    _____

3. Highlight the topic sentence in paragraph 2, and then cross out any sentences that do not support it.

4. An appropriate topic sentence for paragraph 3 is

    a. Reality programs, unlike most sitcoms, soap operas, and made-for-TV movies, cater to a variety of tastes.
    b. Contestants of reality shows must follow a script, so they are not "real."
    c. Reality shows are unpredictable.
    d. Not everyone likes reality shows because their premises are often tedious.

5. What is the introductory style of this essay? _____

6. How does the writer conclude the essay?

   a. with an observation

   b. with a prediction

   c. with a suggestion

Editing

7. In paragraph 2, there is a subject–verb agreement error. Underline and correct the error.

   Correction: _____

   _____

8. In paragraph 3, a sentence has faulty parallel structure. Underline and rewrite the sentence.

   Correction: _____

   _____

9. Underline and correct the misspelled word in paragraph 3.

   Correction: _____

10. Change a slang expression or cliché in paragraph 4 into standard English.

   Correction: _____

   _____

GRAMMAR LINK

See the following chapters for more information about these grammar topics:

Subject–Verb Agreement: Chapter 25
Parallel Structure: Chapter 23
Spelling: Chapter 32
Exact Language: Chapter 31

Writer's Desk **Revise and Edit Your Essay**

Revise and edit the essay that you wrote for the previous Writer's Desk. You can refer to the revising and editing checklists at the end of this chapter and on the inside covers of this book.

A Professional Essay

Ellen Goodman is a Pulitzer-Prize-winning columnist for the *Boston Globe*, and her articles appear in over 370 newspapers. She has also written several books including *Value Judgments* and *Keeping in Touch*. In the next essay, she examines why North Americans are becoming more isolated socially.

Friendless in North America

By Ellen Goodman

1   Lynn Smith-Lovin was listening in the back seat of a taxi when a woman called the radio talk-show hosts to confess her affairs with a new boyfriend and a not-yet-former husband. The hosts, in their best therapeutic voices, offered their on-air opinion, "Give me an S, give me an L, give me a U." You can spell the rest. It was the sort of exchange that would leave most of us wondering why anyone would share her intimate life story with a radio host. Didn't she have anyone else to talk with? Smith-Lovin might have been the only one in the audience with an answer to the question: Maybe not.

2   The Duke University sociologist is co-author of one of those blockbuster studies that makes us look at ourselves. This one is labelled "Friendless in America." A face-to-face study of 1,467 adults turned up some disheartening news. One-fourth reported that they have nobody to talk to about "important matters." Another quarter reported they are just one person away from nobody. But this was the most startling fact. The study is a replica of one done twenty years ago. In only two decades, from 1985–2004, the number of people who have no one to talk to has doubled. And the number of confidants of the average person has gone down from three to two.

3   The people to whom we are closest form our own informal safety net. They're the ones who see us through a life crisis, lend us their spare bedroom, or pick up our kids at school in a pinch. Social isolation is as big a risk factor for premature death as smoking. Robert Putnam has already chronicled the erosion of the ties that bind in *Bowling Alone*. But we've paid less attention to "coping alone" or "suffering alone." Imagine if some other piece of the social safety net had frayed that furiously. Imagine if income had gone down by a third, or divorce doubled, or the medical system halved. We would be setting up commissions and organizing rallies.

4   Not everything in the study was gloomy. Deep in the data is the suggestion that families—husbands and wives, parents and adult children—might be closer. Spouses who call each other "my best friend" might be right. We might have fewer intimates but we're more intimate with them. On average, we see them more than once a week and have known them seven years. Nevertheless, the big news is that circles have tightened, shrunk, and gone nuclear. As Smith-Lovin says, "Literally nothing takes the place of family." The greatest loss has been in neighbours and friends who will provide help, support, advice, and connections to a wider world.

5   There is no shortage of speculation about why our circle of friends is eroding. The usual suspect is the time crunch. It's knocked friendship off the balancing beam of life as we attend to work and family. It's left less time for the groups and associations that bind us. But in the past twenty years, technology has changed the way we use our "relationship time." Walk along any city street and people talking on cell phones are more common than pigeons. Go into Starbucks and a third of the customers are having coffee dates with their laptops. "It could be that talking to people close to us on cell phones has caused our social circle to shrink," says Smith-Lovin. It could be that we are both increasingly in-touch and isolated. It's become easier to keep extensive relationships over time and distance but harder to build the deep ones in our backyard. In the virtual neighbourhood, how many have substituted email for intimacy, contacts for confidants, and Facebook for face to face?

6   A few years ago, when my friend Patricia O'Brien and I wrote a book on the power of friendship in women's lives, we noted that there was no official status for friends, no pro-friendship movement, no cultural or political support system for friends. Yet this voluntary relationship can be the most sustaining one of life.

7   Now we are living in smaller, tighter circles. We are ten degrees of separation from each other and one or two people away from loneliness. And many now outsource intimacy from friends to professional therapists and *gawd* help us, talk shows. Who can we talk to about important matters? Who can we count on? As we search for tools to repair this frayed safety net, we can take poor, paradoxical comfort from the fact that if we are feeling isolated, we are not alone.

PRACTICE 4

1. Who is the audience for this essay? _____

2. The thesis of this essay is not stated directly, but it is implied. Using your own words, write the thesis of this essay. _____

    _____

3. What type of introduction does Goodman use?

    a. historical background

    b. anecdote

    c. general background

4. In your own words, how have the socialization habits of North Americans changed in the past twenty years?

    _____

    _____

5. What specific reasons does Goodman give for this social change?

    _____

    _____

6. Goodman writes, "It could be that we are both increasingly in-touch and isolated." What does she mean?

    _____

    _____

 Writer's Room   **Topics for Cause and Effect Essays**

Writing Activity 1

Write a cause and effect essay about one of the following topics, or choose your own topic.

WRITING LINK

More Cause and Effect Writing Topics

Chapter 18, Writer's Room topic 1 (page 264)
Chapter 20, Writer's Room topic 2 (page 285)
Chapter 26, Writer's Room topic 2 (page 344)
Chapter 31, Writer's Room topic 2 (page 394)

General Topics	Academic and Work-Related Topics
Causes and/or effects of ...	Causes and/or effects of ...
1. a good/bad sports parent	6. a public policy
2. getting married	7. becoming successful
3. a fear of _____	8. giving somebody a second chance
4. road rage	9. learning a skill
5. a natural phenomenon	10. a hostile workplace

Writing Activity 2

Choose a quotation that you agree or disagree with, and then write a cause and effect essay based on it.

> Usually when people are sad, they don't do anything. They just cry over their condition. But when they get angry, they bring about a change.
>
> —Malcolm X, political activist

> Human beings, by changing the inner attitudes of their minds, can change the outer aspects of their lives.
>
> —William James, psychologist

> Those who can make you believe absurdities can make you commit atrocities.
>
> —Voltaire, satirist

> Fire and swords are slow engines of destruction, compared to the tongue of a gossip.
>
> —Richard Steele, essayist

READING LINK

More Cause and Effect Readings

"The Hijab" by Naheed Mustafa, page 460
"Nature Returns to the Cities" by John Roach, page 468
For a more complete list of readings by rhetorical mode, see Appendix 6.

✓ CHECKLIST: CAUSE AND EFFECT ESSAY

As you write your cause and effect essay, review the checklist on the inside front cover. Also, ask yourself these questions.

☐ Does my thesis statement indicate clearly that my essay focuses on causes, effects, or both?

☐ Do I have adequate supporting examples of causes and/or effects?

☐ Do I make logical and valid points?

☐ Do I use the terms *effect* and/or *affect* correctly?

Submit your best essays for possible publication to **thewritersworld@prenhall.com**.

Argument

Fear not those who argue but those who dodge.

—MARIE EBNER VON ESCHENBACH, *writer*

CHAPTER CONTENTS

Exploring
• What Is Argument?
• The Argument Essay
• Explore Topics

Developing
• The Thesis Statement
• The Supporting Ideas

• The Essay Plan
• The First Draft

Revising and Editing
• Revise and Edit an Argument Essay
• A Professional Essay: "Keep Your Roses" by Melonyce McAfee

CHAT ROOM

For this activity, you and a partner will take turns debating an issue. To start, choose which one of you will begin speaking. The first speaker chooses one side of any issue listed below, and then argues about that issue, without stopping, for a set amount of time. Your instructor will signal when to switch sides. After the signal, the second speaker talks non-stop about the other side of the debate. If you run out of ideas, you can switch topics when it is your turn to speak.

Possible topics:

Technology has improved our lives.	Technology has hurt our lives.
It is better to be an only child.	Is it is better to have brothers and sisters.
Adolescence is the best time of life.	Adolescence is the worst time of life.
Our college needs improvements.	Our college does not need improvements.

EXPLORING

WHAT IS ARGUMENT?

When you use **argument**, you take a position on an issue, and you try to prove or defend your position. Using effective argument strategies can help you convince somebody that your point of view is a valid one.

Argument is both a writing pattern and a purpose for writing. In fact, it is one of the most common aims, or purposes, in most academic and work-related writing. For example, in Chapter 10, there is an essay called "On Genius," in which the author uses definition as the predominant pattern. At the same time, the author uses argument to convince the reader that true genius exists all around us. Therefore, in most of your school and work-related writing, your purpose is to persuade the reader that your ideas are compelling and legitimate.

The following examples show arguments people might make every day.

Audience: Mate	Audience: College dean	Audience: Customer
We need to move to a larger home.	**The Graphic Arts Department needs new computers.**	**Our company has the best cell-phone package.**
• My home office space in the corner of our bedroom is not adequate.	• The department has grown, and there are not enough computers.	• We have the lowest rates.
• Our son and daughter are approaching ages where they will need separate bedrooms.	• The existing computers do not support new graphics programs.	• We give more free daytime minutes than the competitors.
• We can have a larger apartment or duplex for the same cost if we are just willing to relocate slightly north of the city.	• To make our education relevant, students must understand current high-tech tools.	• We include call display and voice messaging in all of our packages.

LIFE SNAPSHOT   Argument at Work

Network administrator Octavio Pelaez uses argument writing in this excerpt from a memo to his director.

We need to invest in a new email server. First, the slow speed and unreliability of the present equipment is becoming a serious inconvenience. While the cost of replacing the server and the accompanying software will be very high, the cost of not doing it is going to be much higher in lost time and productivity. It would not be an exaggeration to say that for the last three months, we have lost over a thousand billable hours due to the poor condition of our equipment. The average hourly rate per user is $30, thus those lost hours of productivity have cost the company over $30 000. Also, consider the impact on our company's reputation when the clients have problems communicating with us. We cannot afford to wait any longer to invest in new equipment and technology. In fact, over the long term, replacing the email server would actually increase productivity and profitability.

The Argument Essay

When you write an argument essay, remember four key points.

1. **Consider your readers.** What do your readers already know about the topic? Will they likely agree or disagree with you? Do they have specific concerns? Consider what kind of evidence would be most effective with your audience.

2. **Know your purpose.** In argument writing, your main purpose is to persuade the reader to agree with you. Your specific purpose is more

focused. You may want the reader to take action, you may want to support a viewpoint, you may want to counter somebody else's argument, or you may want to offer a solution to a problem. Ask yourself, *What is my specific purpose?*

3. **Take a strong position and provide persuasive evidence.** The first thing to do in the body of your essay is to prove that there is, indeed, a problem. Then back up your point of view with a combination of facts, statistics, examples, and informed opinions.

4. **Show that you are trustworthy.** Respect your readers by making a serious argument. If you are condescending, or if you try to joke about the topic, your readers may be less inclined to accept your argument. You can also help your readers have more respect for your ideas when you choose a topic that you know something about. For example, if you have been in the military or you know people in the military, you might be able to make a very convincing argument about the lack of proper equipment for soldiers.

A Student Essay

Read the student essay and answer the questions that follow.

Changing Face of Cosmetic Surgery

By Kate Howell

1   Many people who undergo cosmetic surgery are regarded as vapid, shallow, and lacking in self-esteem. The phrases "Be happy with who you are" and "God made you perfect as is" are thrown around to provide assurance. For instance, a woman who attempts to change her appearance is told that such an act signals a level of dishonesty toward herself, her family and, possibly, her creator. The stigma associated with plastic surgery clearly exists—note the negative connotation of the word "plastic." However, such attitudes ignore reality. Anyone who uses cosmetic surgery to enhance his or her appearance should be applauded, not condemned.

2   "It is better to look good than to feel good." This line was made famous in the 1980s by Billy Crystal's "Fernando" character on *Saturday Night Live*, but few would have imagined that it was more than a catchphrase. It was actually an indication of a cultural phenomenon that exploded shortly thereafter. Cosmetic surgery has become popular on TV, in the office, and all around campus. TV shows such as *Extreme Makeover* have become hits. Prices for all kinds of procedures, from eyelifts to liposuction, have gone down, so more and more people can afford them. The age of plastic surgery recipients has also gone down, with college-aged girls opting for breast implants and nose jobs.

3   It is not just women who are body-obsessed. According to *HealthDay News*, men are the newest arrivals to the cosmetic surgery party. In 2000, there was a 16 percent increase in body-altering procedures performed on males. Competition in the business world is fierce, and men are looking for any advantage they can find. Bags under the eyes and a weak chin just won't cut it when there is an army of young bucks with MBAs gunning for every job. The idea that men are not supposed to care or show interest in their personal appearance is outdated and unfortunate. We do not live in a society of cattle ranchers and frontier explorers anymore. The beaten-up faces and callused hands of yore are no longer necessary tools of the trade; in today's society, they

have been replaced by cheek lifts and palm scrubs, and that is not necessarily a bad thing.

4   There remains a degree of disapproval of plastic surgery, yet the importance of personal appearance is everywhere. Consumers spend billions of dollars each year on makeup, haircuts, tanning salons, manicures, and pedicures. Studies show that good-looking people tend to get hired for jobs. In the movies, some distinct qualities belong to the majority of the stars: trim bodies, immaculate grooming, and gleaming teeth. Yet nobody likes to acknowledge the fact that looks matter. Science tells us we are attracted to certain features, and it is ridiculous to deny that fact. Appearance certainly isn't everything, but to downplay its importance is self-righteous hypocrisy.

5   If, as is widely believed, it is what is on the inside that matters, then people should not get in such a huff about altering one's outside. If a person feels unattractive, he or she should not be held back from making a change because friends or family cling to some half-hearted notion of "playing the cards one has been dealt." If people desire to remake their body as they see fit, then more power to them. In this time of laziness and apathy, at least these people are taking steps to try to improve their lot in life. As humans, we adapt to our society, and ours is now one of aesthetics. To borrow an oft-used phrase from hip-hop: Don't hate the player, hate the game.

PRACTICE 1

1.   Highlight the thesis statement.

2.   What introduction style does the author use?

     a.   an anecdote   b.   a definition
     c.   a contrasting position   d.   a description

3.   Highlight the topic sentence in paragraphs 2 and 4. Be careful because the topic sentence may not be the first sentence.

4.   The topic sentence in paragraph 3 is implied but is not stated directly. Choose the most effective topic sentence for this paragraph.

     a.   Men are obsessed about their bodies.

     b.   In 2000, the percentage of males getting cosmetic surgery increased.

     c.   Men no longer want to have wrinkled, beaten-up faces and callused hands.

     d.   To gain an advantage in the competitive workplace, men are increasingly opting to have cosmetic surgery.

5.   What is the author's specific purpose?_____

     _____

     _____

6.   The writer supports her point of view with specific evidence. Underline a quotation and a statistic.

7. In your own words, sum up the writer's main point about cosmetic surgery.

_____

_____

_____

Explore Topics

In the following Writer's Desk, you will try an exploring strategy to generate ideas about different topics.

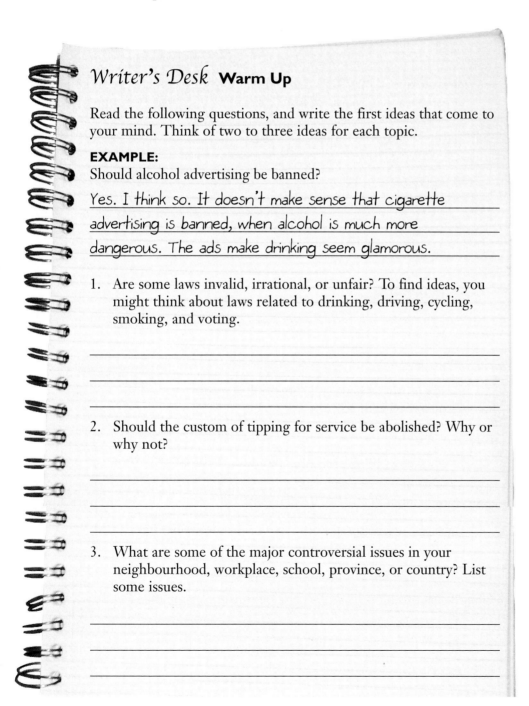

Writer's Desk **Warm Up**

Read the following questions, and write the first ideas that come to your mind. Think of two to three ideas for each topic.

EXAMPLE:
Should alcohol advertising be banned?

Yes. I think so. It doesn't make sense that cigarette advertising is banned, when alcohol is much more dangerous. The ads make drinking seem glamorous.

1. Are some laws invalid, irrational, or unfair? To find ideas, you might think about laws related to drinking, driving, cycling, smoking, and voting.

_____

_____

2. Should the custom of tipping for service be abolished? Why or why not?

_____

_____

3. What are some of the major controversial issues in your neighbourhood, workplace, school, province, or country? List some issues.

_____

_____

THE THESIS STATEMENT

In the thesis statement of an argument essay, state your position on the issue.

topic   controlling idea (the writer's position)

Many corporate executives <u>are overpaid for very substandard work.</u>

A thesis statement should be debatable, not a fact or a statement of opinion.

Fact:	Some car companies have produced electric cars.
	(This is a fact. It cannot be debated.)
Opinion:	I think that people should buy electric cars.
	(This is a statement of opinion. Nobody can deny that you feel this way. Therefore, do not use phrases such as *In my opinion, I think*, or *I believe* in your thesis statement.)
Debatable argument:	To address global warming and energy shortages, the automobile industry should focus on the production of electric cars.
	(This is a debatable statement.)

HINT **Be Direct**

Many students feel reluctant to state their point of view directly. They may feel that it is impolite to do so. However, in academic writing, it is perfectly acceptable, and even desirable, to state an argument in a direct manner.

PRACTICE 2

Evaluate the following statements. Write F for a fact, O for an opinion, or A for an argument.

1. Canada should impose a standard six-week vacation for all workers. _____

2. Many universities permit soft-drink companies to sell their products on campus. _____

3. I disagree with advertising on college campuses. _____

4. The city's major art gallery spent millions of dollars on an abstract painting. _____

5. In my opinion, abstract art is ridiculous. _____

6. Japanese anime should be recognized as an influential art form. _____

7. I think that no one should use racial profiling at borders. _____

8. Racial profiling at borders is a legitimate way to defend the nation. _____

9. In our province, art is not taught in most high schools. _____

10. Art education should be compulsory in our high schools. _____

HINT Making a Guided Thesis Statement

Your instructor may want you to guide the reader through your main points. To do this, mention your main and supporting ideas in your thesis statement. In other words, your thesis statement provides a map for the readers to follow.

Art education should be compulsory in high schools because it encourages creativity, it teaches about culture, and it develops students' analytical skills.

Writer's Desk Write Thesis Statements

Write a thesis statement for the next topics. You can look for ideas in the previous Writer's Desk on page 201. Make sure that each thesis statement clearly expresses your position on the issue.

EXAMPLE: Topic: Alcohol advertising

Thesis statement: Advertisements for alcoholic beverages should be prohibited on television or in any form of mass media.

1. Topic: Unfair laws

Thesis statement: _____

_____

_____

2. Topic: Tipping customs

Thesis statement: _____

_____

_____

3. Topic: A controversial issue

Thesis statement: _____

_____

_____

The Supporting Ideas

To make a logical and reasoned argument, support your main point with facts, examples, and statistics. (For details about adding facts, examples, and statistics, see page 43 in Chapter 4.)

You can also include the following types of support.

- **Quote informed sources.** Sometimes experts in a field express an informed opinion about an issue. An expert's thoughts and ideas can add weight to your argument. For example, if you want to argue that people are becoming complacent about AIDS, you might quote an article published by a respected national health organization.

- **Consider logical consequences.** When you plan an argument, think about the long-term consequences of a proposed solution to a problem. For example, in response to the terrorist attacks of September 11, 2001, many governments enacted anti-terrorism legislation. However, in some cases, the laws have been used to suppress legitimate dissent or free speech. The new laws could also be misused or misinterpreted by future governments.

- **Acknowledge opposing viewpoints.** Anticipating and responding to opposing views can strengthen your position. For instance, if you argue that school uniforms should be mandatory, you might address those who feel that students need freedom to express themselves. Try to refute some of the strongest arguments of the opposition.

Making an Emotional Appeal

Generally, an effective argument appeals to the reader's reason. For example, you could use certain words or descriptions to encourage a reader's sense of justice, humanity, or pride. But sometimes an appeal to the reader's emotions can boost your argument. However, use emotional appeals sparingly. If you use **emotionally charged words** such as *wimp* or *thug*, or if you appeal to base instincts such as fear or cowardice, then you may seriously undermine your argument. Review the next examples of emotional appeals.

Overly emotional: A ferocious, bloodthirsty pit bull broke free of its leash and attacked a defenceless, fragile boy named Jason. The child, who will suffer from lifelong psychological trauma, is disfigured with irreparable facial scars.

Reasonable and more neutral: Pit bulls can be unpredictable. The pit bull attack on nine-year-old Jason caused significant facial scarring and psychological trauma.

HINT **Avoid Common Errors**

When you write your argument essay, avoid the following pitfalls.

- **Do not make generalizations.** If you begin a statement with *Everyone knows* or *It is common knowledge*, then the reader may mistrust what you say. You cannot possibly know what everyone else knows or does not know. It is better to refer to specific sources.

| **Generalization:** | Everyone knows that our nation is too dependent on oil. |
| **Better:** | Prominent MPs have stated that our nation's dependence on oil is a serious problem. |

(continued)

- **Do not make exaggerated claims.** Make sure that your arguments are plausible.

Exaggerated:	If marijuana is legalized, drug use will soar in schools across the nation.
Better:	If marijuana is legalized, drug use may increase in schools across the nation.

PRACTICE 3

You have learned about different methods to support a topic. Read each of the following thesis statements and think of a supporting idea for each item. Use the type of support suggested in parentheses.

1. Volunteer work should be mandatory in all high schools.
    (Logical consequence) _____
    _____

2. Online dating is a great way to meet a potential mate.
    (Acknowledge an opposing view) _____
    _____

3. Children should not be spanked.
    (Emotional appeal) _____
    _____

4. The college dropout rate in this province is too high.
    (Logical consequence) _____
    _____

5. Pointy-toed stilettos are unattractive, uncomfortable, and potentially harmful.
    (Acknowledge an opposing viewpoint) _____
    _____

ABC
ABC

VOCABULARY BOOST

Some words can influence readers because they have positive or negative connotations, which are implied or associated meanings. The meaning often carries a cultural value judgment with it. For example, *macho* may have negative connotations in one country and positive connotations in another country. For the word *thin*, synonyms like *skinny* or *skeletal* have negative connotations, while *slender* and *svelte* have positive ones. Using a thesaurus, try to come up with related terms or descriptions that have either positive or negative connotations for the words in bold.

Gloria is **large**.
Calvin is **not assertive**.
Mr. Wayne **expresses his opinion**.
Franklin is a **conservative**.

Identify terms you chose that might be too emotionally loaded for an argument essay.

Consider Both Sides of the Issue

Once you have decided what issue you want to write about, try to think about both sides of the issue. Then you can predict arguments that your opponents might make, and you can plan your answer to the opposition.

Example:

Arguments *For* Banning Alcohol Advertisements	Arguments *Against* Banning Alcohol Advertisements
• Ads encourage drinking among adolescents.	• Print advertisers will lose significant income from magazine ads.
• Ads are aimed at young males who can become aggressive.	• Sporting events rely on advertising dollars.
• Alcohol kills more people than cigarettes.	• Advertisers should have freedom of speech.

Writer's Desk **Consider Both Sides of the Issue**

Choose one of the topics from a previous Writer's Desk, and write arguments showing both sides of the issue.

Thesis statement: _____

For	Against
_____	_____
_____	_____
_____	_____
_____	_____
_____	_____
_____	_____

HINT **Strengthening an Essay with Research**

In some courses, your instructors may ask you to include supporting ideas from informed sources to strengthen your essays. You can find information in a variety of resources, including textbooks, journals, newspapers, magazines, or the Internet. When researching, make sure that your sources are from legitimate organizations. For example, for information about the spread of AIDS, you might find statistics on the World Health Organization website. You would not go to someone's personal rant or conspiracy theory site.

For more information about evaluating and documenting sources, refer to Chapter 16: The Research Essay.

The Essay Plan

Before you write your argument essay, outline your ideas in a plan. Include details that can help illustrate each argument. Ensure that every example is valid and relates to the thesis statement. Also think about your organization. Many argument essays use emphatic order and list ideas from the least to the most important or compelling.

Thesis statement: Advertisements for alcoholic beverages should be prohibited on television or in any form of mass media.

I.   Banning alcohol ads would reduce excessive drinking and alcohol-related assaults and injuries among youths.
   A. Drinking is like a rite of passage, and ads encourage that belief.
   B. Many binge drinkers die from alcohol poisoning.
   C. Many rapes and assaults are blamed on excessive drinking.

II. Alcohol advertising targets young impressionable males who are the most dangerous drivers.
   A. Beer ads reinforce he-man attitudes.
   B. Young males more likely to drink and drive than any others.
   C. Drunk driving rates are very high among young men.

III. It is hypocritical to ban cigarette advertising but not alcohol advertising.
   A. Cigarette packages carry warnings, but alcohol bottles don't.
   B. Alcohol is addictive.
   C. Alcohol causes many diseases such as cirrhosis of the liver.

Writer's Desk Write an Essay Plan

Choose one of the ideas that you have developed in previous Writer's Desks, and write a detailed essay plan.

The First Draft

Now that you have a refined thesis statement, solid supporting details, and a roadmap of your arguments and the order in which you will present them, you are ready to write the first draft. Remember to write complete sentences and to include transitional words or expressions to lead readers from one idea to the next. Here are some transitions that introduce an answer to the opposition or the supporting ideas for an argument.

To Answer the Opposition	To Support Your Argument
admittedly	certainly
however	consequently
nevertheless	furthermore
of course	in fact
on one hand / on the other hand	obviously
undoubtedly	of course

GRAMMAR HINT **Keeping Pronouns Consistent**

In argument writing, ensure that your pronouns do not switch between *they*, *we*, and *you*. If you are writing about specific groups of people, use *they* to refer to those people. Only change pronouns when the switch is logical.

Many hunters argue that they need large collections of guns. Yet why would ~~you~~ *they* need a semi-automatic to go hunting?

See Chapter 29 for more information about pronoun usage.

Writer's Desk **Write the First Draft**

Write the first draft of your argument essay. Include an interesting introduction. Also, add specific details to flesh out each body paragraph.

REVISING AND EDITING

REVISE AND EDIT AN ARGUMENT ESSAY

When you finish writing an argument essay, carefully review your work and revise it to make the supporting examples as clear as possible to your readers. Check that the order of ideas is logical, and remove any irrelevant details. Before you revise and edit your own essay, practise revising and editing a student essay.

A Student Essay

Kayin Jacobs is a student in Victoria, British Columbia. Read the essay, and then answer the questions that follow. As you read, correct any errors that you find, and make comments in the margins.

Alcohol Advertising

By Kayin Jacobs

1   Magazines feature glossy vodka advertisements. During television sporting events, viewers see one beer ad after another. Alcohol, while society's most accepted drug, is considerably more dangerous than some other substances that cannot be advertised. The current massive promotion of alcoholic beverages has several negative side effects that are ignored because of the cultural significance of alcohol. Advertisements for alcoholic beverages should be prohibited on television or in any form of mass media.

2   Binge drinking is a common pass-time for students entering their first week of university. While some may see drinking as a rite of passage for young people entering adulthood, the reality is that the practice doesn't have no positive benefits. The website *College Drinking: Changing the Culture*, which was created by the U.S. National Institute on Alcohol Abuse and Alcoholism (NIAAA), states that 1400 college students between the ages of eighteen and 24 die every year in alcohol-related incidents, while 500 000 students suffer alcohol-related injuries each year. The East Tennessee State University School of Nursing site mentions that 600 000 college students are physically attacked by a student who has been drinking, while another 70 000 students are raped or sexually assaulted as a result of alcohol. Alcohol is the only recreational drug that is still actively advertised on television, and this is a large part of the reason why so many young people binge on the drug. Elimination of the advertising could result in a lower number of young people that drink, just as removing cigarette advertising from television has helped reduce the number of young smokers.

3   Alcohol advertising targets young impressionable males who are the most dangerous drivers. Beer ads, for example. These advertisements usually allude to a connection between drinking a certain beer and getting attractive females. Yet statistics about drunk driving fatalities indicate that young males are more likely to drink and drive than any other group. For example, according to Transport Canada's report *The Alcohol-Crash* Problem, in the year 2000, 1981 people were killed in alcohol-related crashes, and 87.5 percent of the people that were killed were male. It stands to reason that the elimination of alcohol advertising would result in fewer drunk driving fatalities, as young men are both the primary target of these advertisements and the primary cause of most drunk driving deaths.

4   Cigarette packages contain warnings about negative health effects. Alcohol cans and bottles should also have warning labels explaining the addictive qualities of the product and the long-term effects of excessive drinking. Certainly, both cigarettes and alcohol are highly addictive. A lifetime drinker has health problems that could be compared to a lifetime smoker. Some of the potential health problems that could await an alcoholic include brain cell damage, inflammation and ulcers in the stomach, and cirrhosis, hepatitis, or cancer of the liver. According to the Centers for Disease Control website, in 2003 there were 12 207 deaths from chronic liver disease caused by alcohol.

5   Now, don't get the wrong message. This is not an argument for the prohibition of alcohol but for a pause in the incessant marketing of this product to young people, young males in particular. Let's face it: young guys can become idiots when they have a bottle in their hands. Advertising

promotes our alcohol culture, which results in many preventable deaths every year. Those who want alcohol can buy it, but it should not be actively marketed. A lesson society seems to have learned with cigarettes. Now let's hope the holocaust of people's lives is curbed with the ban of alcohol advertising.

PRACTICE 4

Revising

1. Highlight the thesis statement.

2. Highlight the topic sentence in each body paragraph.

3. a. How does the topic sentence in paragraph 4 fail to support the thesis statement?

   _____

   _____

   _____

   b. Create a topic sentence for paragraph 4 that more effectively links the paragraph to the thesis statement.

   _____

   _____

   _____

4. In the concluding paragraph, the writer uses emotionally charged words and exaggerates. Give examples of each of these problems.

   Emotionally charged language _____

   Exaggeration _____

5. Does the writer acknowledge the opposing viewpoint? ___ Yes   ___ No

Editing

6. Underline and correct a spelling mistake in paragraph 2.

   Correction: _____

GRAMMAR LINK

See the following chapters for more information about these topics:

Spelling: Chapter 32
Numbers: Chapter 36
Double Negatives:
    Chapter 27
Fragments: Chapter 21

7. In paragraph 2, there is an inconsistency in the way the ages are written. Underline and correct the error.

   Correction: _____

8. In paragraph 2, there is a double negative. (Two negative words cancel each other out.) Underline the error and write the correct phrase in the space.

   Correction: _____

9. Identify fragments in paragraphs 3 and 5, and write correct sentences on the lines below.

Paragraph 3: _____

Paragraph 5: _____

Writer's Desk **Revise and Edit Your Essay**

Revise and edit the essay that you wrote for the previous Writer's Desk. You can refer to the checklists at the end of this chapter and on the inside covers of this book.

A Professional Essay

Melonyce McAfee is an editorial assistant at *Slate* magazine. She has written for a variety of publications including the *San Diego Union-Tribune*. In this essay, she argues for the abolition of Administrative Professionals Day. Read the essay and answer the questions that follow.

Keep Your Roses

By Melonyce McAfee

1   Here's a plot line for the writers at NBC's *The Office*: It's April 26. Paper salesman Jim presents a bouquet of tulips to his office crush, Pam, the receptionist. The accompanying card reads, "For all you do. Happy Secretaries Day." Competitive and cringe-inducing boss Michael, until now oblivious to the holiday, sees the card and orders a garish bouquet, large enough to blot out Pam's head and overshadow Jim's arrangement. The bouquet arrives at 4:49 p.m. Eyes roll. Administrative Professionals Day is the Hallmark holiday that leads to interoffice jealousy, discomfort, and not much else.

2   The National Secretaries Association got the ball rolling with Professional Secretaries Week in 1952. The holiday was renamed Administrative Professionals Week in 2000, but I prefer the tell-it-like-it-is Secretaries Day. The NSA (now, naturally, the International Association of Administrative Professionals) claims the day is meant to enhance the image of administrative workers, promote career development, and encourage people to enter the field. But does it really do any of the above?

3   In my first job out of college, I worked as a typist at a title company, a job akin to cryptography. I pecked my way toward carpal tunnel syndrome to turn chicken scratch into property reports. Typists served the entire office, but title officers also had personal secretaries. On Secretaries Day, we typists sucked our teeth at the bouquets on the secretaries' desks. At my next corporate job, I had gained an "assistant" title. But along with the other assistants, I was still

left empty-handed. The office professionals chipped in for a bouquet for the division secretary, who regularly pawned off duties on us assistants and huffed when asked to, well, work. "I can't believe they got *her* flowers," we hissed.

4   My mother, a former hospital administrative assistant, was surprised with three greeting cards and a gorgeous scarf last Secretaries Day. She wasn't aware of the holiday and was touched that the nurses in her department took the opportunity to thank her for working hard on special projects. But she also had to listen to a chorus of "*I* didn't get anything" from other administrators. She says that didn't diminish her pleasure, but it does prove my point. When the holiday makes someone feel appreciated, it almost invariably leaves others out in the cold.

5   Maybe part of the problem is that in the fifty years since the holiday began, the duties of a secretary have been farmed out across the office, and the job definition is no longer clear. A secretary used to be the woman who answered phones, took dictation, typed, picked up dry cleaning, and stole your husband, if she was really good. Now she (or he) might give PowerPoint presentations or build a website. Meanwhile, someone else might do the typing and filing.

6   The confusion over who qualifies as a secretary creates social anxiety about either over-celebrating the holiday or under-celebrating it. One Secretaries Day, a former advertising-sales assistant and co-worker of mine got lovely plants from colleagues who rushed to point out that they'd gotten her a gift even though she wasn't really a secretary. She got the impression they thought she might be offended by being lumped in with the administrative staff. The holiday forces workers, like it or not, to evaluate how they stack up. Mail-room guy, copy clerk, typist, receptionist, administrative secretary, executive assistant—are you low enough on the totem pole to merit a gift? Or are you too low?

7   In some industries, Secretaries Day is less apt to cause confusion. Schools, for example, have it easy—it's obvious that the lady in the front office with her glasses hanging by a chain is the secretary. But in many workplaces, administrative positions are rife with ambiguity. What about legal clerks at law firms and sales assistants at magazines—when you cut them, do they not bleed Wite-Out? In the media business, assistant positions are often a stepping-stone to greater glory. Still, assistants perform the same duties as secretaries. And even if most of them don't do it for long, every publication has a guy who's been an editorial assistant for fifteen years. He can write a dozen screenplays and freelance hundreds of album reviews for the local indie paper, but he's still going to be an assistant ten years from now. Does he deserve the same Benihana gift certificate that the publisher's secretary gets? Of course he does. He just lacks the magic title.

8   Perhaps my impatience with Secretaries Day springs from job dissatisfaction, as an executive assistant at a New York-based magazine suggested when we mused about why the holiday creates bitterness. True—in my mind, I should be the boss. And I resent being reminded of my slow progress up the chain of command every April 26. Those of us who yearn to be professionals, not administrative professionals, tend to bristle at the idea that we're just boosters for the big boys and girls.

9   Some bosses feel compelled to take their secretary, assistant, or whoever out to lunch on Secretaries Day. It's a nice gesture, but who wants to sit

through that awkward meal? Anyone who has seen the *Curb Your Enthusiasm* episode in which Larry David takes his maid on a squirm-worthy lunch date at his country club knows the potential disaster of forced boss–employee **conviviality**. Instead of Secretaries Day, why not just chip in for a big cake on the Friday before Labour Day and toast everyone in the office. Wouldn't that be kinder, not to mention easier? I'd much prefer that to a holiday that's a catch-all for "attagirl," "I'm sorry for being an insufferable employer," and "we should talk about that raise."

conviviality: friendliness

PRACTICE 5

1. Highlight the thesis statement.

2. What technique does the writer use to introduce the topic?

   a. historical background

   b. anecdote

   c. a definition

3. What synonyms does McAfee use for "secretary" in this essay?

   _____

4. In which paragraph does the writer acknowledge an opposing viewpoint?_____

5. Which sentence best sums up the writer's implied argument in paragraph 3?

   a. Typists and assistants are secretaries.

   b. The writer worked as a typist in a small company for many years, and then she became an executive.

   c. Typists do a lot of hard work but are not appreciated.

   d. Many people in offices, such as typists and assistants, feel resentful when they are not rewarded on Secretaries Day.

6. Which sentence best sums up the writer's implied argument in paragraph 8?

   a. Administrative assistants really do the work of the bosses.

   b. Honestly, most administrative assistants dislike their jobs.

   c. Secretaries Day reminds administrative assistants that they have not advanced on the career ladder.

   d. Most administrative assistants want to be professionals.

7. Using your own words, sum up McAfee's three main supporting arguments.

   _____

   _____

   _____

WRITING LINK

More Argument Writing Topics.
Chapter 20, Writer's Room topic 2 (page 285)
Chapter 22, Writer's Room topic 2 (page 303)
Chapter 24, Writer's Room topic 1 (page 316)
Chapter 29, Writer's Room topic 2 (page 377)
Chapter 30, Writer's Room topic 2 (page 385)
Chapter 32, Writer's Room topic 2 (page 406)
Chapter 33, Writer's Room topic 2 (page 416)

READING LINK

More Argument Readings

"Google's China Web" by Frida Ghitis (page 476)
"Medicating Ourselves" by Robyn Sarah (page 505)
For a more complete list of readings by rhetorical mode, see Appendix 6.

Writer's Room   Topics for Argument Essays

Writing Activity 1

Choose any of the following topics, or choose your own topic, and write an argument essay. Remember to narrow your topic and to follow the writing process.

General Topics

1. graffiti
2. gun laws
3. labour unions
4. home schooling
5. same-sex marriage

Academic and Work-Related Topics

6. usefulness of college programs
7. working while going to school
8. minimum wage
9. parental leave
10. working at home

Writing Activity 2

Choose a quotation that you agree or disagree with, and then write an argument essay based on it.

> Many would be cowards if they had courage enough.
>
> —Thomas Fuller, historian

> Advertising is the modern substitute for argument.
>
> —George Santayana, philosopher

> Of all forms of caution, caution in love is perhaps the most fatal to true happiness.
>
> —Bertrand Russell, author and philosopher

> Everything on the earth has a purpose, every disease an herb to cure it, and every person a mission.
>
> —Mourning Dove Salish, author

 CHECKLIST: ARGUMENT ESSAY

After you write your argument essay, review the checklist on the inside front cover. Also, ask yourself these questions.

▢ Does my thesis statement clearly state my position on the issue?

▢ Do I make strong supporting arguments?

▢ Do I include facts, examples, statistics, and logical consequences?

▢ Do my supporting arguments provide evidence that directly supports the thesis statement?

▢ Have I acknowledged and countered opposing arguments?

▢ Are my arguments valid? (Have I avoided making broad generalizations? If I have used an emotional appeal, is it restrained?)

▢ Is my tone courteous?

Other Writing Skills

Source: Understanding Music by Jeremy Yudkin, Third Edition, 2002, Prentice Hall, Upper Saddle River, New Jersey

Page 411. "Jazz singers also deliberately make use of unusual sounds. A special kind of singing in which the vocalist improvises with nonsense syllables . . . is known as 'scat' singing."

423: bebop uses "nonsense syllables used in scat singing." Different from swing-not as predictable.

Sample Research Essay

Single space your name, instructor's name, course title, and date.

Centre the title. (Notice that the title is not underlined, boldfaced, or put in quotation marks.)

Double-space the body of the essay.

Acknowledge sources of borrowed ideas.

Place author's name and page number in parentheses.

Zachary Alapi
Mrs. Wheatcroft
ARH LFA 01
April 24, 2008

Alapi 1

Goya's Greatest Work

Francisco José de Goya y Lucientes (1746–1828) is one of the most renowned and famous Spanish artists whose work has had a tremendous and lasting impact on the world of art. One of Goya's most famous paintings is titled <u>The Shootings of May 3, 1808</u>. It is an extremely powerful and evocative work that captures the brutality of the French occupation of Spain during the reign of Napoleon. There is little doubt that Goya's message regarding his feelings on religious hypocrisy and the elevation of the common Spaniard are clearly visible in <u>The Shootings of May 3, 1808</u>.

<u>The Shootings of May 3, 1808</u> was painted in the context of the French occupation of Spain under Napoleon. For the Spanish, this was a war of independence against the oppression and tyrannical rule of Napoleon, as well as an attempt to rid the country of the political corruption that was so rampant (Gassier and Wilson 205). Spanish guerrilla fighters launched attacks on French troops, which led to French firing squads killing captured Spanish guerrilla fighters (Alexander 194). The Spaniards killed at the hands of the firing squads became heroes and martyrs for the Spanish cause. In the work, Goya elevates the common Spaniard to a seemingly Christ-like status against the faceless, oppressive French soldiers.

The unique and revolutionary techniques in painting used by Goya throughout his career can be seen in <u>The Shootings of M...</u> used a fairly limited colour pal...

and ...

Essay Exam

Answer both Parts A and B. You will have two hours to complete the evaluation.

A. Define two of the following terms. (5 points each)
1. democracy
2. electorate
3. communism
4. industrial revolution
5. gerrymandering

B. Write a well-structured essay on one of the following topics. (20 points)
1. Distinguish between panic and mass hysteria. Can governments ever benefit from either of these phenomena?
2. Evaluate the usefulness of sanctions imposed by Western nations against North Korea.
3. Trace the rise of National Socialism in Germany in the 1930s.

In the next chapters, you will learn about additional writing skills. During your post-secondary career, your instructor may ask you to support your essay ideas using paraphrases or summaries. These useful strategies strengthen your research paper and make it more forceful and convincing. Chapter 15, Paraphrasing and Summarizing, provides you with details about these important skills. Chapter 16 leads you through the process of writing a research essay. Finally, essay exams are perhaps the most common type of writing that you will do in college and university. Chapter 17, Becoming a Successful Student, provides information about study skills and guides you through the exam-writing process.

Paraphrasing and Summarizing

CHAPTER 15

After all, the ultimate goal of all research is not objectivity, but truth.

—HELENE DEUTSCH, *psychoanalyst*

CHAPTER CONTENTS

GRAMMAR LINK

To find out more about using quotations, see Chapter 35.

Integrating Borrowed Information

During your college career, your instructor may ask you to support your essay ideas using quotations, paraphrases, or summaries. These useful strategies strengthen your research paper and make it more forceful and convincing.

A **quotation** permits you to use another person's exact language. A **paraphrase** lets you use your own words to present someone else's essential information or ideas. Finally, a **summary** allows you to use borrowed information by presenting only the main points of one or several works in your own words. A summary is a shortened version of the original work.

All of these strategies are valid ways to incorporate research into your writing, as long as you give credit to the author or speaker.

HINT Avoid Plagiarism

Plagiarism is the act of using—intentionally or unintentionally—someone else's words or images without giving that person credit. Plagiarism is a very serious offence and can result in expulsion from college or termination from work. **Always** acknowledge the source when you borrow material. Here are some ways to avoid plagiarizing someone else's work.

- Do not buy another work and present it as your own.
- Do not use another student's work and present it as your own.
- Do not use someone's exact words or ideas without citing that source.
- Do not make slight modifications to an author's sentences and then present the work as your own.

To avoid plagiarism, keep detailed notes about your sources. Then, when you want to borrow words, phrases, or ideas, you can acknowledge the source.

Paraphrasing

Paraphrasing allows you to support your essay using other people's ideas. By paraphrasing, you can make the ideas of a source clearer in your own paper. In addition, paraphrasing forces you to grasp a text completely, which may be useful for fully understanding the subject of your research paper. Clarifying ideas by paraphrasing may also help when you are studying. When you paraphrase, use only your own words.

How to Paraphrase

- Read the original text carefully and underline any key ideas. You will have to restate the main ideas and supporting details of the text when you paraphrase.
- Use your own words to restate the main and supporting ideas of the original text. To help prevent copying, try not to look again at the original source. Use a dictionary and thesaurus to find exact meanings and synonyms of words in the original text.
- Mention the source of the original text. State the author and title of the original text.
- Put quotation marks around any words or phrases used from the original source. Words that are specific names or generic words do not have to be put into quotation marks.
- Use approximately the same number of words as the original passage. A paraphrase is a restated version of the original text.
- Do not change the meaning of the original text. Do not include your own opinions.
- Verify that your paraphrase expresses the ideas and intent of the author of the original text.

The next paragraph is from a longer article written by Matt Richtel and appeared in the April 11, 2006 edition of the *New York Times* online edition. Read the selection and paraphrase.

Original Selection

Ms. Vargas works not in a restaurant but in a busy call center in this town, 150 miles from Los Angeles. She and as many as 35 others take orders remotely from 40 McDonald's outlets around the country. The orders are then sent back to the restaurants by Internet, to be filled a few yards from where they were placed. The people behind this setup expect it to save just a few seconds on each order. But that can add up to extra sales over the course of a busy day at the drive-through.

Effective Paraphrase

On the *New York Times* website, Matt Richtel states that at least 35 workers who are employed at a call centre near Los Angeles receive take-out food orders from McDonald's restaurants in different parts of the United States. Using the Internet, call centre employees mail the orders back to the McDonald's restaurants, and then employees serve customers. McDonald's owners believe that this system will save time and increase profits each day.

Unacceptable Paraphrase

As many as 35 people take orders from 40 McDonald's outlets around the country. They send back the orders to the original McDonald's restaurants. This method is supposed to save a few seconds on each order and add extra sales to each day.

This unacceptable paraphrase uses exact words from the text and does not put them in quotation marks. It also does not mention the source.

PRACTICE I

Read the following selections and answer the questions. The original selection, written by Mike Oliveira, appeared in the *Montreal Gazette* on December 4, 2006, on page D5.

While Apple has sold 70 million units and has legions of devotees, the iPod has also received unfavourable attention for problems that have been known to kill the pricey gadgets—including screens that break, batteries that fade, damaged headphone jacks that distort sound and failing hard drives. In rare cases, some iPods were even sold with a virus.

Paraphrase 1

In the *Montreal Gazette*, Mike Oliveira writes that iPod sales are in the millions. However, some iPods contain many problems that lead to breakage. Such problems are breaking screens, fading batteries, damaged headphone jacks that distort sound, and failing hard drives. Some iPods even contain a virus.

1. How does this paraphrase plagiarize the original piece of writing?

Paraphrase 2

Apple computers have sold millions of iPods, but some customers are experiencing difficulties with the popular product. Some iPod users complain that screens fracture, batteries weaken, and headphones do not work. Also, iPod hard drives collapse and some have a virus.

2. How does this paraphrase plagiarize the original piece of writing?

_____

_____

Summarizing

Summarizing is a vital skill for writing and studying. When you summarize, you condense a text to its key ideas. Reducing a long work to its bare essentials requires that you fully understand the message of the text. It also helps you understand the organization of the ideas in the text.

How to Summarize

- Read the original text carefully.
- Underline any key ideas. In a summary, you will only present the main ideas of a text.
- Ask yourself *who, what, when, where, why*, and *how* questions. These questions will help you to synthesize the ideas of the original text.
- Restate the essential ideas in your own words. Refer to a dictionary and thesaurus for the meanings of words and for useful synonyms.
- Maintain the original meaning of the text. Do not include your own opinions.
- Mention the author and title of the original source.
- Reread your summary. Verify that you have explained the key message of the text.

PRACTICE 2

The next paragraph is from page 101 of the textbook *Core Concepts in Sociology*, by Linda L. Lindsey, Stephen Beach, and Bruce Ravelli. Compare the paraphrase and summary of the original text. Then answer the questions that follow by underlining the appropriate response.

Original Selection

In much of the world, health care is provided by traditional or folk healers. The ethnocentric notion long prevalent in the Western world that traditional healing would be replaced by scientific medicine is now questioned. Folk healers are successful because they understand patient concerns from the viewpoint of the patient's culture. China's "barefoot doctors" are recruited from the villages they eventually serve. They understand village culture and combine techniques from both traditional and scientific medicine.

Paraphrase

In *Core Concepts in Sociology*, Linda L. Lindsey and others state that indigenous medical practices are used by many societies around the world. Occidental medical experts were wrong when they thought that modern Western medicine would take the place of native health care customs. By being sensitive to culture, health care givers around the world gain the confidence of their patients. Chinese doctors practising in rural areas often are villagers themselves. They are successful because they blend local and Western medicine (101).

Summary

According to Linda L. Lindsey in *Core Concepts in Sociology*, indigenous health care givers around the world are successful in treating patients because they blend local and Western medicine practices (101).

1. Which is about the same length as the original text?
   paraphrase _____
   summary   _____
   both   _____

2. Which contains only the main idea of the original text?
   paraphrase _____
   summary   _____
   both   _____

3. Which maintains the author's intent of the original text?
   paraphrase _____
   summary   _____
   both   _____

4. Which includes all the details of the original text?
   paraphrase _____
   summary   _____
   both   _____

5. Which mentions the source of the original text?
   paraphrase _____
   summary   _____
   both   _____

HINT   Consider Your Audience

When you decide whether to paraphrase or summarize, think about your audience.

- Paraphrase if your audience needs detailed information about the subject.
- Summarize if the audience needs to know only general information.

PRACTICE 3

The following essay is from pages 192–193 of *Cultural Anthropology* by Carol R. Ember and Melvin Ember. Read the essay and then write a summary. You may think that summarizing a longer text is difficult. To make the exercise more manageable, follow these steps.

- Read the complete article.
- Underline the main ideas in the text.
- Write the summary by answering *who, what, when, where, why,* and *how* questions.
- Write a first draft of the summary.
- Remove any unnecessary details.
- Ensure that you have not used the exact words or phrases from the original text.
- Reduce your writing to only a paragraph by revising and condensing your draft.
- Reread your summary to verify that you have stated the essential ideas of the text.

Why Street Gangs Develop

1   The street gangs of young people that we read and hear about so often are voluntary associations. They are a little like age-sets in that the members are all about the same age, but they are unlike age-sets in being voluntary, and they do not "graduate" through life stages together. Nobody has to join,

although there may be strong social pressure to join the neighbourhood gang. Gangs have a clear set of values, goals, roles, group functions, symbols, and initiations. Street gangs are also often like military associations in their commitment to violence in the defence of gang interests.

2   Violent street gangs are found in many U.S. cities, particularly in poor neighbourhoods. But poverty alone does not appear sufficient to explain the existence of gangs. For example, there is plenty of poverty in Mexico, but gangs did not develop there. In Mexico there was a *palomilla* (age-cohort) tradition; age-mates hung out together and continued their friendship well into adulthood, but there were no gangs as we know them. Mexican American gangs did develop in the barrios of cities such as Los Angeles. When we realize that most youths in poor neighbourhoods do not join gangs, it is clear that poor neighbourhoods cannot explain gangs. It is estimated that only 3 to 10 percent of Mexican American young people join gangs.

3   But why do some young people join and not others? If we look at who joins a gang, we see that it seems to be those children who are subject to the most domestic stress. The gang "joiners" are likely to come from poor families, have several siblings, and have no father in the household. They seem to have had difficulty in school and have gotten into trouble early.

4   What about gangs appeals to them? Most adolescents in this country have a difficult time deciding who they are and what kind of people they want to be, but young people who join gangs seem to have more identity problems. One 18-year-old said he "joined the gang for my ego to go higher," reflecting a low self-esteem. Those who are raised in female-centred households seem to be looking for ways to show how "masculine" they are. They look up to the tough male street gang members and want to act like them. But getting into a gang requires initiation. Most gangs have their own stylized rituals; for example, Mexican American gangs physically beat the initiate, who must show bravery and courage. As happens in most initiation ceremonies, the gang initiate identifies even more strongly with the group afterward.

5   So, belonging to a gang may make some youths feel as if they belong to something important. This is a kind of psychological adjustment, but is it adaptive? Does being in a gang help such youth survive in a neighbourhood where young men are often killed? Or are gang members less likely to survive? We really don't know the answers to those questions.

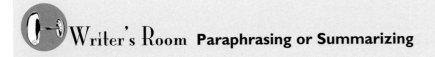

Writer's Room   Paraphrasing or Summarizing

Writing Activity 1

Exchange an essay with a classmate and paraphrase or summarize it.

Writing Activity 2

Summarize the information found in Chapter 17, Becoming a Successful Student.

CHECKLIST: PARAPHRASING AND SUMMARIZING

When you paraphrase or summarize, ask yourself these questions.

- In a paraphrase, have I kept the original intent of the author?

- In a summary, have I kept only the key ideas?

- Have I used my own words when paraphrasing or summarizing?

- Have I mentioned the source when paraphrasing or summarizing?

Submit your best essays for possible publication to **thewritersworld@prenhall.com**.

The Research Essay

16
CHAPTER

*Research is the process of going up alleys to
see if they are blind.*

—MARSTON BATES, *zoologist*

Planning a Research Essay

Conducting **research** means looking for information that will help you better understand a subject. Knowing how to locate, evaluate, and use information from other sources is valuable in your work and day-to-day activities. It is also crucial in college writing because, in many of your assignments, you are expected to include information from outside sources. In this chapter, you will learn some strategies for writing a research paper.

Determining Your Topic

In some courses, your instructor will ask you to write a research paper about a specific topic. However, if you are not assigned one, then you will need to think about issues related to your field of study or to your personal interests.

The scope of your topic should match the size of the assignment. Longer essays might have a broader topic, but a short research essay (of three or four pages) must have a rather narrow focus. For instance, you would not write about the history of Spanish art in a short research paper, but you could write about a particular artwork or artist. To help find and develop a topic, you can try exploring strategies such as freewriting, questioning, or brainstorming. (See Chapter 1 for more information about prewriting strategies.)

Finding a Guiding Research Question

The point of a research essay is not to simply collect information and summarize it; the idea is to gather information that relates directly to your central question. To help you determine your central question, brainstorm a list of questions that you would like your research to answer. For example, Zachary Alapi must write a research essay for his art history class. He might ask himself the following questions in order to narrow his topic.

What is my favourite artwork?

Why is Goya's "firing squad" painting so powerful?

What compelled Goya to paint?

Zachary's next step is to find the most promising research question that can become the focus of his essay.

Why is Goya's "firing squad" painting so powerful?

Writer's Desk Find a Research Topic

Choose a general topic that you might like to write about.

Topic: _____

Now ask five or six questions to help you narrow the topic.

_____

_____

_____

_____

_____

_____

Decide which question will become your guiding research question, and write it here.

_____

_____

Gathering Information

Once you know what information you seek, you can begin gathering ideas, facts, quotations, anecdotes, and examples about the research topic you have chosen. Before you begin to gather information, consider how to find it and how to sort the valid information from the questionable information.

Consulting Library-Based Sources

Today's technological advances in both print and electronic publishing make it easier than ever to access information. For sources, you can consult encyclopedias, online catalogues in libraries, periodical databases, and the Internet. Here are some tips for finding information about your topic through library resources.

- **Ask a reference librarian** to help you locate information using various research tools, such as online catalogues, CD-ROMs, and microfiches. Before meeting with the librarian, write down some questions that you would like the answers to. Possible questions might be *Can I access the library's online databases from my home computer?* and *Can you recommend a particular online database?*

- **Search the library's online holdings.** You can search by keyword, author, title, or subject. The listing gives the call number, which helps you locate the book on the library shelves. If the catalogue is part of a library network, the online listing will explain which library to visit. Because books are organized by topic, chances are good that you will find other relevant books near the one you have chosen.

- **Use online periodical services in libraries.** Your library may have access to *EBSCOhost®* or *INFOtrac*. By typing keywords into EBSCO*host®*, you can search through national or international newspapers, magazines, or reference books. When you find an article that you need, print it or cut and paste it into a word processing file and then email the document to yourself. Remember to print or copy the publication data because you will need that information when you cite your source.

Searching the Internet

Search engines such as *Google* and *Yahoo!* can rapidly retrieve thousands of documents from the Internet. However, most people do not need as many documents as those engines can generate. Here are some tips to help make your Internet searches focused and efficient.

- **Choose your keywords with care.** Imagine you want information about new fuel sources for automobiles. If you type in the words *alternative energy* in Google's keyword search space, you will come up with over ten million entries (also known as "hits"). Think about more precise terms that could help you limit your search. For instance, if you are really interested in fuel sources for automobiles, you might change your search request to *alternative fuel sources*. Other options might be *alternative car fuel*. To limit the search, type in only the keywords that are most relevant to your research question. If you do not find information on your topic, think about synonyms or alternative ways to describe it.

- **Use quotation marks to limit the search.** Remember that you are driving the search engine, and you can control how many hits you get. By putting quotation marks around your search query, you limit the number of sites to those that contain all of the words that you requested. For example, when you input the words *alternative car fuel* into Google without quotation marks, you will have over three million hits. When the same words are enclosed with quotation marks, the number of hits is reduced to about one thousand, and the displayed webpages are more relevant.

- **Use bookmarks.** When you find information that might be useful, create a folder where you can store the information in a "bookmark" or "favourites" list. Then you can easily find it later. (The bookmark icon appears on the toolbar of your search engine.)

- **Use academic search engines.** Sites such as *Google Scholar* (scholar.google.com) or *Virtual Learning Resources Centre* (virtuallrc.com) help you look through academic publications such as theses, peer-reviewed papers, books, and articles. To find more academic sites, simply do a search for "academic search engines."

Conducting Interviews or Surveys

Another excellent way to find information about your topic is to conduct **interviews**. You can speak to an expert in the field or people who are directly affected by the issue. If you record the interview, ensure that your subject gives you permission to do so. Remember to plan the interview before you meet the person, and list key questions that you would like answered. Include the person's complete name and qualifications in your research notes.

Another source of information can be a **survey**, which is an assessment of the views of many people. For example, if you are writing about the tuition fee increase, you can survey students to gather their opinions. When you plan your survey, follow some basic guidelines:

- **Determine your goal.** What do you want to discover?

- **Determine the age, gender, and status of the respondents** (people you will survey). For example, in a survey about the legalization of marijuana, you might decide to survey equal-sized groups of males and females or those over and under twenty-five years of age.

- **Decide how many people you will survey.** Try to survey at least twenty people. If you are working with a partner or a team of students, you can increase that number.

- **Determine the type of survey you will do.** Will you survey people by phone, Internet, or with written forms? Keep in mind that people are more likely to obscure the truth when asked questions directly, especially if the questions are embarrassing or very personal. For example, if you ask someone whether he agrees or disagrees with legalized abortion, he might present a viewpoint that he thinks you or nearby listeners will accept. The same person might be more honest in an anonymous written survey.

- **Plan your survey questions.** If gender, age, marital status, or job status are important, place questions about those items at the beginning of your survey. When you form your questions, do not ask open-ended, essay-type questions because it will be difficult to compile the results. Instead, ask yes/no questions or provide a choice of answers. Sample questions:

What is your gender?
_____ male
_____ female

How often do you use the public transit system (the bus, subway, or train)?
_____ weekdays
_____ about once a week
_____ about once a month
_____ rarely or never

If you want to determine your respondents' knowledge about a topic, include an "I don't know" response. Otherwise, people will make selections that could skew your survey results.

Has Jackson Monroe done a good job as student union leader?
_____ yes
_____ no
_____ I don't know

Writer's Desk **Research Your Topic**

Using the guiding research question that you developed in the previous Writer's Desk, list some keywords that you can use to research your topic.

_____

_____

Using the library and the Internet, find some sources that you can use for your research essay. You might also conduct interviews or prepare a survey.

Evaluating Sources

When you see sources published in print or online, especially when they are attention-grabbing with colour or graphics, you may forget to question whether those sources are reliable. For instance, a company's website advertising an alternative cancer therapy might be less reliable than an article in a scientific journal by a team of oncologists (doctors who treat cancer).

When you evaluate Internet sites, you can often determine which type of sponsor or organization runs the website by looking at the last three letters of the web address.

Common Domain Names and Website Sponsors

domain name	sponsor	example
.edu	educational institution	www.phoenix.edu
.gov	government	www.irs.gov
.com	company	www.nytimes.com
.org	organization (often not-for-profit)	www.magazines.org
.net	network	www.jobs.net

PRACTICE I

Imagine that you are writing an essay about the dangers of Internet dating. Your audience is other college students. To enhance your argument, you want to add some facts, statistics, anecdotes, and quotations to your essay. Answer the questions by referring to the list of websites that follows.

1. Which sites would likely contain useful information? For each site that you choose, explain why it could be useful.

_____

_____

_____

2. Which sites are probably not useful for your essay? For each site you choose, explain why.

_____

_____

_____

A. **Internet Dating Directory: The Yellow Pages of Online Dating**

Interactive Directory of Online Dating Sites and Services. The Most Popular Directory of 2006.

internetdating.net/

B. **Stop Internet Dating Petition: [powered by iPetitions.com]**

Petition Stop Internet Dating. This is a petition to stop Internet Dating.

www.ipetitions.com/petition/endinternetdating/

C. **globeandmail.com: Technology**

Police issue warning on Internet dating. Canadian Press. Toronto — Police forces around the world spend fortunes trolling for and arresting Internet ...

www.theglobeandmail.com/servlet/story/RTGAM.20070225. winternet-dating0225/BNStory/Technology/home

D. **Internet dating: sucks for guys, good for women. Free Dating...**

It is deplorable how much it sucks for guys on dating sites for many reasons. There is usually a hugely uneven ratio of men vs women, with men in the great ...

forums.plentyoffish.com/datingPosts2568515.aspx

E. **CNN.com - Transcripts**

And also with us is CNN.com technology correspondent Daniel Sieberg.... I would say that Internet dating in some fashion or another has been around really ...

transcripts.**cnn**.com/TRANSCRIPTS/0207/28/sm.25.html

F. **Internet Dating Stories: The good, the bad, and the... OH MY GOD...**

Stories from people about their Internet dating experiences, the good, the bad and the bizarre. Includes online safety advice.

www.internetdatingstories.com

> **HINT** **Questions for Evaluating a Source**
>
> Each time you find a source, ask yourself the following questions:
>
> - Will the information support the point that I want to make?
> - Is the information current? Check the date of publication of the material you are considering.
> - Is the information relevant and directly related to my topic?
> - Is the source reliable and highly regarded? For instance, is the source from a respected newspaper, journal, or website?
> - Is the author an expert on the subject?
> - Does the author present a balanced view, or does he or she clearly favour one viewpoint over another? Ask yourself if the author has a financial or personal interest in the issue.
> - On various sites, do different authors supply the same information? Information is more likely to be reliable if multiple sources cite the same facts.

PRACTICE 2

Working on your own or with a partner, complete the following tasks.

1. Use exploring strategies to come up with a narrowed research question about the legalization of marijuana.

2. Searching the Internet, find two websites that you do not consider valid sources. Explain how you determined that the two sources are not useful for an academic research paper.

3. Next, find two websites that you consider valid. Explain how you determined that the two sources are reliable for an academic research paper.

Taking Notes

As you research your topic, keep careful notes on loose-leaf paper, on note cards, or in computer files. Do not rely on your memory! You would not want to spend several weeks researching, only to accidentally plagiarize because you had not adequately acknowledged some sources.

Look for sources that support your thesis statement. Each time you find a source that seems relevant, keep a detailed record of its publication information so that you can easily cite the source when you begin to write your research essay. You will find important information about preparing in-text citations and Works Cited (MLA) or References (APA) lists later in this chapter.

For example, Lenny Bukowski searched for information on jazz, and he created the following note card after finding source material in the library.

Source: *Understanding Music* by Jeremy Yudkin, Third Edition, 2002, Prentice Hall, Upper Saddle River, New Jersey

Page 411. "Jazz singers also deliberately make use of unusual sounds. A special kind of singing in which the vocalist improvises with nonsense syllables . . . is known as 'scat' singing."

423: bebop uses "nonsense syllables used in scat singing." Different from swing—not as predictable.

Finding Complete Source Information

Source information is easy to find in most print publications. It is usually on the copyright page, which is often the second or third page of the book, magazine, or newspaper. On many Internet sites, however, finding the same information can take more investigative work. When you research on the Internet, look for the home page to find the site's title, publication date, and so on. Record as much information from the site as possible.

Book, Magazine, Newspaper	Website
• author's full name	• author's full name
• title of article	• title of article
• title of book, magazine, or newspaper	• title of website
• publishing information (name of publisher, city, and date of publication)	• date of publication or update
• page numbers used	• date that you accessed the site
	• complete website address

> **HINT** **Avoid Plagiarism**
>
> Do not plagiarize. When you use someone else's work without giving that person credit, it is considered stealing, and it is a very serious offence. To eliminate your chances of inadvertently plagiarizing, ensure that your notes contain detailed and clear source information. Then, when you later quote, paraphrase, or summarize another's work, you can cite the source. For more information about plagiarism, paraphrasing, and summarizing, see Chapter 15.

Writer's Desk Take Notes

Use your topic from the previous Writer's Desk. Take notes from the sources that you have found. In your notes, include direct quotations, paraphrases, and summaries. Organize your sources and keep a record of your sources.

Organizing the First Draft

For research essays, as for any other type of essay, planning is essential. After you have evaluated the material that you have gathered, decide how you will organize your material. Group your notes under the main points that you would like to develop. Then arrange your ideas in a logical order. You might choose to use spatial, chronological, or emphatic order.

Writing a Thesis Statement

After taking notes, plan your thesis statement. Remember that the thesis statement expresses the main focus of the essay. One way to form the thesis statement is to convert your guiding research question into a statement. For instance, student writer Zachary Alapi decided to use the following as his guiding question: *Why is Goya's "firing squad" painting so powerful?* After researching and gathering material on the topic, he then reworked the question to create a thesis statement.

> Thesis: Goya's message regarding his feelings on religious hypocrisy and the elevation of the common Spaniard are clearly visible in <u>The Shootings of May 3, 1808</u>.

Creating an Informal Outline

A general **outline** or **plan** will help you organize your ideas. List some of the supporting details that you will insert into your essay. Then, ask yourself the following questions as you evaluate your outline.

- Do I have sufficient supporting examples?
- Is my plan organized in a logical manner?
- Do I need to research more sources?

Zachary's Preliminary Outline

Introduction: General info about Goya
Thesis: Goya's message regarding his feelings on religious hypocrisy and the elevation of the common Spaniard are clearly visible in <u>The Shootings of May 3, 1808</u>.

    Context of French occupation under Spain
        Much bloodshed (Alexander, page 194)
        King Ferdinand VIII's position (See Gasier and Wilson, page 205)
    Revolutionary techniques that Goya used
        Views about colour expressed by Myers (see pages 5–12)
        Description of painting
        Political expressions about war (see Schickel, pages 132–36)
    Goya's relationship with Spanish people
        Shows "religion without mercy" (Lassaigne, page 96)
        Role of church

An outline also helps you check whether you have any "holes" in your research. If you need more support for certain ideas, do more research and fill in any holes before starting on your first draft. For reminders about the writing process, see Chapters 1 through 5.

HINT **Inserting Quotations, Paraphrases, and Summaries**

Using your outline, you can plan your first draft. Smoothly integrate supporting paraphrases, summaries, and quotations. Rather than repeating *Yudkin says* over and over, try to use a variety of verbs when you integrate information from your sources. For instance, you could include the following verbs:

states	suggests	notes	indicates
concurs	reiterates	discusses	mentions

Refer to Chapter 15 for more detailed information about paraphrasing and summarizing, and see Chapter 35 for information about punctuating quotations.

Writer's Desk **Make a Preliminary Plan**

Organize your topic and make a plan. In your preliminary plan, include source information. Remember that this is not a final plan. You can add or remove information afterward.

Incorporating Visuals

Visuals—such as charts, maps, graphs, photos, or diagrams—can provide useful information as you research a topic. They can also enhance your own research essay if you know how to include them and cite them properly. For example, a graph showing the falling crime rate can be an effective way to support an argument that policing methods have become increasingly successful. Visuals help to clarify, summarize, or emphasize a concept. However, use visuals sparingly and only when they help to illustrate a point.

Most word processing programs offer templates for visuals, such as graphs and charts. For example, the toolbar in MS Word allows you to select *Chart* under *Insert* to create line, bar, pie, and other types of charts. Simply input your own data, and the program will create the chart for you. The following are standard examples of what you can create.

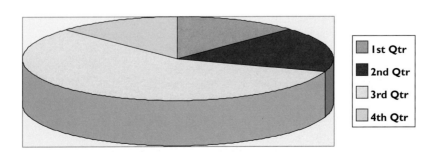

HINT **Using Visuals**

Here are some recommendations for using visuals in an academic research essay:

- Ask your instructor whether you are permitted to use visuals in your essay. If so, find out if you should use them in the body of your essay near the point that you are supporting, or if you should place them in an appendix.
- Include a label above each visual to clearly identify it. For example, you can number figures and tables sequentially: *Figure 1*, *Figure 2*, or *Table 1*, *Table 2*, and so on.
- Place a caption beside or under the visual to help the reader understand it.
- Acknowledge the source of any visual that you borrow.
- Explain how the visual supports a point.

     Example: The crime rate has fallen steadily since the 1990s (see fig. 2).

Citing Sources

Each time you borrow someone's words, ideas, or images, you must **cite** or credit the source. If you fail to properly acknowledge the source of your information, you will be committing a serious academic offence called plagiarism (see page 216 of Chapter 15).

There are two ways you need to cite sources in your research essays. The first is in the body of your essay. When incorporating quotations, paraphrases, or summaries, offset the source information using parentheses. These **in-text citations**, also known as **parenthetical citations**, allow you to acknowledge where you obtained the information. The second place to cite sources is in an alphabetized list at the end of your essay. The title of this source list depends on the documentation style you choose. For example, the Modern Language Association (MLA) refers to the list as Works Cited and the American Psychological Association (APA) refers to it as References.

HINT **Choose a Documentation Style**

A **documentation style** is a method of presenting the material that you have researched.

    The three most common styles for documenting sources are the Modern Language Association (MLA), the American Psychological Association (APA), and the *Chicago Manual of Style* (CMS). Before writing a research essay, check with your instructor about which documentation style you should use and where you can find more information about it.

For more information about where to find the most up-to-date guidelines and samples, check each organization's website: **www.mla.org** or **www.apastyle.org**.

Using MLA Style

MLA: In-Text Citations

In an MLA-style research essay, there are two ways you can show readers that you have borrowed an idea or a quote from a source.

1. **Enclose the author and page number in parentheses.** Include the last name of the author along with the page number where the material appears. If there is more than one author, write both authors' names in parentheses.

Do not use a comma between the name(s) and page reference. Place the final period after the final parenthesis.

> Sometimes a group of rioters will direct their hostility at one person, even if that person has never attacked them or their ideals (Locher 92).

> The consequences of a nuclear attack would be devastating: "Nuclear winter could produce climatic disaster" (Roskin and Berry 236–37).

If you are using several works by the same author, then you can place a shortened version of the title—perhaps the first two or three words—within the parentheses.

> Martin Luther King attended the rally (Kofsky, <u>Black Nationalism</u> 48).

HINT Quoting from a Secondary Source

If your source material includes a quotation, and you do not know the original source of the quotation, then use *Qtd. in* (a shortened form of "quoted in").

> David York, co-founder of Toughlove International, said, "Our society's fearful of our kids" (Qtd. in Schmalleger 533).

---

2. **Introduce the source in the text and write the page reference in parentheses.** You can mention the author's name in the introductory phrase, with only the page number in the parentheses. Place the final period *after* the parentheses.

> "Violent mobs often take out their anger and frustration on any individual," writes David A. Locher (92).

> According to sociologist David A. Locher, mobs display violent behaviour as a way of venting hostility and frustration (92).

HINT Citing Certain Web Sources

If you are using a Web-based source, no page number is necessary. If you cannot find the author's name, then put the title of the site in parentheses.

> Peer support networks are essential: "Many witnesses identified peer support groups as one of the most important services needed on the road to recovery from mental illness" ("Out of the Shadows").

GRAMMAR LINK

To find out more about writing titles, see page 434 in Chapter 35.

MLA: Making a Works Cited List

An MLA-style Works Cited list appears at the end of a research essay. It gives readers details about each source from which you have borrowed material to write your essay. Works Cited is not the same as a running bibliography, which is a list of all of the sources you consulted while you were researching your essay topic. In a Works Cited list, only include works you have quoted, paraphrased, or summarized.

To prepare a Works Cited list, follow these basic guidelines.

1. Write "Works Cited" at the top of the page and centre it. Do not italicize it, underline it, or put quotation marks around it.
2. List each source alphabetically, using the author's last name.
3. Indent the second line and all subsequent lines of each entry five spaces.
4. Double-space all lines.

HINT Writing the Name, Title, and Publishing Information Using MLA Style

Name
On the Works Cited page, write the author's complete last name and first name.

Title
Add quotation marks around the titles of short works. Underline or italicize titles of longer works such as books, newspapers, and magazines.

Place and Year of Publication
Mention the name of the city and the shortened name of the publisher. MLA does not require the name of the province or state. If the work is published outside Canada, add a shortened form of the country name, such as Eng. for England. Also mention the year of publication.

Publisher's Name
Use a shortened form of the publisher's name. Omit *A*, *An*, or *The* from the beginning, and omit words such as *Co.*, *Corp.*, *Books*, *Press*, and *Publishers*. The short form for University Press is UP.

Complete Reference
Here is an example of a basic Works Cited entry. Notice that you do not underline the final period that follows the title.

Brainard, Shirl. <u>A Design Manual</u>. Upper Saddle River: Prentice Hall, 2006.

Sample MLA-Style Works Cited Entries

The following are a few sample entries for various publications. The *MLA Handbook for Writers of Research Papers* has a complete list of sample entries. Before you look at the samples for each type of source, review how the punctuation varies for each.

Books

Last name, First name. <u>Title of the Book</u>. Place of Publication:
    Publisher, Year.

- **one author**

    Findley, Timothy. <u>Famous Last Words</u>. Toronto: Penguin, 1982.

- **two or three authors**

    Write the last name and first name of the first author. Follow with *and*, and then write the first and last name of subsequent authors. If the book is a second, third, or subsequent edition, write just the abbreviated form of the edition after the title.

Bovée, Courtland and John Thill. <u>Business Communication Essentials</u>. 2nd ed. Upper Saddle River: Prentice Hall, 2006.

- **four or more authors**

Add *et al*, which means "and others," after the first author's name.

Coon, Dennis, et al. <u>Psychology, A Journey</u>. Scarborough: Thomson, 2003.

- **book with an editor instead of an author**

Write the editor's name followed by *ed*.

Koppleman, Susan, ed. <u>Old Maids: Short Stories by Nineteenth-Century US Women Writers</u>. Boston: Pandora, 1984.

- **two or more books by the same author**

Write the author's name in the first entry only. In subsequent entries, type three hyphens followed by a period. Then add the title.

Atwood, Margaret. <u>The Tent</u>. Toronto: McClelland, 2006.

- - -. <u>Lady Oracle</u>. Toronto: McClelland, 1976.

- **a work in an anthology**

When your source is a story or article in an anthology, mention the author and title of the article first.

Munro, Alice. "Boys and Girls." <u>Literature</u>. Ed. R. S. Gwynn and Wanda Campbell. Toronto: Longman, 2003.

If you are using several pieces from the same anthology, include separate entries for each piece like the first entry below. Then add another entry for the anthology itself that looks like the second entry below.

Munro, Alice. "Boys and Girls." Gwynn and Campbell 313–326.

Gwynn, R. S. and Wanda Campbell, eds. <u>Literature</u>. Toronto: Longman, 2003.

- **encyclopedia and dictionary**

When encyclopedias and dictionaries list items alphabetically, you can omit volume and page numbers. It is sufficient to list the edition and year of publication.

"Democracy." <u>Columbia Encyclopedia</u>. 6th ed. 2005.

"Legitimate." <u>The Canadian Oxford Dictionary</u>. 2nd ed. 2004.

Periodicals

Last name, First name. "Title of Article." <u>Title of the Magazine or Newspaper</u> Date: Pages.

- **article in a magazine**

Geddes, Don. "Canadian Combat." <u>Maclean's</u> 20 March 2006: 21–22.

- **article in a newspaper**

Devlin, Keith. "Tied in Knots." <u>National Post</u> 7 Dec. 2006: A18.

- **editorial**

    If the editorial is signed, begin with the editor's name. If it is unsigned, begin with the title, followed by the word *Editorial*.

    > "Tax Freedom Day Is Here." Editorial. <u>Montreal Gazette</u> 27 June 2006: A16.

- **article in a journal**

    > Last name, First name. "Title of Article." <u>Title of Journal</u>
    >   Volume. Issue (Date): Pages.

    > Seligman, Martin. "The American Way of Blame." <u>APA Monitor</u> 29.7
    >   (1998): 97.

Electronic Sources Electronic sources include websites, information from subscription services, and reference databases. Electronic communications are frequently updated or moved, so keep track of the date you accessed a site. When using a source published on the Internet, include as much of the following information as you can find. Keep in mind that some sites do not contain complete information. Also, when you write the network address, break the address only at a slash mark.

> Last name, First name. "Title of Article." <u>Title of Site or Online</u>
>   <u>Publication</u>. Date of most recent update. Date you accessed
>   the site <Network Address>.

- **article on a personal website**

    > Krystek, Lee. "Crop Circles from Outer Space?" <u>Museum of</u>
    >   <u>Unnatural Mystery</u>. 16 May 2007 <http://www.unmuseum.org/
    >   cropcir.htm>.

- **article in an online periodical**

    If the site mentions the volume or page reference, include it. If not, include as much information as you can find.

    > Grossman, Lev and Richard Lacayo. "All-Time 100 Novels." <u>Time</u>.
    >   2005. 25 Apr. 2007 <http://www.time.com/time/2005/100books/
    >   the_complete_list.html>.

- **government site (or other sites without author information)**

    If the author is not mentioned on the site, begin with just the title and include as much information as you can find.

    > "The Canadian Refugee System." 2005. Citizenship and Immigration
    >   Canada. 28 May 2006 <http://www.cic.gc.ca/english/refugees/
    >   index.html>.

Other Types of Sources

- **interview that you conducted**

    > Kumar, Nantha. Personal interview. 14 Aug. 2007.

- **film or video**

    Include the name of the film, the director, the studio, and the year of release.

    > <u>Casablanca</u>. Dir. Michael Curtiz. 1942. DVD. Warner Brothers, 2003.

- **radio or television program**

    Include the segment title, the program name, the network, and the broadcast date.

    "Underdogs." <u>The National</u>. CBC. 8 Jan. 2006.

- **sound recording**

    Include the name of the performer or band, the title of the song, the title of the CD, the name of the recording company, and the year of release.

    McLachlan, Sarah. "Shelter." <u>Rarities, B-Sides, & Other Stuff</u>. Nettwerk, 1996.

HINT **Placement and Order of Works Cited**

The Works Cited list should be at the end of the research paper. List sources in alphabetical order of the author's last names. If there is no author, list the title (but ignore *A*, *An*, or *The* which may appear at the beginning of the title).

Bridgman, Rae. <u>Street Cities: Rehousing the Homeless</u>. Peterborough: Broadview Press, 2006.

- - -. <u>Safe Haven: The Story of a Shelter for Homeless Women</u>. Toronto: U of Toronto Press, 2003.

Fiscolanti, Michael. "The Whistle Blower." <u>Maclean's</u>. 20 February 2007.

<u>Godey's Lady's Book</u>. April 1850. 14 July 2006 <www.history.rochester.edu/godeys>.

Nova, Sylvia, et al. <u>Women on the Edge: A Decade of Change for Long-Term Homeless Women</u>. Ottawa: CMHC, 1999.

PRACTICE 3

Imagine that you are using the following sources in a research paper. Arrange the sources for a Works Cited list using MLA style.

- A print article by Shyman Selvaduri in <u>Toronto Life</u> magazine called "About a Boy," which was published in the March 2007 issue, and which appeared on pages 33 to 37.

- A book by Gwynne Dyer called <u>With Every Mistake</u> that was published by Random House Canada in Toronto, in 2005.

- A book called <u>Flashback: A Brief History of Film</u> written by Louis Giannetti and Scott Eyman. The book was published by Prentice Hall in Upper Saddle River, New Jersey, in 2006.

- A book called <u>War</u> by Gwynne Dyer and published by Vintage Canada, Toronto, in 2004.

- An article called "Behind the Diary" on the website <u>Library and Archives Canada</u>, which was created in 2002. You accessed the site on May 10, 2007. The web address is <http://www.collectionscanada.ca/king/ 053201/053201130601_e.html>. Although you have attempted to find more source information, you cannot find the author's name on the site.

Works Cited

_____

_____

_____

_____

_____

_____

_____

_____

_____

_____

_____

_____

Sample Research Essay

Title Pages and Outlines

Although MLA does not insist on a title page or an outline for a research essay, your instructor may recommend or request one or both. Include the following information on your title page.

Title
Your name
Your course
Professor's name
Date

To prepare a formal outline in MLA style, use the following format.

Thesis: Goya's message regarding his feelings on religious hypocrisy and the elevation of the common Spaniard are clearly visible in The Shootings of May 3, 1808.

I.   Context of the French occupation of Spain under Napoleon.
A. Much bloodshed
B. Spanish war of independence against oppression
C. Spanish patriotism and return of the monarchy

II. Unique and revolutionary techniques in painting
A. Limited colour palette
B. Brutally realistic
C. Lit central oval

III. The style has tremendous realism
A. Peasant figure is elevated to Christ-like status
B. Depicts the war as savage and brutal through the faceless members of the firing squad

IV. Religion is depicted without mercy
A. Peasant is martyr
B. Monks and monastery dark, sinister

Sample Research Essay Using MLA Style

Read a complete student essay. Notice how the student integrates paraphrases, summaries, and quotations.

Zachary Alapi
Mrs. Wheatcroft
ARH LFA 01
April 24, 2008

Goya's Greatest Work

Francisco José de Goya y Lucientes (1746–1828) is one of the most renowned and famous Spanish artists whose work has had a tremendous and lasting impact on the world of art. One of Goya's most famous paintings is titled <u>The Shootings of May 3, 1808</u>. It is an extremely powerful and evocative work that captures the brutality of the French occupation of Spain during the reign of Napoleon. There is little doubt that Goya's message regarding his feelings on religious hypocrisy and the elevation of the common Spaniard are clearly visible in <u>The Shootings of May 3, 1808</u>.

<u>The Shootings of May 3, 1808</u> was painted in the context of the French occupation of Spain under Napoleon. For the Spanish, this was a war of independence against the oppression and tyrannical rule of Napoleon, as well as an attempt to rid the country of the political corruption that was so rampant (Gassier and Wilson 205). Spanish guerrilla fighters launched attacks on French troops, which led to French firing squads killing captured Spanish guerrilla fighters (Alexander 194). The Spaniards killed at the hands of the firing squads became heroes and martyrs for the Spanish cause. In the work, Goya elevates the common Spaniard to a seemingly Christ-like status against the faceless, oppressive French soldiers.

The unique and revolutionary techniques in painting used by Goya throughout his career can be seen in <u>The Shootings of May 3, 1808</u>. Goya used a fairly limited colour palette and his scheme of light, shadow, line, and colour was generally subordinate to the cartoon-like subject matter (Myers 20). His aim seems to be to shock the viewer with a harsh and

Single space your name, ➤ *instructor's name, course title, and date.*

Centre the title. ➤ *(Notice that the title is not underlined, boldfaced, or put in quotation marks.)*

Double-space the body of ➤ *the essay.*

Acknowledge sources of ➤ *borrowed ideas.*

Place author's name and ➤ *page number in parentheses.*

Alapi 2

brutally realistic portrayal of the scene. Compositionally, "Goya seems
to have related his form in a positive way to the edge of the canvas or
wall area," which essentially means that the majority of the action in his
work takes place in a lit central oval surrounded by darkness, leaving
the corners of the canvas empty (Myers 24). This focus is important in the
context of the The Shootings of May 3, 1808 because the top half and
bottom right portion of the canvas are completely dark. "Both the night
and symmetrical composition of the subjects emphasize the drama"
("Goya"). The light, which shines specifically on the central peasant
figure, captures the attention of the viewer and places the emphasis on
what is happening to the peasant. This painting technique makes his
defiance toward the firing squad even more poignant and emphatic.

For Internet source, include title of site in parentheses.

Goya identified closely with the Spanish people, and through his
depiction of them in The Shootings of May 3, 1808, he shows how he shares
their sentiments (Lassaigne 96). Goya depicts "religion without mercy."
While the common peasant is the martyr, the monk cowers at his feet,
unable to stand up to the firing squad. Religion, which is supposed to
provide stability and courage for the people, is depicted as weak and not
carrying out its duties, forcing the peasant to stand up to the executioners.
Furthermore, the monastery in the background is shrouded in an
inauspicious darkness, which is juxtaposed by the light shining on a
central peasant figure, thereby suggesting that the courage of the common
man is to be celebrated, not the church, which is weak and hypocritical.

Common knowledge is not documented.

The Shootings of May 3, 1808 is a powerful and important painting
that explores the elevation of the common Spanish peasant to a
seemingly divine status and criticizes the hypocrisy of the church. The
realistic representation of the subject matter accentuates the emotions
and messages depicted. Through his brutally honest depiction of the
shootings, Goya conveys a sense of suffering, courage, and human
emotions by his glorification of the common man, who is the eternal
victim of war and its inhumanity.

Alapi 3

Works Cited

Centre the title of the ➤
Works Cited page.

Double-space sources. ➤

Alexander, Don. "French Replacement Methods During the Peninsular

War, 1808–1814." Military Affairs 44.4 (1980): 192–97.

Place sources in ➤
alphabetical order.

Gassier, Pierre and Juliet Wilson. The Life and Complete Work of

Francisco Goya. New York: Reynal, 1971.

"Goya." Spanish Arts. 22 Jan. 2007 <http://www.spanisharts.com/prado/

Indent second line ➤
of each source.

goya.htm>.

Lassaigne, Jacques. Spanish Painting from Velazquez to Picasso.

Cleveland: World Publishing, 1952.

Myers, Bernard. Goya. London: Spring Books, 1964.

Citing Sources Using APA Style

The American Psychological Association (APA) documentation style is commonly used in scientific or technical fields such as social sciences, economics, and nursing. Before you write a research essay for any course, ask your instructor which style he or she prefers.

> **HINT APA Website**
>
> To get some general information about some basic style questions, you can view the APA's website at **www.apastyle.org**. Use the menu on the left side of the page to direct you to specific style questions and answers.
> On the same website, there is a link to information about online or "electronic" sources. Because the information about online sources is continually being updated, the site has comprehensive information about the latest citing methods. Visit **www. apastyle.org/elecref.html**.

APA: In-Text Citations

Here are two basic options for inserting parenthetical citations in an APA-style research essay.

1. **Enclose the author(s), the publication year, and the page number(s) in parentheses.** Include the last name(s) of the source's author(s). For two authors, separate the authors' names using & (the ampersand sign). For three to five authors, give all names in the first instance; thereafter use *et al* after the first author's name. Follow with the publication year and then the page number or the page range where the material appears, using *p.* or *pp.* Separate the names, date, and page references with commas, and place the sentence's final period *after* the closing parenthesis.

Sometimes rioters lose control and "take out their anger and frustration on any individual" (Locher, 2002, p. 92).

A dozen men are responsible for the development of the movie camera (Giannetti & Eyman, 2006, p. 4).

2. **Introduce the source directly in the text.** When you include a short quotation within a sentence, place the publication year in parentheses immediately after you mention the author's name. Present the quotation, and then write the page number in parentheses immediately after it.

Sociologist David A. Locher (2002) explains, "Violent mobs often take out their anger and frustration on any individual" (p. 92).

As Giannettti and Eyman (2006) explained, a dozen men are responsible for the development of the movie camera (p. 4).

APA: Making a References List

Similar to the MLA Works Cited list, the APA References list gives details about each source you have used, and it appears at the end of your paper. Follow these basic guidelines to prepare References using the APA format.

1. Write "References" at the top of the page and centre it. Do not italicize it, underline it, or put quotation marks around it.

2. List each source alphabetically, using the last names of the authors.

3. Indent the second line and all subsequent lines of each reference 1.25 cm (one-half inch) from the left margin.

4. Double space the list.

HINT Writing the Author, Date, Title, and Place Using APA Style

Author
On the References page, write the complete last name and use the first and middle initials (if provided). Do not write complete first names.

Date
Put the date in parentheses immediately after the name. If you do not have the author's name, then put the date immediately after the title.

Title
Capitalize the first word in the title, the first word in the subtitle, and any proper nouns or adjectives in Reference lists. Do not add quotation marks or any other special marks around the titles of short works. Italicize titles of longer works such as books, newspapers, or magazines.

Place of Publication
Mention the name of the city and the postal abbreviation of the province or state, unless the city is a well-known publishing centre.

Complete Reference
Brainard, S. (2006). *A design manual.* Upper Saddle River, NJ: Prentice Hall.

Book

Carefully review the punctuation of the following example.

Last name, Initial(s). (date). *Title of the book.* City and Province or State of Publication: Publisher.

- **one author**

  Reverse the name of the author. Put the complete last name and the first initial.

  > Findley, T. (1982). *Famous last words*. Toronto, ON: Penguin.

- **two or more authors**

  Reverse the name of each author.

  > Ciccarelli, S. K., & Meyer, G. E. (2006). *Psychology*. Upper Saddle River, NJ: Prentice Hall.

- **book with an editor instead of an author**

  Put the editor's name followed by (Ed.).

  > Koppleman, S. (Ed.). (1984). *Old maids: Short stories by nineteenth-century US women writers*. Boston: Pandora Press.

- **two or more books by the same author**

  Include the author's name in all references. Arrange the works by year of publication, putting the earliest work first.

  > Atwood, M. (2006). *The tent*. New York: Doubleday.

  > Atwood, M. (1976). *Lady Oracle*. New York: Doubleday.

- **a work in an anthology**

  > Munroe, A. (2003). Boys and Girls. In R.S. Gwynn & W. Campbell (Eds.) *Literature* (pp. 313–326). Toronto: Longman.

- **encyclopedia and dictionary**

  > Democracy. (2005). In *Columbia encyclopedia* (6th ed.). New York: Columbia University Press.

  > Legitimate. (2004). In *The Canadian Oxford dictionary*. (2nd ed.). Toronto, ON: Oxford University Press.

Periodicals

> Last name, Initials. (Year, Month and day). Title of article. *Title of the Magazine or Newspaper, Volume number*, Pages.

- **article in a magazine**

  When citing newspapers or magazines, include as much of the following information as is available.

  > Shreeve, J. (2005, March). Beyond the brain. *National Geographic, 207*, 2–31.

- **article in a newspaper**

  > Devlin, K. (2006, December 7). Tied in knots. *National Post*, p. A18.

- **article in a journal**

  > Last name, Initials. (Year, Month).Title of article. *Title of Journal. Volume*(Issue), Pages.

  > Seligman, M. (1998). The American way of blame. *APA Monitor, 29*(7), 97.

Electronic Sources If the source was published on the Internet, include as much of the following information as you can find. Keep in mind that some sites do not contain complete source information.

> Last name, Initials. (date of most recent update). Title of article. *Title of Site or Online Publication.* Retrieved date, from http:// site_address.html

- **article on a personal website**

    Krystek, L. (2006). Crop circles from outer space? *Museum of unnatural mystery.* Retrieved May 16, 2007, from http://www. unmuseum.org/cropcir.htm

- **article in an online journal**

    If the site mentions the volume or page reference, include it. If not, put in as much information as you can find.

    Grossman, L., & Lacayo, R. (2005). All-time 100 novels. *Time.* Retrieved May 25, 2006, from http://www.time.com/time/2005/ 100books the_complete_list.html

- **government site**

    Begin with the complete name of the government agency, followed by the date and title.

    Citizenship and Immigration Canada. (2006). The Canadian refugee system. Retrieved May 28, 2006, from http://www.cic.gc.ca/ english/refugees/ index.html

Other Types of Sources

- **interview that you conducted**

    In APA style, do not include a personal interview in your References list. In the actual text, just include the parenthetical notation (personal communication).

- **film or video**

    Curtiz, M. (Director). (2003). *Casablanca.* [DVD]. United States: Warner Brothers. (Original movie released 1942).

- **sound recording**

    McLachlan, S. (1996). Shelter. On *Rarities, B-sides, & other stuff* [CD]. Vancouver, BC: Nettwerk.

PRACTICE 4

Imagine that you are using the following sources in a research paper. Arrange the sources for a References page using APA style.

- A print article by Shyman Selvaduri in *Toronto Life* magazine called "About a Boy," which was published in the March 2007 issue, and which appeared on pages 33 to 37.
- A book by Gwynne Dyer called *With Every Mistake* that was published by Random House Canada in Toronto, in 2005.

- A book called *Flashback: A Brief History of Film* written by Louis Giannetti and Scott Eyman. The book was published by Prentice Hall in Upper Saddle River, New Jersey, in 2006.
- A book called *War* by Gwynne Dyer and published by Vintage Canada, Toronto, in 2004.
- An article called "Behind the Diary" on the website Library and Archives Canada, which was created in 2002. You accessed the site on May 10, 2007. The web address is <http://www.collectionscanada.ca/king/053201/053201130601_e.html>. Although you have attempted to find more source information, you cannot find the author's name on the site.

References

_____

_____

_____

_____

_____

_____

_____

_____

_____

_____

 Writer's Room   **Research Essay Topics**

Writing Activity 1

Write a research paper about one of the following topics. Ask your instructor what reference style you should use. Put a Works Cited (MLA) or References (APA) page at the end of your assignment.

1. Write about a contemporary issue that is in the news.
2. Write about any issue in your career choice or field of study.

Writing Activity 2

Write a research paper about one of the following topics. First, brainstorm questions about your topic and then find a guiding research question. Then follow the process of writing a research essay.

Abortion	Holistic healing
Affirmative action	Home schooling
Assisted suicide	Immigration
Attention deficit disorder	Legalization of marijuana
Body image	Necessity of military intervention
Carpal tunnel syndrome	Prison reform
Censorship of the Internet	Privacy and the Internet
Date rape	Response to terrorism
Election reform	Same-sex marriage
Executive salaries	Sperm-donor rights
Fast food	Tobacco industry
Foreign adoptions	Consequences of war
Genetically modified food	Waste disposal
Government-sponsored gambling	Youth gangs
Health-care reform	Violence in the media

 CHECKLIST : RESEARCH ESSAY

When you plan a research essay, ask yourself these questions.

☐ Have I narrowed my topic?

☐ Have I created a guiding research question?

☐ Are my sources reliable?

☐ Have I organized my notes?

☐ Have I integrated source information using quotations, paraphrases, and summaries?

☐ Have I correctly documented my in-text or parenthetical citations?

☐ Have I correctly prepared and punctuated my Works Cited page or References list?

Submit your best essays for possible publication to **thewritersworld@prenhall.com**.

Becoming a Successful Student

CHAPTER 17

Being prepared is the best way to reduce exam anxiety.

—ADELE BERRIDGE, *instructor*

Preparing for Exams

All courses in educational institutions measure how much students understand a subject through different forms of evaluation, including oral presentations and essay exams. Learning and practising effective study habits early on will help you achieve success in your college courses.

Here are two tips every student should remember:

- **Do not procrastinate.** If you know that an assignment is due on a given date, then give yourself enough time to complete it. You may want to finish the assignment a couple of days ahead of time so that you will have time to reread it with a fresh eye and make any revisions necessary. If you know that you have a test in a couple of weeks, give yourself enough time to study. Do not wait until the last minute and cram because you may be unable to retain the information that you need.

- **Balance your college, home, and career lives.** If you put too much emphasis on your college career, you may feel stressed or anxious about passing or failing. Such stress will not help you to achieve good grades. If you put too much emphasis on your social life, you may realize too late in the semester that you are failing certain courses. Maintain equilibrium in your life so that you remain motivated to achieve success in your studies.

PRACTICE 1

Write a short paragraph explaining what kind of study habits you have. Be honest with yourself and support your description with specific examples. Then read the rest of this chapter to see how you can develop better study skills.

_____

_____

_____

_____

_____

_____

_____

_____

_____

Take Two Types of Class Notes

Having effective notes will make studying for tests and exams easier. When you take notes, record the primary and secondary ideas of a subject. Always keep notes for each course in a separate binder, or use a binder with dividers so that each subject has its own space. Here are strategies for taking both textbook and lecture notes.

Textbook Notes

- Read the text carefully and underline any key words or phrases.
- Use a dictionary to understand the definitions of unfamiliar words.
- Give a title to your notes. It could just be the chapter of your textbook, or it could be the name of the subject.
- Rewrite all primary and secondary ideas in your own words. (Chapter 15 gives you guidelines on how to paraphrase and summarize.)
- Review your notes to verify that you have understood the key concepts of the text.

Lecture Notes

- Complete all homework and reading assignments before class. Most lecturers use homework reading assignments as a springboard to transmit new concepts.
- Bring your notebook, textbooks, and pens to class. You will need these to take notes and refer to concepts the instructor is explaining.
- Listen carefully. An instructor often gives clues to critical information using statements such as "and most importantly . . ." or "remember to consider . . .".
- Write only the key words or phrases, and use symbols or abbreviations. You probably will not have time to write complete sentences.

- Ask your instructor to repeat what you do not hear or understand. If you have not caught the information, chances are great that others in your class have not either. If it would be inappropriate to interrupt the lecture, put a mark beside the concept to remind yourself to get clarification from the instructor or a classmate later.

- Date your notes. You will want a record of when you wrote them during the semester. The dates might help you to know what to focus on while you are studying.

HINT **Using Abbreviations**

Many abbreviations we use in English derive from Latin terms. Here are some abbreviations to help you take notes more efficiently.

Abbreviation	English	Latin
e.g.	for example	exempli gratia
etc.	and so on	et cetera
i.e.	in other words	id est
N.B.	important	Nota Bene
vs., v.	against	versus

Keep in mind that these abbreviations are useful for note taking. When you write an essay, use the complete English words, not the abbreviations.

Sharpen Your Study Skills

Here are some guidelines for studying effectively.

- **Take meaningful notes.** Follow the previous note-taking tips to learn how to summarize and synthesize the key concepts of an article, textbook, or lecture.

- **Review course material.** Cramming is an ineffective, short-term strategy for college success. Reviewing your course material *regularly*, perhaps every second day or each week, will ensure that you know your subjects well.

- **Organize study time.** Decide regular study times and write your study plan in your agenda. Be strict with yourself and always spend that time studying. As little as thirty minutes a day could be sufficient to become familiar with the subject matter.

- **Ask questions.** All college instructors are available outside class hours. Make regular appointments with your instructor and prepare questions about concepts that you do not understand. Waiting until the day before your exam will be too late.

- **Study with a classmate or friend.** Set a particular time each week, which will motivate you to study during times when you want to do something else. Ask each other questions on key concepts or proofread each other's written work.

HINT **Predict Exam Questions**

An effective study strategy is to predict possible exam questions.

- Look for important themes in your course outline.
- Study your notes and try to analyze what information is of particular importance.
- Look at previous exams for the course. Determine if any questions or subjects are repeated in more than one exam.

Writing Essay Exams

In many of your courses, you will have to answer exam questions with a paragraph or essay. Instructors feel that this type of exam allows you to reveal your understanding of the topic. Although taking any exam can be stressful, you can reduce exam anxiety and increase your chances of doing well by following some of the preparation and exam-writing strategies outlined in this chapter.

Schedule Your Time

Before you write the exam, find out exactly how much time you have, and then plan how much time you will need to answer the questions. For example, if you have a one-hour exam, and you have three questions worth the same value, try to spend no more than twenty minutes on each question.

Determine Point Values

As soon as you get an exam, scan the questions and determine which questions have a larger value. For example, you might respond to the questions with the largest point value first, or you might begin with those that you understand well. Then go to the more difficult questions. If you are blocked on a certain answer, skip to another question, and then go back to that question later.

Carefully Read the Exam Questions

In an exam question, every word counts. Here are two ways you can read actively.

1. Identify Key Words and Phrases When you read an exam question, underline or circle key words and phrases to understand exactly what you are supposed to do. In the next example of an essay question, the underlined words highlight two different tasks.

<u>Explain</u> what is meant by neocolonialism and

1. Define the term neocolonialism.

2. Explain how neocolonialism affects both rich and poor countries.

<u>analyze how it influences the economies of rich and poor.</u>

2. Examine Common Question Words Exam questions direct you using verbs (action words). The following chart gives you several common words that you will find in essay-style questions.

Verb	Meaning
describe discuss review	Examine a subject as thoroughly as possible. Focus on the main points.
narrate trace	Describe the development or progress of something using time order.
evaluate explain your point of view interpret justify take a stand	State your opinion and give reasons to support your opinion. In other words, write an argument essay.
analyze criticize classify	Explain something carefully by breaking it down into smaller parts.
enumerate list outline	Go through important facts one by one.
compare contrast distinguish	Discuss important similarities and/or differences.
define explain what is meant by . . .	Give a complete and accurate definition that demonstrates your understanding of the concept.
explain causes explain effects explain a process summarize illustrate	Analyze the reasons for an event. Analyze the consequences or results of an event. Explain the steps needed to do a task. Write down the main points from a larger piece of work. Demonstrate your understanding by giving examples.

PRACTICE 2

Write the letter of the correct key word in the space provided.

EXAMPLE

1. Explain how the gross national product (GNP) of a country is calculated. _____

2. Explain the events that led to the end of World War I. _____

3. Illustrate alternative energy sources. _____

4. Distinguish between universal health care and privatized medicine. _____

5. Discuss whether euthanasia should be legalized. _____

6. Explain what utilitarianism is. _____

KEY WORD

a. compare and contrast
b. define
c. explain a process
d. argue
e. explain causes
f. give examples

PRACTICE 3

The following sample has been taken from an essay exam. Read the instructions and then answer the questions that follow the sample.

Essay Exam

Answer both Parts A and B. You will have two hours to complete the evaluation.

A. Define two of the following terms. (5 points each)
1. democracy
2. electorate
3. communism
4. industrial revolution
5. gerrymandering

B. Write a well-structured essay on one of the following topics. (20 points)
1. Distinguish between panic and mass hysteria. Can governments ever benefit from either of these phenomena?
2. Evaluate the usefulness of sanctions imposed by Western nations against North Korea.
3. Trace the rise of National Socialism in Germany in the 1930s.

---

1. What is the total point value of the exam? _____

2. Which part of the exam would you do first? Explain why. _____

   _____

3. How much time would you spend on Part A and on Part B? Why? _____

   _____

4. How many definitions and essays should you write? _____

   _____

5. In Part B, which two questions would be answered with an
   argument essay? _____

   _____

Follow the Writing Process

Treat an essay exam as you would any other writing assignment by following the three main steps of the writing process.

Explore　　　■ Jot down any ideas that you think can help you answer the question. Try the prewriting activities suggested in Chapter 1 of this book, such as brainstorming or clustering. Prewriting will help you generate some ideas for your essay.

Develop　　　■ Use the exam question to guide your **topic sentences** and **thesis statement**.

- List supporting ideas, organize your ideas using an essay plan or outline, and then write an essay. Remember to include an introduction with a clear thesis statement and to use transitions such as *first*, *moreover*, or *in addition* to link your ideas.

Revise and Edit
- Read over your essay to verify that all ideas support the thesis statement and to ensure that you have adequate details to support your topic sentences. Also check your spelling, punctuation, and mechanics.

PRACTICE 4

Write a thesis statement for the following questions.

EXAMPLE:

Discuss the influences of the industrial revolution on class structure.

Thesis statement: *The industrial revolution caused a dramatic change in the means of production and transformed traditional class structure.*

1. Explain your point of view on poverty.

   Thesis statement: _____

   _____

2. Distinguish between a religion and a cult.

   Thesis statement: _____

   _____

3. Analyze the effects of globalization on world culture.

   Thesis statement: _____

   _____

PRACTICE 5

College student Seokman Chang wrote the following essay for an exam. Read the essay and answer the questions that follow.

1   Throughout human history, there have been migratory movements of people all over the world. The Polynesians journeyed and stayed in the Hawaiian Islands, the Vikings found homes in Great Britain and Ireland, and the Moguls came and settled in India. Today, the migration trend continues. People migrate to different parts of the world for many reasons and often bring with them benefits to the host region or country.

2   First, many people go to different countries searching for better work opportunities. For example, many groups of professionals migrate to get higher-paying jobs. There are engineers, teachers, lawyers, and computer

specialists who have come to this country to broaden their skills and work experience. One day, in a supermarket line-up, I had a conversation with a woman from China. She and her husband had just arrived in this country. They were both doctors and were preparing to take the qualifying exams. The woman was very excited about being able to continue her career. She felt that she would grow professionally. Unskilled labourers also come to North America because the pay for such jobs is higher than in their homeland. A factory worker usually earns more per hour in an industrialized country than in a developing country. Most skilled and unskilled economic migrants come to new lands seeking a better quality of life.

3   Second, sometimes immigrants leave their homelands unwillingly. They may be forced to leave their homes because of famine or war. For example, many Africans have migrated from one region or country to another for both reasons. There is drought in the sub-Saharan countries and war in Congo, Darfur, Somalia, and other areas. Furthermore, often people are expelled from their homeland. In 1972, the Ugandan dictator Idi Amin expelled the Indian community. They had very little time to pack up and leave. China and other countries have expelled some political activists, while other activists have fled for their lives, claiming political refugee status.

4   Moreover, some people leave their native lands to join family members who have already immigrated. Such cases are especially true of new immigrants. Often first-generation immigrants arrive in the new country alone. When they have settled, they send for their immediate family members. My neighbour came from Vietnam about ten years ago. For the first few years, he was in this country alone. He worked during the day and took night courses. As soon as he got settled, he sent for his parents because they were getting older and had no one to take care of them in Vietnam. Now the family is together again.

5   The receiving country gains many advantages from immigrants. New groups add to the cultural diversity of the country. For example, new immigrants bring their language, culture, and traditions with them. North American cities have a variety of ethnic restaurants, grocery stores, and cultural festivals. In addition, Western countries need immigrants to maintain or increase the population. The birth rates of most Western countries are falling and immigrants are needed to maintain population rates. New immigrants also bring skills that are advantageous to the host country. New immigrants perform many varied jobs, from doctors and engineers to fruit pickers and waiters. Immigrants contribute to the economy of the host country.

6   People leave their homelands for a variety of reasons and their adopted countries gain tremendously from migration. The migrant usually finds a more stable and prosperous life. The adopted countries of new immigrants gain tremendously in social and economic areas. A country that is multicultural is vibrant and flourishing. So the next time you eat at your favourite Italian restaurant, read a novel by Rohinton Mistry, or watch a movie directed by Atom Egoyan, remember that immigration made it all possible.

1. This student essay is an answer to which of the following questions? Circle the best possible answer.

    a. Distinguish the periods of immigration to North America and describe the migrant groups.

    b. Evaluate the current immigration policy of the nation.

    c. Explain why people immigrate and some consequences of their migration.

2. Deconstruct this essay by making an informal essay plan. For the details, just use words or phrases.

Thesis statement: _____

Topic sentence 1: _____

Details: _____

_____

Topic sentence 2: _____

Details: _____

_____

Topic sentence 3: _____

Details: _____

_____

Topic sentence 4: _____

Details: _____

_____

 Writer's Room **Essay Exam Topics**

Writing Activity

1. Predict at least three essay exam questions for one of your courses. Then develop an informal essay plan for one of the questions.
2. Look at an older exam that you completed. Write a paragraph explaining what you should have done to receive a higher mark.

 CHECKLIST: ESSAY EXAM

As you prepare for your essay exam, ask yourself these questions.

▢ Have I taken clear notes during lectures?

▢ Have I reviewed my notes on a regular basis?

▢ Have I organized study time?

▢ Have I asked my instructor questions when I didn't understand a concept?

▢ Have I asked my instructor about the types of questions on the exam?

▢ Have I asked my instructor what material the exam will cover?

Editing Handbook

When you speak, you have tools such as tone of voice and body language to help you express your ideas. When you write, however, you have only words and punctuation to get your message across. Naturally, if your writing contains errors in style, grammar, and punctuation, you may distract readers from your message, and they may focus, instead, on your inability to communicate clearly. You increase your chances of succeeding in your academic and professional life when you write in clear, standard English.

The chapters in this Editing Handbook can help you understand and correct important grammar concepts. Before you begin, review the following themes, which can help you to think about key grammar topics in different ways.

Section 1: Effective Sentences

Theme: Conflict

During times of conflict, competing groups can sit together, share ideas, and seek resolutions to the conflict. By combining various perspectives, perhaps a truce can be attained. In the next chapters, you will learn to combine sentences to make your writing more appealing.

Section 2: Common Sentence Errors

Theme: Urban Development

When an architect makes a mistake, the resulting building can have serious faults. For example, when architects planned and built the Tower of Pisa, they did not take into account the poor soil conditions and the inadequate depth of the foundation. In the same way, a sentence needs to be constructed properly to provide the reader with a complete picture.

Section 3: Verbs

Theme: International Trade

To operate properly, the pieces of a machine must fit together perfectly. If a bolt is missing, or if a piece is not the right size, the machine will malfunction. In the same way, for a sentence to be complete, the parts of the sentence must fit together properly. For example, the subject and verb must agree.

Section 4: More Parts of Speech

Theme: Forces of Nature

During storms, lighthouses transmit signals to passing ships to guide them through dangerous waters. In sentences, certain parts of speech act as signals. If the wrong part of speech is used, the sentence may not transmit a clear signal.

Section 5: Word Use and Spelling

Theme: Flora and Fauna

To preserve endangered types of insects, entomologists must make accurate analyses of population sizes, habitats, and food sources. In the same way, when you write, you should carefully examine your text to ensure that your spelling and choice of words are accurate.

Section 6: Punctuation and Mechanics

Theme: Human Development and Creativity

A musical piece has bridges that link the sections within a movement together. In the same way, a sentence has punctuation that links parts together.

18

Identifying Subjects and Verbs

CONFLICT **Is behaviour learned or genetic? In this chapter, you will learn about the sources of aggressive behaviour.**

CHAPTER CONTENTS

- Identifying Subjects
- Identifying Verbs

GRAMMAR SNAPSHOT **Looking at Subjects and Verbs**

Psychologist Ken Low has given seminars on dealing with aggression. In the following excerpt from a seminar, he discusses the source of anger. Notice that subjects are in bold and verbs are underlined. Also observe that some sentences have no visible subjects.

<u>Understand</u> the source of your anger. <u>Examine</u> your feelings of unhappiness. In my case, the **cause** of the unhappiness <u>was</u> my sense of worthlessness. **Everyone** <u>was succeeding</u>, in my mind, and **I** <u>was</u> not. **I** <u>wanted</u> to blame my boss, my parents, or my wife. **I** <u>was prepared</u> to blame anybody and anything outside of myself. **Recognizing** my unhappiness <u>gave</u> me insight into the source of my anger. **I** <u>held</u> a mistaken conviction: the **world** <u>owed</u> me a good life.

In this chapter, you will identify subjects and verbs.

Identifying Subjects

A **sentence** contains one or more subjects and verbs, and it expresses a complete thought. The **subject** tells you who or what the sentence is about. A **verb** expresses an action or state. If a sentence is missing a subject or a verb, it is incomplete. You will use your ability to identify subjects and verbs in the editing process.

- Subjects may be **singular** or **plural**. A subject can also be a **pronoun**. To determine the subject of a sentence, ask yourself who or what the sentence is about. It may be about a person, place, or thing.

  Detective Marcos will interview the suspects.
  Many **factors** cause people to break laws.
  It is an important case.

- A **compound subject** contains two or more subjects joined by *and*, *or*, or *nor*.

    Reporters and **photographers** were outside the prison gates.

- Sometimes a **gerund** (*-ing* form of the verb) is the subject of a sentence.

    Listening is an important skill.

HINT   Here and There

Here and *There* are not subjects. In sentences that begin with *Here* or *There*, the subject follows the verb.

   There are several **ways** to find a criminal.
   Here is an interesting **brochure** about the police academy.

How to Find the Subject

To find the subject, ask yourself *who* or *what* the sentence is about. The **simple subject** is the noun or pronoun, or the name of a person or organization.

   The **Royal Canadian Mounted Police** is a large organization. **It** has branches in every province.

   When you are identifying the subject, you can ignore words that describe the noun.

                    adjectives   subject
   The pompous and rude **sergeant** left the room.

PRACTICE I

Circle the subject in each sentence. Sometimes there will be more than one simple subject.

EXAMPLE: A behavioural (study) examines genetics and behaviour.

1. Research psychiatrist Carl E. Schwartz works in the Department of Psychiatry at Massachusetts General Hospital.

2. He conducted a study to determine hereditary factors in behaviour.

3. There were over one hundred children in his study.

4. Infants and toddlers were classed into two groups.

5. Objects, strange people, and unfamiliar settings were used to test the children.

6. Talking was not permitted.

7. The outgoing toddlers easily interacted in new surroundings.

8. The inhibited children were more likely to show signs of stress in unfamiliar surroundings.

Prepositional Phrases

A **preposition** is a word that links nouns, pronouns, and phrases to other words in a sentence. It expresses a relationship based on movement, motion, or position. A **prepositional phrase** is made up of a preposition and its object (a noun or a pronoun).

Because the object of a preposition is a noun, it may look like a subject. **However, the object in a prepositional phrase is never the subject of the sentence.**

Section 1
**EFFECTIVE
SENTENCES**

          prepositional phrase   subject

<u>With the parents' approval</u>, the **experiment** began.

HINT **Using "of the"**

In most expressions containing *of the*, the subject appears before *of the*.

    subject

    Each (of the parents) agreed to participate.
    One (of the fathers) was uncomfortable with the process.

Common Prepositions

about	below	in	outside
above	beside	inside	over
across	between	into	through
after	beyond	like	to
against	by	near	toward
along	despite	of	under
among	down	off	until
around	during	on	up
at	except	onto	with
before	for	out	within
behind	from		

To help you identify the subject, put parentheses around prepositional phrases. In each of the following examples, the prepositional phrase is in parentheses. Notice that a sentence can contain more than one prepositional phrase.

(In spite of the storm), **they** drove to the hospital.

The **clinic**, (after 1971), expanded greatly.

(In the late 1990s), (during a period of cost cutting), high-tech **cameras** were placed in the room.

PRACTICE 2

Circle the subject in each sentence. Place any prepositional phrases near the subject in parentheses.

EXAMPLE: **(**For many years**),** (Schwartz) has studied genetics and behaviour.

1. In Schwartz's study, half of the babies were classified as shy. The others in the group were classified as outgoing. In unfamiliar surroundings, the shy and outgoing children reacted differently. For example, in the presence of a stranger, the shy toddlers would freeze. The outgoing toddlers would approach the stranger and interact.

2. The differences in reactions occurred in their heart rate, in the dilation of their pupils, and in the levels of the stress hormone, cortisone. Generally, the differences in the temperament of children persisted to adulthood.

3. After the first study, Carl Schwartz tracked down twenty-two of the original subjects. About one-third of the uninhibited adults showed impulsive and aggressive behaviour. Some of the shy children became extremely shy adults. However, not all outgoing infants become bold or aggressive adults. In fact, most individuals in the study did not develop behavioural problems.

Section 1
EFFECTIVE SENTENCES

Identifying Verbs

Every sentence must contain a verb. The **verb** expresses what the subject does, or it links the subject to other descriptive words.

An **action verb** describes an action that a subject performs.

Detective Rowland <u>attended</u> a seminar in Sudbury. He <u>spoke</u> to some officials.

A **linking verb** connects a subject with words that describe it, and it does not show an action. The most common linking verb is *be*, but other common linking verbs are *appear*, *become*, *look*, and *seem*.

Kim Rossmo <u>is</u> a former detective. His methods <u>seem</u> reliable.

When a subject performs more than one action, the verbs are called **compound verbs**.

In 2003, Rossmo <u>wrote</u> and <u>spoke</u> about his methods.

Helping Verbs

The **helping verb** combines with the main verb to indicate tense, negative structure, or question structure. The most common helping verbs are forms of *be*, *have*, and *do*. **Modal auxiliaries** are another type of helping verb, and they indicate ability (*can*), obligation (*must*), and so on. For example, here are different forms of the verb *ask*, and the helping verbs are underlined.

<u>is</u> asking	<u>had</u> asked	<u>will</u> ask	<u>should have</u> asked
<u>was</u> asked	<u>had been</u> asking	<u>can</u> ask	<u>might be</u> asked
<u>has been</u> asking	<u>would</u> ask	<u>could be</u> asking	<u>could have been</u> asked

The **complete verb** is the helping verb and the main verb. In the following examples, the main verb is double underlined. In **question forms**, the first helping verb usually appears before the subject.

> Criminal profiling techniques <u>have been <u>spreading</u></u> across the continent. <u>Should</u> the detective <u>have <u>studied</u></u> the files?

Interrupting words such as *often*, *always*, *ever*, and *actually* are not part of the verb.

> Rossmo <u>has</u> often <u>returned</u> to Vancouver.

HINT **Infinitives Are Not the Main Verb**

Infinitives are verbs preceded by *to* such as *to fly*, *to speak*, and *to go*. An infinitive is never the main verb in a sentence.

infinitive

The network <u>wanted</u> **to produce** a show about geographic profiling.

PRACTICE 3

In each sentence, circle the subject and underline the complete verb. Remember to underline the helping verbs as well as the main verbs. You can place prepositional phrases in parentheses.

EXAMPLE:

(According to Professor Saundra K. Ciccarelli), many (factors) <u>contribute</u> to aggressive behaviour.

1. The amygdala is located near the base of the brain. Studies have shown the amygdala's role in fear responses. In a 1939 experiment, the temporal lobe was removed from the brains of several monkeys. The lobe contains the amygdala. After the surgery, the monkeys showed absolutely no fear of snakes and humans. This anecdote illustrates the role of the brain in fearful or aggressive behaviour.

2. Why do people harm others? In her book *Psychology*, Ciccarelli discusses the connection between the brain and aggressive behaviour. She gives an example of a specific case. In 1966, Charles Whitman shot and killed fourteen people. Before his death in a shootout with police, Whitman wrote a note and asked doctors to examine the state of his brain. In fact, a later examination revealed the presence of a tumour next to his amygdala.

3. There are also chemical links to aggression, according to Ciccarelli. Testosterone, in high levels, has been shown to cause aggressive behaviour. Also, certain substances have an impact on the brain. Alcohol affects the amount of some brain chemicals and reduces a person's inhibitions.

FINAL REVIEW

Circle the subjects and underline the complete verbs in the following sentences. Underline <u>all</u> parts of the verb. To avoid misidentifying subjects, you can place prepositional phrases in parentheses.

EXAMPLE:

(One) (of the most interesting influences on behaviour) <u>is</u> social roles.

1. Many psychologists and social scientists believe in the importance of social roles on behaviour. Thus, children can be influenced by aggressive characters on television. Young adults may be pressured or manipulated by peers. Basically, people can learn to be aggressive.

2. Most interesting of all, people of all ages can modify their behaviour due to their social roles. Psychologist Philip Zimbardo demonstrated the importance of social roles in his prison experiment at Stanford University. He recruited about seventy volunteers and gave half of them guard roles and the other half prisoner roles. Many volunteers in the guard roles exhibited violent behaviour. Other volunteers in the prisoner roles became meek. Therefore, the behaviour of the students changed due to their roles.

3. History is filled with examples of people behaving badly, often during times of conflict. Soldiers, especially, are in stressful situations and fulfill the obligations of their roles. The prison abuse scandal at Abu Ghraib in Iraq is a real-life example. Prison guards beat and humiliated prisoners. Why did the guards act so cruelly? According to psychologists, a uniform and a specific social role have powerful influences on people's behaviour.

 Writer's Room   **Topics for Writing**

Write about one of the following topics. After you finish writing, identify your subjects and verbs.

1. List various ways in which social roles influence people's behaviour. Support your points with specific examples.
2. Some experts suggest that personality traits are partly inherited. Are your character traits similar to a family member's traits? Compare and contrast yourself with someone else in your family.

✔ CHECKLIST: SUBJECTS AND VERBS

Review this chapter's main points.

To identify **subjects**, look for words that tell you who or what the sentence is about.

To identify **verbs**, look for words that do the following:

   action verbs describe the actions that the subject performs.

   linking verbs describe a state of being or link the subject with descriptive words.

   helping verbs combine with the main verb to indicate tense, negative structure, or question structure.

To identify **prepositional phrases**, look for words that consist of a preposition and its object. Note: the object of a prepositional phrase cannot be the subject.

prepositional phrase   subject   verb
In spite of criticism, the police chief has released the suspect.
                                            helping verb

Sentence Combining

19

CHAPTER

CHAPTER CONTENTS

GRAMMAR SNAPSHOT Looking at Compound and Complex Sentences

The next excerpt is from Criminal Justice Today *by Frank Schmalleger. The underlined sections are called dependent clauses. Why do you think the clauses are called dependent?*

Defendants may choose to be represented in Chinese courts by an attorney, a relative, or a friend, or they may choose to represent themselves. <u>If they desire</u>, a lawyer will be appointed for them. [. . .] <u>While they work to protect the rights of the defendant</u>, attorneys have a responsibility to the court. Defence lawyers are charged with helping the court render a verdict.

In this chapter, you will identify and write complex sentences.

Understanding Key Terms

When you use sentences of varying lengths and types, your writing flows more smoothly and appears more interesting. You can vary sentences and create relationships between ideas by combining sentences.

Before you learn about the types of sentences, it is important to understand some key terms.

A **phrase** is a group of words that is missing a subject, a verb, or both, and is not a complete sentence.

in the morning

acting on her own

the excited witness

A **clause** is a group of words that contains a subject and a verb. There are two types of clauses.

- An **independent clause** is a complete sentence. It stands alone and expresses one complete idea.

    The victims asked for compensation.

- A **dependent clause** has a subject and verb, but it cannot stand alone. It "depends" on another clause to be complete. A dependent clause usually begins with a subordinator such as *after*, *although*, *because*, *unless*, and *when*.

    Because they had lost a lot of money,. . .

    . . . because they had lost a lot of money.

PRACTICE 1

Write S next to each complete sentence. If the group of words is not a complete sentence—perhaps it is a phrase or a dependent clause—then write X in the blank.

EXAMPLE:

Circumstantial evidence is sometimes discounted.   _S_

Although it may be reliable.   _X_

1. Circumstantial evidence is often very reliable.   ____

2. Blood, for example.   ____

3. It may match with the DNA of the victim.   ____

4. Pieces of clothing, hair fibres, and other types of evidence.   ____

5. Such evidence is usually very good.   ____

6. Unless somebody altered the evidence.   ____

7. A credit card may place a criminal at the crime scene.   ____

8. Although the suspect may have an alibi.   ____

Making Compound Sentences

Combining Sentences Using Coordinating Conjunctions

A **coordinating conjunction** joins two complete ideas and indicates the connection between them. The most common coordinating conjunctions are *for*, *and*, *nor*, *but*, *or*, *yet*, and *so*.

complete idea	coordinating conjunction	complete idea

The detective collected the evidence, **and** the lab analyzed it.

Review the following chart showing coordinating conjunctions and their functions.

Conjunction	Function	Example
and	to join two ideas	Anna went to school, **and** she became a forensics expert.
but	to contrast two ideas	The courses were difficult, **but** she passed them all.
for	to indicate a reason	She worked very hard, **for** she was extremely motivated.
nor	to indicate a negative idea	The work was not easy, **nor** was it pleasant.
or	to offer an alternative	She will work for a police department, **or** she will work for a private lab.
so	to indicate a cause-effect relationship	She has graduated, **so** she will look for work.
yet	to introduce a surprising choice	She wants to stay in her town, **yet** the best jobs are in a nearby city.

Section 1
**EFFECTIVE
SENTENCES**

> **HINT   Recognizing Compound Sentences**
>
> To be sure that a sentence is compound, place your finger over the coordinator, and then ask yourself if the two clauses are complete sentences. In compound sentences, always place a comma before the coordinator.
>
> **Simple:** The witness was nervous **but** very convincing.
>
> **Compound:** The witness was nervous, **but** she was very convincing.

PRACTICE 2

Insert coordinating conjunctions in the blanks. Choose from the following list, and try to use a variety of coordinators. (There may be more than one answer for some sentences.)

but   or   yet   so   for   and   nor

EXAMPLE:

In 1969, the FBI introduced criminal profiling as an investigative strategy, _and_ it has been quite successful.

1. Kim Rossmo is a renowned geographic profiler, _____ he is also

   an excellent detective. In the early 1990s, Detective Rossmo could work

   in Canada, _____ he could take a job in the United States. The

Vancouver Police Department did not try to keep Rossmo,
_____ he moved south.

2. Rossmo examines the movements of criminals, _____ he
searches for specific patterns. According to Rossmo, criminals attack
places they know, _____ they generally don't work in their own
neighbourhoods. Most people don't want to travel long distances for
their jobs, _____ they are lazy. Criminals work the same way,
_____ they stay relatively close to home.

3. Rossmo developed a fascinating mathematical formula, _____
many police departments were skeptical about his ideas. He tried to
convince others, _____ he believed strongly in his computer
program. Basically, he inputs the addresses of suspects into a computer,
_____ he also inputs details about the crime scenes. His
program can process a fifteen-square-kilometre area, _____ it
looks for a "hot" area. Suspects may live directly in the centre of the hot
area, _____ they may live within a few blocks.

4. For example, in the late 1990s, there were several sexual assaults in a
town in Ontario, Canada, _____ Rossmo and his associates
created a profile map. One particular suspect's home was compared to
the location of the crime scenes, _____ it was placed in
Rossmo's computer program. Originally, the main offender's name was
low on a list of 316 suspects, _____ it rose to number 6 on the
list after the profiling. The suspect did not admit his guilt,
_____ other evidence tied him to the crime scenes. He was
eventually tried and convicted for the crimes, _____ he went to
prison.

GRAMMAR LINK

For more practice using
semicolons, see
Chapter 22, Run-Ons.

Combining Sentences Using Semicolons (;)

Another way to form a compound sentence is to join two complete ideas with a
semicolon. The semicolon replaces a coordinating conjunction.

complete idea	;	complete idea

The eyewitness was certain; she pointed at the suspect.

Section 1
**EFFECTIVE
SENTENCES**

> **HINT** **Use a Semicolon to Join Related Ideas**
>
> Use a semicolon to link two sentences when the ideas are of equal importance and are closely related. Do not use a semicolon to join two unrelated sentences.
>
> **Incorrect:** Some eyewitnesses make mistakes; I like to watch criminal trials.
> (The second idea has no clear relationship with the first idea.)
>
> **Correct:** One eyewitness misidentified a suspect; the witness was not wearing contact lenses that day.
> (The second idea gives further information about the first idea.)

PRACTICE 3

Make compound sentences by adding a semicolon and another complete sentence to each simple sentence. Remember that the two sentences must have related ideas.

EXAMPLE:

Last year, Eric joined a gang; *he regretted his decision.*

1. Eric rebelled against his parents _____

   _____

2. Some people don't have supportive families _____

   _____

3. At age fifteen, I acted like other teens _____

   _____

4. She didn't commit any crimes _____

   _____

5. His friends tried to influence him _____

   _____

6. Eric entered the court room _____

   _____

Combining Sentences Using Transitional Expressions

A **transitional expression** links two complete ideas together and shows how they are related. Most transitional expressions are **conjunctive adverbs** such as *however* or *furthermore*. When you join two ideas with a transitional expression, place a semicolon before the expression and a comma after it.

Some Transitional Expressions

Addition	Alternative	Contrast	Time	Example or Emphasis	Result or Consequence
additionally	in fact	however	eventually	for example	consequently
also	instead	nevertheless	finally	for instance	hence
besides	on the contrary	nonetheless	later	namely	therefore
furthermore	on the other hand	still	meanwhile	of course	thus
in addition	otherwise		subsequently	undoubtedly	
moreover			frequently		

If the second sentence begins with a transitional expression, put a semicolon before it and a comma after it.

Complete idea **;**   **transitional expression ,**   complete idea

Harper was not guilty; **nevertheless,** he was convicted.

PRACTICE 4

Combine sentences using the following transitional expressions. Choose an expression from the following list, and try to use a different expression in each sentence.

in fact	~~frequently~~	however	of course	for instance
therefore	moreover	nevertheless	thus	eventually

EXAMPLE:

                              ; frequently, it
DNA evidence is useful.~~It~~ has helped clear many innocent people.

1. In the past, many technicians looked at evidence through a microscope. They might examine a strand of hair.

2. In the early 1990s, a comparison of hair samples could deliver a conviction. Scientists developed more sophisticated techniques.

3. Dr. Edward Blake is a leading authority on DNA evidence. He often testifies at trials.

4. According to Dr. Blake, microscopic hair analysis is subjective. It has secured convictions in many cases.

5. Billy Gregory's hair matched a hair found at a crime scene. Both strands of hair appeared identical.

6. The strands of hair had exactly the same colour and width. They were genetically different.

7. In 1993, Gregory was convicted of the crime. He was sentenced to life in prison.

8. In 2000, a DNA test cleared him. He was able to go home.

9. Today, conventional hair comparison evidence is no longer allowed in most courtrooms. It may become an obsolete science.

Making Complex Sentences

When you combine a dependent and an independent clause, you create a **complex sentence**.

An effective way to create complex sentences is to join clauses with a **subordinating conjunction**. "Subordinate" means secondary, so subordinating conjunctions are words that introduce secondary ideas.

If you use a subordinator at the beginning of a sentence, put a comma after the dependent clause. Generally, if you use a subordinator in the middle of the sentence, you do not need to use a comma.

main idea   **subordinating conjunction**   secondary idea

The police arrived **because** <u>the alarm was ringing</u>.

subordinating conjunction   secondary idea ,   main idea

Because <u>the alarm was ringing</u>, the police arrived.

Meanings of Subordinating Conjunctions

Subordinating conjunctions create a relationship between the clauses in a sentence.

Subordinating Conjunction	Indicates	Example
as, because, since, so that	**a reason or a cause**	He paid a lot <u>because</u> he wanted a reliable alarm system.
after, since, until, when, whenever, while	**a time**	<u>After</u> he drove home, he parked on the street.
as long as, even if, if, provided that, so that, unless	**a condition**	The alarm won't ring <u>unless</u> someone touches the car.
although, even though, though	**a contrast**	<u>Although</u> the alarm began to wail, nobody looked at the car.
where, wherever	**a location**	<u>Wherever</u> you go, you will hear annoying car alarms.

> **HINT More About Complex Sentences**
>
> Complex sentences can have more than two clauses.
>
>   1   2
> Although males commit most violent crimes, more and more females engage in violent
>   3
> acts after they have joined gangs.
>
> You can also combine compound and complex sentences. The next example is a
> **compound-complex sentence**.
>
>   complex
> Although Alicia is tiny, she is strong, and she is a dedicated police officer.
>   compound

PRACTICE 5

Add a missing subordinating conjunction to each sentence. Use each subordinating conjunction once.

although	when	because	since
even though	if	unless	whenever

1. _____ a new television program about crime scene investigations is announced, many people watch it. Real-life lawyers and prosecutors get annoyed _____ members of the jury expect to see the same expensive, sophisticated crime-solving techniques used in average cases. _____ the members of the jury are not experts, they believe they know a lot about crime investigations because they have picked up tidbits from crime scene shows.

2. It is very expensive and difficult to get DNA analyses _____ the case is a very high profile and important one. _____ there is no DNA evidence, the case can still be very strong.

3. According to actor Robert Blake's defence lawyer, jurors will listen to detailed scientific evidence _____ they are used to watching those crime scene shows on television. The jury will find the defendant guilty _____ the evidence is solid. _____ the jury is unconvinced, the defendant might be released.

PRACTICE 6

Combine the sentences by adding a subordinating conjunction. Use a different subordinating conjunction in each sentence. Properly punctuate your sentences.

EXAMPLE:

He entered the courtroom. Photographers snapped photos.

As he entered the courthouse, photographers snapped photos.

or

The photographers snapped photos as he entered the courthouse.

1. Stephen was fourteen years old. He was arrested.

   _____

   _____

2. He proclaimed his innocence. The police refused to believe him.

   _____

   _____

3. He was extremely nervous. He appeared to be guilty.

   _____

   _____

4. He was in jail. He finished high school.

   _____

   _____

5. New evidence surfaced. He was released.

   _____

   _____

FINAL REVIEW

The following paragraphs contain only simple sentences. When sentences are
not varied, the essay is boring to read. To give the paragraphs more sentence
variety, combine at least fifteen sentences. You will have to add some words and
delete others.

EXAMPLE:

When the   she
~~The~~ witness is traumatized ~~She~~ might not remember her assailant's face.

1. Each day, you may see many faces. How many will you remember?
   You might recall the ones you see repeatedly. You will forget the others.
   Dr. Rod Lindsay works in Kingston at Queen's University. He is an
   expert on eyewitness testimony. Dr. Lindsay says that it is not easy to

remember faces. During a traumatic moment the brain almost shuts down. Dr. Lindsay is worried. He does not trust the methods used to collect eyewitness testimony.

2. In 1986, the police showed a crime victim a set of six photos. She felt a strong pressure to make a choice. One photo looked different from the others. It was in colour. The other photos were black and white. She picked the colour photo. It was not the guilty man. According to Dr. Lindsay, all photos of suspects should have similar colour and lighting to avoid biasing witnesses.

3. The best way to show photos is to show them sequentially. The witness must look at each photo. The witness must say "yes" or "no." He or she cannot go back to a previous picture. The witness must compare each photo to his or her memory. Dr. Lindsay contacted 33 police departments. Only nine showed photos of suspects sequentially.

4. According to experts, more police departments should use the "double blind" procedure. Sometimes, police officers know about the main suspect. They might cue the witness unconsciously. The double blind procedure ensures that the person showing the photos does not know the main suspect. Dr. Lindsay contacted 33 police departments. Only six used the double blind procedure.

5. Marvin Anderson spent fifteen years in jail. He was convicted of rape. The witness pointed at him during the trial. She identified him as her rapist. Many years later, DNA evidence cleared Anderson. He was released. Today, the lawyers see problems with the ways the photos were presented to the victim. Also, the officer may have "cued" the victim.

6. According to Dr. Lindsay, many people are wrongfully convicted. Witnesses misidentify them. It is unfortunate. The jury tends to believe eyewitness testimony. It can be seriously flawed.

Writer's Room **Topics for Writing**

Write about one of the following topics. Include some compound and some complex sentences.

1. Do you watch crime shows or read about crime? Describe a crime show, movie, or book.
2. What can people do to reduce the risk of being robbed? List several steps that people can take.

Section I
**EFFECTIVE
SENTENCES**

 CHECKLIST: COMBINING SENTENCES

When you edit your writing, ask yourself these questions.

☐ Are my compound and complex sentences complete?

He was arrested because
~~Because~~ of the scandal.

☐ Are my sentences correctly punctuated?

In compound sentences, place a comma before the coordinator.

In complex sentences, place a comma after a dependent introductory clause.

Comma: The case was dismissed, and the suspect was freed.

Comma: After she was released, she tried to find a job.

No comma: She tried to find a job after she was released.

20 Sentence Variety

CONFLICT **In this chapter, you will read about crime and prisons.**

CHAPTER CONTENTS

GRAMMAR SNAPSHOT Looking at Sentence Variety

The next selections, from Crime, a Normal Phenomenon *by sociologist Emile Durkheim, were translated from the original French. The first translation sounds choppy because the sentences are short and uniform in length. When the passage is rewritten with sentence variety, it flows more smoothly.*

No Sentence Variety

Crime is normal. It exists in all societies. The type of crime may change. The form of crime may change. Everywhere and always there have been criminals.

Sentence Variety

Crime, which is normal, exists in all societies. The type or form of crime may change, but everywhere and always there have been criminals.

In this chapter, you will vary the length and structure of sentences to produce sentence variety.

What Is Sentence Variety?

In Chapter 19, you learned about how to write different types of sentences. In this chapter, you will learn to vary your sentences by consciously considering the length of sentences, by altering the opening words, and by joining sentences using different methods.

> **HINT** **Be Careful with Long Sentences**
>
> If your sentence is too long, it may be difficult for the reader to understand. Also, you may accidentally write run-on sentences. If you have any doubts, break up a longer sentence into shorter ones.
>
> **Long and complicated:** In his book *Criminal Justice Today*, Frank Schmalleger describes a practice of the ancient Hebrews who sometimes punished a tribe by sending a sacrificial goat into the wilderness, and the goat, which was supposed to symbolically contain the tribe's sins, became the source of the modern word *scapegoat*.
>
> **Better:** In his book *Criminal Justice Today*, Frank Schmalleger describes a practice of the ancient Hebrews. They sometimes punished a tribe by sending a sacrificial goat into the wilderness. The goat, which was supposed to symbolically contain the tribe's sins, became the source of the modern word *scapegoat*.

PRACTICE 1

Edit each long sentence by breaking it into smaller, more easily understood segments. Each segment must be a complete sentence.

1. Many early punishment methods were designed to publicly humiliate criminals and one of the most common methods was to force an offender to stand in a public square with his or her head and hands secured so that everyone in the community would see that person, and often the local citizens would throw eggs and tomatoes at the offender, but sometimes they would throw rocks which could end the offender's life, however, such retribution was permitted by the community, and ultimately citizens had the power to exact extreme punishment if they believed that the criminal deserved it.

2. In the fifteenth century, England began sending convicts to the North American colonies and to Australia, and the program, which was known as *transportation* had two purposes which included ridding Britain of undesirable criminals but also of providing a captive force of workers who could help build roads, bridges, and housing for the people who were developing the colonies so although many criminals had to go on long journeys and would never see their families again, they also had a much better life than they would have had if they had remained in Great Britain's damp and overcrowded prisons, so some may have been grateful for the chance to build a new life in a different country.

Varying the Opening Words

An effective way to make your sentences more vivid is to vary the opening words. Instead of beginning each sentence with the subject, you could try the following strategies.

Begin with an adverb

An **adverb** is a word that modifies a verb, and it often (but not always) ends in *-ly*. *Quickly* and *frequently* are adverbs. Non *-ly* adverbs include words such as *sometimes* and *often*.

> <u>Quickly</u>, the criminal left the scene.

Begin with a prepositional phrase

A **prepositional phrase** is a group of words made up of a preposition and its object. *In the morning* and *at dawn* are prepositional phrases.

> <u>On the courtroom steps</u>, the defendant covered his head with his jacket.

Begin with an *-ing* verb

You can begin your sentence with a **present participle** or *-ing* word. Only combine sentences using an *-ing* modifier when the two actions happen at the same time.

> <u>Reaching for her wallet</u>, she asked the officer what had happened.

GRAMMAR LINK

For a complete list of past participles, see Appendix 2.

Begin with an *-ed* verb

You can begin your sentence with a **past participle**, which is a verb that has an *-ed* ending. There are also many irregular past participles such as *gone*, *seen*, and *known*.

> <u>Shocked</u>, she stepped into the police cruiser.

PRACTICE 2

Combine the sets of sentences using the indicated words.

EXAMPLE: The attacker was nervous. He grabbed the purse.

(adverb)
Nervously, the attacker grabbed the purse.

1. The bystanders watched the police cruiser arrive. They were anxious.

   (adverb) _____

2. The bystanders were relieved. They left the scene.

   (*-ed* verb) _____

3. The officers saw the people leave. They were annoyed.

   (*-ed* verb) _____

4. One witness gave the officers his name. He was reluctant.

   (adverb) _____

5. The officers looked at the injured woman. They felt upset.

   (*-ing* verb) _____

6. The guilty man raised his hands. He did this with a grin.

   (prepositional phrase) _____

Combining Sentences with an Appositive

An **appositive** is a word or phrase that gives further information about a noun or pronoun. You can combine two sentences by using an appositive. In the example, the italicized phrase could become an appositive because it describes the noun *Mr. Zlatko*.

> **Two sentences:**   Mr. Zlatko was *a middle-aged male.* He lost his savings.

You can place the appositive directly before the word that it refers to or directly after that word. Notice that the appositives are set off with commas.

appositive
Combined: A middle-aged male, **Mr. Zlatko** lost his savings.

appositive
Mr. Zlatko, a middle-aged male, lost his savings.

PRACTICE 3

Combine the following pairs of sentences. In each pair, make one of the sentences an appositive. Try to vary the position of the appositive.

EXAMPLE:

The man ~~was~~ an extravagant spender ~~. He~~ owed money to many people.

1. Charles Dickens was a British novelist. He often wrote about Debtor's Prison.

2. Dickens lived in the 1800s. It was a time when laws were very harsh.

3. His father was John Dickens. John Dickens was a poor businessman who often owed money to others.

4. When Charles was twelve years old, his father was taken to Marshalsea Debtor's Prison. It was an event that changed the life of the boy.

5. The prison was a filthy, crowded place. It had no separate sections for males and females.

6. For the next six months, Charles left school and went to work in a shoe factory. The school was a place where he had been receiving a good education.

7. When he was released from prison, John Dickens paid for Charles to return to school. John Dickens was a thinner, tired man.

8. Charles Dickens wrote about Debtor's Prison in many of his novels. He was a talented writer.

Combining Sentences with Relative Clauses

A **relative pronoun** describes a noun or pronoun. You can form complex sentences by using relative pronouns to introduce dependent clauses. Review the most common relative pronouns.

who	whom	whomever
whose	which	that

Which Use *which* to add non-essential information about a thing. Generally use commas to set off clauses that begin with *which*.

> The crime rate, **which** peaked in the 1980s, has fallen since then.

That Use *that* to add essential information about a thing. Do not use commas to set off clauses that begin with *that*.

> The car **that** was stolen belonged to a police officer.

GRAMMAR LINK

For more information about punctuating relative clauses, refer to Chapter 33.

Who Use *who* (*whom, whomever, whose*) to add information about a person. When a clause begins with *who*, you may or may not need a comma. Put commas around the clause if it adds non-essential information. If the clause is essential to the meaning of the sentence, do not add commas. To decide if a clause is essential or not, ask yourself if the sentence still makes sense without the *who* clause. If it does, the clause is not essential.

> The woman **who** committed the theft did not use a gun.
>
> (The clause is essential. The sentence would not make sense without the *who* clause.)

> The female thief, **who** spent a lot on legal fees, was sentenced to ten years in prison.
>
> (The clause is not essential.)

> **HINT** **Using *That* or *Which***
>
> Both *that* and *which* refer to things, but *which* refers to non-essential ideas. Also, *which* implies that you are referring to the complete subject and not just a part of it. Compare the next two sentences.
>
> **Incorrect:** The amygdala **that** is located near the base of the brain has a role in fear responses.
> (This incorrectly implies that a part of the amygdala is not located near the base of the brain. In fact, all of the amygdala is near the base of the brain.)
>
> **Correct:** The amygdala, **which** is located near the base of the brain, has a role in fear responses.
> (This correctly implies that all of the amygdala is near the base of the brain.)

Section 1
**EFFECTIVE
SENTENCES**

PRACTICE 4

Using a relative pronoun, combine each pair of sentences. Read both sentences before you combine them. Having the full context will help you figure out which relative pronoun to use.

EXAMPLE:

                      , who   ,
Sociologist Emile Durkheim was from France .̶ H̶e̶ believed that deviant behaviour can be good for societies.

1. Crime is difficult for societies. It sometimes forces them to change and adapt.

2. In many countries, people express their opinions about the government. They are breaking the law.

3. Last year, some citizens in China criticized government policies. They were arrested and imprisoned.

4. Rigid governments enact unfair laws. Those governments may eventually perish.

5. Definitions of criminal behaviour are agreed on by citizens. The definitions can change over time.

6. For instance, in the 1960s, Americans broke Jim Crow laws. They were arrested.

7. The activists were treated as criminals. They helped change society.

8. Durkheim reflects about crime. Sometimes there are positive consequences to criminal behaviour.

9. However, Durkheim also warns people. Deviance beyond a certain level can threaten the social order.

PRACTICE 5

Add dependent clauses to each sentence. Begin each clause with a relative pronoun (*who*, *which*, or *that*). Add any necessary commas.

EXAMPLE:

The case *that involved an adolescent boy* was made into a documentary.

1. The boy _____ did not commit the crime.

2. His lawyers _____ did not have all of the evidence.

3. The jury came to a conclusion _____.

4. The judge sentenced the boy _____ to a long prison term.

5. The wrongfully convicted _____ are sometimes never exonerated.

6. Sometimes mistakes _____ can change the lives of individuals.

7. The case _____ brought attention to the wrongfully convicted.

Writing Embedded Questions

It is possible to combine a question with a statement or to combine two questions. An **embedded question** is a question that is set within a larger sentence.

Question:	How old was the victim?
Embedded question:	The detectives wondered <u>how old the victim was</u>.

In questions, there is generally a helping verb before the subject. However, when a question is embedded in a larger sentence, remove the helping verb or place it after the subject. As you read the following examples, pay attention to the word order in the embedded questions.

■ Combine two questions.

Separate:	Why **do** people commit crimes? Do you know?
(In both questions, the helping verb is *do*.)
Combined:	Do you know <u>why people commit crimes</u>?
(The helping verb *do* is removed from the embedded question.)

■   Combine a question and a statement.

Separate: How **should** society treat young offenders? I wonder about it.

(In the question, the helping verb *should* appears before the subject.)

Combined: I wonder how society should treat young offenders.

(In the embedded question, *should* is placed after the subject.)

HINT   **Use the Correct Word Order**

When you edit your writing, ensure that you have formed your embedded questions properly.

she thought

Dr. Alvarez wonders why ~~do~~ people commit crimes. I asked her what ~~did she think~~ about the issue.

PRACTICE 6

Edit six errors in embedded questions.

EXAMPLE:

people can

The writer explains how ~~can people~~ become criminals.

1. Many experts wonder why is the crime rate so high? Parents may ask how are role models a factor. They question how do negative models influence youths. Some blame icons in youth culture. For example, a recent newspaper report linked the hateful words of gangsta rap songs to youth crime.

2. However, it is unclear how can people only criticize singers or other celebrities from youth culture. In fact, they should really ask why are so many "pillars" of society deviant. Corporate executives have stolen from shareholders, and prominent religious figures have promoted intolerance and hatred. A reporter from Yellowknife asks why have so many people in highly-regarded positions of authority abused their power. Psychologists, sociologists, and criminologists are trying to find answers.

FINAL REVIEW

The next essay lacks sentence variety. Use the strategies that you have learned in this chapter, and create at least ten varied sentences.

EXAMPLE:

Criminal profilers study crime scenes. ~~They believe~~ *believing* that they can determine the personality of the perpetrator.

1. Two people were at a bus stop. A large man tried to take a woman's purse. He was very aggressive. An innocent bystander intervened. He asked the man to leave the woman alone. The thief pushed the bystander. This caused the bystander to fall and crack his head on the pavement. The woman got onto the next bus.

2. The police arrived. The witnesses left the scene. They thought that the situation was under control. Susan Helenchild is a prosecutor from Winnipeg. She has advice for witnesses. They should give their names and addresses to police officers. They should remain at the crime scene. A court cannot easily convict a guilty person. The court needs evidence.

3. A girl arrived after the crime had occurred. She was interviewed by the police. She said nothing important. The prosecutor asked the police to interview her again. The girl had seen the thief earlier in the day. He was drunk and aggressive. In court, the thief claimed to be calm and gentle. He blamed the victim for the crime. He called the victim aggressive. The girl's testimony helped the prosecution. Her testimony contradicted the words of the accused.

4. Why do witnesses leave crime scenes? Officers often wonder. Sometimes witnesses believe they have nothing useful to add. Helenchild feels frustrated with such witnesses. She says that any evidence can help the prosecution. Witnesses should always give contact information to police officers.

Writer's Room **Topics for Writing**

Write about one of the following topics. Use a variety of sentence lengths.

1. What are some categories of criminals? Classify criminals into different types.
2. Why does the criminal life seem exciting to some people? What factors contribute to make crime appealing?

 CHECKLIST: SENTENCE VARIETY

When you edit your writing, ask yourself these questions.

☐ Are my sentences varied? Check for problems in these areas:

   ▪ too many short sentences
   ▪ long sentences that are difficult to follow

Police departments examine strategies to lower the crime rate because

they want to show they are being effective in the fight against crime

. *Sometimes*
~~and sometimes~~ they present those strategies to the media.

☐ Do I have any embedded questions? Check for problems in these areas:

   ▪ word order
   ▪ unnecessary helping verbs

I don't know why ~~do~~ people break the law.

Section I
**EFFECTIVE
SENTENCES**

READING LINK

Conflict
These essays contain more information about law, order, and conflict.
"Types of Correctional Officers" by Frank Schmalleger (page 161)
"Little Brother Is Watching You" by Eric Gall (page 80)

21 Fragments

CHAPTER

URBAN DEVELOPMENT In this chapter, you will read about the development of suburbs and cities.

CHAPTER CONTENTS

- What Are Fragments?
- Phrase Fragments
- Fragments with *-ing* and *to*
- Explanatory Fragments
- Dependent-Clause Fragments

GRAMMAR SNAPSHOT **Looking at Sentence Fragments**

In his essay "Every Day Carless," Ewan Schmidt argues for a motorized vehicle-free downtown. The sentence fragments are underlined.

The downtown core is very quiet each Friday. There are no car horns. <u>No screeching of the brakes.</u> <u>No yelling.</u> <u>No loud motor noises.</u>

<u>Because there are no cars.</u> People can walk anywhere they want without worrying about traffic. <u>Even in the middle of the street.</u>

In this chapter, you will identify sentence fragments and write complete sentences.

What Are Fragments?

A **fragment** is an incomplete sentence. It lacks either a subject or verb, or it fails to express a complete thought. You may see fragments in newspaper headlines and advertisements (*overnight weight loss*). You may also use fragments to save space when you are writing a text message. However, in college writing, it is unacceptable to write fragments.

Sentence: More and more people are moving to urban centres.

Fragment: In developing countries.

Phrase Fragments

Phrase fragments are missing a subject or a verb. In each example, the fragment is underlined.

No verb:	<u>The history of cities.</u> It is quite interesting.
No subject:	Ancient civilizations usually had one major city. <u>Specialized in trades.</u>

How to Correct Phrase Fragments

To correct phrase fragments, add the missing subject or verb, or join the fragment to another sentence. The following examples show how to correct the previous phrase fragments.

Join sentences:	The history of cities is quite interesting.
Add words:	Ancient civilizations usually had one major city. **The citizens in that city** specialized in trades.

Section 2
**COMMON
SENTENCE
ERRORS**

> **HINT Incomplete Verbs**
>
> The following example is a phrase fragment because it is missing a helping verb. To make this sentence complete, you must add the helping verb.
>
> | | |
> |---|---|
> | **Fragment:** | Modern cities growing rapidly. |
> | **Sentence:** | Modern cities <u>are</u> growing rapidly. |

PRACTICE 1

Underline and correct ten phrase fragments.

EXAMPLE:

Damascus is one of the world's oldest cities. ~~Founded~~ *It was founded* in 3000 B.C.

1. The first cities began in ancient civilizations. Mesopotamia, the Indus Valley, and China. Those were large ancient civilizations. Ancient cities such as Jericho, Harappa, and Mohenjo-daro had small populations. Compared to modern cities. For example, the first cities had only around 150 000 people. Eventually, ancient empires grew. Rome reached a population of one million. Baghdad. It exceeded that number.

2. During the Middle Ages, some European cities became powerful city states. Venice and Genoa even had their own military and maritime institutions. Around that time. London became the largest city in the world. Paris as populated as Beijing and Istanbul.

3. The Industrial Revolution was an important phenomenon for the growth of cities. In the eighteenth and nineteenth centuries. Many

people migrated from the countryside to the urban centres. Urbanization led to many social problems. Child labour, low wages, and unsanitary living conditions. Those were some common problems. Many reformers worked hard to improve the living conditions. Of the urban poor.

4. By the 1930s, the Great Depression raised the unemployment rate. In rural areas. Many people had to leave their farms and look for work in the cities. After World War II. Economic prosperity helped to increase the migration to the cities. Most of today's cities are growing and prospering.

Section 2
COMMON
SENTENCE
ERRORS

Fragments with *-ing* and *to*

A fragment may begin with a **present participle**, which is the form of the verb that ends in *-ing* (*running*, *talking*). It may also begin with an **infinitive**, which is *to* plus the base form of the verb (*to run*, *to talk*). These fragments generally appear next to another sentence that contains the subject. In the examples, the fragments are underlined.

-ing **fragment:**	<u>Reacting to urban sprawl.</u> City planners started a new movement in the 1980s and 1990s.
to **fragment:**	Urban designers believe in the new urbanism. <u>To help people live better lives.</u>

How to Correct *-ing* and *to* Fragments

To correct an *-ing* or *to* fragment, add the missing words or join the fragment to another sentence. The following examples show how to correct the two previous fragments.

Join sentences:	Reacting to urban sprawl, city planners started a new movement in the 1980s and 1990s.
Add words:	Urban designers believe in the new urbanism. **They want** to help people live better lives.

HINT   When the *-ing* Word Is the Subject

Sometimes a gerund (*-ing* form of the verb) is the subject of a sentence. In the example, *cycling* is the subject of the sentence.

Correct sentence: <u>Cycling</u> is a great form of exercise in urban areas.

A sentence fragment occurs when the *-ing* word is part of an incomplete verb string or when you mention the subject in a previous sentence. In the example, the fragment is underlined.

Fragment: Many city dwellers get exercise. <u>Cycling on bike paths.</u>

PRACTICE 2

Underline and correct ten *-ing* and *to* fragments.

EXAMPLE:
The new urbanism movement has many principles.

One principle is designing
~~Designing~~ walkways in neighbourhoods.

1. New urbanism is a suburban planning movement. To create people-friendly neighbourhoods. To limit the use of cars. Urban planners design self-contained neighbourhoods. Believing in the need to curtail urban sprawl. Architects pattern areas where people can walk to work and choose recreational activities close to home.

2. The new urbanism movement is a reaction against older suburban areas. After World War II, architects designed suburbs that relied heavily on the use of cars. Therefore, most people living in traditional suburbs have to commute to city centres. Creating problems such as traffic congestion and air pollution.

3. Driving to work, school, and shopping areas. Suburban dwellers waste a lot of time travelling in their cars. In addition, urban sprawl creates difficulties for people who cannot drive. Limiting their daily activities. To do errands downtown or at a mall. Non-drivers must find other means of transport.

4. To answer such concerns. Urban designers reconsidered traditional suburban models. Since 1990, the new urbanism movement has become very popular. To improve the quality of suburban life. City planners design beautiful areas for living, working, shopping, and playing. They hire innovative architects who insert skylights and green space in their designs. Presently, there are many communities in North America. Using the principles of the new urban movement.

Explanatory Fragments

An **explanatory fragment** provides an explanation about a previous sentence and is missing a subject, a complete verb, or both. These types of fragments begin with one of the following words.

also	particularly	for instance	especially	except
for example	as well as	such as	including	like

In the examples, the explanatory fragment is underlined.

Fragment: Planners in the 1960s influenced the new urbanism movement. <u>For example, Jane Jacobs.</u>

Fragment: New urbanism planners take into consideration many factors. <u>Especially reducing the use of the automobile.</u>

How to Correct Explanatory Fragments

To correct explanatory fragments, add the missing words, or join the explanation or example to another sentence. The following examples show how to correct the previous explanatory fragments.

Add words: Planners in the 1960s influenced the new urbanism movement. For example, Jane Jacobs **was an important authority on urban planning**.

Join sentences: New urbanism planners take into consideration many factors, especially reducing the use of the automobile.

PRACTICE 3

Underline and correct ten explanatory fragments. You may need to add or remove words.

EXAMPLE:

                                     , such as

Some new urbanism towns are famous. ~~Such as~~ Celebration.

1. New urbanists plan communities with a central downtown area that is walking distance from all neighbourhoods. The first community built on the new urbanism principles is Seaside, Florida. It was started in 1981 and became very famous. For example, *Atlantic Monthly*. It featured Seaside on its cover. Robert Davis bought the land to build the community. He hired many people who followed the principles of the new urbanism philosophy. Such as architects and urban planners.

2. Seaside was relatively easy to build because the area did not have the traditional rules for developing land. For instance, no zoning regulations. The buildings in the town have uniform designs. Particularly the houses. They all have certain features, including porches that must be five metres from the sidewalk. Also, the streets. They must be made of bricks so cars cannot speed.

3. There are many other towns. Like Seaside. The most famous of these is the one Disney has built in Florida called Celebration. It also has strict

rules for conformity. For example, the windows. They must be decorated with white or off-white curtains. The houses are built close together. For instance, only six metres apart. In Celebration, if neighbours complain about a barking dog, the dog can be evicted from the town.

4. Many people criticize those types of communities. Especially regarding the conformity of the design. On the other hand, people moving to those towns hope to live in an ideal community. For example, no crime or social problems. However, critics point out that all communities have some social problems.

Dependent-Clause Fragments

A **dependent clause** has a subject and verb, but it cannot stand alone. It literally depends on another clause to be a complete sentence. Dependent clauses may begin with subordinating conjunctions or relative pronouns. The following list contains some of the most common words that begin dependent clauses.

Common Subordinating Conjunctions				Relative Pronouns
after	before	though	whenever	that
although	even though	unless	where	which
as	if	until	whereas	who(m)
because	since	what	whether	whose

In each example, the fragment is underlined.

Fragment: In the city, houses are close together. <u>Whereas in the suburbs, houses have large yards</u>.

Fragment: <u>Before William Levitt built Levittown</u>. Many people lived in congested neighbourhoods.

How to Correct Dependent-Clause Fragments

To correct dependent-clause fragments, join the fragment to a complete sentence, or add the necessary words to make it a complete idea. You could also delete the subordinating conjunction. The following examples show how to correct the previous dependent-clause fragments.

Delete subordinator: In the city, houses are close together. In the suburbs, houses have large yards.

Join sentences: Before William Levitt built Levittown, many people lived in congested neighbourhoods.

PRACTICE 4

Underline and correct ten dependent-clause fragments.

EXAMPLE:

                                                                  because
William Levitt and his brother built Levittown. ~~Because~~ of a shortage of
affordable housing.

1. In 1948, developer William Levitt built a community in Pennsylvania.
   Which has been designated the first traditional suburb. Levitt wanted to
   give returning soldiers the opportunity to participate in the American
   dream. He called his community Levittown. This town consisted of
   similarly built single-family homes. That attracted young families. People
   wanted to escape the crowds of big cities like New York and Philadelphia.
   Homes in large cities were very expensive. Whereas Levittown contained
   affordable housing. The community grew to approximately 17 000
   houses. Which led to the beginning of urban sprawl.

2. Some people criticized the idea of Levittown. Because all of the houses
   looked similar. Even though the town had four different house styles.
   The first residents sometimes got lost trying to find their homes.
   Although it began with the premise of affordable housing for everyone.
   Levittown initially discriminated against non-whites and did not permit
   them to buy houses in the community. Eventually, Levittown
   abandoned its "whites-only" policy. In 1957, the first African Americans
   to buy a house there were Bill and Daisy Meyers. Who had rocks
   thrown at them by the other residents.

3. Because Levittown is getting older. It has become a more attractive
   suburb. Many homeowners have remodelled their homes, and the
   saplings have grown into mature trees. Although many other suburbs
   have developed. Levittown remains a model of traditional suburban
   living.

FINAL REVIEW

The paragraphs contain the four types of fragments: phrase, explanatory, *-ing* and *to*, and dependent clauses. Correct fifteen fragment errors.

EXAMPLE:

Tourists have been coming to Tokyo. ~~Since~~ *since* World War II.

Section 2
**COMMON
SENTENCE
ERRORS**

1. Tokyo, the world's largest city. It was originally called Edo. The Edo warrior family inhabited a marshy region of Japan. Where there were a few villages. Eventually, the town of Edo grew. It started to gain prominence in the 1600s. In 1603, Edo warrior Tokugawa Ieyasu became shogun or warlord of the region. He was so powerful that he moved the government from Kyoto to Edo. Thinking that he would have more control over politics. He acquired complete control over Japan. Quelling any opposition. His government promoted an isolationist policy. Japan had no contact with other nations. Until the nineteenth century.

2. From the seventeenth century to the nineteenth century, Japan was politically stable, allowing Edo's population to grow rapidly to about one million people. Both London and Paris had a smaller population. At that time. Edo became the economic centre of Japan. Prospering greatly due to industry. Also at that time, Japanese society developed a class system. Based on four levels of hierarchy. The samurai or warriors were at the top of the social system.

3. The Tokugawa Ieyasu family's power collapsed by the 1850s. Because of corruption within its government. At the same time, the Western powers were pressuring Japan. To open trade. England and the United States wanted Japan as a trading post. For example, in 1853, Matthew Perry. He forced Japan to open trade relations with America. Japan westernized rapidly. After its contact with Europe and America. In 1867, Edo's name was changed to Tokyo.

4. Since the late 1800s. Tokyo has modernized like other Western capitals. In 1923, a great earthquake destroyed much of the city, and rebuilding became a priority. Many structures were built. Such as a subway system in 1927, an airport in 1931, and a port in 1941. After World War II, Tokyo greatly expanded. Today, it is a mega metropolis. Inviting visitors from all around the world.

Section 2
**COMMON
SENTENCE
ERRORS**

 Writer's Room   **Topics for Writing**

Write about one of the following topics. Check that there are no sentence fragments.

1. Write about where you live. Describe your neighbourhood.
2. What are some similarities and differences between living in a city and living in a suburb?

 CHECKLIST: SENTENCE FRAGMENTS

When you edit your writing, ask yourself this question.

Are my sentences complete? Check for these types of fragments.

- phrase fragments
- *-ing* and *to* fragments
- explanatory fragments
- dependent-clause fragments

Los Angeles and San Francisco are moving closer together. ~~Because~~ *because* of the San Andreas fault.

The two cities will make the largest urban area in the world. ~~If~~ *if* the movement continues.

Run-Ons

CHAPTER CONTENTS

GRAMMAR SNAPSHOT **Looking at Run-Ons**

Darius Knightely is a freelance travel writer. The next excerpt about his recent trip to Barcelona contains a sentence error. The underlined error is a run-on.

Barcelona is a city of contrasts. <u>Visitors see medieval buildings, narrow streets, and grandiose churches they also see grid-like</u> <u>neighbourhoods, modernist architecture, and glass and steel places of worship.</u> The modern sections of the city contrast with the older areas.

In this chapter, you will learn to correct run-on sentences.

What Are Run-Ons?

A **run-on sentence** occurs when two or more complete sentences are incorrectly joined. In other words, the sentence runs on without stopping. There are two types of run-on sentences.

1. A **fused sentence** has no punctuation to mark the break between ideas.

    Incorrect: Skyscrapers are unusually tall buildings the Taipei 101 tower is among the tallest.

2. A **comma splice** uses a comma incorrectly to connect two complete ideas.

    Incorrect: The CN Tower is located in Toronto, it is the world's tallest communication structure.

PRACTICE I

Read the following sentences. Write C beside correct sentences, FS beside fused sentences, and CS beside comma splices.

EXAMPLE:

Gustave Eiffel was born in 1832 he designed the Eiffel Tower and the
Statue of Liberty.   *FS*

1. One of the most recognizable modern structures is the Eiffel
   Tower, it was built at the end of the eighteenth century.   _____

2. The French government wanted to celebrate the centennial
   anniversary of the French Revolution, which took place in 1789.   _____

3. The government held a competition it invited architects to submit
   designs to commemorate the anniversary of the revolution.   _____

4. Winners of the competition would have their designs displayed at
   the World's Fair of 1889.   _____

5. Many architects submitted designs, Gustave Eiffel's tower design
   won.   _____

6. The tower took twenty-six months to complete it was the tallest
   structure in the world at that time.   _____

7. It was 320 metres tall and weighed 63 500 tonnes.   _____

8. Many Parisians did not like the look of the tower, they wanted
   to destroy it.   _____

9. But it proved to be a very popular tourist attraction people from
   all over the world visit Paris and climb the tower.   _____

10. In fact, tourism experts consider the Eiffel Tower as the number
    one tourist attraction in the world.   _____

Correcting Run-Ons

You can correct both fused sentences and comma splices in a variety of ways.
Read the following run-on sentence, and then review the four ways to correct it.

Run-On: Antoni Gaudí began his career as a secular architect he
               eventually became very religious.

1. Make two separate sentences by adding end punctuation, such as a period.

   Antoni Gaudí began his career as a secular architect. **He** eventually
   became very religious.

2. Add a semicolon (;).

   Antoni Gaudí began his career as a secular architect; he eventually
   became very religious.

3. Add a coordinating conjunction such as *for*, *and*, *nor*, *but*, *or*, *yet*, or *so*.

Antoni Gaudí began his career as a secular architect, **but** he eventually became very religious.

4. Add a subordinating conjunction such as *although*, *because*, *when*, *before*, *while*, *since*, or *after*.

Although Antoni Gaudí began his career as a secular architect, he eventually became very religious.

PRACTICE 2

Correct the run-ons by making two complete sentences.

EXAMPLE:

Antoni Gaudí designed very interesting works, ̶h̶e̶ is considered to be a genius. *(. He)*

1. Antoni Gaudí was born in 1852 in Tarragona, Spain he is considered to be Catalonia's greatest architect.

2. Gaudí became a Catholic he also believed in Catalan nationalism.

3. Gaudí designed the Sagrada Familia he wanted to express his Catholic faith in his work.

4. Nature fascinated Gaudí, he incorporated nature's images into his creations.

5. Classical design used geometric shapes Gaudí's designs mimicked shapes from nature.

6. Gaudí's style evolved from Gothic influences, he created intricate, flowing, asymmetrical shapes.

7. Businessmen in Barcelona commissioned Gaudí to design a modern neighbourhood, he constructed many buildings like the Casa Mila.

8. His work used the *trencadis* style this style involves the use of broken tiles to decorate surfaces.

9. One of Gaudí's most famous designs is Park Guell, the park has dragon-shaped benches and tree-shaped columns.

10. Many people initially laughed at Gaudí's vision eight of his creations are now recognized as World Heritage Sites.

HINT **Semicolons and Transitional Expressions**

Another way to correct run-ons is to connect sentences with a transitional expression. Place a semicolon before the expression and a comma after it.

The construction costs were too high**; therefore,** the town abandoned plans to build city hall.

The design was beautiful**; nevertheless,** it was rejected.

Some common transitional expressions are:

additionally	furthermore	however
meanwhile	moreover	nevertheless
of course	therefore	thus

To practise combining sentences with transitional expressions, see Chapter 19.

Section 2
**COMMON
SENTENCE
ERRORS**

PRACTICE 3

Correct the run-ons by joining the two sentences with a semicolon.

EXAMPLE:

I. M. Pei has designed many famous buildings; the John F. Kennedy Library is just one.

1. The Louvre Palace is one of the most recognized buildings in Paris, it was built in the Renaissance style for French monarchs.

2. The French Revolution abolished the monarchy the Louvre became a museum.

3. French officials wanted to expand the Louvre, they hired a famous architect to modify the building.

4. I. M. Pei was born in China in 1917 he immigrated to the United States to study architecture.

5. The French government commissioned Pei to enlarge the museum he designed three pyramids for the entrance.

6. The main pyramid gives light to the underground entrance, it is made of many glass squares.

7. The pyramid is about twenty-one metres high, it has two smaller pyramids on each side.

8. The pyramids were completed in 1989 many people thought the entrance was unattractive.

9. I. M. Pei is an outstanding architect his innovative designs have won many prizes.

Section 2
**COMMON
SENTENCE
ERRORS**

PRACTICE 4

Correct the run-ons by joining the two sentences with a comma and a coordinator (*for*, *and*, *nor*, *but*, *or*, *yet*, *so*).

EXAMPLE:

, and

Arthur Erickson is a Canadian architect his designs are world famous.

1. The University of British Columbia has many beautiful buildings Arthur Erickson's Museum of Anthropology is the most beautiful.

2. The museum rooms are high and spacious they can house large totems of the northwest First Nations.

3. The museum contains unusual artifacts, its totem pole collection is very interesting.

4. Architect Arthur Erickson considers the environment important his designs must fit into the landscape.

5. Erickson was an inexperienced architect his design won first place in a competition.

6. Many architects entered the competition Erickson's design was the most innovative.

7. The first-place winner was asked to design Simon Fraser University Erickson evaluated the surroundings.

8. The site was on top of a mountain it overlooked the ocean.

9. Erickson could follow the design trend of the time he could design according to his personal vision.

10. Simon Fraser University fits into the landscape its buildings are built into the mountainside.

PRACTICE 5

Correct the run-ons by joining the two sentences with a **subordinator**. Use one of the following subordinators: *because*, *before*, *although*, *when*, *even though*, and *although*. If the dependent clause comes at the beginning of the sentence, remember to add a comma.

EXAMPLE:

even though

European ideas have influenced African architecture ∧ many indigenous designs reveal beauty and practicality.

1. African architecture is not that well known it is very rich and diverse.

2. African architecture was influenced by Arabs they colonized North Africa.

3. Europeans arrived in the sixteenth century Islam provided inspiration for architectural design.

4. Until the twenty-first century, there were very few famous African architects African countries were controlled by European powers.

5. Modern African buildings are beautiful they are not appreciated as World Heritage Sites.

6. The Aswan Dam, one of the most famous dams in the world, was constructed in the twentieth century the Nile River no longer flooded each year.

7. The construction of the Aswan Dam was controversial people were concerned about its impact on the environment.

8. The Eastgate Centre was built in Harare it became the world's first modern building to use natural cooling methods.

9. Modern African architecture is gaining momentum architects are considering the unique needs of Africa.

PRACTICE 6

Use a variety of methods to correct ten run-on errors. Add commas when necessary.

EXAMPLE:

and

Many new buildings are being erected all over China, modern building designs are very popular.
^

Section 2
COMMON SENTENCE ERRORS

1. The Chinese Revolution dominated politics China's government developed policies to minimize class differences. As a result, new buildings were designed for utility, with no regard for beauty.

2. Now, China is industrializing at a great rate businesses are asking architects to design practical but beautiful buildings. The National Theatre building, for example, is controversial, it is also extremely intriguing. It was designed by French architect Paul Andreu, many people have criticized its design. It is shaped like an egg. It has three halls and a lake, it has a bridge. Another highly discussed building in Beijing is the CCTV tower it looks like the letter Z, many Chinese think it is an eyesore.

3. The cost of building these edifices is very expensive, some members of the public complain that such designs are too foreign. Others believe that designing interesting buildings is very important. China hosted the Olympics in 2008. For example, the Olympic Stadium was a necessity, the cost was prohibitive.

4. The Beijing skyline has changed, not everybody has liked the changes. Some say that such change is the price for industrialization, average citizens are eager for Beijing to join the ranks of the most beautiful cities in the world.

FINAL REVIEW

Correct ten run-on errors.

EXAMPLE:

and

The construction industry is the largest in the world, public and private buildings consume a lot of energy.
^

Section 2
**COMMON
SENTENCE
ERRORS**

1. When most people envision cities, they think about houses, roads, and skyscrapers built above ground they do not think about subterranean cities. However, many people use underground public and private buildings every day. In North America, there are at least five hundred public and private underground buildings for example, the Engineering Library at the University of Berkeley and the Vietnam Veterans Memorial Education Center are only two such subterranean structures. More and more underground structures are being built every day.

2. Some of the oldest underground cities are located in Cappadocia, Turkey the first underground city in that area was constructed around 2000 BC. Archaeologists believe that at one time, up to twenty thousand people lived in those underground Turkish cities the early Christians used them as a means to escape persecution.

3. Montreal contains an extremely large modern underground city. It was designed by I. M. Pei in the 1960s other architects have contributed to its expansion. It is located downtown and has around 42 kilometres of tunnels with about 120 exterior access points. More than 500 000 people use the underground city each day they want to avoid Montreal's very cold temperatures in the winter.

4. There are many reasons to build underground. First, underground buildings benefit from better climate control architects say that such buildings can be heated and cooled more efficiently than above-ground buildings. Also, building underground reduces the impact on the environment, forests and fields do not have to be cleared. Moreover, the wind, snow, and rain do not erode the walls, well-constructed underground buildings are resistant to fire and earthquakes.

5. Perhaps in the future, there will be more underground public and private buildings, they are more environmentally friendly and more energy efficient. Certainly it is time to rethink how urban planners design cities.

Writer's Room Topics for Writing

Write about one of the following topics. Edit your writing and ensure that there are no run-ons.

1. Are there any buildings or areas in your neighbourhood, town, or country that you find attractive or unattractive? Describe these buildings and explain why you believe they are beautiful or unsightly.

2. Are there any changes or additions that you would make to the town or city where you live, such as adding a new park or a museum? What suggestions would you make to city planners?

 CHECKLIST: RUN-ONS

When you edit your writing, ask yourself this question.

Are my sentences correctly formed and punctuated? Check for and correct any fused sentences and comma splices.

One of the most successful architects in the world is Ernest
     . He
Cormier—he designed the Supreme Court of Canada building in Ottawa.

Section 2
**COMMON
SENTENCE
ERRORS**

Faulty Parallel Structure

URBAN DEVELOPMENT In this chapter, you will read about landscapes and gardens.

CHAPTER CONTENTS

- What Is Parallel Structure?
- Correcting Faulty Parallel Structure

GRAMMAR SNAPSHOT Looking at Parallel Structure

The Royal Botanic Gardens in Kew, England, supports research on conservation of the environment. The following paragraph summarizes one of the conservation schemes in Peru. Review the underlined ideas to see how they are parallel.

The Huarango (*Prosopis pallida*) forests of the south coast of Peru are among the most highly threatened ecosystems on earth. The remaining trees are important primary producers, forming soil, preventing desertification, and providing the only refuge for biodiversity in large areas of hyperarid desert. They also furnish an extraordinary cornucopia of food, forage, and other products used by local people for thousands of years.

In this chapter, you will identify and correct faulty parallel structure.

What Is Parallel Structure?

Parallel structure occurs when pairs or groups of items in a sentence are balanced. Notice how the following sentences repeat grammatical structures but not ideas.

Parallel nouns: Books, stores, and catalogues give gardeners information.

Parallel tenses: Gardeners dig and plant in the soil.

Parallel adjectives: Kew Garden is large, colourful, and breathtaking.

Parallel phrases: You will find the public garden down the road, over the bridge, and through the field.

Parallel clauses: There are some gardens that have just trees, and some that have only flowers and plants.

Correcting Faulty Parallel Structure

Use parallel structure for a series of words or phrases, for paired clauses, for comparisons, and for two-part constructions. If you see "//" or simply "faulty parallelism" on one of your marked essays, try the following tips for correcting those errors.

Series of Words or Phrases

Use parallel structure when words or phrases are joined in a series.

Not parallel:	The English, the Chinese, and people from Japan create luxurious gardens.
Parallel nouns:	<u>The English</u>, <u>the Chinese</u>, and <u>the Japanese</u> create luxurious gardens.
Not parallel:	I like to read books about gardens, to attend lectures about gardening, and buying plants for my garden.
Parallel verbs:	I like <u>to read</u> books about gardens, <u>to attend</u> lectures about gardening, and <u>to buy</u> plants for my garden.

Section 2
**COMMON
SENTENCE
ERRORS**

Paired Clauses

Use parallel structure when independent clauses are joined by *and*, *but*, or *or*.

Not parallel:	You can find the bonsai garden on the right, and you can look left for the tea garden.
Parallel prepositions:	You can find the bonsai garden <u>on the right</u>, and you can see the tea garden <u>on the left</u>.
Not parallel:	The tourists were dazzled, but they also had feelings of fatigue.
Parallel adjectives:	The tourists were <u>dazzled</u>, but they were also <u>fatigued</u>.

HINT   Use Consistent Voice

When joining two independent clauses with a coordinating conjunction, use a consistent voice. For example, if the first part of the sentence uses the active voice, the other part should also use the active voice.

	active passive
Not parallel:	The bees **flew** to the flowers, and then the nectar **was tasted** by them.
	active active
Parallel active voice:	The bees **flew** to the flowers, and then they **tasted** the nectar.

PRACTICE I

Correct the faulty parallel structure in each sentence.

EXAMPLE:

The Hermitage, which was the winter palace of the Russian Tsars, has a

collection of valuable paintings, rare books, and ~~furniture that is antique~~. *antique furniture*

1. Tsar Peter the Great was cosmopolitan, educated, and he had great determination.

2. In 1703, Peter created plans, and workers were ordered to build a new city.

3. The Tsar commissioned a summer palace and a palace for the winter.

4. The Tsar designed parks, flower gardens, and he was also creating arboretums.

5. The summer garden contains large, exotic trees that are rare.

6. The landscaper, Domenico Trezzini, worked fastidiously, diligently, and he was creative.

7. Tourists can stroll down paths, over bridges, and walking by marble statues.

8. St. Petersburg is called the "window to the west," "the city of the white nights," and people also view it as "the northern Venice."

Comparisons

Use parallel structure in comparisons containing *than or as.*

Not parallel:	Designing an interesting garden is easier than to take care of it.
Parallel *-ing* forms:	<u>Designing an interesting garden</u> is easier than <u>taking care of it.</u>
Not parallel:	The rock garden looks as colourful as the garden where there are roses.
Parallel noun phrases:	<u>The rock garden</u> looks as colourful as <u>the rose garden.</u>

Two-Part Constructions

Use parallel structure for the following paired items.

both . . . and	either . . . or	not . . . but
rather . . . than	neither . . . nor	not only . . . but also

Not parallel:	The lecture on landscaping was both enlightening and of use.
Parallel adjectives:	The lecture on landscaping was both <u>enlightening</u> and <u>useful</u>.
Not parallel:	I could either see the bonsai exhibit or going to a film.
Parallel verbs:	I could either <u>see</u> the bonsai exhibit or <u>go</u> to a film.

PRACTICE 2

Correct ten errors in parallel construction.

EXAMPLE:

Section 2
**COMMON
SENTENCE
ERRORS**

to develop recreational facilities

Cities need parks to create green areas, to prevent overcrowding, and ~~people can use them for recreation~~.

1. During the Industrial Revolution, urban life changed rapidly and in totality. City planners realized that more people were moving to the cities. Planners, politicians, and people who immigrated saw city life changing. Urban designers wanted to create green space rather than filling cities with concrete buildings.

2. One of the most important advocates of city beautification was Frederick Law Olmsted. He was born in 1822, in Hartford, Connecticut. He not only promoted urban planning, but he also was designing beautiful city gardens. He and collaborator Calvert Vaux designed New York's Central Park. Olmstead wanted the park to reflect his personal philosophy, so in it he created open spaces, beautiful views, and paths that wind.

3. Olmsted and Vaux designed many other projects. An important design was the Niagara Falls project. At that time, the falls were not completely visible to tourists. Olmsted wanted to create a harmonious landscape, to allow greater tourist accessibility, and conservation of the area was important to him. Such a park required a great deal of planning. Goat Island separates Canada from the United States. Either the landscapers could buy Goat Island or Goat Island was continuing to be an eyesore. Olmsted and Vaux bought the island and restored it.

4. For Olmsted, contributing to the community was more important than to have fame. He designed Mount Royal Park in Montreal, and the 1893 World's Fair in Chicago was also planned by him. He was known as much for his sense of beauty as for respecting the environment. Olmsted died in 1903, but thousands of people continue to enjoy his legacy.

FINAL REVIEW

Correct fifteen errors in parallel construction. Remember: If you change a compound sentence to a simple sentence, you will have to remove a comma.

EXAMPLE:

Walking through Kew Gardens is more relaxing than ~~to read~~ *reading* a book.

1. One of London's most famous sites is the Royal Botanic Gardens. Kew Gardens contains flower beds, greenhouses, and there are stone sculptures. Kew can be traced back to the 1700s when King George III commissioned and was supporting expanding it. Since then, not only has Kew been enlarged, but it was becoming a World Heritage site. To visit Kew Gardens, travel over the Thames, along the edge of Kew village, and you must go past the Kew Gardens subway station.

2. Today, at Kew Gardens, botanical research is as important as attracting people who are tourists. The site is important for storing seeds, cataloguing plants, and professional gardeners go there for training. But, modernization is creating problems for Kew. Being so close to London, Kew experiences air pollution, hot weather, and the rainfall is in small amounts. Even with such problems, Kew is truly beautiful, very innovative, and it is also extremely impressive.

3. Another famous European garden is the Versailles garden near Paris, France. King Louis XIV moved his court from Paris to Versailles in 1682, and he asked the great landscaper André Le Nôtre to design the gardens. Le Nôtre worked carefully, intuitively, and with passion. Le Nôtre not only had to plan a garden, but water also had to be brought to the site by him. The original soil was neither rich and it was not fertile.

4. Le Nôtre succeeded in his design. It is perfectly laid out adhering to Renaissance principles. The gardens have walkways, fountains, statues, and there are ponds. The gardens reflect the glory of the king, the beauty of nature, and human creativity. Le Nôtre received great fame, honour, and was wealthy. Millions of visitors visit Versailles to enjoy the gardens, to understand a part of history, and seeing the splendour of the age of Louis XIV.

 Writer's Room   **Topics for Writing**

Choose one of the following topics, and write a paragraph. Make sure your nouns, verbs, and sentence structures are parallel.

1. If you could be anywhere right now, where would you be? Describe that place. Include details that appeal to the senses.
2. What do you do to relax? List some steps.

 CHECKLIST: PARALLEL STRUCTURE

When you edit your writing, ask yourself this question.

☐ Are my grammatical structures balanced? Check for errors in these cases:

■ when words or phrases are joined in a series

■ when independent clauses are joined by *and*, *but*, or *or*

■ in comparisons or contrasts

24 Mistakes with Modifiers

GRAMMAR SNAPSHOT **Looking at Mistakes with Modifiers**

Myles Oka, a student in urban planning, wrote about the consequences of urban sprawl. The next excerpt contains some modifier errors.

Because I live in a suburb, I drive many miles each day to work. <u>Last night, stuck in traffic, car</u> <u>horns blared constantly. Commuters inched</u> <u>their cars slowly like caterpillars wanting to get</u> <u>home.</u> I was stressed and anxious.

In this chapter, you will identify and correct misplaced and dangling modifiers.

Misplaced Modifiers

A **modifier** is a word, phrase, or clause that describes or modifies nouns or verbs in a sentence. To use a modifier correctly, place it next to the word(s) that you want to modify.

       modifier   words that are modified

<u>Trying to combat pollution,</u> **city planners** have launched an anti-littering campaign.

A **misplaced modifier** is a word, phrase, or clause that is not placed next to the word that it modifies. When a modifier is too far from the word that it is describing, the meaning of the sentence can become confusing or unintentionally funny.

I saw a pamphlet about littering waiting in the mayor's office.
(How could a pamphlet wait in the mayor's office?)

Commonly Misplaced Modifiers

As you read the sample sentences for each type of modifier, notice how the meaning of the sentence changes depending on where the modifier is placed.

Prepositional Phrase Modifiers   A prepositional phrase is made of a preposition and its object.

Confusing:	Helen read an article on electric cars <u>in a café</u>.
	(Who was in the café: Helen or the cars?)
Clear:	<u>In a café</u>, Helen read an article on electric cars.

Participle Modifiers   A participle modifier is a phrase that contains an *-ing* verb or an *-ed* verb.

Confusing:	Jamal Reed learned about anti-littering laws <u>touring Singapore</u>.
	(Can laws tour Singapore?)
Clear:	While <u>touring Singapore</u>, Jamal Reed learned about anti-littering laws.

Relative Clause Modifiers   A modifier can be a relative clause or phrase beginning with *who*, *whose*, *which*, or *that*.

Confusing:	The woman received a $1000 fine from the officer <u>who dropped a candy wrapper</u>.
	(Who dropped the candy wrapper: the woman or the officer?)
Clear:	The woman who dropped a candy wrapper received a $1000 fine from the officer.

Limiting Modifiers   Limiting modifiers are words such as *almost, nearly, only, merely, just,* and *even*. In the examples, notice how the placement of *almost* changes the meaning of each sentence.

Almost all of the citizens took the steps that solved the littering problem.
(Some of the citizens did not take the steps, but most did.)

All of the citizens **almost** took the steps that solved the littering problem.
(The citizens did not take the steps.)

All of the citizens took the steps that **almost** solved the littering problem.
(The steps did not solve the littering problem.)

Section 2
COMMON SENTENCE ERRORS

> **HINT**   **Correcting Misplaced Modifiers**
>
> To correct misplaced modifiers, follow these steps:
>
> 1. First, identify the modifier.
>   Armando saw the oil slick **standing on the pier**.
>
> 2. Then, identify the word or words being modified.
>   **Armando**
>
> 3. Finally, move the modifier next to the word(s) being modified.
>   Standing on the pier, Armando saw the oil slick.

Section 2
**COMMON
SENTENCE
ERRORS**

PRACTICE 1

Correct the misplaced modifier in each sentence.

EXAMPLE:

    who was fined $500

The man forgot to flush the public toilet who was fined $500.

1. Experts recognize Singapore as the cleanest city in the world from the United Nations.

2. Singaporean police officers will immediately arrest litterbugs who patrol city streets.

3. After littering, officers give a $1000 fine to polluters.

4. For a second littering offence, a polluter must clean a public area such as a park or school yard wearing a bright yellow vest.

5. In 1992, Singapore's new law prohibited the importation, selling, or chewing of gum, which caused a large controversy.

6. Because gum was stuck on them, passengers could not close the doors to the subway trains.

7. In 2004, the law was revised to allow gum into the country that has medicinal purposes.

8. Evangeline dropped her gum on a downtown street not seeing the police officer.

9. She nearly cleaned the park for eight hours on the weekend.

10. Singaporeans with no litter are proud of their city.

Dangling Modifiers

A **dangling modifier** opens a sentence but does not modify any words in the sentence. It "dangles" or hangs loosely because it is not connected to any other part of the sentence.

To avoid having a dangling modifier, make sure that the modifier and the first noun that follows it have a logical connection.

Confusing:	<u>While eating a candy bar</u>, the wrapper fell on the ground.
	(Can a wrapper eat a candy bar?)
Clear:	<u>While eating a candy bar</u>, **Zelda** dropped the wrapper on the ground.
Confusing:	<u>To attend the conference</u>, a background in environmental work is necessary.
	(Can a background attend a conference?)
Clear:	<u>To attend the conference</u>, **participants** need a background in environmental work.

Section 2
COMMON SENTENCE ERRORS

HINT **Correcting Dangling Modifiers**

To correct dangling modifiers, follow these steps:

1. First, identify the modifier.

   <u>When travelling</u>, public transportation should be used.

2. Then, decide who or what the writer aims to modify.

   Who is travelling? **People**

3. Finally, add the missing subject (and in some cases, also add or remove words) so that the sentence makes sense.

   When travelling, people should use public transportation.

PRACTICE 2

Underline the dangling modifier in each sentence. Then, rewrite the sentence keeping the modifier. You may have to add or remove words to give the sentence a logical meaning.

EXAMPLE:

<u>Enjoying parks</u>, it is difficult when there is a lot of litter.

It is difficult for people to enjoy parks when there is a lot of litter.

1. Believing it is not garbage, cigarette butts are left on city streets.

_____

2. With an unconcerned attitude, the hamburger wrapper ended up on the ground.

   _____

3. Unhappy with the garbage in the park, a major cleanup took place.

   _____

4. Playing in the sand, there were pieces of glass from broken bottles.

   _____

5. Sitting on a park bench, all sorts of plastic bags drifted by.

   _____

6. To understand the effects of littering, the cleanup costs must be examined.

   _____

Section 2
**COMMON
SENTENCE
ERRORS**

7. Seeing no available trash can, the cigarette butt can be wrapped up and carried.

   _____

8. While walking barefoot on the grass, a piece of glass cut Pablo's foot.

   _____

9. The car alarm was wailing while reading my newspaper in the park.

   _____

10. By thinking about litter, parks can be kept clean.

    _____

PRACTICE 3

Correct the dangling or misplaced modifiers in the following sentences. If the sentence is correct, write C next to it.

EXAMPLE:

                        Alicia noticed that
Living in Mexico City, the air is extremely bad.   _____

1. Having the highest level of air pollution in the world, people

   suffer from asthma in Mexico City.   _____

2. Coming mainly from the millions of cars on the streets, the

   dangers of the air pollution are well known.   _____

3. Situated in a valley surrounded by mountains, pollution gets

   trapped above Mexico City.   _____

4. Living near Ermita subway, Alicia Gutierrez suffers from

   pollution-related illnesses.   _____

5. Because they are older models, the latest catalytic converters are
   not in many cars.   _____

6. Mexico City planners discussed ways to combat the bad air in a
   meeting.   _____

7. Several years ago, Mexico City's mayor introduced the new
   fuel-efficient buses in a state of excitement.   _____

8. Because of the law requiring motorists to leave their cars home
   one day a week, Luis took a bus to work.   _____

9. Trying to combat the pollution, at least five billion dollars has
   been spent.   _____

10. Appreciating Mexico City's initiatives, the air quality is much
    better.   _____

FINAL REVIEW

Identify fifteen dangling or misplaced modifier errors in this selection. Then, correct each error. You may need to add or remove words to ensure that the sentence makes sense.

EXAMPLE:

                         a young boy found surprising results.
Working on his school project, ~~some surprising results were found~~.

1. Emilio discovered that there are many ways to help the environment in his
   school project. He sat with his parents to discuss energy-saving strategies
   drinking coffee. First, there are things people can do to help the
   environment in their kitchens. When using freezer bags or aluminium foil,
   washing them can reduce waste. Also, people should use cloth napkins and
   dishtowels instead of paper products. With airtight lids, Emilio places food
   in plastic containers.

2. Emilio and his parents also discussed tips for other areas of the home.
   Families can take measures in the bathroom who want to save energy. For
   example, people should take shorter showers. While Emilio is brushing his
   teeth, it is important to leave the faucet turned off as much as possible.
   People can install a toilet dam to reduce water consumption.

3. For their laundry room, Emilio's parents bought energy-efficient appliances with a smile. After washing shirts, the family hangs them out to dry instead of using a clothes dryer. They also buy phosphate-free detergent doing the shopping.

4. When Emilio's father goes to the grocery store, he makes sensible decisions about products near his house. Trying to do fewer trips and buying in bulk, the gas consumption is reduced. He buys incandescent light bulbs at the local hardware store that save energy.

5. The family's furnace needs to be upgraded, which is very old. Based on the latest technology, Emilio's parents are planning to buy an energy-efficient heater. Also, watching only one television, there is a reduction in energy consumption and the family spends more time together. Using the techniques mentioned above, Emilio's family has helped the environment and saved money.

 Writer's Room **Topics for Writing**

Write about one of the following topics. Proofread your text to ensure that there are no modifier errors.

1. What are some steps that your neighbourhood or town could take to combat a littering or pollution problem?

2. What are some types of polluters? Write about three categories of polluters.

CHECKLIST: MODIFIERS

When you edit your writing, ask yourself these questions.

☐ Are my modifiers in the correct position? Check for errors with the following:

- prepositional-phrase modifiers

- participle modifiers

- relative clause modifiers

- limiting modifiers

Wearing overalls, the
~~The~~ urban planner surveyed the garbage ~~wearing overalls~~.

☐ Do my modifiers modify something in the sentence? Check for dangling modifiers.

the tourist got a hefty fine from the police officer
Having thrown the plastic bag onto the street, ~~the police officer gave the tourist a hefty fine~~.

READING LINK

Urban Development
These essays contain more information about urban issues.
"Friendless in North America" by Ellen Goodman (page 194)
"Living Environments" by Avi Friedman (page 465)
"Nature Returns to the Cities" by John Roach (page 468)

Section 2
COMMON SENTENCE ERRORS

25 Subject–Verb Agreement

INTERNATIONAL TRADE In this chapter, you will read about the world of international business.

CHAPTER CONTENTS

GRAMMAR SNAPSHOT Looking at Subject–Verb Agreement

The next excerpt, from "Canadians' Vacation Days Disappearing," is by Suzanne Beaubien. The subjects and verbs are identified. Link each verb with its subject. Do you know why some verbs end in -s?

Piers Steel, a human resources professor at the University of Calgary's Haskayne School of Business, <u>says</u> **he** <u>doesn't</u> <u>think</u> **forfeiting vacation time** necessarily <u>makes</u> businesses more productive.

"Some **people** <u>will take</u> ten hours to do five hours of work," **Steel** <u>said</u>, "but the **need** to take vacation time <u>varies</u> from job to job. Some **people** <u>love</u> their jobs and <u>do</u> not <u>want</u> to take time away."

In this chapter, you will practise making subjects and verbs agree.

Basic Subject–Verb Agreement Rules

Subject–verb agreement simply means that a subject and verb agree in number. A singular subject needs a singular verb and a plural subject needs a plural verb.

Simple Present Tense Agreement

Writers use **simple present tense** to indicate that an action is habitual or factual. Review the following rules for simple present tense agreement.

- **Third-person singular form:** When the subject is *he*, *she*, *it*, or the equivalent (*Mark, Carol, Ottawa*), add an *-s* or *-es* ending to the verb.

  Maria Orlon <u>works</u> as a marketing researcher in Regina.

- **Base form:** When the subject is *I, you, we,* or *they,* or the equivalent (*women, the Rocky Mountains*), do not add an ending to the verb.

  Many **businesses** <u>rely</u> on marketing research.

HINT *Be, Have,* and *Do*

The verbs *be, have,* and *do* have irregular third-person singular forms.

be:	I <u>am</u>	He <u>is</u>	We <u>are</u>
have:	I <u>have</u>	She <u>has</u>	They <u>have</u>
do:	I <u>do</u>	It <u>does</u>	You <u>do</u>

Agreement in Other Tenses

In the past tense, almost all verbs have one past form. The only past-tense verb requiring subject verb agreement is the verb *be,* which has two past forms: *was* and *were.*

I <u>was</u> tired. **Edward** <u>was</u> also tired. That day, **we** <u>were</u> very lazy.

In the present perfect tense, which is formed with *have* or *has* and the past participle, use *has* when the subject is third-person singular and *have* for all other forms.

The **travel service** <u>has raised</u> its booking fees. Other **agencies** <u>have not raised</u> their fees.

In the future tense and with modal forms (*can, could, would, may, might . . .*), use the same form of the verb with every subject.

I <u>will work</u>. **She** <u>will work</u> with me. **We** <u>can work</u> together.

GRAMMAR LINK

For more information about using the present perfect tense, see Chapter 26.

Section 3
VERBS

HINT Use Standard English

In casual conversations and in movies, you may hear people say *He be cool,* or *She don't have the time.* In professional and academic situations, use the correct forms of *be, have,* and *do.*

PRACTICE I

Underline the correct present tense form of the verbs in parentheses.

EXAMPLE:

Many businesses (export / exports) products to other nations.

1. Although several countries (share / shares) the English language, the details

   in the language and culture (be / is / are) different. Business travellers

   (learn / learns) about these differences.

2. For example, Canadians (put / puts) gas in their cars, whereas British citizens (use / uses) petrol. In England, you (do / does) not phone people, you "ring" them. Australians also (have / has) interesting expressions. A "chalkie" (is / are) a teacher, and a "mozzie" (is / are) a mosquito.

3. In England, class-based traditions (is / are) still strong, and many people (support / supports) the monarchy. Australia, on the other hand, (have / has) a very egalitarian culture. Mr. Ian Wynn (have / has) been an Australian real estate agent for seven years, and he (does / do) not like signs of arrogance. Last spring, when some tourists (was / were) arrogant, Wynn said, "Don't be a tall poppy. The tall poppy (get / gets) its head cut off."

4. Spelling also (differ / differs) among English speaking nations. Canada (follow / follows) British spelling much of the time. Thus, we (maintain / maintains) the -*our* ending on words such as *flavour* or *colour*. Americans (drop / drops) the final "u" and (write / writes) *flavor* or *color*.

More Than One Subject

There are special agreement rules when there is more than one subject in a sentence.

and

When two subjects are joined by *and*, use the plural form of the verb.

> High schools, universities, and trade schools **prepare** students for the job market.

or, nor

When two subjects are joined by *or* or *nor*, the verb agrees with the subject that is the closest to it.

> singular
> The layout artists or the editor **decides** how the cover will look.

> plural
> Neither the artist nor her assistants **make** changes to the design.

> **HINT** *As Well as and Along with*
>
> The phrases *as well as* and *along with* are not the same as *and*. They do not form a compound subject. The real subject is before the interrupting expression.
>
> Japan, China, and South Korea **develop** high-tech computer products.
> Japan, as well as China and South Korea, **develops** high-tech computer products.

PRACTICE 2

Underline the correct verb in each sentence. Make sure the verb agrees with the subject.

EXAMPLE:

Japan and China (<u>have</u> / has) interesting types of restaurants.

1. Tokyo and other Japanese cities (have / has) "Maid Cafés."

2. The hostess and the female servers (dress / dresses) in traditional maid uniforms.

3. Recently, in the Otome Road area of Tokyo, a businesswoman and her partner (have / has) opened a Butler Café.

4. Every day, Jin or another waiter (serve / serves) customers.

5. The coffee or the tea (come / comes) on a special tray.

6. The host and the waiters (treat / treats) the customers like British royalty.

7. "Mademoiselle" or "Your Highness" (is / are) said to each customer by the server in the butler uniform.

8. A crumpet as well as a large scone (appear / appears) on each table.

9. Every day, many young and old women (try / tries) to get a table at the Butler Café.

Special Subject Forms

Some subjects are not easy to identify as singular or plural. Two common types are indefinite pronouns and collective nouns.

Indefinite Pronouns

Indefinite pronouns refer to a general person, place, or thing. Carefully review the following list of indefinite pronouns.

Indefinite Pronouns			
Singular	another anybody anyone anything	each everybody everyone everything	nobody no one nothing one	other somebody someone something
Plural	both, few, many, others, several			

Singular Indefinite Pronouns In the following sentences, the verbs require the third-person-singular form because the subjects are singular.

Almost <u>everyone</u> **knows** about the Free Trade Agreement.

You can put one or more singular nouns (joined by *and*) after *each* and *every*. The verb is still singular.

<u>Every</u> client **likes** the new rule. <u>Each</u> man and woman **knows** about it.

Plural Indefinite Pronouns *Both*, *few*, *many*, *others*, and *several* are all plural subjects. The verb is always plural.

A representative from Canada and another from Mexico are sitting at a table. <u>Both</u> **want** to compromise.

Collective Nouns

Collective nouns refer to a group of people or things. Here are some common collective nouns.

army	gang
association	government
audience	group
band	jury
class	mob
club	organization
committee	population
company	public
crowd	society
family	team

Generally, each group acts as a unit, so you must use the singular form of the verb.

The <u>company</u> **is** ready to make a decision.

HINT *Police Is Plural*

Treat the word *police* as a plural noun because the word "officers" is implied but not stated.

The police **have** a protester in custody.

PRACTICE 3

Underline the correct verb in each sentence.

EXAMPLE:

The Executive Planet website (have / <u>has</u>) tips for business travellers.

1. Each large and small nation (have / has) its own gift-giving rules. For example, Singapore (have / has) strict rules against bribery, and the government (pride / prides) itself on being corruption-free. The police (arrest / arrests) officials who accept a bribe.

2. Specific rules (apply / applies) to gift-giving in Singapore. Certainly, everyone (love / loves) to receive a gift. Nobody (like / likes) to be left out while somebody else (open / opens) a present, so in Singapore, every businessman or businesswoman (know / knows) that gifts must be presented to a group. For example, if somebody (want / wants) to thank a receptionist, he or she (give / gives) a gift to the entire department. The group (accept / accepts) the gift graciously.

3. To be polite, most individuals (refuse / refuses) a gift initially. Some (believe / believes) that a refusal (make / makes) them appear less greedy. If the gift-giver (continue / continues) to insist, the recipient will accept the gift.

4. Singaporeans (do / does) not unwrap gifts in front of the giver. It (imply / implies) that the receiver is impatient and greedy. Everyone (thank / thanks) the gift-giver and (wait / waits) to open the gift in privacy.

5. China, as well as Japan, also (have / has) unusual gift-giving rules. In China, nobody (give / gives) a gift in white or green wrapping paper because those colours are unlucky. In Japan, the number four (sound / sounds) like the word meaning "death," so people do not give gifts that contain four items. To avoid insulting their hosts, business travellers should learn about gift-giving rules in other nations.

Section 3
VERBS

Verb Before the Subject

Usually the verb comes after the subject, but in some sentences, the verb is before the subject. In such cases, you must still ensure that the subject and verb agree.

There or Here

When a sentence begins with *there* or *here*, the subject always follows the verb. *There* and *here* are not subjects.

      V   S   V   S
Here **is** the <u>menu</u>.   There **are** many different <u>sandwiches</u>.

Questions

In questions, word order is usually reversed, and the main or helping verb is placed before the subject. In the following example, the main verb is *be*.

        V   S   V   S
Where **is** the <u>Butler Café</u>?   **Is** the <u>food</u> good?

In questions in which the main verb is not *be*, the subject agrees with the helping verb that appears before it.

      HV   S   V   HV   S   V
When **does** the <u>café</u> close?   **Do** <u>students</u> **work** there?

PRACTICE 4

Correct any subject–verb agreement errors. If the sentence is correct, write C in the space.

EXAMPLE:

> Have
> ~~Has~~ you ever visited Turkey?

1. Is there etiquette rules about greetings? _____

2. Do each nation have its own rules? _____

3. There be specific rules in each country. _____

4. In Turkey, do older men or women receive preferential treatment? _____

5. If someone enters a room, he or she greet the oldest person first. _____

6. There be tremendous respect for elders. _____

7. Why is the two women holding hands? _____

8. In Turkey, handholding is a sign of respect and friendship. _____

9. In many companies, there have not been enough attention given to business etiquette. _____

10. On the other hand, there is many business professionals who learn about the customs of their foreign clients. _____

Section 3
VERBS

Interrupting Words and Phrases

Words that come between the subject and the verb may confuse you. In these cases, look for the subject and make sure that the verb agrees with the subject.

> S   interrupting phrase V
> Some <u>companies</u> in the transportation sector **lose** money.

> S interrupting phrase V
> The <u>manager</u> in my office never **wears** a suit and tie.

> **HINT** **Identify Interrupting Phrases**
>
> When you revise your paragraphs, place words that separate the subject and the verb in parentheses. Then you can check to see if your subjects and verbs agree.
>
> > S interrupting phrase V
> > An <u>employee</u> (in my brother's company) **annoys** his co-workers.
>
> When interrupting phrases contain *of the*, the subject appears before the phrase.
>
> > S   interrupting phrase V
> > <u>One</u> (of the most common work-related ailments) **is** carpal tunnel syndrome.

PRACTICE 5

Identify the subject and place any words that come between each subject and verb in parentheses. Then underline the correct form of the verb. (Two possible verb choices are in bold.)

EXAMPLE:

(One) (of the most controversial topics in business circles) <u>is</u> / **are** stress.

1. Canadians **take / takes** very few vacation days. Other nations, including France, England, and Sweden, **have / has** many vacation days. The average employee in France **have / has** about thirty-nine vacation days annually. Canadians, on the other hand, only **receive / receives** twenty-one vacation days each year. The typical Canadian employee, for a variety of reasons, only **use / uses** nineteen of those days each year.

2. Why **do / does** Canadians forfeit vacation days? Some **say / says** that they do not schedule their vacation in advance. Others **is / are** too busy at work and **take / takes** cash instead of vacation days. Journalist Suzanne Beaubien, in a newspaper article, **suggest / suggests** that businesses benefit each time an employee **do / does** not take a vacation. "Over $5 billion in wages is handed back to employers," she **say / says**.

3. One of the problems caused by a lack of time off **is / are** stress-related illness. Some Canadians, according to JobCircle.com, **is / are** beginning to rebel. Workers increasingly **call / calls** in sick when they really **have / has** family responsibilities or other reasons for missing work. For example, Ted Owens, a Toronto-based broker, **admit / admits** to using sick days for other purposes. One of his co-workers **have / has** also lied to the boss on a regular basis.

Interrupting Words—Who, Which, That

If a sentence contains a clause beginning with *who*, *which*, or *that*, then the verb agrees with the subject preceding *who*, *which*, or *that*.

There is a <u>woman</u> in my neighbourhood *who* **works** as an executive.

Sometimes a complete dependent clause appears between the subject and verb.

interrupting clause
The <u>problem</u>, *which* we discussed, **needs** to be solved.

PRACTICE 6

Correct nine subject–verb agreement errors.

EXAMPLE:

discusses

Jeff Geissler ~~discuss~~ maternity leave in an article for the Associated Press.

1. Elisa Elbert, who works for an accounting firm, is expecting a child. Elisa, like other Australian citizens, receive up to twelve months of paid leave. Madhuri Datta, a Canadian, is having her baby next month. Datta, who is due in November, want to share her paid leave with her husband. According to a recent poll, one of the Canadian government's best laws are the one that permits parents to divide thirty-five weeks of paid parental leave.

2. The U.S. *Family and Medical Leave Act*, which only cover workers in large companies, protect new mothers from losing their jobs. The act, according to a Harvard study, only provide for twelve weeks of paid leave.

3. Why do Canada have a parental leave program? Jeanne Brooks-Gunn, a professor at Columbia University, point out that some countries have falling birth rates and need to boost their populations. Canada, Italy, and Japan, for instance, have parental-leave policies that encourages working women to reproduce.

FINAL REVIEW

Correct fifteen errors in subject–verb agreement.

EXAMPLE:

enjoys

The worker ~~enjoy~~ his afternoon nap.

1. Is afternoon naps beneficial? In Spain, the afternoon siesta have been part of the culture for centuries. Many businesses, including shops, restaurants, and offices, close for three hours each afternoon and then opens from 5 to 7 p.m. During the long break, employees return home and has a siesta. However, the siesta culture is changing.

2. Some multinational companies that operates in Spain remain open for business in the afternoons. One of the reasons are the companies' desire to increase productivity. To give sleep-deprived Spaniards the siesta that they crave, a new type of business has opened. There is "siesta shops" throughout Spain. Each shop satisfy a need.

3. Jose Luis Buqueras, a computer programmer, work for a British multinational in Madrid, and he has a one-hour lunch break. Luckily for Buqueras, there be several siesta shops in his neighbourhood that offers short siestas. If he pays 500 pesetas, he can doze in a darkened room for twenty minutes. One of the attendants massage his neck. Then somebody cover him with a blanket. Quiet music plays in the background.

4. Although many Spanish citizens no longer enjoy three-hour breaks, they have not given up their afternoon siestas. Perhaps other nations can benefit from Spain's example. According to many medical professionals, a short afternoon nap helps reduce stress. There is also studies showing that naps reduce heart disease. David Jenkins, a government employee in Ireland, want siesta shops to open in his country.

Section 3
VERBS

 Writer's Room   **Topics for Writing**

Write about one of the following topics. Proofread your text to ensure that your subjects and verbs agree.

1. Do you have afternoon naps? Explain why or why not. Compare yourself to someone who has, or does not have, frequent naps.

2. Describe a visit that you made to a culturally different restaurant. What happened? Use language that appeals to the senses.

CHECKLIST: SUBJECT–VERB AGREEMENT

When you edit your writing, ask yourself these questions.

☐ Do my subjects and verbs agree? Check for errors with the following:

- present tense verbs

- *was* and *were*

- interrupting phrases

The clients, whom I have never met, ~~is~~ ^{are} unhappy with the new ad. It ~~be~~ ^{is} too dull.

☐ Do I use the correct verb form with indefinite pronouns? Check for errors with singular indefinite pronouns such as *everybody*, *nobody*, or *somebody*.

Somebody ~~have~~ ^{has} to modify the photograph.

☐ Do my subjects and verbs agree when the subject is after the verb? Check for errors with the following:

- sentences containing *here* and *there*

- question forms

~~Do~~ ^{Does} she watch commercials? There ~~is~~ ^{are} many funny ads on television.

Verb Tenses

INTERNATIONAL TRADE In this chapter, you will learn about advertising and marketing.

CHAPTER CONTENTS

GRAMMAR SNAPSHOT Looking at Verb Tenses

The next excerpt is from Business Ethics by Richard T. De George. Look at the underlined verbs and try to determine what tense the author has used. What is the difference between was and were? Why do some verbs begin with has? What is the difference between was and has been? You will discover the answers to these questions in this chapter.

The growth of giant corporations <u>has tended</u> to make competition in many areas very costly. The growth of supermarkets, which <u>began</u> in the 1940s, <u>has forced</u> most small grocers and vegetable and fruit markets out of business. The prices a supermarket <u>was</u> able to charge <u>were</u> lower than those the small operators could charge for equal-quality goods. The consequence <u>has been</u> the elimination of small grocers.

In this chapter, you will write using a variety of verb tenses.

What Is Verb Tense?

Verb tense indicates when an action occurred. Review the various tenses of the verb *work*. (Progressive or *-ing* forms of these verbs appear at the end of this chapter.)

Simple Forms

Present:	I <u>work</u> in a large company. My sister <u>works</u> with me.
Past:	We <u>worked</u> in Cancun last summer.
Future:	My sister <u>will work</u> in the Middle East next year.
Present perfect:	We <u>have worked</u> together since 2001.

<table>
<tr><td>**Past perfect:**</td><td>When Maria lost her job, she <u>had worked</u> there for six years.</td></tr>
<tr><td>**Future perfect:**</td><td>By 2020, I <u>will have worked</u> here for twenty years.</td></tr>
</table>

HINT Use Standard Verb Forms

Non-standard English is used in everyday conversation and may differ according to the region in which you live. **Standard English** is the common language generally used and expected in schools, businesses, and government institutions in Canada. In college, you should write using standard English.

Non-standard:	He don't have no money.
	She be real tired.
Standard:	He <u>does not</u> have <u>any</u> money.
	She <u>is</u> really tired.

Present and Past Tenses

Present Tense Verbs

The simple present tense indicates that an action is a general fact or habitual activity. Remember to add *-s* or *-es* to verbs that follow third-person singular forms.

| **Fact:** | Our fee <u>includes</u> mass mail-outs and pamphlet distribution. |
| **Habitual activity:** | Carmen Cruz <u>takes</u> drawing classes every Saturday. |

Past Tense Verbs

The past tense indicates that an action occurred at a specific past time. Regular past tense verbs have a standard *-d* or *-ed* ending. Use the same form for both singular and plural past tense verbs.

Yesterday morning, we **discussed** the campaign.

GRAMMAR LINK

For rules on the spelling of regular past-tense verbs, see Chapter 32, Spelling and Commonly Confused Words.

PRACTICE I

Write the present or past tense of each verb in parentheses.

EXAMPLE:

In the 1960s, some American companies (attempt) _attempted_ to enter the Japanese marketplace.

1. General Mills company (produce) _____ many food products.

   Each year, the company (sell) _____ products around the world.

   Sometimes, a product (succeed) _____ in a foreign

   marketplace, but occasionally, a product (fail) _____.

2. In 2004, Joyce Millet (publish) _____ an article called,

   "Marketing in Japan: What History Can Teach Us." To prepare for her

   article, she (research) _____ examples of product failures.

3. In the late 1960s, General Mills (plan) _____ to market Betty

   Crocker cake mixes in Japan. They (try) _____ to design a

   suitable product. Product developers (learn) _____ that very

   few Japanese homes had ovens, so they (need) _____ to find a

   new way to bake the cakes. At that time, most Japanese homes (contain)

   _____ a rice cooker, so designers (create) _____ a

   spongy cake mix that worked in a rice cooker.

4. At first, sales of the Betty Crocker cake mix were good, but sales quickly

   (tumble) _____. What was the problem? In the past, most

   Japanese citizens (believe) _____ that rice was sacred, so they

   (refuse) _____ to contaminate the rice with cake flavour.

Section 3
VERBS

Irregular Past Tense Verbs

Irregular verbs change internally. Because their spellings change from the present to the past tense, these verbs can be challenging to remember. For example, the irregular verb *go* becomes *went* when you convert it to the past tense.

> The company <u>sold</u> the patent.
> (*sold* = past tense of *sell*)

> Consumers <u>bought</u> the product.
> (*bought* = past tense of *buy*)

be (was or were) Most past tense verbs have one form that you can use with all subjects. However, the verb *be* has two past forms: *was* and *were*. The packing box <u>was</u> not sturdy enough. The plates <u>were</u> fragile.

⌐ **GRAMMAR LINK**

See Appendix 2 for a list of common irregular verbs.

PRACTICE 2

Write the correct past tense form of each verb in parentheses. Some verbs are regular, and some are irregular. If you do not know the past tense form of an irregular verb, consult the chart in Appendix 2.

EXAMPLE:

Long ago, John Pemberton (have) _____*had*_____ a great idea.

1. In 1884, John Pemberton (be) _____ a pharmacist in Atlanta, Georgia. He (know) _____ about a successful French product called a "coca wine." Pemberton (make) _____ his own version of the product and called it Pemberton's French Wine Coca. In 1885, Atlanta (pass) _____ prohibition legislation, so Pemberton created an alcohol-free version of his drink. He (mix) _____ his syrup with carbonated water, and he (bring) _____ some samples to a local pharmacy. Customers (pay) _____ 5 cents a glass for the drink.

2. Pemberton's bookkeeper (be) _____ a marketing wizard. Frank M. Robinson (think) _____ of a name for the drink. He also (feel) _____ certain that the drink required an interesting logo, thus Robinson (develop) _____ the handwritten Coca-Cola logo. In 1886, many stores (have) _____ the red logo on their awnings.

3. Pemberton never (make) _____ a lot of money from his invention. He (sell) _____ his company to Mr. Asa Candler for $2300. Candler (take)_____ the Coca-Cola company to new heights, and it (become) _____ a highly successful international company.

4. In 1889, the Coca-Cola company (do) _____ not patent the formula for Coca-Cola because company executives (do) _____ not want competitors to know the secret formula of the soft drink. It remains one of the best-kept trade secrets in history.

> HINT   **Use the Base Form after *Did* and *To***
>
> Remember to use the base form
>
> ■ of verbs that follow *did* in question and negative forms.
> ■ of verbs that follow the word *to* (infinitive form).
>
>   *invent*   *promote*
> Did he ~~invented~~ a good product? Pemberton wanted to ~~promoted~~ his soft drink.

PRACTICE 3

Correct twelve verb tense and spelling errors in the next essay.

EXAMPLE:

                               like
Consumer groups didn't ~~liked~~ the marketing campaign.

1. In past centuries, breastfeeding be the most common method of feeding children. At the end of the nineteenth century, some parents feeded their children cows' milk. In 1838, a German physician analyzed milk from cows and discover that larger proteins and reduced carbohydrates contributed to the increasing infant mortality rate.

2. The search for a healthy alternative to breast milk preoccupied scientists in the nineteenth century. Finally, in the 1870s, Nestlé Company produced the first infant formula. Consumers just had to mixed water with the formula.

3. In 1973, Nestlé Company wanted to sold the formula in Africa. The company putted advertisements for the product in magazines and on billboards. Nestlé also gave free samples to African women as soon as they had their babies. In hospitals, mothers seen their own breast milk dry up after they gave formula to their babies. When the women returned home, they did not had enough money to continue buying enough formula. They added too much water to the formula, and the water was often contaminated. Babies who drinked formula become malnourished. In many villages, the level of infant malnutrition and mortality rised.

GRAMMAR LINK

For a list of irregular past participles, see Appendix 2.

Past Participles

A **past participle** is a verb form, not a verb tense. The past tense and the past participle of regular verbs are the same. The past tense and the past participle of irregular verbs may be different.

	Base Form	Past Tense	Past Participle
Regular verb:	talk	talked	talked
Irregular verb:	begin	began	begun

HINT **Using Past Participles**

You cannot use a past participle as the only verb in a sentence. You must use it with a helping verb such as *have, has, had, is, was* or *were*.

          helping verb
The company **was** <u>founded</u> in 1863.

          past participle
The products **have** <u>become</u> very popular.

Section 3
VERBS

PRACTICE 4

In the next selection, the past participles are underlined. Correct ten past participle errors, and write C above correct past participles.

EXAMPLE:

                      met
The business ethics students have <u>meeted</u> many times to discuss the case.

1. Since 1973, Nestlé has <u>faced</u> a lot of criticism for its marketing techniques in Africa. According to critics, Nestlé should have <u>knew</u> that the advertising was dangerous and misleading. For instance, by 1980, Nestlé had <u>make</u> hundreds of billboards showing a white woman feeding her child with a bottle. The African women were <u>teached</u> that good mothers don't breastfeed their children.

2. The method of giving free samples to new mothers was also <u>blamed</u> for the problem. According to critics, a company spokesman has <u>admit</u> that the free samples contributed to the drying up of mothers' breast milk. In addition, the colour white was <u>weared</u> by company salespeople when they walked through hospital wards. New mothers could have <u>thinked</u> that the salespeople were nurses.

3. Nestlé's business practices have always <u>being</u> legal. In fact, Nestlé has successfully <u>used</u> the same techniques in many wealthy nations. Nonetheless, in 1977, a worldwide boycott of Nestlé products was <u>organize</u> by a group of concerned citizens.

4. Many business students have <u>studied</u> the Nestlé case. Technically, Nestlé did the same thing in Africa that it has <u>did</u> in the United States for many years. If a marketing technique has <u>work</u> successfully in wealthy countries, is a company <u>obliged</u> to revise its marketing techniques in less developed countries?

Present Perfect Tense (*have* or *has* + past participle)

A past participle combines with *have* or *has* to form the **present perfect tense**.

> Kate **has been** a marketing manager for six years.
> Since 2001, the products **have sold** extremely well.

You can use this tense in two different circumstances.

- Use the present perfect to show that an action began in the past and continues to the present time. You will often use *since* and *for* with this tense.

PAST
(5 years ago, the
factory opened)

NOW

The factory **has flourished** for five years.

- Use the present perfect to show that one or more completed actions occurred at unspecified past times.

PAST

? ? ? ?

NOW

Mr. Jain **has visited** China four times.
(The time of the four visits is not specified.)

Choosing the Past or the Present Perfect

Look at the difference between the past and the present perfect tenses.

Simple past: In 2002, Kumar Jain **went** to Shanghai.
                      (This event occurred at a known past time.)

Present perfect: Since 2002, Jain **has owned** a factory in China.
                      (The action began in the past and continues to the present.)

                      He **has made** many business contacts.
                      (Making business contacts occurred at unknown past times.)

HINT **Use Time Markers**

When you try to identify which tense to use, look for time markers. **Time markers** are words such as *since, for,* or *ago* that indicate when an action occurred.

Simple past: Three weeks **ago**, Parker launched her new perfume.
Present perfect: **Since 2006**, the perfume has been successful.

PRACTICE 5

Write the past or present perfect form of the verb in parentheses.

EXAMPLE:

For the last six years, my cousin Mike (be) ___has been___ a sales representative.

1. Since the beginning of the twentieth century, many companies (try)

   _____ to create memorable advertisements for their products.

   Before the 1920s, most ads (be) _____ on billboards and in

   magazines. Then, in 1922, companies (discover) _____ the

   potential of radio advertising. They (sponsor) _____ radio shows.

   For example, the Lucky Strike Cigarette Company sponsored a music

   show. Since then, many companies (sponsor) _____ artistic and

   sporting events.

2. In the mid 1920s, radio stations (decide) _____ to give short time

   slots to advertisers so that they could promote their products as an

   alternative to the sponsorship of shows. Ever since, commercials (be)

   _____ an effective way for companies to market their products.

   Most people (see) _____ thousands of commercials.

HINT Past or Present Perfect?

Use the past tense when referring to someone who is no longer living or to something that no longer exists. Use the present perfect tense only when the action has a relationship to someone or something that still exists.

$$\text{designed}$$
Leonardo da Vinci <u>has designed</u> many products.

PRACTICE 6

Identify and correct ten verb errors.

EXAMPLE:

$$\text{began}$$
The Coca-Cola Company <u>has begun</u> in 1886.

Section 3
VERBS

1. Since 1986, Coca-Cola is a familiar product throughout the world. For over a century, the company made some very successful marketing decisions. In 1931, Haddon Sunblom has illustrated a Coca-Cola advertisement with a Santa Claus figure that had a white beard, rosy cheeks, and a red suit. Since 1931, Sunblom's drawing is the popular image of the Christmas character.

2. Although the Coca-Cola company been very successful since its inception, occasionally it has made blunders. In 1984, Coca-Cola managers have worried about the increasing popularity of Pepsi. That year, Coke developers modified the original formula and have made the product much sweeter.

3. On April 23, 1985, at a press conference, Coca-Cola's chairman has introduced the New Coke by calling it "smoother, rounder, and bolder." Unfortunately, when the product hit store shelves, consumers complained about the taste.

4. On July 29, 1985, the company pulled the New Coke from the shelves and reintroduced the original product, calling it Coke Classic. Curiously, Coke Classic is very successful since its reintroduction. Since the "New Coke" fiasco, other companies learned from Coca-Cola's mistake. If consumers love a product, do not modify it!

Past Perfect Tense (*had* + past participle)

The **past perfect tense** indicates that one or more past actions happened before another past action. It is formed with *had* and the past participle.

PAST PERFECT	PAST	NOW
↓	↓	↓

Mr. Lo **had spent** a lot on research by the time he **launched** the product.

Notice the differences between the simple past, the present perfect, and the past perfect tenses.

Simple past: Last night, Craig <u>worked</u> at Burger Town.
(The action occurred at a known past time.)

Present perfect: He <u>has owned</u> the restaurant for three years.
(The action began in the past and continues to the present.)

Past perfect: Craig <u>had had</u> two business failures before he bought Burger Town.
(All of the actions happened in the past, but the two business failures occurred before he bought the hamburger restaurant.)

PRACTICE 7

Underline the correct verb form in each sentence. You may choose the simple past or the past perfect tenses.

EXAMPLE:

The Barbosas (were / <u>had been</u>) farmers for ten years when Alex Barbosa decided to sell organic beef.

1. Even though he (never studied / had never studied) marketing, Alex Barbosa decided to promote his organic beef.

2. He printed flyers, and then he (distributed / had distributed) them to private homes.

3. When most residents threw out the flyer, they (did not even read / had not even read) it.

4. The flyer contained a picture that Barbosa (took / had taken) the previous summer.

5. The image of the meat carcass (was / had been) unappealing.

6. After Barbosa received negative feedback about his flyer, he remembered that his daughter (warned / had warned) him about the image.

7. Also, the neighbourhood (had / had had) low-income families who could not afford the high price of the organic meat.

8. Finally, in 2005, Barbosa hired a business graduate who (learned / had learned) how to do effective marketing.

9. By December 2006, Barbosa's organic meat (found / had found) a niche in the marketplace.

Passive Voice (*be* + past participle)

In sentences with the **passive voice**, the subject receives the action and does not perform the action. To form the passive voice, use the appropriate tense of the verb *be* plus the past participle. Look carefully at the following two sentences.

Active:	The boss **gave** documents to her assistant.
	(This is active, because the subject, *boss*, performed the action.)
Passive:	Several documents **were given** to the assistant.
	(This is passive because the subject, *documents*, was affected by the action and did not perform the action.)

To form the passive voice, use the appropriate past tense of the verb *be* plus the past participle.

HINT Avoid Overusing the Passive Voice

Generally, try to use the active voice instead of the passive voice. The active voice is more direct and friendly than the passive voice. For example, read two versions of the same message.

Passive voice: No more than two pills per day should be ingested. This medication should be taken with meals. It should not be continued if headache or nausea are experienced. Any side effects should be reported immediately.

Active voice: Do not ingest more than two pills per day. Take this medication with meals. Do not continue taking it if you experience headache or nausea. Immediately report any side effects to your doctor.

PRACTICE 8

Complete the following sentences by changing the passive verb to the active form. Do not alter the verb tense.

EXAMPLE:

Each department will be visited by the supervisor.

The supervisor will visit each department.

1. A funny commercial *was created* by the advertising agency.

_____

2. The ad *will be seen* by many people.

_____

3. A well-known comedian *was hired* by the company.

_____

4. Many commercials *are created* by Pedro Guzman.

_____

5. Complaints about their commercials *are often ignored* by companies.

_____

> **HINT** **When *be* Is Suggested, Not Written**
>
> In the passive voice, sometimes the verb *be* is suggested but not written. The following sentence contains the passive voice.
>
>   (who was)
> A man ^ **named** Harley Cobb complained about the car company's decision.

Section 3
VERBS

PRACTICE 9

Correct eight errors with past participles.

EXAMPLE:

        found
A problem was ~~find~~ with the design.

1. When Apple Computers first developed the Macintosh, a pull-down screen, or window, was include in the product. The computer also had a variety of icons for different tasks. For instance, useless files were drag to a trashcan icon. A year later, Microsoft Corporation introduced its popular software program name Windows. The software, create in 1988, looked a lot like Apple's software. Apple sued Microsoft for copyright infringement and argued that Microsoft copied the "look and feel" of Apple software.

2. There are strict rules about copyright. A unique product can be patent. However, people cannot copyright an idea. Therefore, Apple's decision to use specific icons could not be protect. Still, Apple argued that its original concept should not have been copy. The case, which lasted for four years, was win by Microsoft.

Progressive Forms (*-ing* verbs)

Most verbs have progressive tenses. The **progressive tense**, formed with *be* and the *-ing* form of the verb, indicates that an action is, was, or will be in progress. For example, the present progressive indicates that an action is happening right now or for a temporary period of time. The following timeline illustrates both the simple and progressive tenses.

Every day, he **sells** leather wallets.
(Simple present)

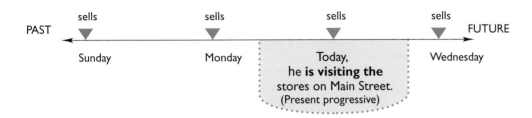

To form the progressive, use the appropriate tense of the verb *be* with the *–ing* verb.

**Section 3
VERBS**

Present progressive:	Right now, I **am** <u>working</u>.
Past progressive:	We **were** <u>sleeping</u> when you phoned us.
Future progressive:	Tomorrow, at noon, I **will be** <u>driving</u>.
Present perfect progressive:	The receptionist **has been** <u>working</u> since 8 a.m.
Past perfect progressive:	She **had been** <u>speeding</u> when the officer stopped her.

Common Errors in the Progressive Form

- Do not use the progressive form when an action happens regularly.

  complains
  Every day he ~~is complaining~~ about his job.

- In the progressive form, use the correct form of the verb *be*.

  is
  Right now, Ron ~~be~~ talking with his manager.

- In the progressive form, always include the complete helping verb.

  is   *have*
  Right now, the manager discussing the problem. They been talking for hours.

Non-Progressive Verbs

Some verbs do not take the progressive form because they indicate an ongoing state or a perception rather than a temporary action.

Examples of Non-Progressive Verbs

Perception Verbs	Preference Verbs	State Verbs	Possession Verbs
admire	desire	believe	have*
hear	doubt	know	own
smell*	hate	mean	possess
see	like	realize	
seem	love	recognize	
taste*	prefer	suppose	
feel*	want	think*	
	care	understand	

*Some verbs have more than one meaning and can be used in the progressive tense. Compare the following pairs of sentences.

Non-Progressive:	He **has** a franchise. (expresses ownership) I **think** it is unethical. (expresses an opinion)
Progressive:	He **is having** a bad day. I **am thinking** about you.

Section 3
VERBS

PRACTICE 10

Underline and correct one verb error in each sentence.

EXAMPLE:

had

She been working in the store for ten years when she was fired.

1. Ellen Peters was producing fragrances in her Toronto basement and give them away when her sister suggested that she try to market her perfume.

2. These days, Peters negotiating with a cosmetics company that hopes to market her product internationally.

3. She been looking for a product name for the last six months.

4. Last May, she be planning to call it Golden Mist when someone told her that "mist" means "manure" in German.

5. While her friends were brainstorm to help her, one of them suggested the name "Pete," which is a shortened form of Peters.

6. Unfortunately, pété is meaning "release of gassy air" in French.

7. Often, companies are having problems with bad translations.

8. For instance, the owner of the Japanese travel agency called Kinki Nippon Tours be complaining about foreign customers who wanted sex tours when a customer told him the English meaning of "kinky."

9. In another case, a Scandinavian vacuum cleaner company was making a mistake when it created the slogan "Nothing sucks like an Electrolux."

10. Ellen Peters wants to her product to sell internationally, so right now she is work with a marketing firm to come up with a good name.

FINAL REVIEW

Underline and correct fifteen errors in verb form or tense.

EXAMPLE:

published

The book *Business Ethics* was <u>publish</u> by Prentice Hall in 2006.

1. Since 1900, many products been defective. In his book *Business Ethics*, Richard T. De George discusses a famous product defect case. In the early 1970s, American automakers lose market share because smaller Japanese imports be flooding the market.

2. Lee Iacocca, the CEO of Ford Motor Company, was wanting the company to produce a lightweight, economical car. Engineers developed the Ford Pinto. Because Ford wanted the product on the market quickly, the car was not test for rear-end impact during the production period. Then, after the Pintos had been produce, they were put in collision tests, and they failed the tests. When the Pinto was hitted from behind, a bolt on the bumper sometimes punctured the fuel tank. It could cause an explosion.

3. Ford conducted a study and determined that a small baffle, worth about $8, could be place between the bumper and the gas tank. The company maked a cost-benefit analysis to compare the cost of adding the baffle against the estimated cost of lawsuits. The company decided that it was less expensive to fight lawsuits than to insert the baffle. For the next seven years, the

design of Ford Pintos did not changed. The company also neglected to offer the baffle to customers.

4. In 1976, Pintos had thirteen explosions from rear-end impacts, which was twice the number of explosions for cars of a comparable size. When it be too late, the Ford Motor Company realized that the lawsuits was much more expensive than the baffle installations.

5. The Pinto was recall in 1978. Since 1978, Ford has make much better business decisions. In the late 1970s, the bad publicity from the Pinto case damaged the company's reputation. Since then, Ford tried to improve its image.

Section 3
VERBS

 Writer's Room **Topics for Writing**

Write about one of the following topics. Proofread your writing and ensure that your verbs are formed correctly.

1. Write a short paragraph describing a useful product that you own. When and where did you get the product? How is it useful?

2. What are the effects of advertising on consumers? How does the deluge of commercials, spam, billboards, and other advertising affect the population?

 CHECKLIST: VERB TENSES

When you edit your writing, ask yourself these questions.

Do I use the correct present and past tense forms? Check for errors in these cases:

- verbs following third-person singular nouns
- irregular present or past tense verbs
- question and negative forms

                      were   *were*
The products which ~~was~~ defective ~~was~~ in his shop.

■ Do I use the correct form of past participles? Check for errors in the following:

  ▪ spelling of irregular past participles
  ▪ present perfect and past perfect verbs
  ▪ passive and active forms

                have made
Since the 1970s, some car companies ~~made~~ bad business decisions.

■ Do I use *-ing* forms correctly? Check for the overuse or misuse of progressive forms. Also ensure that progressive forms are complete.

                   designing   *wanted*
In 1971, while engineers were ~~design~~ the Pinto, nobody ~~was wanting~~ to make an unsafe car.

Problems with Verbs

INTERNATIONAL TRADE **In this chapter, you will read about unusual and dangerous jobs.**

CHAPTER CONTENTS

GRAMMAR SNAPSHOT **Looking at Other Verb Forms**

The next excerpt is from a personal letter written by Garrett Brice, a Kelowna-based software designer who spent a summer working in a fire tower. Conditional sentences are underlined, and some modals are in bold. What types of errors do people make with the underlined or bold sentences?

The strangest job I have ever had was working in a fire tower. Sometimes, I would spend weeks at a time completely alone. <u>I had to alert the base camp if I saw smoke rising in the forest.</u> I brought along a guitar because I wanted to learn how to play it. Probably I **should have tried** harder. <u>Maybe if I had had a teacher with me, I would have learned some songs.</u> As it was, I spent the time playing with my dog, reading, writing, and just watching the birds.

In this chapter, you will identify and write modals, conditionals, gerunds, and infinitives.

Verb Consistency

A verb tense gives your readers an idea about the time that an event occurred. A **tense shift** occurs when you shift from one tense to another for no logical reason. When you write essays, ensure that your tenses are consistent.

Tense shift: Jean Roberts travelled to Santiago, Chile, where she interviews a salon owner.

Correct: Jean Roberts travelled to Santiago, Chile, where she **interviewed** a salon owner.

HINT **Would and Could**

When you tell a story about a past event, use *would* instead of *will* and *could* instead of *can*.

> *couldn't*
> In 2001, Simon Brault wanted to be an actor. At that time, he <u>can't</u> find a good
> *would*
> acting job. To earn extra cash, he <u>will</u> deliver telegrams wearing a costume.

PRACTICE I

Underline and correct ten tense shifts in the following paragraphs.

EXAMPLE:

> *decided*
> In the 1990s, Gretta Zahn made a decision. She <u>decides</u> to work as a parts model.

1. Some people have very unusual jobs. In 1992, a modelling agent noticed seventeen-year-old Gretta Zahn's hands. He signed the young girl to a contract, and he said that he will make her famous as a "hand model." During Zahn's modelling years, her jobs were diverse. She soaked her fingers in dishwashing liquid, wear diamond rings, and demonstrated nail polish.

2. In the 1990s, Zahn's modelling career was lucrative. At the height of her career, she can earn up to $1500 a day. She will start her day at 5 a.m., and sometimes she will have to work for fourteen hours. To get a perfect shot, some photographers will take hundreds of pictures of her.

3. Zahn's agent told her that she will need to take special care of her hands. From 1992 to 2000, she cannot wear jewellery because it would leave tan lines. Also, during those years, she will not do the dishes, and she refused to pump her own gas.

4. In 2000, Zahn gave up modelling. Today, she enjoys gardening, and she likes to wear rings and bracelets. Her hands are no longer flawless, but she did not mind. "I have a life," she says. "I no longer worry about getting a cut or scrape."

Section 3
VERBS

Avoiding Double Negatives

A double negative occurs when a negative word such as *no* (*nothing, nobody, nowhere*) is combined with a negative adverb (*not, never, rarely, seldom,* and so on). The result is a sentence that has a double negative. Such sentences can be confusing because the negative words cancel each other.

> Mr. Lee <u>doesn't</u> want <u>no</u> problems.
>
> (According to this sentence, Mr. Lee wants problems.)
>
> He <u>didn't</u> know <u>nothing</u> about it.
>
> (According to this sentence, he knew something about it.)

How to Correct Double Negatives

There are two ways to correct double negatives.

- Completely remove *one* of the negative forms. Remember that you may need to adjust the verb to make it agree with the subject.

  Correct: Mr. Lee **doesn't** want ~~no~~ problems.

  Mr. Lee ~~doesn't~~ wants **no** problems.

- Change "no" to *any* (*anybody, anything, anywhere*).

  Correct: Mr. Lee doesn't want ~~no~~ ^{any} problems.

PRACTICE 2

Correct five errors with double negatives. You can correct each error in more than one way.

EXAMPLE:

They don't have ~~no~~ ^{any} openings.

or

They ~~don't have~~ ^{have} no openings

Have you ever had a strange job? Jordan Woo has had his share of unusual occupations. In 2005, while he was living in Saskatoon, he couldn't find no summer job. Then he saw an ad for a sign holder. For three months, he stood beside a work crew and held up signs to direct traffic. Occasionally, for an hour or two, he didn't have nothing to do. The crew was working on a rural road, and sometimes there wasn't no traffic. He was bored, but he kept his job because he didn't have no better offers. Eventually, when he couldn't take it no more, he quit.

Non-Standard Forms – *Gonna, Gotta, Wanna*

Some people commonly say *I'm gonna, I gotta,* or *I wanna.* These are non-standard forms, so avoid using them in written communication.

- Write "going to" instead of *gonna.*

  The boss is ~~gonna~~ *going to* hire three new cashiers.

- Write "have to" instead of *gotta* or *got to.*

  We ~~gotta~~ *have to* stay open until midnight.

- Write "want to" instead of *wanna.*

  We ~~wanna~~ *want to* keep our jobs.

PRACTICE 3

Underline and correct eight non-standard verbs.

EXAMPLE:

You and I <u>gotta find</u> a better job. *have to find*

1. If you wanna find work, there are many job-hunting sites on the Internet. One of the oldest and most established sites is Monster.com. The site was created in 1994. Jeff Taylor owned a job-recruitment agency, and he thought that an Internet site could help his business. He decided that his new site was gonna match job seekers with employers. That year, he created Monster Board.

2. In 1995, Taylor sold his business because he didn't wanna pass up a great business offer. The new owners said that they were gonna change the name of the website. They didn't think that consumers would wanna associate "monster" and work. However, Taylor convinced them to keep the name.

3. In 1999, Monster Board joined with Online Career Center and became Monster.com. When you go on the site, you gotta find your region. Monster posts jobs in twenty-three countries. Then you gotta choose the job category that interests you. If you go on the site, you are probably gonna find interesting jobs in your city or area.

Problems in Conditional Forms

In **conditional sentences**, there is a condition and a result. There are three types of conditional sentences, and each type has two parts, or clauses. The main clause depends on the condition set in the *if* clause.

First Form: Possible Present or Future

The condition is true or very possible. Use the present tense in the *if* clause.

> condition (*if* clause)   result
> If you **ask** her, she **will hire** you.

Second Form: Unlikely Present

The condition is not likely, and probably will not happen.

> condition (*if* clause)   result
> If I **had** more money, I **would start** my own business.

Note: In formal writing, when the condition contains the verb *be*, always use "were" in the *if* clause.

> If Katrina **were** younger, she **would change** careers.

Third Form: Impossible Past

The condition cannot happen because the event is over. Use the past perfect tense in the *if* clause.

> condition (*if* clause)   result
> If the business **had closed** in 2002, many people **would have lost** their jobs.

HINT Be Careful with the Past Conditional

In "impossible past" sentences, the writer expresses regret about a past event or expresses the wish that a past event had worked out differently. In the "if" part of the sentence, remember to use the past perfect tense.

    if + past perfect tense → would have (past participle)

                    had stayed
    If the factory ~~would have stayed~~ open, many workers would have kept their jobs.

PRACTICE 4

Write the correct conditional forms of the verbs in parentheses.

EXAMPLE:

If the miners (go, not) ___*had not gone*___ on strike, their working conditions would have remained unsafe.

1. If you do research on the Internet, you (learn) _____ that

truck driving is one of the most dangerous professions. William Roach is a long-distance trucker, and he took a truck-driving course in 1992. If he (fail) _____ the course, he would never have found his passion.

2. Roach loves driving. "On a highway, with nothing but the road in front of me, I feel alive and free. Even if someone offered me a better job, I (remain) _____ a truck driver." Roach claims that the only drawback is the time he spends away from his family. He says, "If I (be) _____ able to, I would bring my wife and son with me."

3. In 2003, Roach was late for a delivery. To save time, he took an unfamiliar route. While driving, Roach fell asleep, and his truck rolled into a ditch. If he (have) _____ a nap earlier that day, perhaps he (not, have) _____ the accident. If he (stay) _____ on the main highway, perhaps the accident (involve) _____ more vehicles. According to medical professionals, if Roach had been awake during the accident, his injuries (be) _____ more severe. Because he was asleep, his body was relaxed and his injuries were minor.

4. Roach claims that even if he (know) _____ about the dangers in truck driving, he would still have chosen to be a long-distance driver. If you could, (you, become) _____ a long-distance driver?

Non-Standard Forms—*Would of, Could of, Should of*

Some people commonly say *would of*, *could of*, or *should of*. They may also say *woulda*, *coulda*, or *shoulda*. These are non-standard forms and you should avoid using them in written communication. When you use the past forms of *should*, *would*, and *could*, always include *have* with the past participle.

Dominique Brown is a nurse, but she really loves real estate. She ~~should of~~ *should have* become a real-estate agent. She ~~woulda~~ *would have* been very successful.

PRACTICE 5

Underline and correct nine errors in conditional forms or in the past forms of *could* and *should*.

EXAMPLE:

have

The workers should <u>of</u> stayed home.

1. One of the world's most successful companies began in a small village in Sweden. In 1943, seventeen-year-old Ingvar Kamprad did well in his studies, and his father gave him a gift of money. Kamprad coulda bought anything he wanted. His mother thought that he shoulda continued his studies. The young man had other ideas. He decided to create a company called IKEA, and he sold small items through a mail-order catalogue.

2. In 1947, Kamprad decided to add furniture to his catalogue. One day, an employee from IKEA removed the legs from a table so that it would fit into his car trunk. Soon, the company created flat packaging designs. If the employee woulda owned a truck, perhaps IKEA would of continued to sell completely assembled furniture. If that had been the case, the company would not of been so successful.

3. Kamprad's extreme youth helped him in his quest to take chances. Maybe if he woulda been older, he woulda been more conservative. If IKEA would not have changed, perhaps it would of remained a small company.

Recognizing Gerunds and Infinitives

Sometimes a main verb is followed by another verb. The second verb can be a gerund or an infinitive. A **gerund** is a verb with an *-ing* ending. An **infinitive** consists of *to* and the base form of the verb.

verb + gerund

Edward <u>finished</u> **installing** the carpet.

verb + infinitive

He <u>wants</u> **to take** weekends off.

Some verbs in English are always followed by a gerund. Do not confuse gerunds with progressive verb forms.

Progressive verb: Julie is working now.
(Julie is in the process of doing something.)

Gerund: Julie <u>finished</u> **working**.
(*Working* is a gerund that follows *finish*.)

Section 3
VERBS

Some Common Verbs Followed by Gerunds

acknowledge	dislike	practise
adore	enjoy	quit
appreciate	finish	recall
avoid	involve	recollect
can't help	justify	recommend
complete	keep	regret
consider	loathe	resent
delay	mention	resist
deny	mind	risk
detest	miss	tolerate
discuss	postpone	

Some Common Verbs Followed by Infinitives

afford	expect	pretend
agree	fail	promise
appear	hesitate	refuse
arrange	hope	seem
ask	learn	swear
claim	manage	threaten
compete	mean	volunteer
consent	need	want
decide	offer	wish
demand	plan	would like
deserve	prepare	

Some Common Verbs Followed by Gerunds or Infinitives Some common verbs can be followed by gerunds or infinitives. Both forms have the same meaning.

begin

continue

like

start

> Elaine <u>likes</u> **to read**. Elaine <u>likes</u> **reading**.
> (Both sentences have the same meaning.)

Stop, Remember, **and** *Used to*   Some verbs can be followed by either a gerund or an infinitive, but there is a difference in meaning depending on the form you use.

Term	Form	Example	Meaning
Stop	+ infinitive	He often stops <u>to buy</u> gas every Sunday.	To stop an activity (driving) to do something else.
	+ gerund	I stopped <u>smoking</u> five years ago.	To permanently stop doing something.
Remember	+ infinitive	Please remember <u>to lock</u> the door.	To remember to perform a task.
	+ gerund	I remember <u>meeting</u> him in 2004.	To have a memory about a past event.
Used to	+ infinitive	Jane used <u>to smoke</u>.	To express a past habit.
	+ gerund	Jane is used to <u>living</u> alone.	To be accustomed to something.

Prepositions Plus Gerunds

Many sentences have the structure *verb + preposition + object*. If the object is another verb, the second verb is a gerund.

verb + preposition + gerund
I dream **about** travelling to Greece.

Some Common Words Followed by Prepositions plus Gerunds

accuse of
apologize for
discourage <u>him</u> from*
dream of
be excited about
be enthusiastic about
feel like
be fond of
forbid <u>him</u> from*
forgive <u>me</u> for*

be good at
insist on
be interested in
look forward to
prevent <u>him</u> from*
prohibit from
succeed in
think about
be tired of
warn <u>him</u> about*

*Certain verbs can have a noun or pronoun before the preposition.

PRACTICE 6

Complete the sentence with the appropriate verb. Underline either the gerund or the infinitive form.

1. Do you remember (using / to use) a cell phone camera for the first time?

   When they first came out, I looked forward (owning / to own / to owning)

   one. When I first got my phone, I remember (to take / taking) pictures of

   myself when I accidentally hit the camera button.

2. A few weeks later, I insisted (to buy / buying / on buying) my grandfather a
   cell phone. I told him that he would need (using / to use) one during
   emergencies. My grandfather (is not used to speaking / didn't used to
   speak) on such tiny phones. Each time I visit him, I plan (to show /
   showing) him how to use it. However, my grandfather is not a
   technophobe. These days, he (used to work / is used to working) on a
   computer. He knows how to send emails, although he wishes that
   salespeople would stop (to send / sending) him spam. However, he just
   can't stand (to use / using / on using) a cell phone.

3. My grandfather is good (to think / thinking / at thinking) up solutions for
   problems. He wrote a letter to the cell phone manufacturer, and he
   explained that some older people dislike (to try / trying / of trying) to read
   the tiny numbers, and they don't want (having / to have) all of the extra
   features such as Internet links. He succeeded (to get / getting / in getting) a
   response. In fact, the cell phone company offered my grandfather a job as
   an advisor for the seniors' market. Now, some cell phone companies are
   excited (to promote / promoting / about promoting) a new larger-model
   cell phone with large numbers and no extra features.

Section 3
VERBS

FINAL REVIEW

Underline and correct fifteen errors with verbs.

EXAMPLE:

going to
Many jobs are <u>gonna</u> become obsolete.

1. Certain jobs disappear because of advances in technology or changing
   habits. For instance, if you would have been born one hundred years ago,
   you would of worn a hat every time you went outside. However, since the
   1950s, hats have not been standard attire and, as a result, hatmaking is no
   longer a popular profession.

2. In 1949, Joseph Wade didn't know nothing about hats, yet he decided to
   open a hatmaking business in Montreal. Wade created men's felt hats and

sold them in his hat store. However, if he would have known what was coming, he woulda chosen another profession. By 1952, when the ducktail haircuts became popular, young men stopped wearing hats because they did not wanna ruin their hair styles. Wade's business eventually closed. He had no idea that hatmaking was gonna become obsolete.

3. In 1964, Theo Malizia enjoyed to deliver milk in his white van. The milk was bottled in glass containers, and it was deposited on the front steps of customers. One day, he hit a pothole, a crate tipped over, and twelve bottles broke. If the bottles would have been made with a less breakable material, they would have been easier to transport. When supermarkets began carrying lighter milk containers, Malizia had to find another job. Home milk delivery wasn't popular no more.

Section 3
VERBS

4. In the 1990s, many people thought that any computer-related job would last for life. Carmen Morales took a nine-month course in website building in 1999. She thought that she was gonna earn a good living. Perhaps she shoulda seen what was coming. New software has become so user-friendly that many businesses simply create their own websites. Perhaps if Morales would have taken a programming course, she would have found a job more easily. Since September, Morales has been taking some business courses because she wants to be an accountant. "People always gotta do their taxes, but very few people wanna do the math," she says. Morales hopes her accounting job will never become obsolete.

 Writer's Room **Topics for Writing**

Write about one of the following topics. Ensure that your verbs are correctly formed.

1. If you had lived one hundred years ago, what job would you have done? Describe the job using details that appeal to the senses.
2. Define one of the following terms or expressions: *mindless work, balancing act, glass ceiling, success, a go-getter,* or *a "suit."*

CHECKLIST: OTHER VERB FORMS

When you edit your writing, ask yourself these questions.

- Are my verb tenses consistent? Check for errors with the following:

  - shifts from past to present or present to past *can/could* and *will/would*

  will → would

  When he drove trucks, he ~~will~~ drive when he was tired.

- Do I use the correct conditional forms? Check for errors in the following:

  - possible future forms (*If I meet . . ., I will go . . .*)

  - unlikely present forms (*If I met . . . , I would go . . .*)

  - impossible past forms (*If I had met . . . , I would have gone . . .*)

  had

  If he ~~would have~~ sold shoes, he would have been successful.

- Do I use standard verbs? Do not write *gonna, wanna, gotta, shoulda,* etc.

  want to   have to

  If you ~~wanna~~ know the truth about the Free Trade Agreement, you ~~gotta~~ do some research.

READING LINK

International Trade
To find out more about the world of international trade, see the following essays.
"Keep Your Roses" by Melonyce McAfee (Page 211)
"Google's China Web" by Frida Ghitis (Page 476)
"I, Telemarketer" by Eugene Henry (Page 470)
"My Head Rolled in Syria" by Josh Freed (Page 479)
"The Rich Resonance of Small Talk" by Roxanne Roberts (Page 473)

Section 3
VERBS

28 Nouns, Determiners, and Prepositions

FORCES OF NATURE **In this chapter, you will read about some unusual weather events.**

CHAPTER CONTENTS

- Count and Non-count Nouns
- Determiners
- Prepositions

GRAMMAR SNAPSHOT **Looking at Nouns, Determiners, and Prepositions**

In her article "Weird Weather: Sprites, Frogs, and Maggots," Pamela D. Jacobson describes unusual weather phenomena. The nouns, determiners, and prepositions are underlined.

<u>Sprites</u> are barely visible <u>to</u> <u>the</u> naked <u>eye</u>. They sometimes look bluish closest <u>to</u> <u>the</u> <u>clouds</u>, but extend red, wispy <u>flashes</u> <u>upward</u>.

Some occur as high as sixty miles <u>above</u> <u>the</u> <u>storm</u>. <u>On</u> <u>images</u> <u>from</u> weather <u>satellites</u> and space <u>shuttles</u>, <u>sprites</u> appear as marvellously complex <u>shapes</u>.

In this chapter, you will identify and write nouns, determiners, and prepositions.

Count and Non-count Nouns

In English, nouns are grouped into two types: count nouns and non-count nouns.

- **Count nouns** refer to people or things that you can count such as *tree*, *house*, or *dog*. Count nouns have both a singular and plural form.

  She wrote three <u>articles</u> about global warming.

- **Non-count nouns** refer to people or things that you cannot count because you cannot divide them, such as *sugar* and *imagination*. Non-count nouns have only the singular form.

  The <u>weather</u> is going to turn cold.

Here are some examples of common non-count nouns.

Common Non-count Nouns

Categories of Objects		Food	Nature	Substances	
clothing	machinery	bread	air	chalk	paint
equipment	mail	fish	electricity	charcoal	paper
furniture	money	honey	energy	coal	
homework	music	meat	environment	fur	
jewellery	postage	milk	radiation	hair	
luggage	software	rice	water	ink	

Abstract Nouns

advice	effort	information	progress
attention	evidence	knowledge	proof
behaviour	health	luck	research
education	help	peace	violence

Determiners

Determiners are words that help to determine or figure out whether a noun is specific or general. Examples of determiners are articles (*a*), demonstratives (*this*), indefinite pronouns (*many*), numbers (*three*), possessive nouns (*Maria's*), and possessive adjectives (*my*).

> Gabriel Daniel Fahrenheit manufactured <u>the</u> first mercury thermometer in 1714.
>
> <u>Fahrenheit's</u> product was <u>his</u> claim to fame.

Commonly Confused Determiners

Some determiners can be confusing because you can only use them in specific circumstances. Review this list of some commonly confused determiners.

a, an, the

A and *an* are general determiners and *the* is a specific determiner.

> I need to buy <u>a</u> new winter coat. <u>The</u> winter coats in that store are on sale.

- Use *a* and *an* before singular count nouns but not before plural or non-count nouns. Use *a* before nouns that begin with a consonant (*a storm*) and use *an* before nouns that begin with a vowel (*an institute*).

- Use *the* before nouns that refer to a specific person, place, or thing. Do not use *the* before languages (*He speaks Italian*), sports (*They watch tennis*), or most city and country names (*Two of the coldest capital cities in the world are Ottawa and Moscow*). Two examples of exceptions are *the United States* and *the Netherlands*).

many, few, much, little

- Use *many* and *few* with count nouns.

> <u>Many</u> **satellites** collect weather information, but <u>few</u> **forecasts** are completely accurate.

■ Use *much* and *little* with non-count nouns.

> Much attention is focused on solar power, but North Americans use very little solar energy.

this, that, these, and *those*

This and *these* refer to things that are physically close to the speaker or in the present time. Use *this* before singular nouns and *these* before plural nouns. *That* and *those* refer to things that are physically distant from the speaker or in the past time. Use *that* before singular nouns and *those* before plural nouns.

> This **book** on my desk and those **books** on that **shelf** are about India. Did you know that in 1861, India had some very wet weather? In that **year**, Cherrapunji received 9300 millimetres of rain. In those **days**, cities had trouble coping with so much rain, but these **days**, they are better equipped.

HINT Latin Nouns

Some nouns borrowed from Latin keep the plural form of the original language.

Singular	Plural	Singular	Plural
alumnus	alumni	medium	media
datum	data	phenomenon	phenomena

Section 4
MORE PARTS OF SPEECH

PRACTICE I

Underline the determiner in parentheses that best agrees with the noun before it. If the noun does not require a determiner, underline *X*.

EXAMPLE:
(The/A/X) driest place on earth is (the/a/X) Arica, Chile.

1. (Much/Many) people all over (the/a/X) world talk constantly about (the/a/ X) weather. (A/ Few/Little) phenomena are as exciting as extreme weather. For example, there are about 80 (the/X) tornadoes each year in (the/X) Canada. (A/The) tornado lasts about fifteen minutes. In 1912, the worst tornado in Canadian history hit (a/the/X) Regina. In (this/that) year, twenty-eight people died and (many/much) others were injured.

2. (Many/Much) people are fascinated with thunderstorms. (A/An/X) interesting fact about (a/the/X) CN Tower is that it is struck by lightning around seventy times per year. (The/X) golfers should be very careful during thunderstorms. They should spend as (few/little) time as possible outdoors if there is lightning. (A/The) lightning bolt can produce a few hundred megawatts of electrical power.

3. (The/X) United States launched its first weather satellite in 1961. In (these/those) early days, satellite pictures amazed weather researchers. Today (much/many) research about weather patterns is being done by meteorologists. (These/Those) days, satellites gather (a/the/X) information about global weather systems that is invaluable for everybody's daily lives.

Prepositions

Prepositions are words that show concepts such as time, place, direction, and manner. They show connections or relationships between ideas.

> <u>In</u> 1998, southern Quebec experienced nearly a week of freezing rain. Freezing rain fell <u>for</u> a few days.

Prepositions of Time and Place

	Prepositions of Time	Prepositions of Place
in	• in a year or month (in February)	• in a city, country, or continent (in Halifax)
on	• on a day of the week (on Monday) • on a specific date (on June 16) • on a specific holiday (on Thanksgiving)	• on a specific street (on Lacombe Ave.) • on technological devices (on TV, on the radio, on the phone, on the cell phone, on the computer)
at	• at a specific time of day (at 9:15) • at night • at breakfast, lunch, dinner	• at a specific address (at 18 Oriole Crescent) • at a specific building (at the hospital)
from ...to	• from one time to another (from 10 a.m. to 1 p.m.)	• from one place to another (from Regina to Saskatoon)
for	• for a period of time (for five hours)	• for a distance (for two kilometres)

Section 4
MORE PARTS OF SPEECH

Commonly Confused Prepositions

to versus *at*

Use *to* after verbs that indicate movement from one place to another. Use *at* after verbs that indicate being or remaining in one place (and not moving from one place to another). *Exception:* Do not put *to* directly before *home*.

> Each day, Suraya **runs** <u>to</u> the gym, and then she goes home and **sits** <u>at</u> the computer.

for, during, and *since*

Use *during* to explain when something happens, *for* to explain how long it takes to happen, and *since* to indicate the start of an activity.

> <u>During</u> the summer, the restaurant closed <u>for</u> one week because of the heat.

> <u>Since</u> 2006, I have been taking skiing lessons <u>during</u> the winter.

PRACTICE 2

Write the correct preposition in the blanks.

EXAMPLE:

_At_ 5:15 a.m. we heard the news.

1. _____ the beginning of human history, people have been trying to predict the weather. Many writers have created almanacs to record weather-related events.

2. _____ 1792, _____ George Washington's second term as president, *The Old Farmer's Almanac* was published. Robert B. Thomas was its first editor. _____ 8:00 a.m. _____ 6:00 p.m., Thomas would work on his magazine. Sitting _____ his desk, he developed a successful formula to forecast weather. He had over an 80 percent accuracy rate. Thomas died _____ 1846, but people can go _____ Dublin, New Hampshire, and view his secret formula _____ the *Almanac*'s office.

3. *The Farmer's Almanac* has been published each year _____ it was first established. _____ World War II, the *Almanac* became notoriously associated with a German spy, whom the FBI captured _____ Long Island. The spy had the *Almanac* _____ his pocket. The U.S. government wanted to discontinue publishing the *Almanac* because it contained information that was useful _____ the Germans. After discussing the issue _____ the telephone, U.S. officials eventually allowed the *Almanac* to be published again.

Common Prepositional Expressions

Many common expressions contain prepositions. These types of expressions usually convey a particular meaning. The meaning of a verb will change if it is used with a specific preposition. Examine the difference in meaning of the following expressions.

to turn on—to start a machine or switch on the lights
to turn off—to stop a machine or switch off the lights
to turn down—to decline something
to turn over—to rotate
to turn up—to arrive

The next list contains some of the most common prepositional expressions.

accuse (somebody) of	forget about	provide (someone) with
acquainted with	forgive (someone) for	qualify for
afraid of	friendly with	realistic about
agree with	grateful for	rely on
apologize for	happy about	rescue from
apply for	hear about	responsible for
approve of	hope for	satisfied with
associate with	hopeful about	scared of
aware of	innocent of	search for
believe in	insist on	similar to
capable of	insulted by	specialize in
comply with	interested in	stop (something) from
confronted with	long for	succeed in
consist of	look forward to	take advantage of
count on	participate in	take care of
deal with	patient with	thank (someone) for
depend on	pay attention to	think about / of
dream of	pay for	tired of
escape from	prevent (someone) from	willing to
excited about	protect (someone) from	wish for
familiar with	proud of	worry about
fond of		

Section 4
MORE PARTS OF SPEECH

PRACTICE 3

Write the correct prepositions in the next paragraphs. Use the preceding list of prepositional expressions to help you.

EXAMPLE:
Many people were upset _about_ the damage from the storm.

1. In southern Asia, many people look forward _____ the monsoon. The word monsoon comes from Arabic *mausin*, which means "the season of the winds." During the wet season from June to September, India receives an average of 300 millimetres of rain each month. During the monsoon, people get tired _____ dealing with the rain.

2. Throughout the year, South Asians depend _____ the monsoon. Farmers hope _____ adequate rainfall for their crops. Children love the monsoon because it provides them _____ the opportunity to play

in the rain and the puddles. Although South Asians are often grateful
_____ a good rainy season, they are also realistic _____ nature's
forces and think _____ possible flooding, transportation delays, and
malaria.

FINAL PRACTICE

Correct fifteen errors in singular nouns, plural nouns, determiners, and
prepositions.

EXAMPLE:

Many   electricity
~~Much~~ houses lost ~~electricities~~ during the ice storm.

1. One of the most interesting weather phenomenon is the ice storm.
    Freezing rain coats all surfaces with a heavy layer of ice. On January 1998,
    Quebec and parts of the New England experienced the worst ice storm of
    the century. About 100 millimetres of freezing rain fell in the region since a
    few days. There were much consequences because of the ice.

2. Over 900 000 households had no electricity for about a week. About
    100 000 people had to leave their homes and go at refuge centres. Many
    people worried of the damage to their homes. Some people stayed at the
    home, but it was difficult without electricity. Others relied of their
    neighbours. Also, the authorities were concerned about some people
    getting hypothermia.

3. The environments looked like a disaster scene from a science fiction movie.
    Farmers lost pigs, sheep, and other livestock. Some business lost income
    because they had no electricity to remain open. Citizens received few
    information from the authorities.

4. Although this time has passed, many friends and neighbours still talk about
    the ice storm. Those days, it is just a distant memory.

Writer's Room **Topics for Writing**

Write about one of the following topics. Proofread your text to ensure that there are no errors in singular or plural forms, determiners, and prepositions.

1. What should people do to prepare for severe weather? List some steps.
2. What are some types of severe weather phenomena? Classify severe weather into three different types.

 CHECKLIST: NOUNS, DETERMINERS, AND PREPOSITIONS

When you edit your writing, ask yourself these questions.

Do I use the correct singular or plural form of nouns? Check for errors with the spelling of regular and irregular plurals and count and non-count nouns.

Many children ~~Much childrens~~ love to play ~~on~~ the ~~snows~~ in snow.

Do I use the correct determiners? Check for errors with *a, an, the, much, many, few, little, this, that, these,* and *those.*

These ~~This~~ days, there is too ~~many~~ much information about ~~a~~ the impact of global warming.

Do I use the correct prepositions? Check for errors with *in, on, at,* and *to,* with *for* and *during,* and with prepositional expressions.

For ~~During~~ three months each winter, the town depends ~~of~~ on tourists who stay ~~to~~ at the ski resorts.

29 Pronouns

FORCES OF NATURE **In this chapter, you will read about nature's power.**

CHAPTER CONTENTS

- Pronoun and Antecedent Agreement
- Indefinite Pronouns
- Vague Pronouns
- Pronoun Shifts
- Pronoun Case
- Relative Pronouns

GRAMMAR SNAPSHOT **Looking at Pronouns**

The following quotation is from the article "The Weather: Friend and Tyrant," in which William Renaurd discusses the effects of weather on people's health. The pronouns are underlined.

"I can feel a cold weather front coming days ahead of its arrival," says Jane. "My teeth begin to hurt, and my entire lower jaw aches. I've

been x-rayed, prodded by dentists, filled with pain-killing drugs, and examined by half a dozen neurologists. They can find no reason for my pain. I've decided that it's the weather and just try to bear it while waiting for the weather to change."

In this chapter, you will identify and write pronouns.

Pronoun and Antecedent Agreement

Pronouns are words that replace nouns (people, places, or things) and phrases. Use pronouns to avoid repeating nouns.

> *They*
> Hurricanes are large tropical storms. ~~Hurricanes~~ commonly form in the Caribbean.

A pronoun must agree with its **antecedent**, which is the word to which the pronoun refers. Antecedents are nouns and phrases that the pronouns have replaced, and they always come before the pronoun. Pronouns must agree in person and number with their antecedents.

Sarah was late for **her** meeting because **she** drove slowly in the blinding rain.

GRAMMAR LINK

For a list of common collective nouns, see page 322 in Chapter 25.

> **HINT Using Pronouns with Collective Nouns**
>
> Collective nouns refer to a group of people or things. The group acts as a unit; therefore, it is singular.
>
> The <u>organization</u> is very popular. Many people belong to **it**.
>
> The <u>company</u> was fined for polluting. **It** had to pay a large sum of money.

PRACTICE 1

Circle the pronoun and underline its antecedent.

EXAMPLE:

Although hurricane <u>names</u> used to be only female, now (they) may also be male.

1. Anna Petrowski works for the World Meteorological Organization (WMO) where she helps to select hurricane names.

2. The WMO makes a list of distinctive names because they are easier to remember.

3. An Atlantic hurricane can have an English, a Spanish, or a French name because it mirrors the nationalities of people that may be affected.

4. In fact, when hurricanes become famous, the WMO retires their names.

5. The army usually sends its personnel to help with emergency relief during a hurricane.

Section 4
MORE PARTS OF SPEECH

Indefinite Pronouns

Use **indefinite pronouns** when you refer to people or things whose identity is not known or is unimportant. This chart shows some common singular and plural indefinite pronouns.

Indefinite Pronouns				
Singular	another	each	nobody	other
	anybody	everybody	no one	somebody
	anyone	everyone	nothing	someone
	anything	everything	one	something
Plural	both, few, many, others, several			
Either singular or plural	all, any, half (and other fractions), some, none, more, most			

Singular

When you use a singular indefinite antecedent, also use a singular pronoun to refer to it.

<u>Nobody</u> remembered to bring **his** or **her** raincoat.

Plural

When you use a plural indefinite antecedent, also use a plural pronoun to refer to it.

Hurricanes and tornadoes arrive each year, and <u>both</u> have **their** own destructive power.

Either Singular or Plural

Some indefinite pronouns can be either singular or plural depending on the noun to which they refer.

Many meteorologists spoke at the conference. <u>All</u> gave important information about **their** research.
(*All* refers to meteorologists; therefore, the pronoun is plural.)

I read <u>all</u> of the newspaper and could not find **its** weather section.
(*All* refers to the newspaper; therefore, the pronoun is singular.)

HINT **Avoid Sexist Language**

Terms like *anybody*, *somebody*, *nobody*, and *each* are singular antecedents, so the pronouns that follow must be singular. At one time, it was acceptable to use *he* as a general term meaning *all people*; however, today it is more acceptable to use *he or she*.

Sexist:	<u>Everyone</u> should stay inside **his** house during a tornado.
Solution:	<u>Everyone</u> should stay inside **his or her** house during a tornado.
Better Solution:	<u>People</u> should stay inside **their** houses during a tornado.

Exception: If you know for certain that the subject is male or female, then use only *he* or only *she*.

In the men's prison, everyone has his own cell.

Section 4
**MORE PARTS
OF SPEECH**

PRACTICE 2

Correct nine errors in pronoun antecedent agreement by changing either the antecedent or the pronoun. If you change any antecedents, make sure that your subjects and verbs agree.

EXAMPLE:

their
Some of the workers had ~~his~~ own skis.

1. Everyone should know what to do if they are caught in extreme weather conditions. For example, people should be aware of lightning storms. All need to avoid open spaces, and he should get inside a building. No one should remain in the open because they could be struck by lightning. If lightning is nearby, each person who is outside should get into a crouching position but never lie down.

2. In the winter months, snowstorms can be dangerous. Somebody stranded in a blizzard should stay with their car. Nobody should wander outside on their own during a blinding snowstorm. It is very dangerous if a car gets stuck in a snowbank. One of the most common problems is carbon monoxide poisoning, which happens when snow blocks the back of the car and carbon monoxide gas backs up in their exhaust pipe. To solve this problem, everyone should clear the snow from their exhaust pipe.

3. Many have heard his or her weather stations reporting on tornadoes. During a tornado warning, everybody should go into a basement or windowless room in their home. Knowing what to do during extreme weather can save people's lives.

Vague Pronouns

Avoid using pronouns that could refer to more than one antecedent.

Vague: My father asked my brother where <u>his</u> umbrella was.
            (Whose umbrella? My father's or my brother's?)

Clearer: My father asked my brother where **my brother's** umbrella was.

Avoid using confusing pronouns such as *it* and *they* that have no clear antecedent.

Vague: <u>They</u> say that thousands of people lost their lives during the 1995 earthquake in Kobe, Japan.
            (Who are *they*?)

Clearer: **Government officials** say that thousands of people lost their lives during the 1995 earthquake in Kobe, Japan.

Vague: <u>It</u> stated in the newspaper that the scientific name for a thundercloud is cumulonimbus.
            (Who or what is *it*?)

Clearer: **The journalist** stated that the scientific name for a thundercloud is cumulonimbus.

This, *that*, and *which* should refer to a specific antecedent.

Vague: My girlfriend said that the roads were icy. I was glad she told me <u>this</u>.
            (What is *this*?)

Clearer: My girlfriend said that the roads were icy. I was glad she told me **this information**.

HINT **Avoid Repeating the Subject**

When you clearly mention a subject, do not repeat the subject in pronoun form.

Thunder ~~it~~ occurs when cold air collides with hot air.

PRACTICE 3

The following paragraphs contain vague pronouns or repeated subjects. Correct the nine errors in this selection. You may need to rewrite some sentences.

EXAMPLE:

The journalist reported
~~They said on television~~ that most tornadoes occur in agricultural areas around the world.

1. Meteorologist Patricia Bowles told her friend Sheila that her photo of the tornado would appear in the newspaper. They say that tornadoes are the most powerful storms on earth. Tornado winds they can often exceed 100 miles per hour. This can cause a lot of damage to property and sometimes kill people.

2. It says that tornadoes form during thunderstorms when cool air moves downward and hot air rises very quickly, creating a funnel effect. When this touches the ground, it becomes a tornado. The United States it has a "Tornado Alley." This consists of Texas, Oklahoma, Kansas, and Nebraska. These states they have more tornadoes than other parts of North America because cold air from Canada meets the warm air from the Gulf of Mexico over the flat prairies.

Pronoun Shifts

If your essays contain unnecessary shifts in person or number, you may confuse your readers. They will not know exactly who or how many you are referring to. Carefully edit your writing to ensure that your pronouns are consistent.

Making Pronouns Consistent in Number

If the antecedent is singular, then the pronoun must be singular. If the antecedent is plural, then the pronoun must be plural.

    singular   *his or her*
A **meteorologist** and ~~their~~ team spend years keeping meticulous records of weather patterns.

               plural   *they*
When there are storm **warnings**, ~~it~~ should be taken seriously.

Making Pronouns Consistent in Person

Person is the writer's perspective. For some writing assignments, you might use the first person (*I, we*). For other assignments, especially most college essays and workplace writing, you might use the second person (*you*), or the third person (*he, she, it, they*).

Shifting the point of view for no reason confuses readers. If you begin writing from one point of view, do not shift unnecessarily to another point of view.

$\qquad$ *They*

Many tourists like to travel, but **they** should be careful. ~~You~~ never

$\qquad$ *They*

know when there will be bad weather. ~~You~~ should always be prepared

for emergencies.

PRACTICE 4

Correct five pronoun shift errors.

EXAMPLE:

Many people were saddened when they heard that thousands of people had died in the 2001 Indian earthquake. ~~One~~ donated money, clothes, and blankets to the victims. *They*

In 2005, we were travelling in Pakistan. We had just finished our breakfast

when you felt the ground moving. Everything in our tenth floor apartment

started to shake and fall. We knew we should not panic, but one really didn't

know what to do. We knew you had to get out of the high-rise and onto the

ground because one could never be certain that the building would remain

standing. There were no guarantees that you could make it out in time.

Section 4
**MORE PARTS
OF SPEECH**

Pronoun Case

Pronouns are formed according to the role they play in a sentence. A pronoun can be the subject or object of the sentence, or it can show possession. This chart shows the three main pronoun cases: subjective, objective, and possessive.

Pronouns				
Singular	**Subjective**	**Objective**	**Possessive Adjective**	**Possessive Pronoun**
First person	I	me	my	mine
Second person	you	you	your	yours
Third person	he, she, it, who, whoever	him, her, it, whom, whomever	his, her, its, whose	his, hers
Plural **First person**	we	us	our	ours
Second person	you	you	your	yours
Third person	they	them	their	theirs

Subjective Case and Objective Case

When a pronoun is the subject of the sentence, use the subjective form of the pronoun. When a pronoun is the object in the sentence, use the objective form of the pronoun.

subject   subject   object
He left the umbrella at work, and **I** asked **him** to bring it home.

Possessive Case

A possessive pronoun shows ownership.

■ **Possessive adjectives** come before the noun that they modify.

She finished **her** research on the polar ice caps, but we did not finish **our** research.

■ **Possessive pronouns** can replace the possessive adjective and the noun that follows it. In the next sentence, the possessive pronoun *ours* replaces both the possessive adjective *our* and the noun *research*.

possessive adjective
She finished **her** research about the polar ice caps, but we did not
possessive pronoun
finish **ours**.

Problems with Possessive Pronouns

Some possessive adjectives sound like certain contractions. When using the possessive adjectives *their*, *your*, and *its*, be careful that you do not confuse them with *they're* (they are), *you're* (you are), and *it's* (it is).

hers   theirs
The book on clouds is ~~her's~~. The weather almanac is ~~their's~~.

Section 4
MORE PARTS OF SPEECH

GRAMMAR LINK

For more information about apostrophes, see Chapter 34.

> **HINT** Choosing *His* or *Her*
>
> To choose the correct possessive adjective, think about the possessor (not the object that is possessed).
>
> ■ If something belongs to a female, use *her* + noun.
>
> Helena and **her** dog like to walk in the snow.
>
> ■ If something belongs to a male, use *his* + noun.
>
> Cliff used **his** new camera to photograph storm clouds.

PRACTICE 5

Underline the correct possessive adjective or possessive pronoun in each set of parentheses.

EXAMPLE:
Dr. Jane Woody wondered whether (his / <u>her</u>) theories would be accepted.

1. Scientists study volcanoes and (its / it's / their) effects on weather patterns. When a volcano erupts and throws (his / its / it's) ash particles into the surrounding air, the explosion causes a lot of lightning and thunderstorms in the region nearby.

2. I have just joined the International Society on Volcanic Studies. The members and (there / they're / their) governments fund research into volcanic activity. A researcher and (their / his or her / its) assistants gather information about volcanic eruptions.

3. My assistant Judith, because of (her / hers) enthusiasm, painstakingly collects data from volcanic eruptions around the world. A lot of research is being done in this field. (Our / Ours) is just one small part of this study.

4. One day, we would like to present (our / ours) observations to climate scientists because we think this research will be important to (they / them). Will you be in (you're / your / yours) office next Tuesday? Let's discuss (our / ours) work and (your / yours) when we meet.

Pronouns in Comparisons with *than* or *as*

Avoid making errors in pronoun case when the pronoun follows *than* or *as*. If the pronoun is a subject, use the subjective case, and if the pronoun is an object, use the objective case.

If you use the incorrect case, your sentence may have a meaning that you do not intend it to have. Review the next two examples. Notice that when the sentence ends with the subjective pronoun, it is advisable to add a verb after the pronoun.

Section 4
MORE PARTS OF SPEECH

objective case
I like rainy days as much as **him**.
(I like rainy days <u>as much as I like him</u>.)

subjective case
I like rainy days as much as **he** [does].
(I like rainy days <u>as much as he likes rainy days</u>.)

HINT **Complete the Thought**

To test which pronoun case to use, complete the thought.

He likes winter more than **I** [like winter].
(Do I want to say that he likes winter more than I like winter?)

He likes winter more than [he likes] **me**.
(Or, do I want to say he likes winter more than he likes me?)

Pronouns in Prepositional Phrases

In a prepositional phrase, the words that follow the preposition are the objects of the preposition. Therefore, always use the objective case of the pronoun after a preposition.

> <u>To</u> **him**, global warming is not a big deal.
> <u>Between</u> **you** and **me**, I think he's misinformed.

Pronouns with *and or or*

Use the correct case when nouns and pronouns are joined by *and* or *or*. If the pronouns are the subject, use the subjective case. If the pronouns are the object, use the objective case.

> She and I
> ~~Her and me~~ had to read about the causes of desertification, and then the
>   her and me
> instructor asked ~~she and I~~ to summarize the information.

> **HINT** **Finding the Correct Case**
>
> To determine that your case is correct, try saying the sentence with either the subjective case or the objective case.
>
> | | |
> |---|---|
> | **Sentence:** | The professor asked her and (**I** or **me**) to research the topic. |
> | **Possible answers:** | The professor asked **I** to research the topic. (This would *not* make sense.) |
> | | The professor asked **me** to research the topic. (This would make sense.) |
> | **Correct answer:** | The professor asked **her** and **me** to research the topic. |

PRACTICE 6

Correct any errors with pronoun case.

EXAMPLE:

                           I
Last summer, my friend and ~~me~~ visited Mexico.

1. Last year, my brother and me took a vacation together.

2. He likes exotic travel more than me but convinced me to accompany him to Antarctica.

3. The tour guide told my brother and I that at its thickest point, Antarctica has an ice cap five kilometres deep. If it were to melt, it would raise the oceans' water level by many metres.

4. Between you and I, it is frightening to think about melting ice caps.

5. My brother is a photographer. Him and me took a lot of photographs.

6. I will have good memories when my brother and me look at our photo album.

Relative Pronouns

Relative pronouns can join two short sentences. They include *who*, *whom*, *whoever*, *whomever*, *which*, *that*, and *whose*.

> **GRAMMAR LINK**
>
> **For more information about relative pronouns, see Chapters 20 and 33.**

Choosing who or whom

To determine whether to use *who* or *whom*, replace *who* or *whom* with another pronoun. If the replacement is a subjective pronoun such as *he* or *she*, use *who*. If the replacement is an objective pronoun such as *her* or *him*, use *whom*.

I know a man **who** studies icebergs.
(<u>He</u> studies icebergs.)

The man to **whom** you gave your résumé is my boss.
(You gave your résumé <u>to him</u>.)

PRACTICE 7

Underline the correct relative pronoun in the parentheses.

EXAMPLE:

People (<u>who</u> /which) live in the arctic are used to harsh weather.

1. Ruth, (who / whom) I met in school, has been my best friend for twenty years.

2. Ruth, (who / whom) is a journalist, recently spent some time on Baffin Island.

3. The people on Baffin Island about (who / whom) Ruth is writing are mostly Inuit.

4. The Inuit (who / whom) are accustomed to extreme weather are active year round.

5. Ruth, (who / whom) loves the sun, sometimes feels depressed during the winter when there is very little daylight.

6. Many people (who / whom) Ruth has interviewed are worried about climate change.

Section 4
MORE PARTS OF SPEECH

FINAL REVIEW

Correct the fifteen pronoun errors in the following paragraphs.

EXAMPLE:

their

Many people around the world have lost ~~one's~~ relatives and property because of severe weather.

1. In 2004 and 2005, severe weather and natural disasters they caused havoc in the lives of people around the world. They say that the forces of nature are uncontrollable and unpredictable. But with increasingly sophisticated technology, climatologists and there assistants should be able to improve natural disaster warnings around the world.

2. In December 2004, my friend and me were on holiday in Thailand. At that time, the strongest earthquake in forty years occurred in the Indian Ocean. It caused a tsunami that annihilated cities, villages, and holiday resorts. My friend, whom is from Indonesia, said that all members of his uncle's family lost his homes. Many people have suffered more than me.

3. Some months after the Asian tsunami, New Orleans experienced one of their worst hurricanes in history. Hurricane Katrina caused the levees to break and flood the city. This caused severe property damage and loss of life. Almost everybody in New Orleans had to leave their home.

4. Also in 2005, a severe earthquake in the mountainous regions of Pakistan caused death and destruction to the people of the region. They say that around 100 000 people died. I watched television reports of people living in tents and wanted to help them because you could see they had lost everything. So I collected donations from students at my college, and my brother, to who I sent the donations, passed them along to an aid organization in Pakistan.

5. The forces of nature are more powerful than us. We have no ability to control inundations, hurricanes, or earthquakes. With better warning systems and relief infrastructures, maybe one can reduce the misery caused by natural disasters.

Writer's Room **Topics for Writing**

Write about one of the following topics. Proofread your text to ensure there are no pronoun errors.

1. Describe a severe weather event that you or someone you know experienced. What happened? Try to use descriptive imagery.

2. Argue that bicycles should be the only type of vehicle allowed in city centres. Support your argument with specific examples.

 CHECKLIST: PRONOUNS

When you edit your writing, ask yourself these questions.

☐ Do I use the correct pronoun case? Check for errors with the following:

- subjective, objective, and possessive cases
- comparisons with *than* or *as*
- prepositional phrases
- pronouns following *and* or *or*

              me   *I (do)*
Between you and <u>I</u>, my sister watches the weather reports more than <u>me</u>.

☐ Do I use the correct relative pronouns? Check for errors with *who* or *whom*.

              whom
My husband, <u>who</u> you have met, is a meteorologist.

☐ Do my pronouns and antecedents agree in number and person? Check for errors with indefinite pronouns and collective nouns.

                    its
The bad weather and <u>their</u> aftermath were reported on the news.

☐ Are my pronoun references clear? Check for vague pronouns and inconsistent points of view.

Scientists   *I*
<u>They</u> say the weather will change rapidly. I read the report and <u>you</u> could not believe what it said.

Section 4
MORE PARTS OF SPEECH

30 Adjectives and Adverbs

CHAPTER

CHAPTER CONTENTS

- Adjectives
- Adverbs
- Comparative and Superlative Forms

Section 4
MORE PARTS OF SPEECH

GRAMMAR SNAPSHOT Looking at Adjectives and Adverbs

In his article "Iceland's Ring Road: The Ultimate Road Trip," Mark Sundeen describes aspects of that country's landscape. The adjectives and adverbs are underlined.

<u>Occasionally</u> an iceberg floated beneath the highway bridge, was carried to sea, then was dashed on the beach by the <u>windswept</u> waves.

We walked along the <u>grey</u> strand where the blocks of glacier rocked <u>gently</u> in the tide, and we gathered in our hands the <u>cocktail-size</u> ice cubes that had washed up on shore and flung them back to the sea.

In this chapter, you will identify and write adjectives and adverbs.

Adjectives

Adjectives describe nouns (people, places, or things) and pronouns (words that replace nouns). They add information explaining how many, what kind, or which one. They also help you appeal to the senses by describing how things look, smell, feel, taste, and sound.

> The **young** <u>students</u> convinced their **imposing** <u>principal</u> to start an **important** <u>project</u> on air quality in the schools.

HINT Placement of Adjectives

You can place adjectives either before a noun or after a linking verb such as *be, look, appear, smell,* or *become.*

Before the noun: The **nervous** <u>environmentalist</u> gave a suitable speech.

After the linking verb: The biologist <u>was</u> **disappointed**, and he <u>was</u> **angry**.

Problems with Adjectives

You can recognize many adjectives by their endings. Be particularly careful when you use the following adjective forms.

Adjectives ending in *-ful* or *-less* Some adjectives end in *-ful* or *-less*. Remember that *ful* ends in one *l* and *less* ends in double *s*.

> The Blue Oceans Club, a **peaceful** environmental organization, has promoted many **useful** projects. Protecting the environment is an **endless** activity.

Adjectives ending in *-ed* and *-ing* Some adjectives look like verbs because they end in *-ing* or *-ed*. When the adjective ends in *-ed*, it describes the person's or animal's expression or feeling. When the adjective ends in *-ing*, it describes the quality of the person or thing.

> The **frustrated** but **prepared** lobbyist confronted the politician, and his **challenging** and **convincing** arguments got her attention.

HINT Keep Adjectives in the Singular Form

Always make an adjective singular, even if the noun following the adjective is plural.

> Lucia was a forty-five-~~years~~ ^year^ old woman when she sold her five-thousand-~~dollars~~ ^dollar^ car and rode a bicycle to work.

Adverbs

Adverbs add information to adjectives, verbs, or other adverbs. They give more specific information about how, when, where, and to what extent an action or event occurred. Some adverbs look exactly like adjectives, such as *early, late, soon, often,* and *hard*. However, most adverbs end in *-ly*.

> verb   adverb
> Biologists <u>studied</u> the statistics on climate change **carefully**.

> adverb   adverb
> They released the results **quite** <u>quickly</u>.

> adverb   adjective
> The **very** <u>eloquent</u> speaker was Dr. Ying.

Forms of Adverbs

Adverbs often end in *-ly*. In fact, you can change many adjectives into adverbs by adding *-ly* endings.

If you add *-ly* to a word that ends in *l*, then your new word will have a double *l*.

> professional + ly
> The journalist covered the story **professionally**.

If you add *-ly* to a word that ends in *e*, keep the *e*. Exceptions to this rule are true ➔ *truly* and *due* ➔ *duly*.

> close + ly
> Scientists monitor the polar ice caps **closely**.

> **HINT** **Placement of Frequency Adverbs**
>
> **Frequency adverbs** are words that indicate how often someone performs an action or when an event occurs. Common frequency adverbs are *always*, *ever*, *never*, *often*, *sometimes*, and *usually*. They can appear at the beginning of sentences, or they can appear in the following locations.
>
> ■ Place frequency adverbs before regular present and past tense verbs.
>
>   Politicians **sometimes** <u>forget</u> the importance of the environment.
>
> ■ Place frequency adverbs after all forms of the verb *be*.
>
>   She <u>is</u> **often** an advisor for environmental agencies.
>
> ■ Place frequency adverbs after helping verbs.
>
>   They <u>have</u> **never** donated to an environmental group.

PRACTICE I

Correct eight errors with adjectives or adverbs.

EXAMPLE:

                    quietly
I entered the room ~~quiet~~ because the lecture had started.

1. Many people frequent debate the issue of climate change. There are two clearly sources that cause global warming: natural and human. People forget often that natural forces have contributed to climate change throughout the history of the world. Scientists know that ice ages have developed and diminished rapid.

2. Global temperature increases naturaly for several reasons. For instance, explosions in the sun generate heat that causes the earth's temperature to rise abrupt. Another natural source for global warming is volcanic eruptions. A strong eruption gives off smoke and gases. These elements may act sometimes as a shield preventing sunlight from entering the atmosphere. A minor change in the earth's orbit may affect also the earth's temperature. So when debating climate change, also keep in mind the natural causes of temperature fluctuations.

Problems with Adverbs

Many times, people use an adjective instead of an adverb after a verb. Ensure that you always modify your verbs using an adverb.

                              really quickly   slowly
The snowstorm developed ~~real quick~~. We had to drive very ~~slow.~~

PRACTICE 2

Underline and correct ten errors with adjective and adverb forms.

EXAMPLE:

         really

Climate change is a <u>realy</u> controversial issue.

1. Human activity contributes great to global warming. With modernization,

   lifestyles are changing real quick. More people are driving cars, and more

   industries are consuming largely amounts of energy. When humans burn

   fossil fuels such as gasoline, coal, and oil, gases in the atmosphere that trap

   heat rise steady. This condition creates a dangerously greenhouse effect,

   which means that heat cannot escape the earth's atmosphere.

2. There is a general consensus by knowing scientists around the world that

   the earth is experiencing global warming. Rising temperatures could have

   extremelly profound consequences for future generations. For instance,

   with melting ice caps, ocean levels could rise dramatical. Other areas in the

   world may experience harmfull desertification.

Section 4
**MORE PARTS
OF SPEECH**

Using *good/well* and *bad/badly*   *Good* is an adjective, and *well* is an adverb. However, as an exception, you can use *well* to describe a person's health (for example, *I do not feel well*).

Adjective:	We will have **good** weather tomorrow.
Adverb:	She slept **well** even though the storm was noisy.

Bad is an adjective, and *badly* is an adverb.

Adjective:	The **bad** weather remained during the past week.
Adverb:	The meteorologist spoke **badly** during the nightly forecast.

PRACTICE 3

Underline the correct adjectives or adverbs.

EXAMPLE:

Generally, public servants who listen (good / <u>well</u>) make (<u>good</u> / well) policies.

1. My biology professor explains subjects (good / well). Yesterday, he spoke

   about the (bad / badly) effects of greenhouse gases. The sunlight heats the

   earth's surface really (good / well), but not all of the heat is absorbed. The extra heat is reflected back into the earth's atmosphere, and greenhouse gases prevent this heat from escaping into the atmosphere.

2. The students in my class reacted (good / well) to a personal challenge for reducing global warming. Nobody thought (bad / badly) of the need for taking personal responsibility. They came up with (good / well) ideas to change their lifestyles, including writing a newsletter about the public's need to change (bad / badly) habits. Two (good / well) ways to reduce greenhouse gases are to reduce driving times and to recycle. Most people have (good / well) intentions and know (good / well) that humans must reduce greenhouse gases.

Comparative and Superlative Forms

Use the **comparative form** to compare two items. Use the **superlative form** to compare three or more items. You can write comparative and superlative forms by remembering a few simple guidelines.

Using -er and -est endings Add -*er* and -*est* endings to one-syllable adjectives and adverbs.

short	short**er** than	the short**est**

Double the last letter when the adjective ends in *one vowel + one consonant*.

hot	hot**ter** than	the hot**test**

When a two syllable adjective ends in -*y*, change the -*y* to -*i* and add -*er* or -*est*.

happ**y**	happ**ier** than	the happ**iest**

Using *more* and *the most* Add *more* and *the most* to adjectives and adverbs of two or more syllables.

beautiful	**more** beautiful than	the **most** beautiful

Using Irregular Comparative and Superlative Forms Some adjectives and adverbs have unique comparative and superlative forms. Study this list to remember some of the most common ones.

GRAMMAR LINK

Farther indicates a physical distance. *Further* means "additional." For more commonly confused words, see Chapter 32.

good/well	better than	the best
bad/badly	worse than	the worst
some/much/many	more than	the most
little (a small amount)	less than	the least
far	farther/further	the farthest / the furthest

PRACTICE 4

Fill in the blanks with the correct comparative and superlative forms of the words in parentheses.

EXAMPLE:

The problems of global warming are (serious) _more serious_ than we previously believed.

1. The international community is trying to deal with one of the (urgent)

   _____ environmental problem the world is facing. Global

   warming is one of the (debated) _____ issues in the

   scientific community. The Kyoto Protocol is an international agreement

   made under the United Nations. Nations agree to reduce their greenhouse

   gas emissions and prevent the greenhouse effect from becoming (bad)

   _____ than in previous years.

2. Dr. Anif Mohammed is a famous climatologist. His presentation was

   (short) _____ than some of the others, but it was also the

   (clear) _____. In fact, he seemed to be the (little)

   _____ nervous speaker at the conference.

Problems with Comparative and Superlative Forms

Using *more* and *-er* In the comparative form, never use *more* and *-er* to modify the same word. In the superlative form, never use *most* and *-est* to modify the same word.

> The photographs of the tornado were ~~more~~ better than the ones of the rain storm, but the photos of the huge waves were the ~~most~~ best in the exhibition.

Using *fewer* and *less* In the comparative form, use *fewer* before count nouns (*fewer people*, *fewer houses*) and use *less* before non-count nouns (*less information*, *less evidence*).

> Diplomats have **less** <u>time</u> than they used to. **Fewer** <u>agreements</u> are being made.

GRAMMAR LINK

For a complete list of non-count nouns, refer to page 359 in Chapter 28.

Section 4
MORE PARTS OF SPEECH

HINT Using *the* in the Comparative Form

Although you would usually use *the* in superlative forms, you can use it in some two-part comparatives. In these expressions, the second part is the result of the first part.

action   result
<u>The more</u> you recycle, <u>the better</u> the environment will be.

PRACTICE 5

Correct the nine adjective and adverb errors in the next paragraphs.

EXAMPLE:

   fewer   less

If ~~less~~ people drove cars, we would have ~~fewer~~ air pollution.

1. The Amazon rainforest is the most largest in the world. It plays a vital role in regulating the global climate. Forests, such as the Amazon, create more better air quality for humans. Trees and plants remove carbon dioxide from the air and release oxygen into the air. The Amazon rainforest has been experiencing deforestation real rapidly.

2. There are several reasons for the deforestation of the Amazon. The most biggest causes for it are cattle ranching and road construction. Roads provide more greater access for logging and mining companies. Clearing the forest, farmers obtain more land for their cattle.

3. The depletion of the Amazon rainforest is one of the worse problems for our global climate. Less politicians than environmental activists are concerned with this issue. The more humanity waits to tackle this problem, the worst it will become. Perhaps over time, governments and the general public will try more harder to save the Amazon rainforest.

FINAL REVIEW

Correct fifteen errors in adjectives and adverbs.

EXAMPLE:

We need to find ~~more~~ better sources of renewable energy.

1. Our society has depended economic on oil for the past two hundred years. Oil is a non-renewable energy source. Many politicians have reacted bad to the suggestion that we need to reduce our reliance on oil. They are concerned about economic progress, which is presently fuelled by oil. Yet worrying scientists and environmentalists believe that burning fossil fuels is causing temperatures around the world to become more warmer. Because

of the threat of global warming, scientists are trying to develop alternative energy sources real quickly.

2. Wind energy is one powerfull alternative. Historically, countles efforts have been made to use wind to power millstones for grinding wheat and running pumps. Today, wind-powered turbines produce electricity 25 percent of the time because winds might not blow strong or continual. Therefore, the wind is not a dependable source of energy.

3. Less people use geothermal energy to heat homes in North America than in some other parts of the world. Nevertheless, it is also one of the most finest alternative energy sources. Steam and hot water from under the earth's surface are used to turn turbines quick enough to create electricity. Around the world, there are a few areas that have steam or hot water close to the earth's surface, making geothermal energy cost effective. Iceland uses geothermal energy to heat about 80 percent of its buildings.

4. The preceded energy sources are just a few of the alternative approaches that researchers are working on perfecting. These alternatives do not substitute completely for the versatility of oil. Scientists, government officials, and concerned citizens know good that our society must reduce its dependence on oil. The more money we spend on research, the best the results will be to develop and promote energy alternatives.

Section 4
MORE PARTS OF SPEECH

Writer's Room Topics for Writing

Write about one of the following topics. Proofread your text to ensure that there are no adjective and adverb mistakes.

1. Compare two types of transportation that you have owned. Explain which one you prefer.
2. Argue that our government should or should not address the issue of global warming.

READING LINK

Forces of Nature
These essays contain more information about the weather and climate issues.
"Into Thin Air" by Jon Krakauer (page 485)
"Monsoon Time" by Rahul Goswami (page 488)
"The Rules of Survival" by Laurence Gonzales (page 482)

Section 4
MORE PARTS OF SPEECH

 CHECKLIST: ADJECTIVES AND ADVERBS

When you edit your writing, ask yourself these questions.

Do I use adjectives and adverbs correctly? Check for errors in these cases:

- the placement, order, and spelling of adjectives

- the placement of frequency adverbs, and spelling of adverbs ending in *-ly*

- the adjective and adverb form

- the use of *good/well* and *bad/badly*

 quietly   interesting
Magnus Forbes spoke very ~~quiet~~ about the ~~interested~~ article on El Niño at
 often
the news conference. He was asked to speak ~~often~~ on environmental topics.

 really well
The environmental lobbyist hid his concern ~~real good~~.

Do I use the correct comparative and superlative forms? Check for errors in these cases:

- *more* versus *-er* comparisons

- *the most* versus *-est* comparisons

- *fewer* versus *less* forms

The ~~most~~ quickest tornado trackers take the first photographs.

 fewer   less
The organization had ~~less~~ members, but it also has ~~fewer~~ bad publicity.

Exact Language

31
CHAPTER

FLORA AND FAUNA **In this chapter, you will read about plants.**

CHAPTER CONTENTS

- Using Specific and Detailed Vocabulary
- Avoiding Wordiness and Redundancy
- Avoiding Clichés
- Using Standard English

GRAMMAR SNAPSHOT Looking at Exact Language

In his article "Deep in the Jungle of Suriname," Conger Beasley describes the beauty of a tropical jungle. The descriptive language is underlined.

The view from the summit over the <u>rippling</u> tree canopy was impressive. The upper parts of the canopy <u>were drenched</u> in sunlight; it's here where the foliage is thickest that the majority of birds and animals range, not down on the floor where the sun rarely <u>penetrates</u> and <u>the air seems to hold its breath like a whale at the bottom of the sea.</u>

In this chapter, you will identify and write exact language.

Using Specific and Detailed Vocabulary

Effective writing evokes an emotional response from the reader. Great writers not only use correct grammatical structures, but they also infuse their writing with precise and vivid details that make their work come alive.

When you proofread your work, revise words that are too vague. **Vague words** lack precision and detail. For example, the words *nice* and *bad* are vague. Readers cannot get a clear picture from them.

Compare the following sets of sentences.

Vague: The flower smelled nice.

Precise: The crimson rose smelled musky sweet.

Vague: The gardener planted some flowers.

Precise: The gardener, Mr. Oliver, planted azaleas, hyacinths, and irises.

HINT **Some Common Vague Words**

The following is a list of some frequently used vague words. Try to find substitutes for overly familiar and vague words.

good	small
bad	great
nice	happy
pretty	sad
big	thing

Creating Vivid Language

When you choose the precise word, you convey your meaning exactly. Moreover, you can make your writing clearer and more impressive by using specific and detailed vocabulary. To create vivid language, do the following:

- **Modify your nouns.** If your noun is vague, make it more specific by adding one or more adjectives. You could also rename the noun with a more specific term.

  Vague: the child

  Vivid: the angry orphan   the tearful and frightened toddler

- **Modify your verbs.** Use more vivid, precise verbs. You could also use adverbs.

  Vague: talk

  More vivid: bicker   debate passionately

- **Include more details.** Add information to make the sentence more detailed and complete

  Vague: Some herbs are good for the health.

  Precise: Garlic has antibiotic properties that can fight bacteria and viruses.

Section 5
WORD USE AND SPELLING

WRITING LINK

You can find more information about appealing to the five senses in Chapter 8, Description.

PRACTICE I

Underline vague words in the following sentences. Then replace them with more precise and detailed vocabulary.

EXAMPLE:

Our town's garden is <u>pretty</u>.

The pond in our town's garden is filled with pink and white water lilies and surrounded by ferns and wild poppies that attract the green frogs, mallard ducks, and cardinals.

1. My neighbour likes to garden.

_____

_____

2. She has planted many flowers and plants.

_____

_____

3. There are also vegetables.

_____

_____

4. The herbs she has planted smell nice.

_____

_____

5. She has fun in her garden.

_____

_____

Avoiding Wordiness and Redundancy

Sometimes students fill their writing assignments with extra words to meet the length requirement. However, good ideas can get lost in work that is too wordy. Also, if the explanations are unnecessarily long, then readers will become bored.

To improve your writing style, use only as many words or phrases as you need to fully explain your ideas.

> The farm was big ~~in size~~.
> (*Big* is a measure of size, so it is unnecessary to repeat it.)

Correcting Wordiness You can cut the number of words needed to express an idea by substituting a wordy phrase with a single word. You could also remove the wordy phrase completely.

> *because*
> I don't like gardening ~~due to the fact that~~ I spend most of the time just pulling out weeds.

\multicolumn{4}{c}{**Some Common Wordy Expressions and Substitutions**}			
Wordy	**Substitution**	**Wordy**	**Substitution**
at this point in time	now, nowadays,	gave the appearance of being	looked like
at that point in time	presently, currently	in order to	to
	then, at that time	in spite of the fact	in spite of
big / small in size	big/small	in the final analysis	finally, lastly
in close proximity	close *or* in proximity	period of time	period
a difficult dilemma	a dilemma	past history	past *or* history
due to the fact	because	still remain	remain
equally as good as	as good as	a true fact	a fact
exactly the same	the same	the fact of the matter is that	in fact
exceptions to the rule	exceptions		
final completion	end		
for the purpose of	for		

PRACTICE 2

Edit the following sentences by crossing out all unnecessary words or phrases. If necessary, find more concise substitutes for wordy expressions.

EXAMPLE:

Medical researchers are conducting experiments with herbs ~~in order~~ to examine their medicinal value.

1. One true fact is that herbs have played an important part in the lives of human beings through the ages.

2. For example, in past history, the Romans put laurel in the crowns of the emperors.

3. The ancient Greeks ate parsley for the purpose of curing stomach aches.

4. During the Middle Ages, mint was popular due to the fact that people used it to purify drinking water.

5. The fact of the matter is that during the Middle Ages, people thought that herbs had magical powers.

6. The early settlers to North America grew herbs in close proximity to their houses.

7. At that point in time, the new immigrants also used herbs as medicine.

8. Today, some people believe that herbal medicines are equally as good as synthetic medicines.

Section 5
WORD USE AND SPELLING

Avoiding Clichés

Clichés are overused expressions. Avoid boring your readers with clichés and use more direct and vivid language instead.

Clichés	**Direct words**
<u>In this neck of the woods,</u> she is considered an expert on orchids.	In this area

Other Common Clichés

a drop in the bucket	death trap
add insult to injury	easier said than done
as luck would have it	go with the flow
at a loss for words	in the nick of time
axe to grind	keep your eyes peeled
between a rock and a hard place	time and time again
better late than never	tried and true
break the ice	under the weather
calm, cool, and collected	work like a dog
crystal clear	

HINT Modifying Clichés

To modify a cliché, change it into a direct term. You might also try playing with language to come up with a more interesting description.

Cliché:	She was as happy as a lark.
Direct language:	She was thrilled.
Interesting description:	She was as happy as a teenager whose parents had gone away for the weekend.

PRACTICE 3

Cross out the clichéd expression in each sentence. If necessary, replace it with fresh or direct language.

EXAMPLE:

greatly impressed
I was ~~blown away~~ by my neighbour's garden.

1. My neighbour threw caution to the wind and planted some strange plants.

2. She was playing with fire planting a ginkgo tree.

3. When I smelled something putrid, I was sure beyond a shadow of a doubt that it was the ginkgo tree.

4. To add insult to injury, she had also planted a corpse flower in her greenhouse.

5. I was at a loss for words when she asked me how I liked her new plants.

6. In the nick of time, my boyfriend arrived, so I could avoid answering her question.

Using Standard English

Most of your instructors will want you to write using **standard English**. The word "standard" does not imply better. Standard English is the common language generally used and expected in schools, businesses, and government institutions in Canada.

Slang is non-standard language. It is used in informal situations to communicate common cultural knowledge. In any academic or professional context, do not use slang.

Slang: Me an some bros wanted to make some dough, so we worked on a farm picking apples. We made a bit of coin, and our grub was included. It was real cool. On the weekends, we mostly chilled.

Standard Canadian English: My friends and I wanted to make some money, so we worked on a farm picking apples. We were well paid, and our food was included. We had a memorable time. On the weekends, we mostly relaxed.

HINT Reasons to Avoid Slang

Slang changes depending on generational, regional, cultural, and historical influences. For example, one group might say "upset" whereas others might say "freaked out" or "having a fit." You should avoid using slang expressions in your writing because they can change very quickly—so quickly, in fact, that you might notice that this textbook's examples of slang are "lame."

Section 5
WORD USE AND SPELLING

PRACTICE 4

Substitute the underlined slang expressions with the best possible choice of standard English.

EXAMPLE:

                                                                    excellent

Over five thousand years ago, the Chinese cultivated roses that were ~~bad~~.

1. The history of roses is <u>sweet</u>.

2. An <u>awesome</u> fact is that the rose is about 35 million years old.

3. I was <u>blown away</u> when I learned that there are 150 species of roses.

4. Throughout history, famous <u>chicks</u>, such as Napoleon's wife Josephine, cultivated roses.

5. From the eighteenth century onwards, Europeans thought it was <u>tight</u> to grow roses in their gardens.

6. Cultivating a successful rose garden is <u>no cakewalk</u>.

7. Roses need a lot of <u>TLC</u> to blossom.

8. The roses in my garden are <u>fly</u>.

FINAL REVIEW

Edit twenty examples of wordiness, slang, clichés, and vague language.

1. At this point in time, many people are freaking out about genetically modified foods. Genetic modification (GM) is a technology that lets scientists fool around with the genetic composition of plants. Historically, people have always tried to change the characteristics of plants for the purpose of making them more disease resistant. That process has traditionally been done through hybridization, a tried-and-true method. That is, two parent plants from the same genus are bred to create an improved hybrid plant. One true fact is that hybrid wheat is hardier than traditional wheat.

2. Today, in North America, hundreds of things that we use daily are genetically modified. In the final analysis, there is great controversy about genetically modified foods. Proponents of this technology say time and time again that food will contain higher levels of nutrition, be resistant to disease, and produce higher yields.

3. In spite of the fact of such arguments, opponents are all fired up about genetically modified foods because they say that there is not enough knowledge about how such foods will affect human health. They believe such modified foods might become a death trap. For example, will humans who are allergic to peanuts have a reaction if they are eating tomatoes that have been genetically modified with a peanut gene? Furthermore, opponents also believe that the loss of diversity in crops and plants really bites. Another worry is that food production will go into the hands of super-sized agricultural companies who will control the growth and distribution of food. Moreover, the bigwigs in this debate have their knickers in a twist about the ethics of mixing genes from species to species.

Section 5
WORD USE AND SPELLING

4. The genetically modified food industry is growing rapidly in size. But it is important to have a healthy and open debate over this issue. Presently, consumers are faced with a difficult dilemma. Most people are in a fog and are unknowingly buying genetically modified foods because such foods lack complete labelling. For example, most cooking oil comes from genetically modified grains. The public should be in the know about this technology. Consumers need to be clued in so that they can make the right choices.

 Writer's Room **Topics for Writing**

Write about one of the following topics. Proofread your text to ensure that you have used detailed vocabulary and avoided wordiness, clichés, and slang.

1. Write about one of the following terms:

   family farm, agribusiness, healthy living, back to basics, farm aid, or *green thumb.*

2. Why are fast foods and other unhealthy foods so popular? Think of some reasons.

Section 5
WORD USE AND SPELLING

 CHECKLIST: EXACT LANGUAGE

When you edit your writing, ask yourself the next questions.

Have I used specific and detailed vocabulary? Check for errors with vague words.

My son likes to garden. (Vague)

My fifteen-year-old son, Kiran, is an enthusiastic gardener. (Detailed)

Have I used exact language? Check for errors with wordiness, clichés, and slang.

Julian works in the garden centre ~~at this point in time~~.   *now*

It is ~~as plain as black and white~~ that many people like organic food.   *evident*

The biology exam was ~~a no-brainer~~.   *easy*

Spelling and Commonly Confused Words

FLORA AND FAUNA **In this chapter, you will read about insects.**

CHAPTER CONTENTS

- Spelling Rules
- 120 Commonly Misspelled Words
- Look-Alike and Sound-Alike Words

GRAMMAR SNAPSHOT Looking at Spelling

In this excerpt from the article, "Songs of Insects," writer Sy Montgomery discusses how insects communicate. Writers often misspell the underlined words.

If you share this poet's <u>sensibilities</u>, now is the time to <u>fulfill</u> your longing. Though <u>widely</u> loved for <u>its</u> changing <u>leaves</u> and migrating birds, early fall is, in some circles anyway, yet more <u>renowned</u> for the sweetness of <u>its</u> insect voices.

In this chapter, you will identify and correct misspelled words.

Spelling Rules

It is important to spell correctly because spelling mistakes can detract from important ideas in your work. Here are some strategies for improving your spelling skills.

How to Become a Better Speller

- **Look up words** using the most current dictionary because it will contain new or updated words. For tips on dictionary usage, see page 457.
- **Keep a record of words that you commonly misspell.** For example, write the words and definitions in a spelling log, which could be in a journal or binder. See Appendix 5 for more information about your spelling log.
- **Use memory cards or flash cards** to help you memorize the spelling of difficult words. With a friend or a classmate, take turns asking each other to spell difficult words.

■ **Write out the spelling of difficult words at least ten times** to help you remember how to spell them. After you have written these words, try writing them in a complete sentence.

Six Common Spelling Rules

Memorize the following common rules of spelling. If you follow these rules, your spelling will become more accurate. Also try to remember the exceptions to these rules.

1. Writing *ie* or *ei*

Write *i* before *e*, except after *c* or when *ei* is pronounced as *ay*, as in *neighbour* and *weigh*.

i **before e:**	chief	field	grief
ei **after c:**	receipt	deceit	receive
ei **pronounced as *ay*:**	weigh	beige	vein

Here are some exceptions:

ancient	science
either	species
neither	society
foreigner	seize
leisure	their
height	weird

2. Adding *-s* or *-es*

Add *-s* to form plural nouns and to create present-tense verbs that are third-person singular. However, add *-es* to words in the following situations.

■ When words end in *s*, *sh*, *ss*, *ch*, or *x*, add *-es*.

Noun: box ➔ boxes
Verb: miss ➔ misses

■ When words end in consonant *y*, change the *y* to *i* and add *-es*.

Noun: baby ➔ babies
Verb: marry ➔ marries

■ When words end in *o*, you usually add *-es*. Exceptions are *pianos*, *radios*, *logos*, *stereos*, *autos*, *typos*, and *casinos*.

Noun: tomato ➔ tomatoes
Verb: go ➔ goes

■ When words end in *f*, or *fe*, change the *f* to a *v* and add *-es*. Exceptions are *beliefs* and *roofs*.

life ➔ lives
wolf ➔ wolves

3. Adding Prefixes and Suffixes

A **prefix** is added to the beginning of a word, and it changes the word's meaning. For example, *con-*, *dis-*, *pre-*, *un-*, and *il-* are prefixes. When you add a prefix to a word, keep the last letter of the prefix and the first letter of the main word.

> i**m** + **m**ature = i**mm**ature
> mi**s** + **s**pell = mi**ss**pell

A **suffix** is added to the ending of a word, and it changes the word's tense or meaning.

For example, *-ly*, *-ment*, *-ed*, and *-ing* are suffixes. When you add the suffix *-ly* to words that end in *l*, keep the *l* of the root word. The new word will have two *l*s.

> casua**l** + **l**y = casua**ll**y
> factua**l** + **l**y = factua**ll**y

4. Adding Suffixes to Words Ending in e

If the suffix begins with a vowel, drop the *e* on the main word. Some common suffixes beginning with vowels are *-ed*, *-er*, *-est*, *-ing*, *-able*, *-ent*, and *-ist*.

> bak**e** ➜ baking
> creat**e** ➜ created

Some exceptions are words that end in *ge*, which keep the *e* and add the suffix.

> outrag**e** ➜ outrag**e**ous
> manag**e** ➜ manag**e**able

If the suffix begins with a consonant, keep the *e*. Some common suffixes beginning with consonants are *-ly*, *-ment*, *-less*, and *-ful*. Some exceptions are *acknowledgment*, *argument*, and *truly*.

> sur**e** ➜ sur**e**ly
> awar**e** ➜ awar**e**ness

5. Adding Suffixes to Words Ending in y

If the word has a consonant before the final *y*, change the *y* to an *i* before adding the suffix. Some exceptions are *ladybug*, *dryness*, and *shyness*.

> prett**y** ➜ prett**i**est
> happ**y** ➜ happ**i**ness

Section 5
**WORD USE AND
SPELLING**

If the word has a vowel before the final *y*, if it is a proper name, or if the suffix is *-ing*, do not change the *y* to an *i*. Some exceptions are *daily*, *laid*, and *said*.

> emplo**y** ➜ emplo**y**ed
> appl**y** ➜ appl**y**ing
> Levinsk**y** ➜ Levinsk**y**s

6. Doubling the Final Consonant

Double the final consonant of one-syllable words ending in a consonant-vowel-consonant pattern.

> shi**p** ➜ shi**pp**ing
> swi**m** ➜ swi**mm**er
> ho**p** ➜ ho**pp**ed

Double the final consonant of words ending in a stressed consonant-vowel-consonant pattern.

refer → preferred
occur → occurred

Do not double the final consonant in two syllable words ending in consonant-vowel-consonant pattern if the stress falls on the first syllable.

enter → entering
open → opening

Exceptions: travel → travelling
label → labelling

120 Commonly Misspelled Words

This list contains some of the most commonly misspelled words in English.

Section 5
WORD USE
AND SPELLING

absence	definite	maintenance	rhythm
absorption	definitely	mathematics	schedule
accommodate	desperate	medicine	scientific
acquaintance	developed	millennium	separate
address	dilemma	minuscule	sincerely
aggressive	disappoint	mischievous	spaghetti
already	embarrass	mortgage	strength
aluminum	encouragement	necessary	success
analyze	environment	ninety	surprise
appointment	especially	noticeable	technique
approximate	exaggerate	occasion	thorough
argument	exercise	occurrence	tomato
athlete	extraordinarily	opposite	tomatoes
bargain	familiar	outrageous	tomorrow
beginning	February	parallel	truly
behaviour	finally	performance	Tuesday
believable	foreign	perseverance	until
business	government	personality	usually
calendar	grammar	physically	vacuum
campaign	harassment	possess	Wednesday
careful	height	precious	weird
ceiling	immediately	prejudice	woman
cemetery	independent	privilege	women
clientele	jewellery	probably	wreckage
committee	judgment	professor	writer
comparison	laboratory	psychology	writing
competent	ledge	questionnaire	written
conscience	leisure	receive	zealous
conscientious	licence (n.)	recommend	
convenient	license (v.)	reference	
curriculum	loneliness	responsible	

PRACTICE I

Edit the following paragraphs for twenty misspelled words.

EXAMPLE:

strength

Some insects have an incredible amount of ~~strenght~~.

1. Throughout history, humans have either been fascinated or repulsed by insects. In fact, humans have developed a close connection to insects and recognize the power and importance of insects for sustaining life. For example, insects pollinate plants and aerate soil. Without such help, the enviroment would suffer. Thus, human cultures have acknowleged insects through art, literature, and religion.

2. First, the ancient Egyptians honoured different insects. The dung beetle or scarab was definatly an important religious symbol. The Egyptians called it Khepera, the god of virility and rebirth. They beleived that he was responsable for pushing the sun along the horizon. To honour Khepera, the Egyptians wore scarab amulets as precious jewlry and buried them in pots and boxs with the dead. The ancients thought that the scarabs helped the dead who were enterring the afterlife. Furthermore, ancient Egyptian kings took the name of Khepera when they became rulers. For example, Tutankhamen's royal name was Neb Kheperu Ra.

3. Another insect, the cricket, was valued in Chinese culture. The Chinese kept both singing and fighting varieties. Singing crickets were expecialy crucial to farmers. They knew it was time to plough when crickets and other insects began to wake and sing. Wealthy ladyes and palace concubines kept crickets as pets in cages. People surmised that the crickets represented the women themselfs who had very little status in the community. Fighting crickets were also very popular, and many people lost much of their savings beting on cricket fights.

4. Western artists are also fascinated with insects. There are many fables that feature different speceis as the main characters. In modern literature,

Section 5
WORD USE AND SPELLING

insects play a noticable role. For example, in Franz Kafka's *Metamorphosis*, the main character turns into a giant cockroach. Insects are common symbols in modern film. Jiminy Cricket is Pinocchio's consceince. In the movie *The Fly*, a scientist is unaturaly transformed into a six-foot human fly. Flys and other insects can also symbolize human fear and repugnance.

5. Humans and insects have had a truely unique relationship for many millennia. Different cultures have integrated insects into the fields of art, music, religion, and history. Indeed, some people say that the teeny creepy crawlers are survivors and will surly outlive humans.

Look-Alike and Sound-Alike Words

Sometimes two English words can sound the same but have different spellings and meanings. These words are called **homonyms**. Here are a few commonly confused words and basic meanings. (For more specific definitions for these and other words, consult a dictionary.)

Section 5
WORD USE AND SPELLING

accept	to receive; to admit	We must <u>accept</u> the vital role that insects play in our culture.
except	excluding; other than	I like all insects <u>except</u> ants.
allowed	permitted	We were not <u>allowed</u> to view the exhibit.
aloud	spoken audibly	We could not speak <u>aloud</u>, so we whispered.
affect	to influence	Pesticides <u>affect</u> the environment.
effect	the result of something	Scientists are examining the <u>effects</u> of pesticides on our health.
been	past participle of the verb *to be*	He has <u>been</u> to the Imax film about caterpillars.
being	present progressive form (the -*ing* form) of the verb *to be*	She was <u>being</u> kind when she donated to the butterfly museum.
by	preposition meaning *next to, on,* or *before*	A bee flew <u>by</u> the flowers. <u>By</u> evening, the crickets were making a lot of noise.
buy	to purchase	Will you <u>buy</u> me that scarab necklace?
complement	to add to; to complete	The film about the monarch butterfly was a nice <u>complement</u> to the exhibit.
compliment	to say something nice about someone	The film was informative and the director received many <u>compliments</u>.
conscience	a personal sense of right or wrong	After spraying pesticides, the gardener had a guilty <u>conscience</u>.
conscious	to be aware; to be awake	He made us <u>conscious</u> of the important role insects play in our society.

PRACTICE 2

Underline the correct word in parentheses.

EXAMPLE:

Many people (by / <u>buy</u>) clothes made out of silk.

1. Silk has (been / being) produced (by / buy) the Chinese for at least four
thousand years. The silkworm is actually a caterpillar that eats nothing
(accept / except) mulberry leaves, grows quickly, and then encircles itself
into a cocoon of raw silk. The cocoon contains a single thread about 300 to
900 metres in length, so it's not surprising that it takes about 2000 cocoons
to make one pound of silk. (Been / Being) very (conscious / conscience) of
the long and intense silk-making process, most people (accept / except) the
high cost of the material.

2. The Chinese valued silk and guarded the secret of its making carefully. In
ancient China, only the emperor and his family were (allowed / aloud) to
wear silk garments. Sometimes, members of royalty wore the fabric as a
(complement / compliment) to their regular clothes. Of course, less
fortunate people admired the emperor's beautiful clothes and always
(complimented / complemented) him on them.

3. By the fifth century, the secret of silk making had been revealed to Korea,
Japan, and India. How did the secret get out? Legend says that a princess
with no (conscious / conscience) smuggled out silkworm larvae to Korea by
hiding them in her hair. The emperor was outraged (by / buy) the actions
of the princess, and there was great debate about her treachery.

Section 5
WORD USE AND
SPELLING

everyday	ordinary or common	Swatting mosquitoes is an <u>everyday</u> ritual of camping.
every day	each day	<u>Every day</u>, I check my roses for aphids.
imply	to suggest	The entomologist <u>implied</u> that he received a large grant.
infer	to conclude	His students <u>inferred</u> that they would have summer jobs because of the grant.
imminent	soon to happen	The journalist reported that the arrival of locusts in parts of Africa was <u>imminent</u>.
eminent	distinguished; superior	Professor Maurice Kanyogo is an <u>eminent</u> entomologist.

its	possessive case of the pronoun *it*	The worker bee went into <u>its</u> hive.
it's	contraction for *it is*	<u>It's</u> well-known that the queen bee is the largest in the colony.
knew	past tense of to know	I <u>knew</u> that I should study for my test on worms.
new	recent or unused	But my <u>new</u> book on honey making was more interesting.
know	to have knowledge of	The beekeepers <u>know</u> that there has been a decline of bees in recent years.
no	a negative	There were <u>no</u> books on beekeeping in the library.
lose	to misplace or forfeit something	Do not <u>lose</u> the mosquito repellent.
loose	too baggy; not fixed	You should wear <u>loose</u> clothes when camping.
loss	a decrease in an amount; a serious blow	Farmers would experience a <u>loss</u> if there were no bees to pollinate crops.
peace	calmness or an end to violence	The <u>peace</u> in the woods was wonderful.
piece	a part of something else; one item in a group of items	The two <u>pieces</u> of amber had insects in them.
principal	director of a school; main	The <u>principal</u> of our school is an expert on beetles. They are his <u>principal</u> hobby.
principle	rules or standards	Julius Corrant wrote a book about environmental <u>principles</u>.
quiet	silent	The crickets remained <u>quiet</u> this evening.
quite	very	They usually make <u>quite</u> a noise.
quit	stop	I would like them to <u>quit</u> making so much noise.

Section 5
**WORD USE
AND SPELLING**

PRACTICE 3

Identify and correct ten word choice errors.

EXAMPLE:

                     peace
I need some ~~piece~~ and quiet.

1. I am reading a book on pollination by Professor Zoe Truger, an imminent

   entomologist who specializes in butterfly behaviour. Its very interesting.

   On it's cover, there is a beautiful photograph of a butterfly. Everyday,

   during the summer, thousands of monarch butterflies are found in southern

Canada, their summer home. As autumn arrives, these butterflies know that migration to warmer climates is eminent.

2. The principle of Jake's school took the students on a nature walk to look for earthworms. The students were very quit when the guide told them there are 2700 species of earthworms.

3. Did you no that beekeeping is one of the world's oldest professions? Some beekeepers may loose their businesses because bees are dying due to pesticide overuse. Citizens need to quite spraying their fields, parks, and gardens with pesticides.

taught	past tense of *to teach*	I <u>taught</u> a class on pollination.
thought	past tense of *to think*	I <u>thought</u> the students enjoyed it.
than	word used to compare items	There are more mosquitoes at the lake <u>than</u> in the city.
then	at a particular time or after a specific time	He found the termite nest. <u>Then</u> he called the exterminators.
that	word used to introduce a clause	They told him <u>that</u> they would come immediately.
their	possessive form of *they*	They wore scarab amulets to show <u>their</u> respect for the god Khepera.
there	a place	The ant colony is over <u>there</u>.
they're	contraction of *they are*	The ants work hard. <u>They're</u> very industrious.
to	part of an infinitive; indicates direction or movement	I want <u>to</u> hunt for bugs. I will go <u>to</u> the hiking path and look under some rocks.
too	also; very	My friend is <u>too</u> scared of bugs. My brother is <u>too</u>.
two	the number after *one*	There were <u>two</u> types of butterflies in the garden today.
where	question word indicating location	<u>Where</u> did you buy the book on ladybugs?
were	past tense of *be*	There <u>were</u> hundreds of ladybugs on the bush.
we're	contraction of *we are*	<u>We're</u> wondering why we have this infestation.

Section 5
WORD USE AND SPELLING

write	to draw symbols that represent words	I will <u>write</u> an essay about the common earthworm.
right	correct; the opposite of the direction left	In the <u>right</u> corner of the garden, there is the compost bin with many worms in it. You are <u>right</u> when you say that earthworms are necessary for composting.
who's	contraction of *who is*	Ishbelle, <u>who's</u> a horticulturist, also keeps a butterfly garden.
whose	pronoun showing ownership	<u>Whose</u> garden is that?

PRACTICE 4

Identify and correct sixteen word choice errors.

EXAMPLE:

There
~~Their~~ are many different types of hobbies.

1. Their are both professional and amateur beekeepers. Beekeepers wear special clothes, but even with protective gear, there usually stung at least once while practising there profession. Some beekeepers have a greater resistance to stings then others have. All of them know than there is a small danger of death from anaphylactic shock because of a bee sting. A person whose interested in beekeeping should know the risks. Than he or she can make the write choices about hobbies.

2. We recently read to books on ladybugs. We went to the library were an expert thought us about ladybugs. The expert, who's bug collection was on display, said each ladybug controls pests because it eats around 5000 aphids in its lifetime. Ladybugs eat other pests to. We where extremely surprised when we heard that fact. Were going to do more research on ladybugs. I will right an email to the expert asking for more information.

FINAL REVIEW

Correct the twenty spelling errors and mistakes with commonly confused words in the following essay.

EXAMPLE:

       carries

The bee ~~carrys~~ pollen grains from one plant to another.

1. Around the world, unatural causes such as climate change, pollution, and human activities are threatening the enviroment. Forests are expecialy vulnerable to these pressures because of loging, increasing pests, and global warming. Conserving biodiversity is important for protecting forests.

2. Biodiversity, a contraction of the words *biological diversity*, means that a variety of plants, animals, and micro-organisms co-exist in an ecosystem. Today, imminent scientists concerned with species' extinction refer to the necesity of maintaining biodiversity on our planet. Scientists are conscience of the value of each species. Argueing for conserving biodiversity, scientists believe that if species become extinct, than the ecosystem will become unstable.

3. Insects are crucial to sustain the biodiversity of an ecosystem and are the most diverse life form on earth. Currently, there are approximately 800 000 identified species of insects, all of which are usefull in balancing the ecosystem. For example, they pollinate plants, and they eat other insects and plants. Their also important to the global economy. For instance, insects are used for honey production, silk making, and agricultural pest control. If an insect species becomes extinct, they're will be a variety of consequences on the remaining species in the ecosystem, such as an increase in predatory insects or a lost of another species higher on the food chain. Such a change in the ecosystem would have an eminent effect on all life forms.

Section 5
**WORD USE AND
SPELLING**

4. Most people think that insects are troublesome and should be eradicated. Of course, insects such as mosquitos carry diseases, including malaria and West Nile Virus, which are harmfull to human health. But its important to keep in mind that most insects provide important services for the natural world, to. Were there are insects, there is a thriving ecosystem. Extinction of an insect species will have a serious affect on nature, so the next time you are tempted to swat a fly or step on an ant, you might think twice.

WRITING LINK

Flora and Fauna
These readings contain more information on plants and insects.
"Living Among the Bees" by Lucie L. Snodgrass (page 114)
"The Zoo Life" by Yann Martel (page 493)
"Songs of Insects" by Sy Montgomery (page 490)

 Writer's Room   **Topics for Writing**

Write about one of the following topics. Proofread your text to ensure there are no spelling and commonly confused word errors.

1. Discuss types of insects that are particularly annoying, repulsive, or frightening.
2. Are laws banning the use of pesticides on lawns a good idea? Explain your views.

 CHECKLIST: SPELLING RULES

When you edit your writing, ask yourself these questions.

☐ Do I have any spelling errors? Check for errors in words that contain these elements:

   ▪ any *ie* or *ei* combinations

   ▪ prefixes and suffixes

~~Dragonflys~~ are ~~lovly.~~ ~~There~~ wings are transparent, but ~~they're~~ bodies
Dragonflies   lovely   Their   ... their
are a variety of colours. They eat other insects such as ~~mosquitos~~.
                                                          mosquitoes

☐ Do I repeat spelling errors that I have made in previous assignments? I should check my previous assignments for errors or consult my spelling log.

Section 5
WORD USE AND SPELLING

Commas

HUMAN DEVELOPMENT In this chapter, you will read about life stages.

CHAPTER CONTENTS

GRAMMAR SNAPSHOT Looking at Commas

On an episode of the ABC news program Primetime, Connie Chung interviewed citizens from Yuzuri Hara, Japan, a small mountainous village two hours outside of Tokyo. In the excerpt that follows, the commas are highlighted.

Mr. Takahashi attributes his smooth skin, even after working fifty years in the sun, to sticking to the local traditional diet. The skin on his arms felt like a baby's, and the skin on his legs barely had a wrinkle. Some of what Mr. Takahashi eats is on the menu every day at a hotel in Yuzuri Hara. The innkeeper, Mrs. Ishi, is eighty and looks pretty good herself.

In this chapter, you will learn to use commas correctly.

What Is a Comma?

A **comma** (,) is a punctuation mark that helps identify distinct ideas. There are many ways to use a comma. In this chapter, you will learn some helpful rules about comma usage.

Notice how comma placement changes the meanings of the following sentences.

The baby hits, her mother cries, and then they hug each other.

The baby hits her mother, cries, and then they hug each other.

Commas in a Series

Use a comma to separate items in a series of three or more items. Remember to put a comma before the final "and."

| Unit 1 | , | unit 2 | , | and/or | unit 3. |

Canada, the United States, and Mexico have psychology conferences.

The experiment required patience, perseverance, and energy.

Some teens may do part-time work, volunteer in the community, and maintain high grades at school.

HINT **Comma Before *and***

There is a trend in the media to omit the comma before the final *and* in a series. However, in academic writing, it is preferable to include the comma because it clarifies your meaning and makes the items more distinct.

PRACTICE I

Underline series of items. Then add fifteen missing commas.

EXAMPLE:

Some psychological studies are <u>simple</u>, <u>obvious</u>, and <u>extremely important</u>.

1. Mary Ainsworth was born in Ohio attended the University of Toronto and worked in Uganda. She became an expert in the childhood development field. Ainsworth's most significant research examined the attachment of infants to their caretakers.

2. Ainsworth designed an experiment called *The Strange Situation*. She measured how infants reacted when the primary caretaker left the room a stranger entered and the primary caretaker returned. She determined that children have four attachment styles. They may be secure avoidant ambivalent or disoriented.

3. Secure children may leave their mother's lap explore happily and return to the mother. Avoidant babies are not upset when the mother leaves do not look at the stranger and show little reaction when the mother returns.

Ambivalent babies are clinging unwilling to explore and upset by strangers. Disoriented infants react oddly to their mother's return. They look fearful avoid eye contact and slowly approach the returning mother.

Commas After Introductory Words or Phrases

Place a comma after an **introductory word** or **phrase**. Introductory words include interjections (*well*), adverbs (*usually*), or transitional words (*therefore*). Introductory phrases could be transitional expressions (*of course*), prepositional phrases (*in the winter*), or modifiers (*born in Egypt*).

Introductory word(s)	,	sentence.

Introductory word: <u>Yes</u>, the last stage of life is very important.

Introductory phrase: <u>After the experiment</u>, the children returned home.

<u>Feeling bored</u>, he volunteered at a nearby clinic.

PRACTICE 2

Underline each introductory word or phrase. Then add twelve missing commas.

EXAMPLE:

<u>Before leaving home</u>, adolescents assert their independence.

1. In *Childhood and Society* Erik Erikson explained his views about the stages of life. According to Erikson there are eight life stages. In his opinion each stage is characterized by a developmental crisis.

2. In the infancy stage babies must learn to trust others. Wanting others to fulfill their needs babies expect life to be pleasant. Neglected babies may end up mistrusting the world.

3. During adolescence a young man or woman may have an identity crisis. Confronted with physical and emotional changes teenagers must develop a sense of self. According to Erikson some adolescents are unable to solve their identity crisis. Lacking self-awareness they cannot commit to certain goals and values.

4. In Erikson's view each crisis must be solved before a person develops in the next life stage. For example a person may become an adult chronologically. However that person is not an adult emotionally.

Commas Around Interrupting Words or Phrases

Interrupting words or phrases appear in the middle of sentences, and while they interrupt the sentence's flow, they do not affect its overall meaning. Some interrupters are *as a matter of fact*, *as you know*, and *for example*. Prepositional phrases can also interrupt sentences.

| **Sentence** | , | **interrupter** | , | **sentence continued.** |

The doctor, <u>for example</u>, has never studied child psychology.

Adolescence, <u>as you know</u>, is a difficult life stage.

The child, <u>with no prompting</u>, started to laugh.

HINT **Using Commas with Appositives**

An appositive gives further information about a noun or pronoun. The appositive can appear at the beginning, in the middle, or at the end of the sentence. Set off appositives with commas.

beginning
<u>A large hospital</u>, the Hospital for Sick Children has some of the world's best researchers.

middle
Gail Sheehy, <u>a journalist</u>, has written about life passages.

end
The doctor's office is next to Sims Wholesale, <u>a local grocery store</u>.

PRACTICE 3

The following sentences contain introductory words and phrases, interrupters, and series of items. Add the missing commas. If the sentence is correct, write C in the space provided.

EXAMPLE:

Erik Erikson, a child development expert, wrote about his identity crisis. _____

1. Erik Erikson during his youth, had an identity crisis. _____

2. At the age of sixteen, he learned more about his past. _____

3. His mother admitted that Erik was the result of an extramarital affair. _____

4. He felt surprised, confused and angry. _____

5. At that time, he did not know his birth father. _____

6. Erikson's mother a Danish woman had moved to Germany. _____

7. His adopted father a pediatrician named Theodore Homburger was Jewish. _____

8. Erikson felt confused about his nationality his religion, and his genealogy. _____

9. In the early 1920s, Erikson went to Vienna. _____

10. Erikson, at a conference met Anna Freud. _____

11. Anna Freud Sigmund Freud's daughter, analyzed Erikson. _____

12. Using psychoanalysis she helped him resolve his identity crisis. _____

Commas in Compound Sentences

In compound sentences, place a comma before the coordinating conjunction (*for*, *and*, *nor*, *but*, *or*, *yet*, *so*).

| **Sentence** | **,** | **and** | **sentence.** |

Adulthood has three stages, **and** each stage has its particular challenge.

Carolina lives with her mother, **but** she is very independent.

She goes to school, **yet** she also works forty hours a week.

HINT Commas and Coordinators

To ensure that a sentence is compound, cover the conjunction with your finger and read the two parts of the sentence. If one part of the sentence is incomplete, then no comma is necessary. If each part of the sentence contains a complete idea, then you need to add a comma.

No comma: Ben still lives with his parents **but** is very self-sufficient.

Comma: Ben still lives with his parents, **but** he is very self-sufficient.

PRACTICE 4

Edit the following paragraphs and add ten missing commas.

EXAMPLE:

She is not an adult, yet she is not a child.

1. Adulthood is another stage in life but the exact age of adulthood is unclear.

   Some cultures celebrate adulthood with high school graduation ceremonies and others celebrate with marriage. Some people define adulthood as the moment a person has full-time work and is self-sufficient yet many people become independent only in their thirties.

2. Cultures treat early adulthood differently. Irene Berridge, who was born and raised in Medicine Hat, Alberta, has a culturally mixed background. Her mother is German and her father is British. She was encouraged to leave home and get an apartment at age nineteen. Today, twenty-one-year-old Irene washes her clothing at a laundromat and she does her own cooking. She has a part-time job and she splits the bills with her roommate.

3. Alexis Khoury's parents are recent immigrants from Greece and they want their daughter to stay home until she marries. Alexis is a thirty-one-year-old Montrealer and she sometimes feels embarrassed to be living at home. She does not feel like an adult and her parents encourage her dependence. However, Alexis will respect her parents' wishes and she will not leave home until she has found a life partner.

Commas in Complex Sentences

A **complex sentence** contains one or more dependent clauses (or incomplete ideas). When you add a **subordinating conjunction**—a word such as *because*, *although*, or *unless*—to a clause, you make the clause dependent.

      dependent clause   independent clause
After Jason graduated from college, he moved out of the family home.

Use a Comma After a Dependent Clause

If a sentence begins with a dependent clause, place a comma after the clause. Remember that a dependent clause has a subject and a verb, but it cannot stand alone. When the subordinating conjunction comes in the middle of the sentence, it is not necessary to use a comma.

Dependent clause	,	main clause.

Comma: When I find a better job, I will move into an apartment.

	Main clause	**dependent clause.**

No comma: I will move into an apartment when I find a better job.

PRACTICE 5

Edit the following sentences by adding or deleting commas.

EXAMPLE:

Although twenty-eight-year-old Samuel Chong lives at home, he is not
ashamed.

1. When he examined the 2001 Census Mark Noble noticed a clear trend.

2. Although most people in their twenties lived on their own about forty
   percent of young adults still lived with their parents.

3. In 1981, the results were different, because only twenty-five percent of
   young adults lived at home.

4. After examining the statistics Noble determined several causes for the shift.

5. Because the marriage rate is declining fewer people buy their own homes.

6. When the cost of education increases people cannot afford to study and pay
   rent.

7. Other young adults stay with their parents, because the rents are so high.

8. Because these conditions are not changing many young adults will likely
   continue to stay with their parents.

Use Commas to Set Off Non-restrictive Clauses

Clauses beginning with *who*, *that*, and *which* can be restrictive or non-restrictive.
A **restrictive clause** contains essential information about the subject. Do not
place commas around restrictive clauses. In the following example, the
underlined clause is essential to understand the meaning of the sentence.

No commas: The only local company that creates computer graphics has no
job openings.

A **non-restrictive clause** gives non-essential or additional information
about the noun but does not restrict or define the noun. Place commas around
non-restrictive clauses. In the following sentence, the underlined clause contains
extra information, but if you removed that clause, the sentence would still have
a clear meaning.

Commas: Her book, which is in bookstores, is about successful
entrepreneurs.

GRAMMAR LINK

For more information about
choosing *which* or *that*, see
Chapter 20, Sentence Variety.

Section 6
**PUNCTUATION
AND
MECHANICS**

HINT   *Which, That, and Who*

Which
Use commas to set off clauses that begin with *which*.

   The brain, **which** is a complex organ, develops rapidly.

That
Do not use commas to set off clauses that begin with *that*.

   The house **that** I grew up in was demolished last year.

Who
If the *who* clause contains non-essential information, put commas around it. If the *who* clause is essential to the meaning of the sentence, then it does not require commas.

Essential: Many people **who** have brain injuries undergo subtle personality changes.

Not essential: Dr. Jay Giedd, **who** lives in Maryland, made an important discovery.

PRACTICE 6

Edit the following sentences by adding twelve missing commas.

EXAMPLE:

The neurologist, whom I have never met, made an exciting discovery.

1. Twenty years ago, scientists thought that the brain stopped changing at an early age. They believed that after children reached twelve years of age their brains would stop growing. In 1997, a team of doctors who specialized in brain research made an exciting discovery. Neuroscientist Dr. Jay Giedd who works at the National Institute of Mental Health realized that brain cells have a growth spurt just before puberty. Scientists discovered that myelin which connects brain cells increases during adolescence. However, not all parts of the brain receive myelin at once, and the last region to receive it is the frontal lobe.

2. The frontal lobe, which is responsible for rational decision making stops an individual from making impulsive choices. For example imagine that you are driving your car. When another car cuts you off the primitive part of your brain wants to hurt the other driver. The frontal lobe helps you to think about alternatives. Thus, you may simply accept that all drivers make mistakes.

3. According to specialists the delay in receiving myelin to the frontal lobe affects many teens, and they may have trouble curbing their impulses. They may react quickly violently or irrationally, and are more likely than people in other age groups to engage in risky behaviour. When the frontal lobe has fully developed people generally become less impulsive.

FINAL REVIEW

Edit this essay by adding seventeen missing commas and removing three unnecessary commas.

EXAMPLE:

If people want to have longer lives they can exercise, eat well, and avoid risky behaviour.

1. In 350 BCE, Aristotle wrote an essay about life spans. Everybody has a maximum life span and nothing can be done to prolong that span. Until recently scientists agreed with Aristotle. They would argue that today's life expectancies are about as high as they can possibly get. However a group of researchers believes that human life expectancy will increase significantly in the future.

2. Dr. James Vaupel a researcher at Duke University, believes that our lifespan can be extended significantly. He gives a concrete example. In 1840, Swedish women had the world's longest life expectancy and the average Swedish woman lived to age forty-five. Today, Japanese women, who live to an average age of eighty-five have the world's longest life expectancy. This huge increase in life expectancy was partly due to the decrease in infant mortality. In 1800, about 25 percent of babies died in the first year of life. Surgery vaccines and antibiotics have helped to lower the childhood death rates. Also, because they have access to new medical interventions people over age sixty-five are living longer. Still, only about 2 percent of the population lives to one hundred years of age.

3. According to Dr. Vaupel, today's babies will have much longer life expectancies than their parents had and half of all newborns could live to

one hundred years of age. Dr. Aubrey De Grey, a professor at Cambridge University believes that human life expectancy will increase to five hundred years or more. Certainly, there are very promising discoveries on the horizon. Cures for cancer, and heart disease will help increase life expectancy. Also, because so many women delay childbirth the period of human fertility may lengthen which could have an eventual impact on life expectancy.

4. Some experts disagree with Vaupel and De Grey. Leonard Hayflick, discovered that human cells divide and reproduce about fifty times before slowing down and stopping. The longest average lifespan humans can attain in Hayflick's view is 120 years of age. However, some research labs are experimenting with ways of increasing the lifespan of cells. For example scientists have isolated a part of the chromosome that shrinks with age. If scientists find a way to slow down cell aging the results could significantly increase life expectancies of all humans.

5. A very long life expectancy, would force humans to rethink life stages. When would childhood end? Would you want to live to 150 years of age or more?

Section 6
**PUNCTUATION
AND
MECHANICS**

 Writer's Room **Topics for Writing**

Write about one of the following topics. After you finish writing, make sure that you have used commas correctly.

1. What problems could occur if human life expectancy were to become a lot longer? Think about the effects of an increased lifespan.
2. Which life stage is the most interesting? Give anecdotes to back up your views.

CHECKLIST: COMMAS

When you edit your writing, ask yourself these questions.

Do I use commas correctly? Remember to use commas in these situations:

- between words in a series of items
- after an introductory word or phrase
- around an interrupting word or phrase

The conference will be in Halifax, Edmonton, or Vancouver.

Beyond a doubt, many psychologists will attend.

The key speaker, in my opinion, is extremely interesting.

Do I use commas correctly in compound and complex sentences? Remember to use commas in these situations:

- before the coordinator in a compound sentence
- after a dependent clause in a complex sentence

She will discuss brain development, and she will present case studies.

When her presentation ends, participants can ask questions.

Section 6
**PUNCTUATION
AND
MECHANICS**

Apostrophes

CHAPTER CONTENTS

GRAMMAR SNAPSHOT Looking at Apostrophes

In an interview with Diane Sawyer for ABC News, musician Paul McCartney discusses his art show and his initial feelings about painting. Review the highlighted words. Discuss what the long form of each contraction is.

The way I was brought up, in the working class, only people who went to art school painted. It **wasn't** for us to paint. We **didn't** ride horses. They did. You know, **we'd** ride bikes if we were lucky. I **would've** felt like I was a bit uppity to paint, you know. "Oh, **you're** painting now, are you?"

In this chapter, you will learn to use apostrophes correctly.

What Is an Apostrophe?

An **apostrophe** is a punctuation mark showing a contraction or ownership.

> Emma **Chong's** art gallery is very successful, and **it's** still growing.

Apostrophes in Contractions

To form a **contraction**, join two words into one and add an apostrophe to replace the omitted letter(s). The following are examples of common contractions.

- **Join a verb with *not*.** The apostrophe replaces the letter *o* in not.

is + not = isn't	does + not = doesn't
are + not = aren't	has + not = hasn't
	have + not = haven't

could + not = couldn't   should + not = shouldn't
do + not = don't   would + not = wouldn't

Exceptions: will + not = <u>won't</u>   can + not = can't

- **Join a subject and a verb.** Sometimes you must remove several letters to form the contraction.

I + will = I'll   she + will = she'll
I + would = I'd   Tina + is = Tina's
he + is = he's   they + are = they're
he + will = he'll   we + will = we'll
Joe + is = Joe's   who + is = who's
she + has = she's   who + would = who'd

Exception: Do not contract a subject with the past tense of *be*. For example, do not contract *he + was* or *they + were*.

HINT Common Apostrophe Errors

- Do not use apostrophes before the final -s of a verb or a plural noun.

     wants   *galleries*
Mr. Gaudet ~~want's~~ to open several ~~gallery's~~.

- In contractions with *not*, remember that the apostrophe usually replaces the missing *o*.

     doesn't
He ~~does'nt~~ understand the problem.

PRACTICE 1

Edit the next sentences for fifteen apostrophe errors. Each word counts as one error.

EXAMPLE:

            isn't
Making a great work of art ~~isnt~~ a simple process.

1. Whos a great artist? Why do some people have amazing artistic abilities whereas others do'nt? Researchers in biology, sociology, and psychology haven't unlocked the keys to human creativity. However, expert's in each field have proposed theories about creativity.

2. Sigmund Freud proposed that creativity is an occurrence of the subconscious. If someones in pain, he or she may create an artwork to relieve the suffering. Near the end of his life, Freud changed his mind. He said that he didnt believe that suffering was a prerequisite to creativity.

3. Neurologists look inside the brain to answer questions about creativity. Theyve said that the left portion of the brains responsible for logical processing and verbal skills. The right sides responsible for artistic, abstract thinking. In the past, neurologists did'nt believe that the left side of the brain had an impact on creative impulses, but recent brain scan's have shown that both sides of the brain are used in creative thinking.

4. Whats the source of creativity? Maybe its never going to be understood. What everybody know's for certain is that artistic talent isnt evenly distributed. Some people are'nt as talented as others.

HINT **Contractions with Two Meanings**

Sometimes one contraction can have two different meanings.

I'd = I had *or* I would

He's = he is *or* he has

When you read, you should be able to figure out the meaning of the contraction by looking at the words in context.

Joe's working on a painting.
(Joe is)

Joe's been working on it for a month.
(Joe has)

PRACTICE 2

Look at each underlined contraction, and then write out the complete words.

EXAMPLE:

They <u>weren't</u> ready to start a business.   _____were not_____

1. Rachel <u>Wood's</u> very happy with her sculpture.   _____

2. <u>She's</u> been a professional artist since 2002.   _____

3. <u>She's</u> an extremely creative woman.   _____

4. I wish <u>I'd</u> gone to art school.   _____

5. <u>I'd</u> like to be an artist, too.   _____

Apostrophes to Show Ownership

You can also use apostrophes to show ownership. Review the following rules.

Possessive Form of Singular Nouns

Add -'s to the end of a singular noun to indicate ownership. If the singular noun ends in s, you add -'s if you would pronounce it (boss's). If you would not pronounce the additional s, then just add an apostrophe (Moses').

> **Lautrec's** artwork was very revolutionary.
>
> **Morris's** wife is a professional dancer.

Possessive Form of Plural Nouns

When a plural noun ends in -s, just add an apostrophe to indicate ownership. Add -'s to irregular plural nouns.

> Many **galleries'** websites contain images of some of the artworks.
>
> The **men's** and **women's** paintings are in separate rooms.

Possessive Form of Compound Nouns

When two people have joint ownership, add the apostrophe to the second name. When two people have separate ownership, add apostrophes to both names.

> **Joint ownership:** Marian and **Jake's** gallery is successful.
>
> **Separate ownership: Marian's** and **Jake's** studios are in different buildings.

PRACTICE 3

Write the possessive forms of the following phrases.

EXAMPLE:

the sister of the doctor   _the doctor's sister_

1. the brush of the artist

2. the brushes of the artists

3. the lights in the studio

4. the room of the child

5. the rooms of the children

6. the entrances of the galleries

7. the photo of Ross and Anna

8. the photo of Ross and the photo of Anna

Section 6
PUNCTUATION AND MECHANICS

> **HINT** **Possessive Pronouns Do Not Have Apostrophes**
>
> Some contractions sound like possessive pronouns. For example, *you're* sounds like *your* and *it's* sounds like *its*. Remember that possesive pronouns never have apostrophes.
>
>   *its*
>
> The conference is on ~~it's~~ last day.
>
>   *yours*   *hers*
>
> The document is ~~your's~~ and not ~~her's~~.

PRACTICE 4

Correct nine errors. You may need to add, move, or remove apostrophes.

1. Many artist's paintings are unique. Have you ever heard of Fernando Botero? The Colombian painters work has been exhibited in a Quebec City museum. Several of his painting's have also appeared in Vancouver galleries.

2. Botero's paintings usually contain images of people. What makes his work unique is it's humour. He makes generals, religious figures, and dictators look like children. Theyre small and bloated, and the images are filled with colour.

3. Another great artist is Georgia O'Keeffe. Its not difficult to recognize an artwork that is her's. Shes known for her paintings of white bones, bull skulls, and flowers. In many art collections, youll find her artwork.

Apostrophes in Expressions of Time

If an expression of time (*year*, *week*, *month*, *day*) appears to possess something, you can add -'*s*.

    Alice Ray gave two **weeks'** notice before she left the dance company.

When you write out a year in numerals, an apostrophe can replace the missing numbers.

    The graduates of the class of **'99** hoped to find good jobs.

However, if you are writing the numeral of a decade or century, do not put an apostrophe before the final -*s*.

    In the **1900s**, many innovations in art occurred.

PRACTICE 5

Correct ten errors. You may need to add, move, or remove apostrophes.

EXAMPLE:

             doesn't

Octavio Cruz ~~doesnt~~ have a studio.

1. In the summer of 2000, Winnipeg construction worker Octavio Cruz did a years worth of painting. He felt incredibly inspired. In the early 1990's, hed sold some artworks, but his paintings were uninspired, and he had trouble becoming motivated. Then, in 1999, he was in a car accident. He spent three week's in a hospital. Since then, hes been extremely creative. His wife's astonishment is evident: "Hes a different man," she says. "His paintings are so much more vivid and colourful."

2. Cruz has been studied by a neurologist, Dr. Wade. The doctors theory is that Cruzs injury "disinhibited" his right brain, thus allowing him to become more creative. Many other peoples stories are similar to Cruz's. In fact, since the 1970's, scientists have recognized that certain brain injuries can stimulate creativity.

FINAL REVIEW

Edit the next paragraphs and correct fifteen apostrophe errors. You may need to add, remove, or move apostrophes.

EXAMPLE:

          artist's

What is an ~~artists~~ motivation to create?

1. In 1982, Dr. Teresa Amabile made an interesting study in creativity. For Amabiles study, she divided schoolgirl's into two groups. Both groups rooms were filled with collage material, including coloured paper, paste, and construction paper. The doctor chose collage-making because it doesnt require drawing skills.

2. Each group was invited to an "art party" in a separate room. The first groups goal was to create art to win a prize, such as a toy. The doctor

offered toys to the best three artists. Thus, the childrens motivation to create was to win the exciting prize. The girls in the second group didnt have to compete for a prize. They were simply told that three name's would be randomly drawn for prizes.

3. The doctors hypothesis was that a persons creativity would lessen if he or she were motivated by a reward. Amabile asked local artists and art critics to judge the collages when the children werent in the room. The judges scores for the first group were consistently lower than those for the second group. Thus, the doctors hypothesis was correct. A reward, such as money or a prize, isnt helpful to the creative process. When people create art for arts sake, they tend to be more imaginative.

 W͞riter's R͞oom   **Topics for Writing**

Write about one of the following topics. After you finish writing, make sure that you have used apostrophes correctly.

1. Describe the work of a painter, illustrator, photographer, or sculptor that you like. Explain what is most interesting about that artist's work.
2. Define one of these terms: *creativity*, *graffiti*, *art*, *vandalism*, or *beauty*.

Section 6
**PUNCTUATION
AND
MECHANICS**

✓ CHECKLIST: APOSTROPHES

When you edit your writing, ask yourself these questions.

▢ Do I use apostrophes correctly? Check for errors in these cases:

- ▪ contractions of verbs + *not* or subjects and verbs

- ▪ possessives of singular and plural nouns (*the student's* versus *the students'*)

- ▪ possessives of irregular plural nouns (*the women's*)

- ▪ possessives of compound nouns (*Joe's and Mike's cars*)

         shouldn't   Wong's

You ~~should'nt~~ be surprised that Chris ~~Wong~~ going to exhibit his paintings.

Chris's

~~Chris'~~ artwork will be on display next week.

▢ Do I place apostrophes where they do not belong? Check for errors in possessive pronouns and present tense verbs.

     looks   its

It ~~look's~~ as if the gallery is moving ~~it's~~ collection to Houston.

Section 6
**PUNCTUATION
AND
MECHANICS**

Quotation Marks, Capitalization, and Titles

CHAPTER CONTENTS

- Quotation Marks
- Using Quotations in Research Essays
- Capitalization
- Titles

GRAMMAR SNAPSHOT **Looking at Quotation Marks**

This excerpt is translated from Paul Gauguin's book, Avant et Après. It recounts when Vincent Van Gogh cut off part of his own ear. Notice that the quotation marks and some capital letters are highlighted.

The man in the bowler hat harshly questioned me: "**W**ell, sir, what have you done to your friend?"

"I don't know," I replied.

"But you know that he is dead," he said.

I would not wish such a moment on anyone, and it took me a while before I could think. My heart pounded, and I was choking with anger and pain. I felt everyone's eyes staring at me. I stammered, "**S**ir, let's go upstairs and discuss it there."

Vincent [Van Gogh] was curled up in bed, covered by a sheet, and he appeared lifeless. I very gently touched his body, and its warmth showed that he was still alive. I felt as if I had been given a second chance. I whispered to the chief of police, "**K**indly wake this man very carefully, and if he asks for me, tell him that I've left for Paris. The sight of me could kill him."

In this chapter, you will learn how to use direct quotations correctly. You will also learn about capitalization and title punctuation.

Quotation Marks (" ")

Use **quotation marks** to set off the exact words of a speaker or writer. When you include the exact words of more than one person in a text, then you must make a new paragraph each time the speaker changes. If the quotation is a complete sentence, punctuate it in the following ways.

- Capitalize the first word of the quotation.

- Place quotation marks around the complete quotation.
- Place the end punctuation inside the closing quotation marks.

> Oscar Wilde declared, "All art is useless."

Generally, attach the name of the speaker or writer to the quotation in some way. Review the following rules.

1. Introductory phrase

When the quotation is introduced by a phrase, place a comma after the introductory phrase.

> Pablo Picasso said, "Art is a lie that makes us realize the truth."

2. Interrupting phrase

When the quotation is interrupted, place a comma before and after the interrupting phrase.

> "In the end," says dancer Martha Graham, "it all comes down to breathing."

3. End phrase

When you place a phrase at the end of a quotation, end the quotation with a comma instead of a period.

> "Great art picks up where nature ends," said Marc Chagall.

If your quotation ends with other punctuation, put it inside the quotation mark.

> "Who is the greatest painter?" the student asked.

> "That question cannot be answered!" the curator replied.

4. Introductory sentence

When you introduce a quotation with a complete sentence, place a colon (:) after the introductory sentence.

> Choreographer George Balanchine explains his philosophy about dance: "Dance is music made visible."

5. Inside quotations

If one quotation is inside another quotation, then use single quotation marks (' ') around the inside quotation.

> To her mother, Veronica Corelli explained, "I am not sure if I will succeed, but you've always said, 'Your work should be your passion.'"

Section 6
PUNCTUATION AND MECHANICS

HINT Integrated Quotations

If the quotation is not a complete sentence, and you simply integrate it into your sentence, do not capitalize the first word of the quotation.

> Composer Ludwig van Beethoven called music "the mediator between the spiritual and the sensual life."

PRACTICE I

In each sentence, the quotation is set off in bold. Add quotation marks and periods, commas, or colons. Also, capitalize the first word of the quotation, if necessary.

EXAMPLE:

Professor Wayne Johnson asks ,"Where are the great female artists?"

1. Art student Alex Beale says **the lack of great female artists throughout history is puzzling**

2. Professor Aline Melnor states **one must consider the conditions for producing art**

3. **Art schools did not accept women** she points out.

4. **Until a hundred years ago, the only alternative to family life for women was the convent** proclaimed writer and feminist Germaine Greer.

5. **Suzanne Valadon** says historian Maria Sage **went from being an artist's model to being an artist**

6. Historian Andre Villeneuve writes that sculptor Camille Claudel was **the mistress of Auguste Rodin**

7. Germaine Greer shows the connection between female and male artists **the painter Rosa Bonheur learned about art from her father, who was also an artist**

8. **In the twentieth century, the numbers of female artists exploded** declared gallery owner Jon Sidell.

9. Angel Trang told her mother **I know that I shouldn't have drawn on the walls, but you always say Express yourself**

10. Louise Otto-Peters has a strong opinion about women in the arts **women will be forgotten if they forget to think about themselves**

PRACTICE 2

Correct ten punctuation errors in the next dialogue.

EXAMPLE:

She told me ⨪ "Your future is in your hands ⸺⸳

Jamilla was concerned about her son, "I don't understand why you are leaving college".

Omar looked at her and replied: "I need to try and make it as a musician."

"How will you make a living in the arts" she asked?

He replied, "I do not need to earn a lot of money to be happy."

"You're being very naïve." Jamilla retorted.

Shocked, Omar said, "I'm simply following your advice. You always say, "Find work that you love." "

"Perhaps you have to take some chances" his mother responded, "and learn from your own mistakes."

Omar stated firmly, "my decision will not be a mistake!"

Using Quotations in Research Essays

Use quotations to reveal the opinions of an expert or to highlight ideas that are particularly memorable and important. When quoting sources, remember to limit how many you use in a single paper and to vary your quotations by using both direct and indirect quotations.

Direct and Indirect Quotations

A **direct quotation** contains the exact words of an author, and the quotation is set off with quotation marks.

A shopping tip from *Consumer 4 Kids Reports* states, "The name brands are always displayed up front, when you first walk into the department."

An **indirect quotation** keeps the author's meaning but is not set off by quotation marks.

A shopping tip by the *Consumer 4 Kids Reports* states that name brand clothes are always put on view at the front of the clothing department.

Integrating Quotations

Short Quotations Introduce short quotations with a phrase or sentence. (Short quotations should not stand alone.) Read the following original selection, and then view how the quotation has been introduced using three common methods. The selection, written by Mary Lou Stribling, appeared on page 6 of her book *Art from Found Materials*.

Original Selection

> Picasso is generally acknowledged as being the first major artist to use found objects in his paintings. About the same time, however, a number of other artists who were active in the Cubist movement began to make similar experiments. The collages of Braque and Gris, which were made of printed letters, newspapers, wallpaper scraps, bottle labels, corrugated cardboard, and other bits of trivia, are especially notable.

1. **Phrase introduction**
   In *Art from Found Materials*, Mary Lou Stribling writes, "Picasso is generally acknowledged as being the first major artist to use found objects in his paintings" (6).

2. **Sentence introduction**
   In her book, *Art from Found Materials*, Mary Lou Stribling suggests that Picasso was not the only artist to use found objects in his work: "About the same time, however, a number of other artists who were active in the Cubist movement began to make similar experiments" (6).

3. **Integrated quotation**
   In *Art from Found Materials*, Mary Lou Stribling reveals that artists incorporated everyday objects into their paintings, including "wallpaper scraps, bottle labels, corrugated cardboard, and other bits of trivia" (6).

HINT **Words That Introduce Quotations**

Here are some common words that can introduce quotations.

admits	mentions
claims	observes
comments	reports
concludes	speculates
explains	suggests
maintains	warns

The doctor **states**, "_____."

"_____," **observes** Dr. Hannah.

Dr. Hannah **speculates** that _____.

Long Quotations If you use a quotation in MLA style that has four or more lines or in APA style (more than forty words), insert the quotation in your research paper in the following way.

- Introduce the quotation with a sentence ending with a colon.
- Indent the entire quotation about ten spaces from the left margin of your document.
- Use double spacing.

- Do not use quotation marks.
- Cite the author and page number in parentheses after the punctuation mark in the last sentence of the quotation.

Review the next example from a student essay about art history. The quotation is from page 132 of Germaine Greer's *The Obstacle Race*. The explanatory paragraph introduces the quotation and is part of an essay.

Much great art has been lost due to a variety of factors:

> Panels decay as wood decays. Canvas rots, tears, and sags. The
> stretchers spring and warp. As color dries out it loses its
> flexibility and begins to separate from its unstable ground; dry
> color flakes off shrinking or swelling wood and drooping canvas.
> (Greer 132)

HINT Using Long Quotations

If your research paper is short (two or three pages), avoid using many long quotations. Long quotations will only overwhelm your own ideas. Instead, try summarizing a long passage or using shorter quotations.

Using Ellipses (...)

If you want to quote key ideas from an author, but do not want to quote the entire paragraph, you can use **ellipses**. These three periods show that you have omitted unnecessary information from a quotation. Leave a space before and after each period, and if the omitted section includes complete sentences, add a period before the ellipses.

The original selection, written by Jeremy Yudkin, appeared in his book *Understanding Music* on page 446. Notice how the quotation changes when the essay writer uses ellipses.

Original Selection

> In his early years, Elvis Presley symbolized something very
> important for American youth. He was the symbol of freedom and
> rebellion. His unconventional clothes, the messages of his music, and
> especially his raw sexuality appealed to the new and numerous
> groups of American teenagers. The spirit of rebellion was in the air.

Quotation with Omissions

> In his book <u>Understanding Music</u>, Jeremy Yudkin describes the
> impact of Elvis: "In his early years, Elvis Presley symbolized
> something very important for American youth. . . . The spirit of
> rebellion was in the air" (446).

PRACTICE 3

Read the following selection and then use information from it to write direct and indirect quotations. The selection, written by David G. Martin, appeared on page 567 of his book *Psychology*.

> Until fairly recently, up to the early or mid-nineteenth century, events that could not be explained were often attributed to supernatural causes. Human behaviour that was bizarre was thought to be the work of demons. Demonology is the study of the ancient belief that mental disorders are caused by possession by demons. Autonomous evil beings were thought to enter a person and control his or her mind and body.

1. Make a direct quotation.

   _____

   _____

   _____

2. Make an indirect quotation.

   _____

   _____

   _____

Capitalization

Remember to capitalize the following:

- the pronoun *I*
- the first word of every sentence

     My brothers and **I** share an apartment.

   There are many other instances in which you must use capital letters. Always capitalize in the following cases.

■ Days of the week, months, and holidays

   Thursday   June 22   Labour Day

Do not capitalize the seasons: summer, fall, winter, spring

■ Titles of specific institutions, departments, companies, and schools

   Bombardier   Department of Finance   Elmwood Collegiate

Do not capitalize general references.

   the company   the department   the school

■ Names of specific places such as buildings, streets, parks, cities,

provinces, and bodies of water

Eiffel Tower	Yonge Street
Times Square	Saskatchewan
Edmonton, Alberta	Lake Erie

Do not capitalize general references.

the street	the state	the lake

■ **Specific languages, nationalities, tribes, races, and religions**

Greek	Mohawk	Buddhist	a French restaurant

■ **Titles of specific individuals**

General Dallaire	Professor Sayf
the President	Prime Minister Blair
Doctor Blain	Mrs. Robinson

If you are referring to the profession in general, or if the title follows the name, do not use capital letters.

my doctor	the professors	Elise Roy, a doctor

■ **Specific course and program titles**

Physics 201	Marketing 101	Advanced German

If you refer to a course, but do not mention the course title, then it is not necessary to use capitals.

He is in his math class.	I study engineering.

■ **Major words in titles of literary or artistic works**

the *Calgary Herald*	*Corner Gas*	*The Lord of the Rings*

■ **Historical events, eras, and movements**

World War II	Post-Impressionism	Baby Boomers

HINT **Capitalizing Computer Terms**

Always capitalize the following computer terms and brands.

Internet	Microsoft Office
World Wide Web	Netscape

PRACTICE 4

Add twenty missing capital letters to this selection.

EXAMPLE:

$$S$$

Mozart was born in ~~s~~alzburg, Austria.

1. Erich Schenk describes the life of Wolfgang Amadeus Mozart in his book <u>Mozart and his times</u>. Mozart, born on january 27, 1756, was a gifted musician who composed his first pieces at age five. By the age of thirteen, he had written a german and an italian opera. In Salzburg, his employer was prince-archbishop Colloredo. Then, in Vienna, he wrote compositions for emperor joseph II. At that time, Austria was a part of the holy roman empire.

2. Mozart's best-known works include <u>the marriage of figaro</u> and <u>the magic flute</u>. Mozart, a catholic, died mysteriously at the age of thirty-five, and his body was put into a communal grave, which was the common practice for paupers in Vienna at that time. His final resting place is near a river called the danube.

Titles

Place the title of a short work in quotation marks. Underline (or italicize, if you are using a computer) the title of a longer document.

Short Works		Long Works	
Short story:	"The Hockey Sweater"	**Novel:**	<u>The Blind Assassin</u>
Web article:	"Music Artists Lose Out"	**Website:**	<u>CNET News.com</u>
Chapter:	"Early Accomplishments"	**Book:**	<u>The Art of Emily Carr</u>
Newspaper article:	"The City's Hottest Ticket"	**Newspaper:**	<u>the Globe and Mail</u>
Magazine article:	"New Artists"	**Magazine:**	<u>Rolling Stone</u>
Essay:	"Hip-Hop Nation"	**Textbook:**	<u>Common Culture</u>
TV episode:	"The Search Party"	**TV series:**	<u>Lost</u>
Song:	"Mouths to Feed"	**CD:**	<u>Release Therapy</u>
Poem:	"Howl"	**Anthology:**	<u>Collected Poems of Beat Writers</u>
		Movie:	<u>Mission Impossible</u>
		Artwork:	<u>The Mona Lisa</u>

Capitalizing Titles

When you write a title, capitalize the first letter of the first and last words and all the major words.

<u>To Kill a Mockingbird</u>

"Stairway to Heaven"

<u>Eight Men Out</u>

Do not capitalize the word ".com" in a web address. Also, do not capitalize the following words, unless they are the first or last word in the title.

Articles: a, an, the

Coordinators: but, and, or, nor, for, so, yet

Prepositions: of, to, in, off, out, up, by . . .

HINT Your Own Essay Titles

In essays that you write for your courses, do not underline your title or put quotation marks around it. Simply capitalize the first word and the main words.

Why Music Is Important

PRACTICE 5

Add twelve capital letters to the next selection. Also, add quotation marks or underlining to five titles.

EXAMPLE:

The magazine ~~business week~~ featured successful female entrepreneurs.

B   W

1. The singer known as Pink was born Alecia Moore on september 8, 1979. During her teen years, she regularly performed at Club fever near girard street in Philadelphia. One saturday night, after her five-minute slot, a representative from MCA records spotted her and asked her to audition for the band, Basic instinct.

2. After some time playing in bands, Pink decided to become a solo artist. Her first album, called Can't take me home, was released in 2000. It was a double platinum hit, and spun off three singles. Pink then went on to record Patti LaBelle's hit song Lady Marmalade with three other artists. In the april 2006 issue of Rolling Stone, Barry Walter reviewed Pink's fourth album I'm Not Dead. He had particular praise for her song Stupid girls.

FINAL REVIEW

Identify and correct twenty-five errors. Look for capitalization errors. Also ensure that titles and quotations have the necessary capital letters, quotation marks, punctuation, and underlining.

EXAMPLE:

The marketing manager said, "Each generation is distinct."

1. People who belong to a generation may have wildly different life experiences. Nonetheless, as Ted Rall points out in his book Marketing Madness, "you are more likely to share certain formative experiences and attitudes about life with your age cohorts".

2. In the last century, each generation was anointed with a title. F. Scott Fitzgerald named his cohorts when he wrote the book, The Jazz Age, which described 1920s flappers who frequented jazz clubs. Tom Brokaw, in his book <u>The greatest generation</u>, discussed people who came of age in the 1930s. Born between 1911 and 1924, they grew up during the Great depression. However, perhaps the best-known spokesperson for a generation is Douglas Coupland.

3. Douglas Coupland was born in 1961 and raised in Vancouver, british Columbia. Even as a young student at Sentinel secondary school, Coupland knew that he would be an artist. When he got older, he took Sculpture classes at Vancouver's Emily Carr institute of Art and design. He also studied at the European Design Institute in italy. As a sculptor, Coupland had some success and, in november 1987, he had a solo show called "The floating world" at an art gallery in Vancouver.

4. Most know Coupland from his second career. While writing a comic strip for the magazine Vista, Coupland was approached by St. Martin's press and asked to write a guidebook about his generation. Instead, he wrote a complete novel called <u>generation X</u>.

5. Coupland's novel, which describes the generation that came of age in the 1970s and 1980s, is filled with original terminology. For instance,

Coupland writes: "Clique maintenance is the need of one generation to see the generation following it as deficient so as to bolster its own collective ego". One chapter in his book is called "Our Parents had more." On page 27, a character has a mid-twenties breakdown that occurs because of "An inability to function outside of school or structured environments coupled with a realization of one's essential aloneness in the world."

6. Every current generation has unique characteristics. Music, clothing, and slang words help define a generation. What name will define the youths who are growing up today?

 Writer's Room **Topics for Writing**

Write about one of the following topics. Include some direct quotations. Proofread to ensure that your punctuation and capitalization is correct.

1. List some characteristics of your generation. What political events, social issues, music, and fashion bind your generation?
2. List three categories of art. Describe some details about each category.

 CHECKLIST: QUOTATION MARKS

When you edit your writing, ask yourself these questions.

☐ Are there any direct quotations in my writing? Check for errors with these elements:

  ☐ punctuation before or after quotations
  ☐ capital letters
  ☐ placement of quotation marks

  "Art is making something out of nothing and selling it," said musician Frank Zappa.

☐ Do my sentences have all the necessary capital letters?

  Carr's greatest works were painted after World ~~war~~ War I.

☐ Are the titles of small and large artistic works properly punctuated?

  Emily Carr's painting was called ~~Above the Trees.~~ <u>Above the Trees.</u>

36 Numbers and Additional Punctuation

CHAPTER CONTENTS

- Numbers
- Additional Punctuation

GRAMMAR SNAPSHOT **Looking at Numbers and Hyphens**

This excerpt is taken from History of Photography and the Camera *by Mary Bellis. Abbreviations, numbers, and hyphenated words are in bold. Why do some numbers appear as numerals and some as words?*

Nitrate film is historically important because it allowed for the development of roll films. The first flexible movie films measured **35-mm** wide and came in long rolls on a spool. In the mid-**1920s**, using this technology, **35-mm** roll film was developed for the camera. By the late **1920s**, **medium-format** roll film was created. It measured **six** centimeters wide and had a paper backing making it easy to handle in daylight. This led to the development of the **twin-lens-reflex** camera in **1929**.

In this chapter, you will learn about using numbers and punctuation such as hyphens.

Numbers

When using numbers in academic writing, follow these rules.

- Spell out numbers that can be expressed in one or two words.

  We spent **eighteen** days in Mexico City.
  There were **forty-seven** people waiting for another flight.
  The airline had room for **four hundred**.
  That day, **thousands** of people cleared customs.

- Use numerals with numbers of more than two words.

  The manager booked rooms for **358** guests.

- Spell out fractions.

  Only **one-third** of the residents have their own homes.

- When the sentence begins with a number, spell out the number. If the number has more than two words, do not place it at the beginning of the sentence.

  Three hundred people were invited to the gallery.
  There were **158** guests.

- Spell out *million* or *billion* if the word appears in a sentence.

  There were about four **million** residents in the surrounding suburbs.

- Use numerals when writing addresses, dates, times, percentages, degrees, pages, or divisions of a book. Also use numerals with prices and percentages. However, write out the word "dollar" or "percent."

  A yearly subscription costs **29** dollars, which is about **15** percent less than the cover price.

HINT **Several Numbers in a Sentence**

When writing two consecutive numbers, write out the shorter number.

  We used **two 35-mm** rolls of film.

  Be consistent when writing a series of numbers. If some numbers require numerals, then use numerals for all of the numbers.

  The gallery guests consumed **300** appetizers, **8** pounds of cheese, and **120** glasses of wine.

PRACTICE 1

Correct any errors with numbers in the next sentences.

EXAMPLE:

                nine
She was just 9̶ years old when she picked up a camera.

1. Montreal photographer Moyra Davey has six cameras, 184 rolls of film, and thirty-three different lenses.

2. She has worked professionally as a photographer for 10 years.

3. A small art gallery in Edmonton exhibited 25 of Davey's photos.

4. 40 people came to the opening.

5. Davey would like to publish her photos and sell each book for one hundred and twenty nine dollars.

6. She wants to self-publish 20 168-page books.

Additional Punctuation

Semicolon (;)

Use a semicolon

- between two complete and related ideas.

  The photograph was stunning; Sherman was very pleased.

- between items in a series of ideas, if the items have internal punctuation or are very long.

  Sherman's works were exhibited in Birmingham, Alabama; Fort Worth, Texas; Toronto, Ontario; and London, England.

Colon (:)

Use a colon

- after a complete sentence that introduces a quotation.

  The photographer Henri Cartier Bresson stated his view: "Photographers are dealing with things that are continually vanishing."

- to introduce a series or a list after a complete sentence.

  Canada has produced some great photographers: Yousuf Karsh, Sam Tata, and Tanya Schmidt.

- to introduce an explanation or example

  The tiny sculpture is outrageously expensive: it costs $2.5 million.

- after the expression "the following."

  Please do the following: read, review, and respond.

- to separate the hour and minutes in expressions of time.

  The exhibit will open at 12:30 p.m.

Hyphen (-)

Use a hyphen

- with some compound nouns. (Note that *compound* means "more than one part.") The following nouns always require a hyphen.

  sister-in-law   mother-in-law   show-off

- when you write the complete words for compound numbers between twenty-one and ninety-nine.

  twenty-five   ninety-two   seventy-seven

- after some prefixes such as *ex-*, *mid-*, or *self-*.

  self-assured   mid-December   ex-husband

- when you use a compound adjective before a noun. The compound adjective must express a single thought.

  <u>one-way</u> street   <u>well-known</u> actor   <u>thirty-year-old</u> woman

There is no hyphen if the compound adjective appears elsewhere in the sentence.

> The street is one way. The actor was well known. The woman is thirty years old.

HINT Non-hyphenated Compound Adjectives

Some compound adjectives never take a hyphen, even when they appear before a noun. Here are some common examples.

World Wide Web   high school senior   real estate agent

Dash (—)

You can use a dash to set off information that you want to emphasize.

> Marge Stranton raised her camera to take the picture, but it was too late—the moment had passed.

Parentheses ( )

You can use parentheses to set off incidental information such as a date or abbreviation. Use parentheses sparingly!

> Lange's photo of the migrant mother, which was taken during the height of the Depression era (1936), has become an enduring image.

> The United Press Photographer's Association (UPPA) was founded in 1946.

HINT Using Abbreviations

Sometimes you will not want to repeat the name of an organization over and over in an essay. To use abbreviations correctly, mention the complete name of an organization the first time you mention it, put the abbreviation in parentheses immediately after the full name, and then use only the abbreviation throughout the rest of the essay.

> The North Atlantic Treaty Organization (NATO) supports an international security that was signed in 1949 in Washington, DC. Today, NATO's headquarters are in Brussels, Belgium.

> There are two types of abbreviations: **initialisms** and **acronyms**. When saying an initialism, pronounce each of the first letters of an organization's title individually. Examples are RCMP and CSIS. When saying an acronym, pronounce it as a full word. Examples of acronyms are NATO (pronounced "nay-toh") and WHO (pronounced "hoo").

Section 6
PUNCTUATION AND MECHANICS

PRACTICE 2

Add a colon, a hyphen, a dash, or a set of parentheses to each sentence.

EXAMPLE:

Dorothea Lange rushed home and printed the photos ‸ a decision that would change her life.

1. In 1936, Dorothea Lange had joined the Farm Security Administration FSA and was travelling around Nipomo Valley in California.

2. Lange described what happened on a warm day in March "I saw and approached the hungry and desperate mother, as if drawn by a magnet."

3. Sitting in her dust covered canvas tent, Florence Thompson was holding her baby, and her children were crowded around her.

4. Florence and her children took many low wage-wage jobs they struggled and rarely had enough to eat.

5. Florence and the other migrant workers stooped over in fields to pick the following items strawberries, peas, corn, and asparagus.

6. Florence Thompson described her encounter with Lange "She just took my picture. She did not ask me my name."

7. The next day, Lange delivered the photos to a San Francisco newspaper the photos appeared on the front page.

8. The front page story described the migrant workers and their suffering.

9. Immediately, concerned citizens sent the following to the migrant camp 184 tins of food, 40 tents, and 3 boxes of tools.

10. However, Florence Thompson was not there to see the outpouring of generosity because her brother in law had brought her to his home.

11. The photo—an iconic image of the Depression has been reproduced in thousands of books and magazines.

12. The compassionate photographs of Dorothea Lange 1895–1965 have influenced modern documentary photography.

FINAL REVIEW

Identify and correct any errors in numbers, semi-colons, hyphens, dashes, or parentheses. Write C next to correct sentences.

EXAMPLE:

> well–known
>
> Some ~~well known~~ people risk their careers to do the right thing.

1. Yousuf Karsh 1908 2002 was born in Turkey of Armenian parents. _____

2. When he was a sixteen year old boy, he moved to Canada to avoid the persecution of Armenians in Turkey. _____

3. His first photography job was in his uncle's shop in Sherbrooke a job that changed his life. _____

4. The shop contained twelve cameras, 170 rolls of film, ten camera stands, and 7 lights. _____

5. Karsh went to Boston to apprentice with John Garo, Karsh learned about photographic techniques. _____

6. Soon, Karsh opened up a studio on Sparks Street and began doing portrait photography. _____

7. He photographed Albert Einstein 1948 and Pablo Picasso 1954. _____

8. One of his best known portraits was of the British prime minister, Winston Churchill. _____

9. He described his encounter with the prime minister "Churchill marched into the room scowling, regarding my camera as you might regard the German enemy." _____

10. Karsh removed the cigar from Churchill's mouth an act that enraged the prime minister. _____

11. Karsh sold his Churchill negative to *Life* magazine for the small sum of a hundred and twenty dollars. _____

12. Karsh's biggest-regret was missing the opportunity to photograph Chairman Mao. _____

13. He photographed 1000s of famous people including politicians, artists, musicians, writers, and members of royalty. _____

14. His career lasted for more than sixty years. _____

15. Karsh died on July 13, two thousand and two. _____

Section 6
PUNCTUATION AND MECHANICS

Writer's Room Topics for Writing

Write about one of these topics. Proofread for errors in numbers or punctuation.

1. Describe a personal photograph that you cherish. When was the photo taken? What is in the photo? Why is it so compelling?

2. Compare two art forms. For example, you could compare a photograph and a painting.

CHECKLIST: NUMBERS AND PUNCTUATION

When you edit your writing, ask yourself these questions.

☐ Are there any numbers in my writing? Check that your numbers are consistently written, and verify that you have used words rather than numerals when necessary.

       thousands
Lange took ~~1000s~~ of photographs.

☐ Are my semicolons, colons, hyphens, dashes, and parentheses used in a correct and appropriate manner?

                  :   *well-used*
She brought the following supplies~~,~~ a camera, a ~~well used~~ chair, and a camera stand.

Section 6
**PUNCTUATION
AND
MECHANICS**

Editing Practice

Why Bother Editing?

After you finish writing the first draft of an essay, always make time to edit it. Editing for errors in grammar, punctuation, sentence structure, and capitalization can make the difference between a failing paper and a passing one or a good essay and a great one. Editing is not always easy; it takes time and attention to detail. But it gets easier the more you do it. Also, the more you edit your essays (and your peers' essays, too), the better your writing will be, and the less time you will need to spend editing!

PRACTICE I   EDIT AN ESSAY

Correct fifteen errors in this student essay. An editing symbol appears above each error. To understand the meaning of each symbol, refer to the revising and editing symbols on the inside back cover of this book.

Climbing Everest

1   The Nepalese and Indians name it Sagarmatha, and people from Tibet
//

call it Qomolangma. The rest of the world knows it as mount Everest.
cap

In 1852, a geological survey of the Himalayan mountain range identified

the highest peak as "Peak XV." By 1865, the British named the peak

"Everest" after a surveyor named Sir George Everest. For mountain

climbers, Everest became a challenge as soon as it is named the highest
shift

peak in the world.

2   By 1921, Tibet opened it's [sp] borders to the outside and gave climbers easy access to Everest. The first Europeans to attempt to climb Everest were George Mallory and Andrew Irvine in 1924, [ro] unfortunately, they both perished in the attempt. Many other unsuccessful endeavours were made to reach the Everest summit. Then in 1953, Edmund Hillary, a New Zealander, and Tenzing Norgay, a Nepalese Sherpa, became the first climbers to reach the top of the world at 8848 metres above sea level. Both men became world-famous heros [sp]. In addition, in 1978, two Austrian climbers, Reinhold Messner and Peter Habeler, reached the Everest summit without the aid of supplemental oxygen. Two years later, Messner again attained the summit without extra oxygen. A solo climb. [frag]

3   Since 1921, around 2200 mountaineers reached [vt] the summit; others have paid a great price. About 185 climbers have died in the attemt [sp]. There is a graveyard on the ascent to the summit. Mountaineers see the remains of corpses, tents, and bottles that were filled with oxygen. [//] The dead remain on Everest. Even ifclimbers wanted to carry the corpses down, you could not [shift] because of thealtitude.

4.   The popularity of climbing the world's most highest [ad] peak has become so great that critics call Everest just another tourist trap. Many climbers set up businesses as guides. A Nepalese businessmen [pl] is planning to develop a cyber café at the base camp, and some snowboarders want to surf down from the summit. There are [agr] also a lot of trash on the summit trail. Nonetheless, Everest still catches the imagination of persons [pl] all over the world.

PRACTICE 2   EDIT AN ESSAY

Correct fourteen errors in this student essay. An editing symbol appears above each error. To understand the meaning of each symbol, refer to the revising and editing symbols on the inside back cover of this book.

The Man Who Discovered King Tutankhamen

1   Howard Carter's persistence helped him make a great contribution to the history of human civilization. Carter was born in 1874 near London, England. He became interested in Egyptology at the age of 17, when he [sp] was working in Egypt on an archaeological sight. His job was to trace [wc] drawings and inscriptions. Howard Carter discovered one of the greatest archaeological finds in history: the tomb of King Tutankhamen.

2   At the age of twenty-five Carter became the first inspector general for monuments in Upper Egypt. He was responsible for supervising digs around the area of the Valley of the Kings. Which had a great number of [frag] tombs. He became very fascinating by the story of the young pharaoh, [ad] King Tutankhamen, and he was absolutly certain that the king's tomb was [sp] located in the general area of the Valley of the Kings.

3   For excavations, Carter received funding from Lord Carnarvon, a wealthy patron of many digs. From 1914 to 1922, Carnarvon funded Carters search [sp] for the legendary tomb of King Tut. By 1922, Lord Carnarvon became frustrated at the lack of success and decided that he would support the search for only one more year. Carter got real lucky when, one [ad] morning, one of his workers tripped over a flat rock, when Carter went to [ro] see what it was, he realized that it was the top of a staircase.

4   Carter was elated by the discovery but his workers had a completely [p] different reaction. They were convinced that the tomb had a curse on it. Whoever broke the door seal was doomed for death. Carter ignored the superstition. And went inside the tomb. Inside he found everything intact [frag] and spent the next ten years cataloguing his find. Some people continued to believe at the curse and blamed it for the death of six workers. An [wc] urban legend eventually formed called the Mummy's Curse, which exagerated the power of the curse. Carter never believed in no curse, and [sp]   [wc] he dies of natural causes at the age of sixty-six. [shift]

PRACTICE 3 EDIT A FORMAL LETTER

Correct twelve errors in this formal business letter.

George Bates
5672 Manet street west
St.-Jérôme, QC J7Z 4V2

August 15, 2008

Customer Service
The Furniture store
1395 Division Street
Montreal, QC H3T 1L9

Subject: Desk

Attention: Sales manager

I bought a desk from your store on august 13 2008, and the store delivered it thursday morning. After the delivery people had left, I discovered a large scratch on the surface of the desk. Its also lopsided. Since I have always found your products to be of excellent quality I would like to have replacement desk delivered to my home and the damaged desk taken away. If you do not have replacement desk of the same model, then I would like to have a full reimbursement.

Thank you very much for your cooperation in this matter I look forward to receiving my new desk.

Yours sincerly,

George Bates

George Bates

PRACTICE 4 EDIT AN ESSAY

Correct twenty errors in the following essay.

Discovering Venice

1   My brother and me are spending this summer in one of the most beautiful

city in the world. Venice, Italy. It is unique because it is composed of a number

of small islands in the Adriatic sea. It has over one hundred canals and over

four hundred bridges. One of Italy's must-see places, Venice has an intriguing

history.

2   Venice was founded in the fifth century by Romans escaping the

ferocious Gothic tribes. According to legend. In the tenth century, Venice

became a city of wealthy merchants who profited from the Crusades. By the

twelfth century, after its successful war against Genoa, Venice had become a

powerful city-state, trading with the Byzantines, the Arabs, and many others.

3   One of it's most famous citizens was the explorer Marco Polo (1254 1324), a

businessman who was one of the first europeans to reach China. Him and his

father spent about twenty-four years in China and was reputedly friends and

confidants of Kublai Khan, the emperor of China. Polo may have brought back

noodles from China. Which have become the basis for italian pasta.

4   When the Polos returned from China, they recounted the adventures they

had had. The citizens of Venice did not believe them. Even today, scholars

differ about weather Marco Polo actually reached China. Some say it was

highly unlikly because he did not mention things such as chopsticks tea, or

Chinese script. Others think that Polo reached China because he talked about

paper money and the Chinese postal system.

5   Venice been written about in many works of fiction. For example,

Shakespeare's Merchant of Venice is set in that city. Shakespeare also set the first part of his tragedy <u>Othello</u> in Venice. In fact, the first scenes of the Shakespearean tragedy takes place in the Duke's palace. Another famous book, Thomas Mann's Death in Venice, takes place on a Venetian island that is popular among tourists.

6   My brother has travelled more than me, and he says that of all the cities he's seen, Venice is his absolute favourite. If I would have known how fascinating the city is, I would have visited it a long time ago.

PRACTICE 5   EDIT A WORKPLACE MEMO

Correct ten errors in the next excerpt from a memo.

To: Career development faculty members

From: Maddison Healy

Re: Internships

I'm gonna take this opportunity to remind you that their are financial resources to hiring two new interns for the Career development Program. If anyone wishes to participate in this collaboration, please let Danielle or I know. The current deadline for applying to the internship program is the beginning of april. The internship program, provides valuable mentoring to college students. Treating an intern with respect, it is very important. If you hire an intern, you are responsible for training them. Also, you must provide constructive feedback to the intern and to the college administrator. For those who are interested, please let me know as quick as possible.

PRACTICE 6   EDIT A SHORT ARTICLE

Correct fifteen errors in the next selection.

Forget What Your Fifth Grade Teacher Taught You

1   The solar system no longer has nine planets, on August 24, 2006, the International Astronomical union, which has a voting membership of about 2500 scientists, met in Prague. It decided to demote Pluto from a planet to a dwarf planet. The astronomers said that Pluto does not exhibit the same characteristics as the other major planets. According to scientists, a planet must orbit the sun, it must be having a spherical shape, and it must have a clear orbit. Unfortunatly, Pluto's orbit overlaps Neptune's orbit, so it does not meet the third criterion for a planet.

2   At the begining of the twentieth century, much astronomers suspected the possibility of another planet in the solar system. In 1930, while working for the Lowell Conservatory in Flagstaff, Arizona, astronomer Clyde Tombaugh took photographs of a sphere that was composed mainly of ices and rocks. It also had a satellite, Charon, orbiting it. Eventualy, this sphere became the nineth planet in the solar system.

3   Scientists were very exciting about the discovery. People from all over the world suggested names for the new planet. The scientists from the observatory received so many suggestions that they had difficulty choosing one. An eleven-years-old girl from Oxford, England, suggested the name Pluto. Venetia Burney was interested in Greek and Roman mythology, and Pluto is the Roman name for Hades, the Greek god of the Dead. She was giving her suggestion to her grandfather, who then wired it to the Lowell Observatory.

4   The scientific community and the public have had a mixed reaction to the declassification of Pluto. As a planet. Some refuse to accept it. But I wonder why are they resistant. Perhaps teachers don't wanna change astronomy textbooks. Maybe humans feel particularly wary when the scientific community "revises" what it once asked them to accept as fact.

Reading Strategies and Selections

In this chapter, the essays are organized according to theme. The predominant writing pattern is in parentheses.

CHAPTER

From Reading to Writing

You don't have to burn books to destroy a culture. Just get people to stop reading them.

—RAY BRADBURY, *author*

Reading Strategies

The reading strategies discussed in this chapter can help you develop your writing skills. They can also help you become a more active reader. You will learn about previewing, finding the main and supporting ideas, understanding difficult words, and recognizing irony. When you read, you expand your vocabulary and learn how other writers develop topics. You also learn to recognize and use different writing patterns. Finally, reading helps you find ideas for your own essays.

Previewing

Previewing is like glancing through a magazine in a bookstore; it gives you a chance to see what the writer is offering. When you **preview**, look quickly for the following visual clues so that you can determine the selection's key points:

- titles or subheadings (if any)
- the first and last sentence of the introduction
- the first sentence of each paragraph
- the concluding sentences
- any photos, graphs, or charts

Finding the Main Idea

After you finish previewing, read the selection carefully. Search for the **main idea**, which is the central point that the writer is trying to make. In an essay, the main idea usually appears somewhere in the first few paragraphs in the form of a thesis statement. However, some professional writers build up to the main idea and only state it in the middle or at the end of the essay. Additionally, some professional writers do not state the main idea directly.

> **HINT   Making a Statement of the Main Idea**
>
> If the reading does not contain a clear thesis statement, you can determine the main idea by asking yourself *who, what, when, where, why,* and *how* questions. Then, using the answers to those questions, make a statement that sums up the main point of the reading.

Making Inferences

If a professional writer does not state the main idea directly, you must look for clues that will help you to **infer** or figure out what the writer means to say. For example, the next paragraph does not have a topic sentence. However, you can infer the main idea. Underline key words that can lead you to a better understanding of the passage.

> Algie Crivens III was 18 and fresh out of high school in 1991 when he was sentenced to twenty years in prison for a murder he did not commit. He spent the next eight-and-a-half years consumed with educating himself while his appeals crawled through the courts. Crivens is nothing if not energetic; he tends to speak in paragraphs, not sentences. While in prison, he channeled this energy into earning an associate's degree in social science and a bachelor's in sociology. He also took courses in paralegal studies and culinary arts. His fellow prisoners used to ask how he could spend so much time reading. But, to him, reading was a way to escape the boredom of prison life.
>
> —from "Righting a Wrong" by Liliana Ibara

PRACTICE I

Ask yourself the following questions.

1. What is the subject of this text?

   _____

2. What points can you infer that the writer is making?

   _____

   _____

Finding the Supporting Ideas

Different writers use different types of supporting ideas. They may give steps for a process, use examples to illustrate a point, give reasons for an argument, and so on. Try to identify the author's supporting ideas.

Highlighting and Making Annotations

After you read a long text, you may forget some of the author's ideas. To help you remember and quickly find the important points, you can highlight key ideas and make annotations.

An **annotation** is a comment, question, or reaction that you write in the margins of a passage.

Each time you read a passage, follow these steps:

- Look in the introductory and concluding paragraphs. Underline sentences that sum up the main idea. Using your own words, rewrite the main idea in the margin.
- Underline or highlight supporting ideas. You might even want to number the arguments or ideas. This will allow you to understand the essay's development.
- Circle words that you do not understand.
- Write questions in the margin if you do not understand the author's meaning.
- Write notes beside passages that are interesting or that relate to your own experiences.
- Jot down any ideas that might make interesting writing topics.

Here is an example of a highlighted and annotated passage from an essay titled "Sprawl Fallout" by Patricia L. Kirk.

What is a euphemism?
General background for the introduction

1   For suburbanites who spend hours in traffic each day commuting to city jobs, the concept of urban sprawl is more than a (euphemism) batted around by city planners. <u>Many commuters know the psychological tolls of their long, slow journeys—irritation, anxiety, less time at home—but the negative impacts might be broader than most realize.</u>

Main point suggests urban sprawl is not good
Definition of sprawl
Shows the effects of sprawl

Traffic jams drive me crazy.

2   Urban sprawl—a phenomenon that results in people living far from their work places—has been linked to asthma, obesity, and just plain foul moods. In one study, people with long commutes reported more headaches, stomach problems, and fatigue than people with shorter drives. Irritability from long commutes was also shown to transfer to job performance, resulting in lower productivity.

Understanding Difficult Words

When you come across an unfamiliar word in a passage, do not stop reading to look up its definition in the dictionary. First, try using context clues to figure out the term's meaning on your own. If you still do not understand the word, circle it to remind you to look up the word's meaning in the dictionary when you have finished reading through the passage. You can keep a list of new vocabulary in the Vocabulary Log in Appendix 5.

Using Context Clues

Context clues are hints in the selection that help to define a word. To find a word's meaning, try the following:

- **Look at the word.** Is it a noun, a verb, or an adjective? Knowing how the word functions in the sentence can help you guess its meaning.
- **Look at surrounding words.** Look at the entire sentence and try to find a relationship between the difficult word and those that surround it. There may be a **synonym** (a word that means the same thing) or an **antonym** (a word that means the opposite), or other terms in the sentence that help define the word.

- **Look at surrounding sentences.** Sometimes you can guess the meaning of a difficult word by looking at the sentences, paragraphs, and punctuation marks surrounding it. When you use your logic, the meaning becomes clear.

In most cases, you can guess the meaning of a new word by combining your own knowledge of the topic with the information conveyed in the words and phrases surrounding the difficult word.

PRACTICE 2

Can you define the words *strewn, emanate,* or *haven?*

Perhaps you are not quite sure. Looking at the words in context makes it much easier to guess the definitions of the words.

> When I arrived in my hometown, I was baffled by the changes in my old neighbourhood. Garbage was **strewn** across front lawns, paint peeled on the greying wooden homes, and roofs sagged. The auto body shop on the corner **emanated** horrible fumes of turpentine and paint, forcing me to cover my nose when I passed it. I wondered what had happened to my former safe **haven**.

Now write your own definition of the words as they are used in the context.

strewn _____

emanated _____

haven _____

HINT Cognates

Cognates (also known as word twins) are English words that may look and sound like words in another language. For example, the English word *responsible* is similar to the French word *responsable*, although the words are spelled differently.

If English is not your first language, and you read an English word that looks similar to a word in your language, check how the word is being used in context. It may, or may not, mean the same thing in English as it means in your language. For example, in English, *sensible* means "to show good sense," but in French, *sensible* means "emotional." In German, *bekommen* sounds like "become" but it really means "to get," and the German word *gift* means "poison" in English. If you are not sure of a word's meaning, you can always consult a dictionary.

Using a Dictionary

If you cannot understand the meaning of an unfamiliar word even after using context clues, then look up the word in a dictionary. A dictionary is useful if you use it correctly. Review the following tips for proper dictionary usage:

- **Look at the dictionary's front matter.** The preface contains explanations about the various symbols and abbreviations. Find out what your dictionary has to offer.

- **Read all of the definitions listed for the word.** Look for the meaning that best fits the context of your sentence.
- **Look up root words, if necessary.** For example, if you do not understand the word *unambiguous*, remove the prefix and look up *ambiguous*.

Here is an example of how dictionaries set up their definitions:

Word-Break Divisions

Your dictionary may indicate places for dividing words with heavy black dots.

Stress symbol and pronunciation

Some dictionaries provide the phonetic pronunciation of words. The stress symbol lets you know which syllable has the highest or loudest sound.

Parts of Speech

The *adj* means that *incisive* is an adjective. If you do not understand the "parts of speech" symbol, look in the front or the back of your dictionary for a list of symbols and their meanings.

in•ci′•cive / in-cī-siv / *adj* showing intelligence and a clear understanding of something

—from *The Longman Dictionary of Contemporary English*, Pearson Education, 2003.

Determining Connotation and Denotation

A **denotation** is the literal meaning for a word that may be found in the dictionary. For example, the dictionary definition of *mother* is "a female parent." A **connotation** is the implied or associated meaning. It can be a cultural value judgment. For instance, the word *mother* may trigger feelings of comfort, security, anger, or resentment in a listener, depending on that person's experience with mothers.

Authors can influence readers by carefully choosing words that have specific denotations. For example, review the next two descriptions. Which one has a more negative connotation?

Terry left his family. Andrew abandoned his family.

PRACTICE 3

Read the following passages and underline any words or phrases that have strong connotations. Discuss how the words support a personal bias.

1. Furthermore, in too many states, welfare keeps flowing while the kids are in jail, or middle-class parents continue to claim children as tax deductions even as the state pays for their upkeep in detention facilities. We must demand that parents reimburse the state for housing their failures.

    —from "Enough Is Enough" by Judy Sheindlin

2. There is no question about whom Ms. Politkovskaya held responsible in years of unflinching reporting from Chechnya: the Russian Army and Mr. Putin himself. When he finally got around to acknowledging her death yesterday, it was in a cold-blooded statement that the authorities "will take every step to investigate objectively the tragic death of the journalist Politkovskaya."

    —from "Another Killing in Moscow" (*New York Times* editorial)

3. Rohe could have chosen to give a substantive speech detailing why she believes "pre-emptive war is dangerous and wrong"—or as she so categorically put it, how she "knows" that it is. Instead she took the easy way out by insulting the speaker and throwing out some leftist chestnuts about the still missing Osama bin Laden and weapons of mass

destruction. But the former would have required her to grapple with
ideas; she chose to take potshots.

—from "The Real Meaning of Courage" by Linda Chavez

Recognizing Irony

Irony is a technique that some writers use to make a point. When an author is
being ironic, he or she says one thing but really means the opposite. When the
author uses an ironic tone, he or she does not intend the reader to interpret the
words literally. Sarcasm is a type of verbal irony.

EXAMPLE:

The charred burger lay in a grease-soaked bun. "That looks
wonderful," he muttered.

PRACTICE 4

Gary Lautens was managing editor and columnist at the *Toronto Star*. Read the
next selection from his essay called "The Greatest Player." Then answer the
questions.

Occasionally, I run into sports figures at cocktail parties, on the street,
or on their way to the bank. "Nice game the other night," I said to an
old hockey-player pal.
"Think so?" he replied.
"You've come a long way since I knew you as a junior."
"How's that?"
"Well, you high-stick better for one thing—and I think the way
you clutch sweaters is really superb. You may be the best in the
league." He blushed modestly. "For a time," I confessed, "I never
thought you'd get the hang of it."
"It wasn't easy," he confided. "It took practice and
encouragement. You know something like spearing doesn't come
naturally. It has to be developed."
"I'm not inclined to flattery but, in my book, you've got it made.
You're a dirty player," I continued. . . . "There isn't a player in the
league who knows as many obscene gestures."

How is the selection ironic? What does the author really mean?

_____

_____

From Reading to Writing

After you finish reading a selection, you could try these strategies to make sure
that you have understood it.

- **Summarize the reading.** When you summarize, you use your own words to
  write a condensed version of the reading. You leave out all information
  except for the main points. You can find a detailed explanation of summaries
  in Chapter 15.

- **Outline the reading.** An outline is a visual plan of the reading that looks like an essay plan. First, you write the main idea of the essay, and then write down the most important idea from each paragraph. You could make further indentations, and under each idea, include a detail or example.

- **Analyze the reading.** When you read, look critically at the writer's arguments and evaluate them, point by point. Also analyze how the writer builds the argument and ask yourself questions such as *Do I agree? Are the author's arguments convincing?* Then, when you write your analysis, you can break down the author's explanations and either refute or agree with them, using your own experiences and examples to support your view.

- **Write a response.** Your instructor may ask you to write about your reaction to a reading. These are some questions you might ask yourself before you respond in writing.

  - What is the writer's main point?
  - What is the writer's purpose? Is the writer trying to entertain, persuade, or inform?
  - Who is the audience? Is the writer directing his or her message at someone like me?
  - Do I agree or disagree with the writer's main point?
  - Are there any aspects of the topic to which I can relate? What are they?

  After you answer the questions, you will have more ideas to use in your written response.

Reading Selections

Theme: Conflict

READING I
The Hijab
Naheed Mustafa

> Naheed Mustafa, a North-America-born Muslim woman, has taken to wearing the traditional hijab scarf. She wrote this article while studying in a Canadian university.

1   I often wonder whether people see me as a radical, fundamentalist Muslim terrorist packing an AK-47 assault rifle inside my jean jacket. Or maybe they see me as the poster girl for oppressed womanhood everywhere. I'm not sure which it is. I get the whole gamut of strange looks, stares, and covert glances. You see, I wear the hijab, a scarf that covers my head, neck, and throat. I do this because I am a Muslim woman who believes her body is her own private concern.

2   Young Muslim women are reclaiming the hijab, reinterpreting it in light of its original purpose—to give back to women ultimate control of their own bodies. The Qur'an teaches us that men and women are equal, and that individuals should not be judged according to gender, beauty, wealth, or privilege. The only thing that makes one person better than another is her or his character.

3   Nonetheless, people have a difficult time relating to me. After all, I'm young, Canadian born and raised, and university-educated. Why would I do this to myself, they ask. Strangers speak to me in loud, slow English and often appear to be playing charades. They politely inquire how I like living in Canada and whether or not the cold bothers me. If I'm in the right mood, it can be very amusing. But, why would I, a woman with all the advantages of a North American upbringing, suddenly, at 21, want to cover myself so that only my face and hands show?

4   Women are taught from early childhood that their worth is proportional to their attractiveness. Women feel compelled to pursue abstract notions of beauty, half realizing that such a pursuit is futile. When women reject this form of oppression, they face ridicule and contempt. Whether it is women who refuse to wear makeup or to shave their legs or to expose their bodies, others have trouble dealing with them.

5   In the Western world, the hijab has come to symbolize either forced silence or radical, unconscionable militancy. Actually, it's neither. It is simply a woman's assertion that judgment of her physical person is to play no role whatsoever in social interaction. Wearing the hijab has given me freedom from constant attention to my physical self. Because my appearance is not subjected to public scrutiny, my beauty, or perhaps lack of it, has been removed from the realm of what can legitimately be discussed. No one knows whether my hair looks as if I just stepped out of a salon, whether or not I can pinch an inch, or even if I have unsightly stretch marks. And because no one knows, no one cares.

6   Feeling that one has to meet the impossible male standards of beauty is tiring and often humiliating. I should know; I spent my entire teenage years trying to do it. I was a borderline bulimic and spent a lot of money I didn't have on potions and lotions in hopes of becoming the next Cindy Crawford. The definition of beauty is ever-changing; waifish is good, waifish is bad, athletic is good—sorry, athletic is bad. Narrow hips? Great. Narrow hips? Too bad.

7   Women are not going to achieve equality with the right to bear their breasts in public, as some people would like to have you believe. That would only make us party **to** our own objectification. True equality will be had only when women don't need to display themselves to get attention and won't need to defend their decision to keep their bodies to themselves.

COMPREHENSION AND CRITICAL THINKING

1.   In paragraph one, find a synonym for "the whole range or scope."

     _____

2.   Find a word in paragraph 4 that means pressured.

     _____

3.   Describe the author's background.

     _____

4.   Why does Mustafa choose to wear the hijab?

     _____

     _____

5. How does Mustafa define the hijab? Give both the literal and symbolic meanings.

_____

_____

6. According to Mustafa, what does the hijab symbolize to non-Muslim North Americans?

_____

7. Using inferences, what assumptions is the author making about men?

_____

_____

8. In paragraph 6, the author argues that women have to meet "impossible standards of beauty." Respond to her opinion.

_____

9. Who is the intended audience for this essay?

_____

WRITING TOPICS

Write about one of the following topics. Remember to explore, develop, and revise and edit your work.

1. What causes women to think they are being judged on their beauty?
2. The author describes being judged because of the hijab. Write about how people are judged based on the clothing they wear.

READING 2

Seeing Red Over Myths
Drew Hayden Taylor

> Drew Hayden Taylor is an Ojibway playwright and novelist, and he is a regular contributor to _Now_ magazine. He discusses common misconceptions about Canadian Natives in the following essay.

1   A year and a half ago, my Mohawk girlfriend and I (a fellow of proud Ojibway heritage) found ourselves in the history-rich halls of Europe, lecturing on Native issues, the propaganda and the reality, at a university deep in the heart of northeastern Germany. Then one young lady, a student at this former communist university, put up her hand and asked an oddly naïve question, something like, "Do Indian women shave their legs and armpits like other North American women?" This was not the strangest question I've had put to me. I keep a list, which includes, "I'm phoning from Edinburgh, Scotland, and am doing research on natives in the 1930s. Can you send information?" or "Where can I get my hands on some Inuit throat singers?"

2   But unbeknownst to me, the shaving of extremities in Europe is a largely unexplored area of female hygiene; evidently this topic warranted investigation as to its possible Aboriginal origin. But the question presented a

rather obvious example of the issue that permeates North America: the myth of pan-Indianism. The young lady had begun her question with "Do Indian women . . . ?" Sometimes the questioner substitutes First Nations/Native/Aboriginal/Indigenous for Indian. However it's worded, it reveals a persistent belief that we are all one people.

3   Within the borders of what is now referred to as Canada, there are more than fifty distinct and separate languages and dialects. And each distinct and separate language and dialect has emerged from a distinct and separate culture. I tried to tell this woman that her question couldn't be answered because, technically, there is no "Indian/First Nations/Aboriginal." To us, there is only the Cree, the Ojibway, the Salish, the Innu, the Shuswap, and so on.

4   I find myself explaining this point with annoying frequency, not just in Europe, but here in Canada, at the Second Cup, Chapters, or the bus station. The power of that single myth is incredible. When people ask me, "What do First Nations people want?" how do I answer? Some of the Mi'kmaq want to catch lobster, some of the Cree want to stop the flooding and logging of their territory in northern Manitoba, Alberta and Quebec, the Mohawk want the right to promote their own language, and I know bingo is in there somewhere.

5   That's why every time I see a TV news report talking about the plight of the Aboriginal people, I find myself screaming "Which people? Be specific!" That's why I never watch television in public.

6   Such is the power of myths. By their very definition, they're inaccurate or incomplete. Now you know why we as Native people (see, I do it myself) prefer not to use the term "myth" when referring to the stories of our ancestors, as in "The Myths and Legends of Our People." There is something inherently wrong about starting a traditional story with "This is one of the myths that was passed down from our grandfathers. . . ." Literally translated, it means, "This is a lie that was handed down by our grandfathers. . . ."

7   The preferred term these days is *teachings*—as in, "Our teachings say. . . ." It's certainly more accurate because it recognizes the fact that most teachings exist for a purpose—that there's some nugget of metaphor or message within the subtext. And in the Native (there I go again!) way, we like to accentuate the positive. (Important note: The word *legend* can also be used instead of *teachings*, provided you have oral permission from a recognized elder, or written permission from an Aboriginal academic—any Nation will do.)

8   The myth of pan-Indianism is not the only one rooted in the Canadian psyche. A good percentage of Canadians believe that there's a strong Aboriginal tradition of alcoholism. In Kenora, a decade or so ago, someone told me that in one month alone there had been almost three hundred arrests of Aboriginals for alcohol-related offences. And Kenora's not that big a town. The statistic frightened me—until it was explained that rather than confirming the mind-boggling image of three hundred drunken Indians running through the Kenora streets, it signified the same dozen people who just got arrested over and over and over again. It's all in how you read the statistic. And nobody told me how many white people had been arrested over and over again. It's all in how you read that statistic.

9   While acknowledging that certain communities do, indeed, suffer from substance-abuse problems (like many non-Native communities, I might add), I can safely say that not myself, my girlfriend, my mother, my best friend, and most of the other people of Aboriginal descent I consider friends and acquaintances are alcoholics. I wonder why this myth is so persuasive.

10 It's also believed by a good percentage of Canadians that all Native people are poor. Unfortunately, many communities do suffer from mind-numbing poverty, as do many non-Native communities. But contrary to popular belief, capitalism was not a foreign concept to Canada's earliest inhabitants. There were levels of wealth and status back then; today, instead of counting their horses, the rich might count their horsepower.

11 Several weeks ago, a Toronto newspaper attacked a rumour about a coalition of Aboriginal people who had expressed interest in buying the Ottawa Senators [hockey team]. The columnist thought the idea preposterous: "These are the same people who can't afford to pay tax on a pack of smokes; the same people who are so poor they claim government policy is forcing them to live in neighbourhoods where a rusted car with more than one flat tire is considered a lawn ornament." Well, the ratio of rusted-car-on-lawn to no-rusted-car-on-lawn is so disproportionate it's hardly worth mentioning.

12 Yes, there are some wealthy Native people out there (I wish I knew more of them personally). But their existence is a hard idea to accept when the media only feature First Nations stories on the desperate and the tragic.

13 So where does this leave us? I was asked to write an essay on the "myths of a common Indian identity," which, as I translate it, means that I was asked to comment on lies about something that doesn't exist. That sounds more like politics to me. But if you're still curious about whether Indian women shave their legs and armpits, you'll have to ask one. I'm not telling.

COMPREHENSION AND CRITICAL THINKING

1. In paragraph 2, what is the meaning of *permeates*? _____

2. Find a word in paragraph 11 that means "ridiculous." _____

3. What are some alternative terms for *Native*?

   _____

4. How does the author introduce his essay?

   a. historical information
   b. contrasting position
   c. anecdote

5. Using your own words, write a thesis statement for this essay.

   _____

   _____

6. According to Taylor, what are some incorrect beliefs that people have about Natives?

   _____

   _____

7. What is the difference between a *teaching* and a *myth*?

   _____

8. Paragraph 11 is missing a topic sentence. Which sentence best expresses the main idea of that paragraph?

   a. Aboriginal people wanted to buy the Ottawa Senators.

   b. Many people have the mistaken notion that all Aboriginals are poor.

   c. Aboriginals do not have rusted cars on their lawns.

   d. People make broad generalizations about Aboriginals.

9. Taylor refutes common misconceptions with factual, anecdotal, and statistical support. Give an example of each one.

   Fact: _____

   Anecdote: _____

   Statistic: _____

WRITING TOPICS

Write about one of the following topics. Remember to explore, develop, and revise and edit your work.

1. Define a term that relates to your race, religion, or nationality.
2. How do people from other nations view Canadians? How do Canadians view themselves? Compare the stereotypes about Canadians with the reality.

Theme: Urban Development

READING 3

Living Environments
Avi Friedman

> Avi Friedman is professor at the McGill School of Architecture. In the following article, which appeared in the *Montreal Gazette*, Friedman reflects on designing an appropriate house for the individual needs of families.

1   When invited to design a home, I first like to know what kind of dwellers my clients are. In our first meeting, I ask them to take me on a guided tour of their current residence and describe how each room is used—when and by whom. Walking through hallways, scanning the interior of rooms, peeping into closets, looking at kitchen cupboards, and pausing at family photos have helped me devise several common categories of occupants.

2   The "neat" household regards the house as a gallery. The home is spotless. The placement of every item, be it hanging artwork, a memento on a shelf, or furniture is highly choreographed. The colour scheme is coordinated and the lighting superb. It feels as if one has walked into an *Architectural Digest* magazine spread. Recent trends, professional touches, and carefully selected pieces are the marks of the place.

3   The "utilitarian" family is very pragmatic. They are minimalists, believing that they get only what they need. Environmental concerns play an important role in buying goods. The place, often painted in light tones, is sparsely decorated with very few well-selected items. Souvenirs from a recent trip are displayed and some photos or paintings are on the wall. They will resist excess consumption and will squeeze as much use as they can from each piece.

4 The home of the "collector" family is stuffed to the brim. It is hard to find additional space for furniture or a wall area to hang a painting. Books, magazines, and weekend papers are everywhere. Newspaper cutouts and personal notes are crammed under magnets on the fridge door. The collector family seems to pay less attention to how things appear and more to comfort. Stress reduction is a motto. Being an excessively clean "show house" is not a concern. Placing dirty breakfast dishes in the sink and the morning paper in the rack before leaving home is not a priority as long as things are moving along.

5 Of course, these are only a few household types, but at the end of a house tour, I have a pretty good idea about my clients. More than the notes that I take during a meeting, these real-life images tell me all about my client's home life and desired domestic environment. When I began practising, I quickly realized house design is about people more than architecture. As hard as I might try, I will never be able to tailor a new personality to someone by placing him or her in a trendy style, one that does not reflect who he or she really is. I can attempt to illustrate options other than their current life habits and decorating choices. But in the end, when they move into their new place, they will bring along their old habits.

6 My experience has taught me some homeowners have been trying hard to emulate lifestyles and décors that are really not theirs. The endless decorating shows on television and the many magazines that crowd supermarket racks provide a tempting opportunity to become someone else. Some homeowners are under constant pressure, it feels, to undergo extreme makeovers and borrow rather than mature into their natural selves. They search for a readymade packaged interior style rather than discovering their own.

7 I am often at a loss when clients ask me what style I subscribe to, or solicit advice on the style they are to adopt. I reply that styles are trendy and comfort is permanent, and that they should see beyond the first day of occupancy into everyday living. Sipping a freshly brewed coffee on the back porch on a summer Sunday and letting the morning paper litter the floor while watching a squirrel on the tree across the yard is a treasured moment. It will never be able to fit into a well-defined architectural style. Home design needs to create the backdrop for such opportunities. It is these types of moments that make us enjoy life.

8 If someone wants to read, why not have a wall of books? Does someone love listening to music? Then a music room or corner should be created, even if it is not trendy. Does someone want to interact with the children? He or she might add a hobby space, even if it is outdated and cannot be found in most magazines.

9 Referring to technological advances, the renowned French architect Le Corbusier once described the home as a "machine for living." It is partially true. Home is the site where mundane and utilitarian activities take place. It is also where special moments, uniquely ours, are created and treasured.

COMPREHENSION AND CRITICAL THINKING

1. Find a four-word expression in paragraph 4 that means "completely filled."_____

2. Find a word in paragraph 6 that means "to copy."_____

3. Underline the thesis statement.
4. Underline the topic sentences in paragraphs 2 to 7.
5. Paragraph 8 is missing a topic sentence. Which sentence best expresses the main idea of that paragraph?

    a. People can create a music room in their homes.

    b. Everybody should think about his or her likes and dislikes.

    c. People should create spaces in their homes to accommodate their personal interests.

    d. Hobby rooms and bookshelves can help make a home feel unique.

6. How does Friedman assess the needs of families when designing a house?

    _____

    _____

    _____

7. What are the three categories of households that Friedman describes in this article?

    _____

8. In your own words, describe the characteristics for each type of household.

    _____

    _____

    _____

9. a. What influences families when they choose a design for their homes?

    _____

    b. Does Friedman think that such influences are positive or negative? Explain your answer.

    _____

10. According to Friedman, what is the most important factor that home design should take into consideration?

    _____

    _____

WRITING TOPICS

Write about one of the following topics. Remember to explore, develop, and revise and edit your work.

1. Use a different classification method to describe types of living environments.

2. Friedman writes, "Home is the site where mundane and utilitarian activities take place. It is also where special moments, uniquely ours, are created and treasured." Write about different categories of special or memorable moments.

READING 4

Nature Returns to the Cities

John Roach

> John Roach is a writer for *National Geographic News*, and he has written many articles about nature. In the next essay, he describes animal life in our concrete jungles.

1   The concrete jungle isn't just for people anymore. Thirty years of good environmental stewardship combined with wildlife's innate ability to adapt has given rise to a resurgence of nature in America's urban centres. In New York City, raccoons have walked through the front door and into the kitchen to raid the refrigerator. In southern California, mountain lions have been seen cooling off under garden sprinklers and breaking into homes near Disneyland. In Chicago, beavers gnaw and fell trees and snarl traffic. In her book *Wild Nights: Nature Returns to the City*, Anne Matthews describes such incidents as she explores the resurgence of wildlife in New York and other cities. "Thirty years of environmental protection and absence of hunting [in cities] have allowed animal populations to soar," she notes.

2   The implications of the wildlife resurgence in cities vary. People may marvel at the presence of a falcon nest on the twenty-seventh floor of New York Hospital. On the other hand, some people were literally sickened to death in the fall of 2000 by the West Nile virus, which had been carried to the city by migrating birds and transmitted to mosquitoes, which passed it on to humans.

3   Overcrowded cities and urban sprawl have put more people and wild animals in close proximity than at any other time in our history, says Matthews. Encounters between these two groups are beginning to exceed what scientists call the cultural carrying capacity, defined in *Wild Nights* as "the moment humans stop saying 'Aww' and start calling 911." This change in the nature of the relationship between people and wildlife, says Matthews, is forcing people to reconsider their ethical and practical role as top predator.

4   Nature's return to U.S. cities has resulted in part from passage of the *Clean Air Act* in 1970 and the *Clean Water Act* in 1972. These laws of environmental protection that helped make air safer to breathe and water safer to drink also made cities more hospitable to wildlife, according to Matthews. After being cleaned up, New York Harbor is now home to booming populations of blue crabs and fiddler crabs, which in turn attract thousands of long-legged wading birds such as herons and egrets. With the air now cleaner, owls have flocked in growing numbers to the suburbs in search of easy prey: pets such as schnauzers, chihuahuas, and cats. In parts of the South and Midwest, forests that were logged in the nineteenth century have grown back over the last hundred years, allowing animal populations to recover. Car collisions with moose are now common along Interstate 95, the main East Coast traffic corridor. Crocodiles, who were all but erased by development pressure in Florida, are now breeding at four times their normal rate in the cooling canals of Florida's nuclear power plants.

5   Some creatures, such as rats, never really left the city. Today, an estimated 28 million rats—which are non-native, like much of the city's human population—inhabit New York. The greater New York area is home to eight million people, which means there are more than three rats to every person. Matthews explains how it happened. "Rats are smart," she writes.

"Although a fast-forward version of natural selection has made rats in many big cities immune to nearly all conventional poisons, they still may press one pack member into service as a taster; if the test rat dies, the others resolutely avoid the bait."

6   Matthews says the strong adaptive ability of non-native species has begun to change the definition of wilderness. Rats were introduced into U.S. cities in the 1700s after arriving as stowaways on merchant ships. Zebra mussels, which have caused major problems in the Great Lakes by clogging intake pipes, were imported in the ballast water of international ships. "The most important thing is to realize that a city is wilder than we tend to imagine and the land we think of as untouched or wild really isn't," says Matthews. "There has been so much human interference and reshaping that we really don't know what a pristine planet is." Matthews thinks people should not try to undo the effects of this increased interference with wildlife, but to improve their understanding of it and continue to make room for nature in their lives.

7   Matthews says it's crucial that people consider what kind of world they want their grandchildren to inherit, and act to ensure that such a world will exist. One immediate concern is what the impacts of global warming will be in fifty years. Citing the results of computer models showing future conditions if no action is taken to mitigate global warming, Matthews says much of New York will be under water, as sea levels rise three feet. New Orleans, Louisiana, already eight feet below sea level, might become the next Atlantis. What can we do? "What you can do is as small as don't use air conditioning as much, don't use your gas-guzzling [sport utility vehicle], walk more," says Matthews. "On the macro level, urge your congressperson to do something about environmental issues."

COMPREHENSION AND CRITICAL THINKING

1.   In paragraph 1, find a word that means "reappearance."_____
2.   Define *prey*. Look in paragraph 4 for context clues. _____

     _____

3.   Underline the thesis statement.
4.   What are at least two reasons the author gives for animals returning to urban environments?

     _____

     _____

5.   What are at least three effects of wildlife in cities?

     _____

     _____

6.   In paragraph 4, the author implies that

     a. The *Clean Air Act* and *Clean Water Act* did not help the environment.
     b. The *Clean Air Act* and *Clean Water Act* were quite effective in helping to improve the quality of the air and water.
     c. Logging practices are much more detrimental to the environment today than they were in the past.
     d. Many dangerous predators such as crocodiles now roam the cities.

7. What is Matthews's opinion about abundant wildlife in the city?

_____

_____

8. In paragraph 6, what is Matthews's definition of wilderness?

_____

9. Although this is mainly a cause and effect essay, there are also elements of process. Which paragraph gives the readers clear steps to take to help the environment?_____

10. What incorrect assumption or belief do many people today have about the relationship between wildlife and cities?

_____

_____

Writing Topics

Write about one of the following topics. Remember to explore, develop, and revise and edit your work.

1. Describe your own experiences with wildlife in your home, yard, or neighbourhood. What caused the bird, animal, or insect to invade your area? How did it affect you and your neighbours?
2. Do you have a pet in your home? Why or why not? Describe the causes and/or effects of your decision to have or not have pets.

Theme: International Trade

READING 5

I, Telemarketer

Eugene Henry

> Journalist Eugene Henry contributes to many Canadian newspapers. Henry spent nine months as a telemarketer.

1   It's a familiar experience: The phone rings, and you find yourself listening to a telemarketer. Depending on your resolve, you might end the unwanted communication in ten or twenty seconds—maybe as long as a minute for the weak-willed or those with especially good manners. Either way, the call usually comes as an annoying interruption in your busy life. However, there's a whole world on the other end of your phone cord, a world in which telemarketing is not one of life's interruptions, but life itself. In late 2003, I became part of that world when I became a telemarketer.

2   Montreal is North America's call-centre capital, and despite the impression one gets from investigative news reports, many are perfectly respectable employers. Some even recruit at career fairs—which is where, fresh out of university, I came across a promising-looking outfit that offered me a modest signing bonus and a respectable salary. The firm was part of a large, publicly traded telemarketing company based in the United States, with call centres in twenty-six countries. The size was comforting: It meant I

wouldn't have to worry about working at the sort of fly-by-night operation that ends up being raided by the police.

3   During my training, I learned more than I ever wanted to know about cable television packages. Our goal was to sell premium movie channels to existing cable customers, and this would become my professional mission over the next few months.

4   Workers at a call centre are divided into a day shift and a night shift, and everyone works from a desk with a computer and a phone in a large, colourless room. The work isn't pleasant, and the days go by slowly.

5   The pressure to sell is intense. Telemarketers who don't make quota tend to disappear. Someone you've worked with for a while and talked with on breaks or at lunch will one day simply stop showing up. They are usually fired, though sometimes they quit.

6   I almost lost my own job in November, shortly after I started. There was an incentive prize of fifty dollars for the employee with the best "conversion"—the ratio of sales to calls—which is a lot of money for a telemarketer. I wasn't a bad salesman, mainly because I didn't push. (A casual manner on the phone works better than someone who sounds desperate or aggressive.) But to win the fifty dollars, I knew I needed to cheat. So I put down people who rejected my pitch as wrong numbers, which meant they would be kept out of my conversion ratio, artificially boosting it. Unfortunately, a "quality assurance monitor"—the big brothers of the call centre—discovered my ruse. It was grounds for immediate dismissal, but my sales were decent, so they kept me on.

7   Others weren't so lucky. Over our Christmas break, almost all of my colleagues were laid off. We were all supposed to return from our Christmas break on January 5; instead, Human Resources called most of us on January 4 to instruct us not to come in the next day.

8   I felt guilty about surviving the **purge**. Most telemarketers are hard-luck cases who live on the margins of the job market. In other words, the people who lost their jobs needed the work more than I did. I didn't have a family to feed—like my single-mother colleague who had no way to pay the bills that had piled up over the holidays.

purge: elimination of employees

9   As March and April wore on, I fell in love with one of the "big brothers." Kelly was a twenty-six-year-old graphic designer. We had a lot to talk about—mostly how she'd rather be designing things, and I'd rather be writing things.

10   I found that being in a secret relationship with the person monitoring your calls helps make telemarketing easier. I had carte blanche to slack off. I even started writing at my desk between calls. Kelly told me there was nothing to worry about, as long as I made enough sales to pass under the radar of her managers. It was a high-stakes sacrifice on her part: She could have lost her job if anyone found out she was cutting someone slack on the floor.

11   Despite Kelly's help, May, which would become my last full month on the job, was a difficult one. The cable company was trying to move everyone to digital, and so we were schooled on the superiority of digital television technology. The job meant calling retired people who had no idea what digital was. Notwithstanding their ignorance, it was our job to "increase their bill a few dollars" so they could enjoy digital splendour.

12   One guy on the floor found an effective strategy. Salman, a Pakistani Muslim, had recently arrived in Montreal by way of Florida. His strategy for

selling digital was to find "specialty channels" that he knew would catch old people's interest. There were a few channels that focus on Christian programming, and Sal found it amusing that he, of all people, had so much success pitching them to pensioners. "It's easy," he told me. "All you have to do is sell Jesus. Jesus sells himself."

13 By the end of May, I'd been on the job nine months, and I'd had enough. I asked Human Resources how to quit. They told me to write a notice and give it to my team manager. When I actually did this, everyone seemed surprised. Apparently, I'm among the small minority of telemarketers who actually give two weeks' notice. Consistent with the disposable employment ethos that governs the profession, many simply stop showing up.

14 Nine months may not seem like a long time. But I think I learned more during that period than I did during four years of university. Certainly, I learned to be more respectful when the phone rings and I hear a stranger's voice. The next time you talk to a telemarketer, think about a polite "no thanks" instead of the all-too-common expletive or hang-up. Sometimes that's enough to get a telemarketer through the day with at least a half-smile on his or her face.

COMPREHENSION AND CRITICAL THINKING

1. Find a word in paragraph 6 that means "reason" or "justification."_____
2. In paragraph 6, what is the meaning of *ruse*?

_____

3. Why did Henry take a job as a telemarketer?
   a. He wanted to work with his girlfriend.
   b. At a job fair, a company made him a good offer.
   c. He thought that he would be very good in sales, and he wanted to have a career in telemarketing.

4. Which statement is *not* true about paragraph 6?
   a. Henry wanted to win a fifty-dollar prize.
   b. Henry lied and pretended that people who did not want to buy from him were really wrong numbers.
   c. Henry's supervisor did not discover that Henry was cheating.
   d. Henry did not lose his job because his sales were quite good.

5. What is Henry's special sales technique?

_____

6. What is ironic about Salman's sales pitch? See paragraph 12.

7. Why were Henry's employers surprised when he gave two weeks' notice?

_____

8. Henry says that he learned more at his job "than at four years of university," but he does not state explicitly what those lessons are. Read between the lines. Think of some positive and negative lessons that he learned.

_____

9. How does the author conclude his essay?
   a. suggestion   b. quotation   c. prediction

10. What is the author's attitude toward his job? You will have to make inferences.

_____

_____

WRITING TOPICS

Write about one of the following topics. Remember to explore, develop, and revise and edit your work.

1. Write about a memorable job that you had in the past. Describe your experiences and explain what you learned.
2. Have you ever had a workplace romance, or do you know someone who has? What happened?

READING 6

The Rich Resonance of Small Talk
Roxanne Roberts

> Roxanne Roberts is a staff writer for the _Washington Post_. In the next article, she muses about the importance of small talk.

1   I talk too much. The good news is that I can enter a room full of strangers, walk up to anyone, and start yammering away. The bad news is . . . well, you can guess that I bore people. All things considered, this has worked out pretty well. In my sixteen years as a social reporter for a newspaper, I've marched up to presidents, movie stars, and kings and felt unafraid to make small talk, otherwise known as the mother's milk of party coverage. I have an advantage, of course, in that I have a press pass and a notebook.

2   But small talk is a big deal for everyone; it is one of those essential social skills that separate the men from the boys. The ability to connect in short, casual conversations can make or break careers, friendships, and romances—it's how we gather information, and hopefully, make a favourable impression. There are only three golden rules for small talk: First, shut up and listen; second, when in doubt, repeat Rule 1; third, get others to talk about themselves.

3   First, Rule 1 and Rule 2 take a lifetime for the average extrovert or egomaniac to master. To listen that intently, to focus with every muscle, takes not only great skill but also great discipline, which is why mere mortals fall short. It is so easy to respond to a casual comment by unwittingly turning the spotlight back on yourself: "You're going to Italy? We stayed at this great little place outside of Florence." It seems so natural—your small talk might be helpful, witty, and even relevant, but you're nonetheless talking instead of listening—and you can never learn anything while talking, except that you talk too much.

4   In the meantime, there are a few other tricks for small talk with strangers and acquaintances. For example, introduce yourself by name, even if you think they know it. "I don't think we've met. I'm Queen Elizabeth II." It's gracious, it's efficient, and it's smart. It's very awkward when someone starts a conversation with "Remember me?" and you don't. Second, ask simple

questions. "What do you think of the [party, conference, cheese puffs]?" Then listen. When you run into a casual acquaintance, ask what he or she has been doing lately. Then listen. Ask follow-up questions based on the answers. If you are genuinely interested, most people will be surprised and flattered. Resist the temptation to display your own special brand of brilliance, and when you catch yourself doing so, shift the focus back. Later on, when the relationship has evolved beyond small talk, you can strut your fabulousness.

5   Furthermore, mastering the art of small talk is important for drawing shy people into a conversation. If this is done right, they walk away thinking *you're* great. "A great small talker is someone who has three to four open-ended questions that make the person open up," says Ann Stock, former White House social secretary for the Clintons and currently the vice president of the Kennedy Center. "It ignites something in them that makes them start talking. After that, you ask leading questions."

6   Use your body language. There's nothing worse than chatting with people who simultaneously scan the room for someone more important. Give someone your full and real attention during your conversation. Face him or her directly, and look in his eyes. Never underestimate small talk—even though many people dread it or think it's silly, boring, or superficial.

7   Once in a rare while, someone comes along who innately gets it and turns a brief, casual moment into a truly memorable encounter. Former president Bill Clinton is a genius at it. In the course of two minutes, he can lock eyes with a person, ask a seemingly simple question, and make a person feel like the centre of the universe. Clinton's remarkable memory for names and faces means he can meet someone and—months or years later—ask about his or her family or golf game. People are shocked and delighted.

8   Another legendary master at the art of small talk was the late Pamela Harriman, Democratic fundraiser, ambassador to France, and the woman once called the "greatest courtesan of the century"—a nod to her many high-profile lovers. What set her apart was her laser-like ability to make anyone feel like the most important person in the room. She wanted to know everything about the people she met. She hung on every word and seldom talked about herself. She made people feel like brilliant, under-appreciated jewels. "She had the power to make people want to talk with her," William Pfaff wrote in the *International Herald Tribune* shortly after her death in 1997. "She was—or certainly made herself seem to be—interested in everyone with whom she spoke, and in what they had to say. She, in turn, had something intelligent to say to them." She was not, he wrote, an intellectual or particularly sophisticated in matters of international relations. She knew enough to ask the right questions. But mostly she let others do the talking: "The willingness to listen is seduction itself—certainly to vain men, and in the world in which she functioned, all men are vain."

9   Finally, consider the famous story about British Prime Minister Benjamin Disraeli and his great political rival, William Gladstone. Legend has it that a lady was taken to dinner one evening by Gladstone and the next by Disraeli. When asked her impression of the two men, she replied, "When I left the dining room after sitting next to Mr. Gladstone, I thought he was the cleverest man in England. But after sitting next to Mr. Disraeli, I thought I was the cleverest woman in England."

COMPREHENSION AND CRITICAL THINKING

1. What is the meaning of *nod to* in paragraph 8?
   a. acknowledgment of
   b. indication of agreement
   c. falling asleep

2. Underline the thesis statement.

3. Why does the author begin the introductory paragraph with the first-person pronoun *I*, but use third-person pronouns for the rest of the essay?

   _____

4. Why does the author think that learning the art of small talk is important?

   _____

   _____

5. Using your own words, list at least five pieces of advice the author gives to master the art of small talk.

   _____

   _____

6. According to Roberts, why is it difficult for people to follow the first rule of small talk?

   _____

   _____

7. Why does the author use Bill Clinton and Pamela Harriman as examples to support her thesis?

   _____

8. How are Clinton's and Harriman's strategies for making small talk similar?

   _____

   _____

9. How are Clinton's and Harriman's strategies for making small talk different?

   _____

   _____

   _____

   _____

10. How is the anecdote in the concluding paragraph a good support for mastering the art of small talk?

_____

_____

_____

WRITING TOPICS

Write about one of the following topics. Remember to explore, develop, and revise and edit your work.

1. Explain steps that people can take to have better relationships with their life partners.
2. Describe a process people can go through to make their guests feel more comfortable. You can discuss houseguests, dinner guests, or party guests.

READING 7

Google's China Web
Frida Ghitis

> Frida Ghitis is a journalist, businesswoman, and writer. She is the author of *The End of Revolution: A Changing World in the Age of Live Television*. In the next essay, Ghitis examines the role that Google and other Internet providers play in supporting China's severe censorship laws.

1   A few years ago, I walked into an Internet room in Tibet's capital, Lhasa. There were no Chinese soldiers in the room and no visible government censors nearby. A sign on the wall, however, reminded Web users that even after entering the stateless world of the Web, China's all-seeing eye had not disappeared. "Do not use Internet," the warning instructed crassly, "for any political or other unintelligent purposes."

2   Since then, China's ruling regime has perfected the science of controlling what the Chinese can read or write on the Internet to such a degree that it has become the envy of tyrants and dictators the world over. We might have expected that from a regime that has proven it will do whatever it takes to stay in power. What we never expected was to see Google, the company whose guiding motto reads, "Don't be evil," helping in the effort. Google's decision to help China censor searches on the company's Chinese website is not only a violation of its own righteous-sounding principles, and it's not just an affront to those working to bring international standards of human rights for the Chinese people. No, Google's sellout to Beijing is also a threat to every person who has ever used Google anywhere in the world.

3   Google saves every search, every email, every fingerprint we leave on the Web when we move through its Google search engine, or its Gmail service, or its fast-growing collection of Internet offerings. Google knows more about us than the **FBI** or the **CIA** or the **NSA** or any spy agency of any government, and nobody regulates it. When a company that holds digital dossiers on millions of people decides profits are more important than principles, we are all at risk. Google will now participate actively in a

FBI: Federal Bureau of Investigation
CIA: Central Intelligence Agency
NSA: National Security Agency

censorship program whose implications, according to Harvard's Berkman Center for Internet and Society, "are profound and disturbing." The Chinese government blocks thousands of search terms—including censorship.

4   To be fair, Google is hardly alone in its decision to capitulate to Beijing's rulers in order to gain a Web share of China's 1.3 billion inhabitants. The country's tantalizing market has tested the ethics of many Western corporations—and almost all have failed the test. That is particularly true in the Internet business. Just last year, Yahoo helped Beijing's Web goons track down the identity of a Chinese journalist who wrote an email about the anniversary of the 1994 Tiananmen Square massacre—a massacre of thousands of Chinese democracy advocates perpetrated by the same regime whose efforts Google now abets. The journalist, Shi Tao, was sentenced to ten years in prison. Reporters Without Borders labelled Yahoo an "informant" that has "collaborated enthusiastically" with the Chinese regime. Microsoft, too, plays by the dictatorship's rules. Bloggers on MSN's service cannot type words such as "democracy" or "freedom." Internet users cannot read or write about anything that even hints of opposition to the ruling Communist Party. Even pro-Western commentary can trigger a block. And forget anything about Tibet or the Dalai Lama. Chinese bloggers, incidentally, must all register and identify themselves to authorities.

5   Neither Yahoo nor Microsoft claims to have higher ethical standards than the competition. The often-stated desire to "do good" and make the world a better place was one of the traits that endeared Google to the public. It was one of the reasons we trusted them to guard the precious and valuable contents of their thousands of servers. Now Google has become a company like all others, one with an eye on the bottom line before anything else. The company has decided to help China's censors even as it fights a request for records from the U.S. Justice Department's investigation of online child pornography. Skeptics had claimed Google was resisting the request to protect its technology, rather than to protect users' privacy. That explanation now sounds more plausible than ever.

6   We've long known about China's disdain for individual freedoms. But Google, we hardly knew you. It's definitely time to rethink that Gmail account and demand some safeguards from a potentially dangerous company. Perhaps here, too, we will need to heed the Tibetan cybercafé warning, "Do not use Internet for any political or unintelligent purposes."

COMPREHENSION AND CRITICAL THINKING

1. Find a word in paragraph 4 that means "to give in to."_____
2. The verb *abet* in paragraph 4 means
    a. hurt
    b. encourage
    c. help or assist

3. Underline the thesis statement.
4. In your own words, explain the author's main point.

    _____

    _____

5. How does the author introduce the text?
   a. general background
   b. historical background
   c. anecdote
   d. contrasting position

6. Why is the author so upset about Google's actions in China? Give at least two reasons.

   _____

   _____

   _____

7. According to the author, how are Google's policies in China hypocritical?

   _____

   _____

   _____

8. Examine paragraph 4. Is the author acknowledging the opposing position? Explain your answer.

   _____

   _____

   _____

9. Why do western businesses agree to participate in the violation of personal freedoms in China?

   _____

   _____

10. In which paragraph(s) does the author use an anecdote to support her point of view? _____

11. Name two informal sources that the author quotes.

    _____   _____

12. What is the author's predominant tone? Underline one or more answers.

contemplative	lighthearted
humorous	casual
outraged	sarcastic
friendly	supportive

WRITING TOPICS

Write about one of the following topics. Remember to explore, develop, and revise and edit your work.

1. Take the opposite position to the author, and argue that Google has every right to act as it does in China.
2. Argue that the censorship rules should (or should not) be more severe. Consider Internet, music, film, or television.

READING 8

My Head Rolled in Syria
Josh Freed

> Josh Freed is a columnist for the *Montreal Gazette*. Winner of Canada's Stephen Leacock Award for Humour, Freed has published many books, including *Fear of Frying and Other Fax of Life*. In the next essay, Freed uses narration and some description to recount an adventure during his vacation in Syria.

1   It's not every vacation I get involved with grave-robbers and jail threats, so let me tell you a story from my recent Middle East travels: the *Tale of the Supposedly Stolen Syrian Statue*.

2   We had been visiting Syria awhile and had just hired a driver to take us to two famous ruins in the countryside. The first was called Apamea, an ancient Roman-era city of 500,000, which is now deserted. Our driver left us in the middle of nowhere, at a breathtaking kilometre-long colonnade of giant pillars, and said he'd meet us at the other end. Soon we were wandering alone down a 2,000-year-old street.

3   "Pssst, mister!" said a voice. "You want to buy antiques? Coins? Statues?" Behind some pillars, a man in a headscarf was hawking dusty relics with Roman designs. Or maybe they were fakes he had made at home that morning—who knew? A second man on a motor scooter showed us bigger treasure—a sculpted white marble head, almost as big as my fist.

4   It was a haunting Roman-style bust with a gentle face and a mysterious smile—the sort of thing you see in museums. They wanted $250 U.S. but quickly came down to $150, even though I wasn't bargaining. Suddenly, one of them hissed "Guard!" and they disappeared.

5   In the distance, I saw a guard approaching in a red headscarf, and I went back to ruin watching. He ignored me, but when he was gone the statue salesmen popped up behind another pillar. By then, my wife and I had decided we were not taking artifacts out of Syria. It was wrong—and besides, it could lead to a cold Syrian jail. For the rest of our walk, we tried to ignore the hawkers who literally chased us from pillar to post lowering their price and playing peek-a-boo with the guard.

6   Eventually, we reached the end of the columns, where our driver, Omar, was waiting. A group of British tourists was there, too, with an English-speaking guide from Damascus, and I asked his advice. He said many Syrian archaeological sites were still undiscovered and grave-robbing was common. The old coins were probably real, though the head was more likely a fake. "If you like the head, buy it anyway. It's probably an imitation—and no one will care either way."

7   Unsure of the complications, we decided against it and drove off to our second location. But we had not gone far when three motorcycles appeared behind us, and our salesman-on-a-scooter waved the statue head, shouting, "Mister! For you, special price—only $70!" They raced up beside us, bargaining through our window. Omar put his foot to the gas and left them behind, but two kilometres on they were waiting around a bend.

8   They drove beside us again, shouting, "$40—very good!" And when the price fell to $30, we impulsively stopped the car and gave in. Why not? At this price, the head was obviously fake and would make a nice memento. I paid them and put the head into my pocket, but just before leaving, the salesman leaned into our car and said, "If anyone sees it at the border, say you got it at the Damascus market. Don't say it's from a grave."

9   And so we drove away, suddenly unsure whether we had bought a cheap fake or a 2,000-year-old treasure. We started to worry about what to do at the Syrian border—declare it, or hope no one noticed? Maybe we should just throw it out? I had barely owned it and the head hung over my soul like an ancient curse.

10   For the next three hours we raced across the country toward our next stop: a 1,500-year-old Christian ruin that is a well-known Syrian attraction. We arrived there in the late afternoon, and a sleepy guard told us the ticket office had just closed. We pleaded, but the guard said, "Sorry—my boss very bad man. If he find you inside, big trouble." Omar wouldn't give in. He offered the guard a bit of **baksheesh** and the man opened the gate. "Quick—go inside," the guard said, "but if problem, you leave quickly."

baksheesh: bribe

11   We found ourselves alone in a lovely Byzantine complex. We spent ten minutes admiring it all when the guard came racing back. "Car coming—maybe boss!" he shouted. "Must leave—please run!" The next thing we knew, we were racing after him. Ten minutes later, we found ourselves outside the site.

12   I breathed a sigh of relief, but it was premature. As we came around the wall near the parking lot, we saw a tall man dressed in black with a moustache like Saddam Hussein's. He looked as "bad" as our guard had warned, a cinema-style villain, who barked, "Where have you been?"

13   "Walking around the church," I said.

14   "No! You were inside the church. You break law. Now you come to police station. You go to jail."

15   Suddenly I remembered the head—it was still in my pocket—and a chill went down my spine. It was bad enough to be arrested sneaking into ruins after hours, but worse if you had an artefact on you that might be 2,000 years old. And at that moment the head felt all too authentic.

16   Either event could be explained alone, but together they would be enough to send us to the Syrian Political Prison for Grave Robbers. I could see the headlines back home: "Montreal journalist caught in grave-robbing ring; Canadian embassy refuses to intervene."

17   Ahead in the parking lot, I saw a white police wagon and made a decision. As the "bad man" marched in front of us, I slipped the head from my pocket and threw it quietly onto the ground. If the trouble blew over, maybe I would come back for it later.

18   In the parking lot there was a heated debate in Syrian among Omar, our guard, and the "bad man." The bad man said he was going for the police and ordered us to wait; then he drove away in his white wagon.

19   Omar offered some quick advice: "We must go—before the man comes back." I ran back to find the head, but to my amazement the white stone of the statue was the same colour as much of Syria: I saw small white stones everywhere, and when I turned them over, none had a gentle face. The head had vanished.

20   As twilight turned to darkness, we packed into our car and drove away, leaving the head in the land it had come from. Was it genuine or fake? Priceless or worthless? It was best not to know. We had let ourselves be tempted by zany circumstances and a touch of greed, and had made a mistake we were lucky to escape.

21   In the car, Omar was laughing merrily. "Statue no go to Canada," he chuckled, as we drove down the road. "Statue stay home."

22   We joined him in laughter. The head was back where it belonged—in the ruins of Syria.

COMPREHENSION AND CRITICAL THINKING

1.   What is the meaning of *hawking* in paragraph 3? _____

2.   Underline the thesis statement.

3.   Why does Freed feel anxious about buying the white statue?

       _____

4.   Even though Freed feels reluctant, he ends up buying the statue. Why does he change his mind?

       _____

       _____

5.   How is the ending of Freed's adventure appropriate?

       _____

6.   What can you infer, or guess, about Freed's character?

       _____

       _____

7.   What larger issues does this story raise?

       _____

8.   The author uses dialogue in several paragraphs. How does the dialogue enhance the story?

       _____

9.   This essay mainly narrates a story, but it also shows some causes of grave robberies. What are some causes?

       _____

       _____

10.   In your opinion, was the white sculpted head real or a fake?

       _____

       _____

WRITING TOPICS

Write about one of the following topics. Remember to explore, develop, and revise and edit your work.

1. What is the most interesting place that you have travelled to? Describe that place.
2. Think about an ethical dilemma that you have faced. Describe what happened.

Theme: Forces of Nature

READING 9

The Rules of Survival
Laurence Gonzales

> Laurence Gonzales won the National Magazine Award in 2001 and 2002. His work has appeared in such publications as *Harper's*, *National Geographic Adventure*, and *Smithsonian Air and Space*, to name a few. The next excerpt is from his latest book, *Deep Survival*.

1   As a journalist, I've been writing about accidents for more than thirty years. In the last fifteen or so years, I've concentrated on accidents in outdoor recreation, in an effort to understand who lives, who dies, and why. To my surprise, I found an eerie uniformity in the way people survive seemingly impossible circumstances. Decades and sometimes centuries apart, separated by culture, geography, race, language, and tradition, the most successful survivors—those who practise what I call "deep survival"—go through the same patterns of thought and behaviour, the same transformation and spiritual discovery, in the course of keeping themselves alive. It doesn't seem to matter whether they are surviving being lost in the wilderness or battling cancer; the strategies remain the same.

2   Survival should be thought of as a journey, a vision quest of the sort that Native Americans have had as a rite of passage for thousands of years. Once people pass the precipitating event—for instance, they are cast away at sea or told they have cancer—they are enrolled in one of the oldest schools in history. Here are a few things I've learned about survival.

STAY CALM

3   In the initial crisis, survivors are not ruled by fear; instead, they make use of it. Their fear often feels like (and turns into) anger, which motivates them and makes them feel sharper. Aron Ralston, the hiker who had to cut off his hand to free himself from a stone that had trapped him in a slot canyon in Utah, initially panicked and began slamming himself over and over against the boulder that had caught his hand. But very quickly he stopped himself, did some deep breathing, and began thinking about his options. He eventually spent five days progressing through the stages necessary to convince him of what decisive action he had to take to save his own life.

THINK, ANALYZE, AND PLAN

4   Survivors quickly organize, set up routines, and institute discipline. When Lance Armstrong was diagnosed with cancer, he organized his fight against it the way he would organize his training for a race. He read

everything he could about it, put himself on a training schedule, and put together a team from among friends, family, and doctors to support his efforts. Such conscious, organized effort in the face of grave danger requires a split between reason and emotion in which reason gives direction and emotion provides the power source. Survivors often report experiencing reason as an audible "voice."

5   Steve Callahan, a sailor and boat designer, was rammed by a whale, and his boat sank while he was on a solo voyage in 1982. Adrift in the Atlantic for seventy-six days on a five-and-a-half-foot raft, he experienced his survival voyage as taking place under the command of a "captain" who gave him his orders and kept him on his water ration, even as his own mutinous (emotional) spirit complained. His captain routinely lectured "the crew." Thus under strict control, he was able to push away thoughts that his situation was hopeless and take the necessary first steps of the survival journey: to think clearly, analyze his situation, and formulate a plan.

CELEBRATE EVERY VICTORY

6   Survivors take great joy from even their smallest successes. This attitude helps keep motivation high and prevents a lethal plunge into hopelessness. It also provides relief from the unspeakable strain of a life-threatening situation.

7   Lauren Elder was the only survivor of a light plane crash in High Sierra. Stranded on a 12,000 foot peak, one arm broken, she could see the San Joaquin Valley in California below, but a vast wilderness and sheer and icy cliffs separated her from safety. Wearing a wrap-around skirt and blouse but no underwear, with two-inch heeled boots, she crawled "on all fours, doing a kind of sideways spiderwalk," as she put it later, "balancing myself on the ice crust, punching through it with my hands and feet." She had thirty-six hours of climbing ahead of her—a seemingly impossible task. But Elder allowed herself to think only as far as the next big rock. Once she had completed her descent of the first pitch, Elder said that she looked up at the impossibly steep slope and thought, "Look what I've done! Exhilarated, I gave a whoop that echoed down the silent pass." Even with a broken arm, joy was Elder's constant companion. A good survivor always tells herself, "Count your blessings—you're alive."

ENJOY THE SURVIVAL JOURNEY

8   It may seem counterintuitive, but even in the worst circumstances, survivors find something to enjoy, some way to play and laugh. Survival can be tedious, and waiting itself is an art. Elder found herself laughing out loud when she started to worry that someone might see up her skirt as she climbed. Even as Callahan's boat was sinking, he stopped to laugh at himself as he clutched a knife in his teeth like a pirate while trying to get into his life raft. And Viktor Frankl ordered some of his companions in **Auschwitz** who were threatening to give up hope to force themselves to think of one funny thing each day. Singing, playing mind games, reciting poetry, and doing mathematical problems can make waiting tolerable, while heightening perception and quieting fear.

Auschwitz: a Nazi concentration camp

NEVER GIVE UP

9   Yes, you might die. In fact, you will die—we all do. But perhaps it doesn't have to be today. Don't let it worry you. Forget about rescue. Everything you need is inside you already. Dougal Robertson, a sailor who was cast away at

sea for thirty-eight days after his boat sank, advised thinking of survival this way: "Rescue will come as a welcome interruption of . . . the survival voyage." One survival psychologist calls that "resignation without giving up. It is survival by surrender."

10   Survivors are not easily discouraged by setbacks. They accept that the environment is constantly changing and know that they must adapt. When they fall, they pick themselves up and start the entire process over again, breaking it down into manageable bits. When Apollo 13's oxygen tank exploded, apparently dooming the crew, Commander Jim Lovell chose to keep on transmitting whatever data he could back to mission control, even as they burned up on re-entry. Elder and Callahan were equally determined and knew this final truth: If you're still alive, there is always one more thing that you can do.

COMPREHENSION AND CRITICAL THINKING

1. What is the meaning of *precipitating* in paragraph 2?
    a. ending
    b. unexpected
    c. initiating or beginning

2. In paragraph 7, what is the meaning of *pitch*?
    a. throw
    b. slope
    c. tone

3. How does the author introduce the text?
    a. general background
    b. historical background
    c. anecdote
    d. contrasting position

4. In this process essay, the author describes the experiences of several survivors. Briefly explain what challenge the following people faced.

    Aron Ralston: _____
    Lance Armstrong: _____
    Lauren Elder: _____
    Viktor Frankl: _____
    Dougal Robertson: _____

5. a. What do most of the stories of survival have in common? What kinds of threats were they surviving?

    _____

    b. How is Frankl's journey different from those of the others mentioned in the essay?

    _____

    _____

6. This process essay uses elements of narration and cause and effect. What are some of the effects of positive thinking while in a dangerous situation?

    _____

    _____

7. What is the author's specific purpose?

_____

_____

8. Who was likely the targeted audience for this essay?
   a. an academic or intellectual audience
   b. children
   c. a general audience

   Give some reasons for your choice.

_____

_____

9. What lessons does this essay have for the reader?

_____

_____

_____

10. Using your own words, explain why it is important to enjoy the survival journey.

_____

WRITING TOPICS

Write about one of the following topics. Remember to explore, develop, and revise and edit your work.

1. Describe a difficult physical ordeal that you know went through. What happened? What steps did you take to get through the ordeal?
2. Explain the steps people should take when they have an emotional crisis. For example, how can they survive a breakup, a public humiliation, or the loss of a friend?

READING 10

Into Thin Air
Jon Krakauer

> Jon Krakauer is a mountaineer and writer. In his memoir, *Into Thin Air*, Krakauer recounts the tragic tale of the 1996 Mount Everest climbing expedition in which he participated. During this expedition, many people who were Krakauer's climbing companions died when a sudden ferocious storm engulfed them. The next reading is an excerpt from Krakauer's best-selling book.

1   The literature of Everest is rife with accounts of hallucinatory experiences attributable to hypoxia and fatigue. In 1933, the noted English climber Frank Smythe observed "two curious looking objects floating in the sky" directly above him at 27,000 feet: "[One] possessed what appeared to be squat underdeveloped wings, and the other a protuberance suggestive of a beak. They hovered motionless but seemed slowly to pulsate." In 1980, during his solo ascent, Reinhold Messner imagined that an invisible companion was climbing beside him. Gradually, I became aware that my mind had gone

haywire in a similar fashion, and I observed my own slide from reality with a blend of fascination and horror.

2   I was so far beyond ordinary exhaustion that I experienced a queer detachment from my body, as if I were observing my descent from a few feet overhead. I imagined that I was dressed in a green cardigan and wingtips. And although the gale was generating a windchill in excess of seventy below zero Fahrenheit, I felt strangely and disturbingly warm.

3   At 6:30, as the last of the daylight seeped from the sky, I'd descended to within 200 vertical feet of Camp Four. Only one obstacle now stood between me and safety: a bulging incline of hard, glassy ice that I would have to descend without a rope. Snow pellets borne by 70-knot gusts stung my face; any exposed flesh was instantly frozen. The tents, no more than 650 horizontal feet away, were only intermittently visible through the whiteout. There was no margin for error. Worried about making a critical blunder, I sat down to marshal my energy before descending further.

4   Once I was off my feet, inertia took hold. It was so much easier to remain at rest than to summon the initiative to tackle the dangerous ice slope; so I just sat there as the storm roared around me, letting my mind drift, doing nothing for perhaps forty-five minutes.

5   I'd tightened the drawstrings on my hood until only a tiny opening remained around my eyes, and I was removing the useless, frozen oxygen mask from beneath my chin when Andy Harris suddenly appeared out of the gloom beside me. Shining my headlamp in his direction, I reflexively recoiled when I saw the appalling condition of his face. His cheeks were coated with an armour of frost, one eye was frozen shut, and he was slurring his words badly. He looked in serious trouble. "Which way to the tents?" Andy blurted, frantic to reach shelter.

6   I pointed in the direction of Camp Four, and then warned him about the ice just below us. "It is steeper than it looks!" I yelled, straining to make myself heard over the tempest. "Maybe I should go down first and get a rope from camp—." As I was in midsentence, Andy abruptly turned away and moved over the lip of the ice slope, leaving me sitting there dumbfounded.

7   Scooting on his butt, he started down the steepest part of the incline. "Andy," I shouted after him, "it's crazy to try it like that! You're going to blow it for sure!" He yelled something back, but his words were carried off by the screaming wind. A second later he lost his purchase, flipped ass over teakettle, and was suddenly rocketing headfirst down the ice.

8   Two hundred feet below, I could just make out Andy's motionless form slumped at the foot of the incline. I was sure he'd broken at least a leg, maybe his neck. But then, incredibly, he stood up, waved that he was O.K., and started lurching toward Camp Four, which at the moment was in plain sight, 500 feet beyond.

9   My backpack held little more than three empty oxygen canisters and a pint of frozen lemonade; it probably weighed no more than sixteen or eighteen pounds. But I was tired and worried about getting down the incline without breaking a leg, so I tossed the pack over the edge and hoped it would come to rest where I could retrieve it. Then I stood up and started down the ice, which was as smooth and hard as the surface of a bowling ball.

crampon: steel spikes attached to the soles of mountain-climbing boots to create a better grip on ice and prevent slipping

10   Fifteen minutes of dicey, fatiguing **crampon** work brought me safely to the bottom of the incline, where I easily located my pack, and another ten minutes after that I was in camp myself. I lunged into my tent with my

crampons still on, zipped the door tight, and sprawled across the frost-covered floor too tired to even sit upright. For the first time I had a sense of how wasted I was: I was more exhausted than I'd ever been in my life. But I was safe.

COMPREHENSION AND CRITICAL THINKING

1. In paragraph 1, *protuberance* means
    a. a bulge
    b. a disturbance
    c. a bird

2. Find a word in paragraph 4 that means "inactivity."_____

3. What type of narrator is telling this story?
    a. first-person narrator
    b. third-person narrator

4. What can you infer or guess about his personality?

    _____

    _____

5. In your own words, sum up the story in a couple of sentences. Remember to answer *who, what, when, where, why,* and *how* questions.

    _____

    _____

    _____

6. Describe the author's physical and mental state at the beginning of the essay.

    _____

    _____

7. What were some obstacles that the narrator faced during his descent to Camp Four?

    _____

    _____

8. This excerpt contains examples of imagery (description using the senses). Give examples of imagery that appeal to touch, sight, and hearing.

    touch   _____

    sight   _____

    hearing _____

9. Which organizational method does the author use in this essay?

    a. time order   b. space order   c. emphatic order

10. The author uses dialogue in this essay. What is the purpose of the dialogue?

    _____

    _____

WRITING TOPICS

Write about one of the following topics. Remember to explore, develop, and revise and edit your work.

1.   Have you or someone you know participated in a risky activity? What happened? Include descriptive details that appeal to the senses.
2.   In Krakauer's story, he describes his reactions during a challenging moment from his past. Think about a time when you felt extremely excited, ashamed, or moved. Where were you and what were you doing? Describe what happened and include descriptive details.

READING 11

Monsoon Time
Rahul Goswami

> Rahul Goswami is a journalist for *Orientation: Middle East*. In the following essay, he reminisces about the weather in his homeland. Pay close attention to the descriptive details.

1   My father used to tell me about the monsoon in Bangladesh. He was born in Handiyal, a village in the north-central district of the country. Behind his parents' house was a river, the Padma, a part of the immense water system that crisscrosses Bangladesh. Big even during the sweltering dry months, the Padma would become an inland ocean at the height of the monsoon. My father would talk about the river swelling day after day as the rain drove down. He loved the monsoon, despite the inevitable annual floods, the misery, and the hardship.

2   Years later, I moved to Dubai, where I lived until just recently. It is a modern metropolis—built on the edge of the great Arabian sand sea— glittering with glazed glass and proud of its impeccably maintained highways. It scarcely ever rains here. On perhaps five days a year, a few millimetres of rain will reluctantly descend. More frequent are the sandstorms, which clog drains that are tested no more than annually. This past year was my first full one in Dubai and the first time in my life I have missed an entire monsoon.

squalls: sudden violent gusts of wind

3   By June in India, when the first wet **squalls** explode over Bombay [Mumbai], one has been anticipating the rain for a month and more. Then in July, the massive, heavy cloud systems have settled immovably over the subcontinent, and they let fall torrents of rain, day after day. Indoors a patina of moisture coats everything, clothes will not dry, and head colds make one miserable. Outside, the city struggles with its everyday routines. Suburban trains do not run, their tracks submerged under feet of muddy water. City drains, routinely untended and choked with tons of garbage, refuse to do their work. Housing

archipelagos: groups of small islands

colonies turn into **archipelagos**. Mosquitoes assume fearsome proportions.

4   By August, the monsoon has dulled the world. Trees appear a uniform drab green, the sea stays grey and forbidding, and the city stinks. When, in September, the rains have at last weakened into ineffectual evening drizzles, one is relieved.

5   The monsoon season has, I discovered, a rhythm that the mind and body grow accustomed to. In Dubai last June, when the temperature reached 48° Celsius, I would catch myself glancing at the sky, wondering idly if there was a hint of interesting cloud. My rational self knew there could not be a monsoon here, but the subconscious would not be denied. Some mornings I would

awake in my darkened, air-conditioned room and imagine rain drumming on the window. It was an illusion that persisted several seconds into wakefulness, and even after I rose I would resist drawing the curtain aside, preferring instead to retreat to the even darker bathroom. Then I'd tell myself there is no rain, and I'd lace my shoes and step outside into the pitiless heat of Arabia.

6   Late in July, I noticed that the illusions persisted at work, too. With the window blinds down and the central air-conditioning humming along at a cool 22° Celsius, I occasionally caught myself wondering whether I'd find a cab that would be willing to drive me home in the rain. After all, it must be raining outside by now. At these times it took some courage to walk into the passageway between the office suites, face the window, stare at the Dubai skyline carelessly shimmering in the late evening sun, and remind myself that the monsoon lay on the other side of the Indian Ocean.

7   The sounds of rain would still visit, sometimes surprising, always comforting, while outside Dubai still blazed with heat and light. August slipped into September and as the body readjusted itself, the mind played along. As the Gulf's fall months began, the harsh absence of monsoon faded. I no longer looked for that high and lonely cloud in the sky. The time for rain had passed, and I wondered whether next year my longing would be the same.

COMPREHENSION AND CRITICAL THINKING

1. Define *monsoon*. _____

2. Find a word in paragraph 3 that means "violent flow or downpour."
    _____

3. In paragraph 3, what is a *patina*? _____

4. What are some effects of the author's decision to move to Dubai?
    _____

5. Using your own words, sum up the main idea of the essay.
    _____
    _____

6. What impression does the writer give of Dubai? Using your own words, describe that place.
    _____
    _____

7. What impression does the writer give of Mumbai during the monsoon season? Using your own words, describe what the city is like.
    _____
    _____

8. What is the dominant impression in Goswami's essay?
    a. joy
    b. tension
    c. homesickness
    d. anger
    e. despair

9. The writer appeals to more than one sense. Give an example for each type of imagery.

    sight   _____

    hearing _____

    smell   _____

10. Monsoons disrupt everyday life with intense and unending rainfall. Moreover, the extreme humidity is unpleasant. Why would the author prefer the chaos and rain of his homeland over the dryness and order of Dubai? You will have to make inferences.

    _____

    _____

    _____

WRITING TOPICS

Write about one of the following topics. Remember to explore, develop, and revise and edit your work.

1. Which season do you like the most? Describe that season using vivid imagery.
2. Describe an extreme weather phenomenon that you lived through. What happened? Include descriptive details that appeal to the senses.

Theme: Flora and Fauna

READING 12

Songs of Insects
Sy Montgomery

Sy Montgomery is a naturalist and writer. She has written many articles about animals and their environments. In the next article, Montgomery reflects on the methods of communication used by insects.

1   In his poem "Conversational Insects," H. I. Phillips has a confession to make:

> I long to interview the little Insects,
> and get the drift of what they're driving at:
> To chat with Wasps and Crickets
> In bushes, trees and thickets
> And understand the language of the Gnat.

2   If you share this poet's sensibilities, now is the time to fulfill your longing. Though widely loved for its changing leaves and migrating birds, early fall is, in some circles anyway, yet more renowned for the sweetness of its insect voices.

3   The insects' songs tell of longing and pursuit, rivalry and battle. If the song of the autumn field cricket suddenly becomes louder, more rapid, and higher pitched, he's located a lady and is calling to her. If his calls soften, she has come to him and is ready to mate. (Unlike grasshoppers, the female

cricket usually mounts the male.) If he encounters a rival, he chirps more loudly and the chirps get longer and less rhythmic. A vicious battle may ensue—so vicious that cricket fights were the entertainment extravaganza of the Sung dynasty in 10th-century China. The victors earned the title *shou lip*—"conquering cricket"—and were ceremoniously buried in little silver caskets when they died of old age.

4　Some insect songs convey information people can use. Because the insect's metabolism speeds up with the heat, the hotter the weather, the faster the chirping. The male snowy tree cricket, which begins singing in September and continues until the killing frost, tracks temperatures so accurately that, in 1897, Tufts College professor A. E. Dolbear developed a measurement formula accurate to within one degree Fahrenheit: count the number of chirps in 15 seconds and add 39.

5　Songs may have X-rated lyrics. Some species of grasshoppers, for instance, explicitly announce the moment of copulation with a distinct, sharp noise just before the male leaps onto the back of the female—a sound that one **entomologist** interprets as the **orthopteran** equivalent of "Oh, boy!" and terms it "the shout of triumph."

entomologist: a scientist who specializes in insects

orthopteran: a term for insects with folded hind legs

6　The autumn songs of these hopping insects are among the most lovely and lyrical sounds of the natural world, appreciated around the globe. For centuries, the Japanese have given one another gifts of singing insects. These tiny pets were so popular around 1820 that fishermen and peasants used to sell them in pushcarts door-to-door. Today, autumn *suzumushi* (bell crickets) and *kirigirisu* (grasshoppers) are sold in nearly every post office in Japan. In Africa, the songs of crickets are said to have magic powers. And perhaps they do. Henry David Thoreau described the song of one species as "a slumberous breathing," an "intenser dream." Nathaniel Hawthorne, describing the autumn music of the snowy tree cricket, wrote, "If moonlight could be heard, it would sound like that."

7　If it takes some effort for us to listen for insect song, it is because the songs are not meant for us; they are meant for creatures that wear their skeletons on their outsides and whose ears are on their elbows. Members of the grasshopper family, including crickets, locusts, and katydids, hear with small disks near one of the front leg joints. On the inside of the hind leg, grasshoppers have a comb-like structure with a row of teeth. They rub this comb against a ridge on the wing to produce a sound. And these songs are perfect for their purposes. Over the relatively long distances that these little animals must travel to find one another, looks mean nothing; songs call out the identity of the musician. For this reason, entomologists can sometimes better classify these insects by their songs than by their appearance.

8　Most autumn-singing insects prefer to perform on warm mornings, afternoons, and early evenings. But if you listen carefully, you may be able to hear one or another singing almost anytime. The greenish yellow marsh meadow locust prefers to sing on hot, quiet forenoons from moist ditches and grassy banks. At night, in areas that have been spared aerial spraying, listen for the katydids. They'll be squawking from the lindens, elms, and maples where cicadas sang during summer days.

COMPREHENSION AND CRITICAL THINKING

1. In paragraph 3, what is the meaning of *pitch*?
    a. throw
    b. slope
    c. tone

2. Find a word in paragraph 5 that means *overtly* or *clearly*. _____

3. How is the author's introduction unusual?

    _____

4. According to the author, why is fall the best season to appreciate singing insects?

    _____

5. In your own words, list some messages that singing insects communicate to each other.

    _____

    _____

6. What do singing insects communicate to humans?

    _____

7. How do people in different cultures value singing insects?

    _____

    _____

8. What type of singing insect is the author mainly describing?

    _____

9. The author mainly uses examples to support her main point, but she also describes a process. How do singing insects make their sounds?

    _____

10. What is the main idea of this essay?

    _____

    _____

WRITING TOPICS

Write about one of the following topics. Remember to explore, develop, and revise and edit your work.

1. List some elements in nature that inspire you or move you. Support your essay with examples.
2. How is your personality similar to certain birds, mammals, or insects? Give examples to support your main point.

READING 13

The Zoo Life
Yann Martel

Yann Martel, the son of diplomats, was born in Spain and currently lives in Canada. In 2002, he won the prestigious Man Booker Prize for his novel *The Life of Pi*, from which this excerpt is taken.

1   If you went to a home, kicked down the front door, chased the people who lived there out into the street and said, "Go! You are free! Free as a bird! Go! Go!"— do you think they would shout and dance for joy? They wouldn't. The people you've just evicted would sputter, "With what right do you throw us out? This is our home. We own it. We have lived here for years. We're calling the police, you scoundrel."

2   Don't we say, "There's no place like home?" That's certainly what animals feel. Animals are territorial. That is the key to their minds. Only a familiar territory will allow them to fulfill the two relentless imperatives of the wild: the avoidance of enemies and the getting of food and water. A biologically sound zoo enclosure—whether cage, pit, moated island, corral, terrarium, **aviary**, or aquarium—is just another territory, peculiar only in its size and in its proximity to human territory. That it is so much smaller than what it would be in nature stands to reason.

aviary: an enclosure for birds

3   Territories in the wild are large not as a matter of taste but of necessity. In a zoo, we do for animals what we have done for ourselves with houses: we bring together in a small space what in the wild is spread out. Whereas before for us the cave was here, the river over there, the hunting grounds a kilometre that way, the lookout next to it, the berries somewhere else—all of them **infested** with lions, snakes, ants, leeches, and poison ivy—now the river flows through taps at hand's reach and we can wash next to where we sleep, we can eat where we have cooked, and we can surround the whole with a protective wall and keep it clean and warm.

infested: invaded by

4   A house is a compressed territory where our basic needs can be fulfilled close by and safely. A sound zoo enclosure is the equivalent for an animal (with the noteworthy absence of a fireplace or the like, present in every human habitation). Finding within it all the places it needed—a lookout, a place for resting, for eating and drinking, for bathing, for grooming, etc.—and finding that there is no need to go hunting, food appearing six days a week, an animal will take possession of its zoo space in the same way it would lay claim to a new space in the wild, exploring it and marking it out in the normal ways of its species, with sprays of urine perhaps. Once this moving-in ritual is done and the animal has settled, it will not feel like a nervous tenant, and even less like a prisoner, but rather like a landholder, and it will behave in the same way within its enclosure as it would in its territory in the wild, including defending it tooth and nail should it be invaded.

5   Such an enclosure is neither better nor worse for an animal than its condition in the wild; so long as it fulfills the animal's needs, a territory, natural or constructed, simply *is*, without judgment, a given, like the spots on a leopard. One might even argue that if an animal could choose with intelligence, it would opt for living in a zoo, since the major difference between a zoo and the wild is the absence of parasites and enemies and the

abundance of food in the first, and their respective abundance and scarcity in the second. Think about it yourself. Would you rather be put up at the Ritz with free room service and unlimited access to a doctor or be homeless without a soul to care for you? But animals are incapable of such discernment. Within the limits of their nature, they make do with what they have.

6   A good zoo is a place of carefully worked-out coincidence: exactly where an animal says to us, "Stay out!" with its urine or other secretion, we say to it, "Stay in!" with our barriers. Under such conditions of diplomatic peace, all animals are content and we can relax and have a look at each other.

COMPREHENSION AND CRITICAL THINKING

1. In paragraph 5, what is the meaning of *scarcity*?
2. Martel doesn't state his thesis directly. Using your own words, write a thesis statement for this essay.

   _____

   _____

3. Using your own words, list the author's main arguments.

   _____

   _____

   _____

4. Martel compares a house and an animal's enclosure. What are the similarities?

   _____

5. In paragraph 5, the author refers to a leopard. What type of figurative language is he using?
   a. simile
   b. metaphor
   c. personification

6. In the last paragraph, the author argues that a good zoo creates a *diplomatic peace*. What does he mean?

   _____

   _____

7. Reread paragraph 1. The author suggests that people would not want to be kicked out of their homes. He then goes on to suggest that a zoo enclosure is an animal's home. Do you think this is a fair comparison? Explain your answer.

   _____

   _____

8. In paragraph 5, the author asks, "Would you rather be put up at the Ritz with free room service and unlimited access to a doctor or be homeless without a soul to care for you?" How would you answer the question? Explain why.

   _____

   _____

WRITING TOPICS

Write about one of the following topics. Remember to explore, develop, and revise and edit your work.

1.   Compare and contrast a zoo enclosure and life in the wild. What are some similarities and differences?
2.   Do you visit zoos? Why or why not? Write an essay giving your opinion of zoos.

Theme: Human Development

READING 14

Twixters

Betsy Hart

> Betsy Hart is a journalist for the *Chicago Sun-Times*. In the next essay, she examines adults who do not want to grow up.

1   Meet the Twixters: "Michelle, Ellen, Nathan, Corinne, Marcus, and Jennie are friends. All of them live in Chicago. They go out together three nights a week, sometimes more. Each of them has had several jobs since college; Ellen is on her seventeenth." They are all ages twenty-four to twenty-eight. They don't own homes, they are not married, and they don't have kids. Most telling: They don't want to own homes, be married, or have kids. As one Twixter, charming twenty-seven-year-old Matt—who took six and a half years to graduate from college—put it, "I do not ever want a lawn . . . I do not want to be a parent. I mean, hell, why would I? There's so much fun to be had while you're young." Ah, out of the mouths of babes. Why would he want such things, indeed? He's still a child, just in a man's body. It used to be that our culture presented adulthood as something valuable, so there was prestige in attaining it. Now we teach our children to fear adulthood—and so they stay children.

2   All of this comes from the current *Time* magazine cover story, "They Just Won't Grow Up." Well put. *Time* reports, "Everybody knows a few of them—full-grown men and women who still live with their parents, who dress and talk and party as they did in their teens, hopping from job to job and date to date, having fun but seemingly going nowhere." Ten years ago, they might have been called, well, losers. But not anymore. There are just too many of them. As *Time* puts it, "This is a much larger phenomenon, of a different kind and a different order." Now, the age from eighteen to twenty-five—and often much later—is seen as a distinct phase in life.

3   Some sociologists who observe this trend say growing up is just harder than it used to be. They are wrong. The problem is, growing up is easier and cushier than ever. And so, the 20 percent of all twenty-six-year-olds who live with their parents—you read right, one-fifth, typically rent-free or heavily subsidized—don't want to go. (How does one put a price on someone doing or helping you with the laundry, anyway?) No one is making them leave the family nest. It's incredibly cushy there, and why in the world would they go through the hard work of building their own nest when they have access to a much fancier one ready-made?

4   The idea that this is all about finances is silly. We're living in a great economy. And the Twixters are such big spenders, on eating out, new cars, and flat-screen TVs, that advertisers are now targeting these adult

adolescents, seeing them as something of a gold mine. The twixters have money. They just want to spend it on the fun toys and leisure activities.

5   Fewer young adults want to take a job they are not crazy about, one that isn't "meaningful enough," or perhaps live in an efficiency apartment and do their laundry down the street, while saving and working for something better. It is more fun to live better now, often at someone else's expense: mom and dad's.

6   Look, I'm not suggesting there should not be a place in the family nest for young adults during a trauma. Sure, parents should help those who are truly getting on their feet—meaning they are working, paying rent, helping around the house—and making plans to move on. I do know some young adults who move in with their parents to help take care of them. It might even be that some generations enjoy living together as equals. I'm just lamenting the adults who want to stay kids, whether they are living with mom and dad or not—and the parents who not only encourage it but subsidize it.

7   Growing up, becoming an adult and taking on adult responsibilities brings joy and satisfaction and disappointment and heartache and even fun. As a culture, the less we encourage that transition, the more we encourage young adults to stay in their "it's all about me" cocoon. The real problem? If we as a culture make it easy for these young adults to have no real responsibilities either for themselves or to others, we rob them of a tangible way to be plugged into and connected to their community and their world—and something bigger than just themselves.

COMPREHENSION AND CRITICAL THINKING

1. Find a word in paragraph 6 that means "mourning" or "grieving."
    _____

2. Find a word in paragraph 7 that means the opposite of "elusive and vague." _____

3. What are the main characteristics of a twixter?
    _____

4. Underline the thesis statement.

5. The author is defining a twixter, but she is also making an argument. What is her point of view?

    _____

    _____

6. What is the author implying in paragraph 3?
    a. It is society's fault that some people never grow up.
    b. Parents contribute to the problem of twixters by making home too comfortable.
    c. Young adults can't easily move out because it is too expensive these days.

7. What is the author's main point in paragraph 4?
    a. Twixters have a lot of money.
    b. Twixters spend a lot of money on games and toys.
    c. Our economy is doing extremely well.
    d. Twixters would rather spend money on themselves than move out of their parents' home.

8.   According to the author, how does delayed adulthood hurt the twixters?

_____

_____

_____

WRITING TOPICS

Write about one of the following topics. Remember to explore, develop, and revise and edit your work.

1.   Choose a term that refers to a particular type of adolescent or young adult and write a definition essay about that term. For example, you might write about *rappers*, *punks*, *skaters*, or *jocks* or you can define a new term that people in your area use.
2.   Define adulthood. What are the main characteristics of an adult?

READING 15

Guilt-Free Goofing Off

Brian Bergman

> Brian Bergman is a Calgary-based writer and editor who spent sixteen years as a bureau chief for *Maclean's* magazine. In the next article, he muses about the importance of procrastination.

1   Mark Twain once said, "The secret of getting ahead is getting started." He's right, of course. But it's not always as easy as all that. Think about it: how often have you put off some unpleasant or unrewarding task until it is nearly too late, or worse? The deadline looms, the pressure mounts, and, finally, you swing into action. In the end, more often than not, the deed gets done. But the stress is draining. You swear you will never put yourself through that again, but the vow is soon broken. Why, oh why, do we keep doing this to ourselves?

2   Piers Steel knows the answer. Or, at least, he has some extremely educated guesses. An assistant professor at the University of Calgary's Faculty of Management, Steel, 36, has spent more than three years conducting a "meta-analysis" of practically everything ever written on procrastination. He's pored over nearly seven hundred professional papers from the fields of psychology, economics, philosophy, and sociology, and examined historical documents dating back three thousand years. His conclusion? "Procrastination is our normal state of being," says Steel. "It's *not* procrastinating that requires effort."

3   Steel argues that, in terms of evolutionary psychology, humans were hard-wired from the beginning to attend to present rewards and dangers, rather than future possibilities. When life revolved around hunting and gathering, such behaviour made perfect sense. "It meant you were going to survive, mate, and feed," says Steel. But priorities started to change, first with the move to an agrarian economy, again during the Industrial Revolution and, most dramatically, in the current high-tech era. Goals and deadlines became increasingly long-term, as did the rewards for meeting them. Meanwhile, a tantalizing array of possible diversions—think television and, especially, the Internet—presented themselves.

4   Small wonder, then, that we have become a society of dilly-dallyers. A series of surveys taken since 1978 show the number of people who say they are moderate procrastinators has increased from about 15 to 60 percent, while those who admit to frequent procrastination jumped from 1 to 6 percent. It's also the rare individual who is entirely free of the vice; fully 95 percent of respondents say they put off the avoidable at least occasionally.

5   While there are many dictionary definitions of procrastination, Steel has come up with his own: "to voluntarily delay an intended course of action despite expecting to be worse off for the delay." The point is, the decision is not rational. The delay isn't for strategic reasons (as is often the case in military conflicts) or because of a lack of information. We know we should act, and that failing to do so will bring us grief. And yet we do nothing. "When we procrastinate, it's almost always about long-term objectives," says Steel. "Instead of attending to those, we go with what is more pleasurable or less painful right now."

6   Men are slightly more likely to procrastinate than women. Young people are far more likely to do so than their elders (high-school and university students are among the worst offenders). Impulsive people are especially vulnerable because they are so easily diverted. Different people procrastinate about different things. Workaholics, for example, almost always meet their job-related deadlines. But many of them will put off going to a doctor, doing their taxes, or seeking counselling for a troubled marriage. Typically, people feel bad about their inaction. "Often they are struggling against it, much like an addiction," says Steel. "People will say, 'No matter what I do, I can't seem to stop putting things off.'"

7   One of the earliest references Steel found is from Hesiod, a Greek poet, who wrote around 700 BCE. "Industry makes work go well," observed Hesiod, "but a man who puts off work is always at hand-grips with ruin." The Hindu text, the *Bhagavad-Gita*, which took written form about 100 CE, lumps procrastination in with a host of other personality flaws, including vulgarity, stubbornness, malice, and laziness.

8   A tad more recently, one of the giants of English letters, Samuel Johnson, wrote in 1751 that procrastination is "one of the general weaknesses, which, in spite of the instruction of moralists, and the remonstrances of reason, prevail to a greater or lesser degree in every mind." The esteemed author of one of the first English dictionaries was no exception. Legend has it that Johnson was once so late in delivering an essay for the periodical *The Rambler* that the publisher sent an errand boy to retrieve the manuscript. Johnson scrambled to pen the article as the courier waited patiently outside his door.

9   Writers through the ages have been particularly prone to procrastination. And in recent years, says Steel, the Internet has given them, and many others, yet another reason to dawdle. So much to surf, so little time to do, well, much of anything else. Perhaps it's only fitting, then, that the Web is home to several tongue-in-cheek pro-procrastination sites. Typical is the Saskatchewan-based International Society for the Promotion of Procrastination. Visitors are told that prospective members (the only kind they have, it's noted) should put their personal information as well as an unsigned cheque (post-dated, of course) into an envelope and send it to an address in Findlater, Saskatchewan. Alas, when one clicks to open the society's alleged postal code, nothing happens.

10   So if you are saddled with the curse of procrastination, what can be done about it? There are, says Steel, several possible remedies. It helps to understand the link between energy levels and delay: the more tired you are, the more likely you are to dither. So get plenty of sleep and exercise and deal with particularly aversive tasks in the morning, when energy levels tend to be higher. Another tip is to break down large projects into several staggered goals; as you complete each one, you are motivated to tackle the others. Personal routines are also good. By establishing a set of steps for doing things automatically, there's less chance for diversion. Steel offers the example of brushing teeth: children have to be constantly reminded to do it, but by adulthood it's become an ingrained behaviour.

11   Steel admits that his abiding interest in procrastination—he plans to write a book on the subject—has some personal roots. As a high school and university student, he would often pull all-nighters, cramming for a test because he had put off studying. And even now, he keeps temptation at bay by making sure his office computer is clear of all video games. But the Calgary academic has some encouraging words for fellow sufferers. "There's enough slack in our society that people can goof off occasionally," says Steel. "Most people can moderately procrastinate and still live pretty good lives."

12   Okay, then, take a break. Just make it a short one, eh?

COMPREHENSION AND CRITICAL THINKING

1. In paragraph 4, find an informal word that means "procrastinator."_____

2. The word *abiding* as it is used in paragraph 11 means

    a. living
    b. enduring
    c. tolerating

3. According to the article, humans procrastinate because

    a. in the past, their priorities were only hunting and gathering.
    b. humans cannot think in terms of long- and short-term goals.
    c. there are no rewards for meeting deadlines.
    d. their basic instinct is to consider their present needs.

4. What three stages of human history helped to create the problem of procrastination?

    _____

5. Find an example of a statistic, an expert opinion, and historical documentation the author uses to support his main idea.

    Statistic: _____

    Expert opinion: _____

    Historical documentation: _____

6. In your opinion, what is the purpose of giving historical examples?

    _____

    _____

7. What possible solutions does the author give to overcome human tendency to procrastinate?_____

    _____

8.   What does the title suggest?

_____

_____

WRITING TOPICS

Write about one of the following topics. Remember to explore, develop, and revise and edit your work.

1.   List types of different human frailties and give examples for each type.
2.   Describe common human characteristics that people view negatively. For example, you could write about jealousy. Support your ideas with examples.

READING 16

Fads
David A. Locher

David A. Locher is an author and college professor. The next excerpt about fads is from his book *Collective Behavior*.

1   Fads can take a wide variety of forms. However, almost all fads have a common pattern. They always appear quickly. They seem to come from nowhere and suddenly occupy the attention of virtually everyone. Then, as quickly as they came, they fade from popularity. Most fads can be placed into one of three general categories: activity fads, product fads, and fashion or apparel fads.

2   Activity fads center on some leisure activity like breakdancing or rollerblading. People suddenly feel excited about taking part in an activity that has never seemed appealing before. Prior to the 1950s, nobody felt the urge to stuff themselves into a phone booth with a large number of other people, and few have done it since then. However, it was all the rage for several years in the 1950s. Disco dancing came and (thankfully) went. Manufacturers often capitalize on these fads by producing a range of accessories to go with the activity. Often, music and movies that relate to the activity are rushed into production in an attempt to cash in on the fad before it ends. The song "The Streak," by Ray Stevens, and the film *Wheels* (a skateboarding film) are both good examples of attempts to make money from fad participants.

3   Useful product fads center on the acquisition of products that serve some purpose, however unimportant. In late 1998, "onion-bloom machines" suddenly became popular. Millions of people bought this kitchen tool designed to cut a large onion into a ready-to-fry "bloom" similar to the popular fried "onion blooms" served in restaurants. They were advertised on television almost every night. Stores quickly sold out their supply of the devices. The product itself is relatively useful, or at least serves some function. In this case, it makes a kind of variation of onion-rings. However, the product is neither particularly necessary nor terribly important. The vast majority of onion-bloom machines are probably gathering dust in kitchen cabinets and closets all over North America. Like many products at the center

of these fads, onion bloom machines remain on the market, but prices and demand dropped dramatically once the initial excitement wore off and people no longer felt the need for such a product in their lives.

4 Frivolous product fads may be the most interesting of all. People may stand in line for hours, fight with each other, and spend hundreds or thousands of dollars just so they can own something that is useless. The Pet Rock is the ideal example of this type of fad. In late 1975, an entrepreneur marketed a plain rock in a cardboard box called "The Pet Rock" and sold over one million at five dollars each (Marum & Parise 1984). The Pet Rock was not decorated, nor did it do anything. It was, in fact, an ordinary rock. Today it may seem difficult to understand why one million people would pay five dollars for a stone, particularly in 1975 when five dollars could buy a meal or two tickets to the movies. Such is the nature of useless product fads. They are always difficult to explain or understand after they end.

5 Fashion fads may or may not involve the purchase of a particular item. For example, millions of women purchased and wore "leg warmers" in the 1980s. These woolly socks without feet were worn over pants or stockings and were used for their look, rather than practical function. Other fashion-related fads may not involve buying anything. In late 1999, at the University of Missouri in Columbia, Missouri, hundreds of young women on campus began wearing their hair loosely gathered into a small ponytail that stuck straight up from the top of their head. The only accessory required was a rubber band. No products were purchased. The rapid adoption of the unflattering look and its relatively rapid disappearance would categorize the hairstyle as a fad.

6 Fads usually seem strange or even ridiculous in hindsight. Looking back, it is hard to believe that hundreds, thousands, or even millions of people took part in bizarre fads such as pole sitting, phone booth stuffing, and breakdancing. What drives otherwise normal people to pay money for a rock, to jump from a bridge or crane attached to a bungee cord, or to stand in freezing weather for hours in order to run, push, shove, and fight over a thirty-dollar talking toy? According to Turner and Killian, in their book *Collective Behavior*, there is nothing wrong with the participants in fads. Most of them are ordinary people. It is the situation that is abnormal. Once confusion and uncertainty set in, people can potentially be led into unusual behavior.

COMPREHENSION AND CRITICAL THINKING

1. In paragraph 6, what is the meaning of *hindsight*?
   a. the recollection of a past event
   b. an idea
   c. a more complete understanding of an event after it has occurred

2. Using your own words, define the term *fad*. _____
   _____

3. Underline the thesis statement.

4. Underline the topic sentences in body paragraphs 2 and 3.

5. Which type of fad does Locher divide into two categories?_____
   What are the two categories?_____

6. In paragraph 4, the author calls frivolous product fads the "most interesting of all." Why are they interesting?
   _____

7. Which of the following is not an example of a fashion fad.
    a. platform shoes
    b. ponytail hairdo
    c. rubber charity bracelets
    d. miniskirts

8. Look at the examples of fads that Locher presents. Which fads, in your opinion, are most ridiculous?

    _____

9. Using inferences, determine how marketers can help make a product become a fad.

    _____

    _____

    _____

10. Why do fads disappear?

    _____

    _____

WRITING TOPICS

Write about one of the following topics. Remember to explore, develop, and revise and edit your work.

1. What fads have you followed? Have you bought something silly, or joined in an activity that was suddenly popular, or worn your hair in a trendy style? Describe one or more fads that you have followed.
2. Write a classification essay about other types of fads. Make sure the fads are linked by a common classification principle. For example, you might write about types of body improvement fads or types of hair fads, or you might break down fashion fads or activity fads into categories.
3. "A fashion is nothing but an induced epidemic." (George Bernard Shaw, author) Reflect on this quotation. Why do you think some people are motivated to create or follow fads?

READING 17

Religious Faith versus Spirituality

Neil Bissoondath

Neil Bissoondath, a journalist and writer, immigrated to Canada from Trinidad when he was eighteen years old. He has written novels, essay collections, and short story collections. His works include *A Casual Brutality* and *Digging Up the Mountains*. In the next essay, he contrasts religion and spirituality. As you read this comparison and contrast essay, also look for elements of argument writing.

1   *Wait till someone you love dies. You'll see. You'll know God exists. You'll want Him to.*

2   The prediction, repeated with minimal variation through the years by believers challenged by my non-belief, was never offered as a promise but as a vague threat, and always with a sense of satisfied superiority, as if the speakers relished the thought that one day I would get my comeuppance.

3   They were, without exception, enthusiastic practitioners of their respective faiths—Roman Catholics, Presbyterians, Hindus, Muslims, God-fearing people all. Which was, to me, precisely the problem: Why all this fear?

4   And then one day, without warning, my mother died. Hers was the first death to touch me to the quick. Her cremation was done in the traditional Hindu manner. Under the direction of a **pundit**, my brother and I performed the ceremony, preparing the body with our bare hands, a contact more intimate than we'd ever had when she was alive.

pundit: Hindu priest

5   As I walked away from her flaming **pyre**, I felt myself soaring with a lightness I'd never known before. I was suddenly freed from days of physical and emotional **lassitude**, and felt my first inkling of the healing power of ritual, the solace that ceremony can bring.

pyre: a pile of burning wood used to cremate a dead body
lassitude: weariness, fatigue

6   Still, despite the pain and the unspeakable sense of loss, the oft-predicted discovery of faith eluded me. I remained, as I do today, a non-believer, but I have no doubt that I underwent a deeply spiritual experience. This was when I began to understand that religious faith and spirituality do not necessarily have anything to do with each other—not that they are incompatible but that they are often mutually exclusive.

7   Western civilization has spent two thousand years blurring the distinction between the two, and as we enter the third millennium we are hardly more at peace with ourselves than people were a thousand years ago. Appreciating the distinction could help soothe our anxieties about the days to come.

8   Spirituality is the individual's ability to wonder at, and delight in, the indecipherable, like a baby marveling at the wiggling of its own toes. It is to be at ease with speculation, asking the unanswerable question and accepting that any answer would necessarily be incomplete, even false. It is recognizing that if scientific inquiry has inevitable limits, so too do religious explanations, which base themselves on unquestioning acceptance of the unprovable: neither can ever fully satisfy.

9   A sense of the spiritual comes from staring deep into the formation of a rose or a hibiscus and being astonished at the intricate delicacy of its symmetry without needing to see behind its perfection of form the fashioning hand of deity.

10   It comes from watching your child being born and gazing for the first time into those newly-opened eyes, from holding that child against your chest and feeling his or her heartbeat melding with yours.

11   It comes from gazing up into the sparkling solitude of a clear midnight sky, secure in the knowledge that, no matter how alone you may feel at moments, the message of the stars appears to be that you most indisputably are not.

12   At such moments, you need no **dogma** to tell you that the world seen or unseen, near or distant, is a wonderful and mysterious place.

dogma: principle, tenet

13   Spirituality, then, requires neither science nor religion, both of which hunger after answers and reassurance—while the essence of spirituality lies in the opening up of the individual to dazzlement. Spirituality entails no worship.

14   At the very moment of my mother's cremation, her brother, trapped thousands of miles away in England by airline schedules, got out his photographs of her and spread them on his coffee table. He reread her old letters and spent some time meditating on the life that had been lived—his way, at the very moment flames consumed her body, of celebrating the life and saying farewell, his way of engaging with the spiritual.

COMPREHENSION AND CRITICAL THINKING

1. In paragraph 2, *comeuppance* means:
    a. rising up
    b. punishment
    c. reward

2. Write a synonym for the word *solace* in paragraph 5. _____

3. Underline the thesis statement. Be careful because it may not necessarily be in the first paragraph.

4. How does Bissoondath define spirituality? Give examples from the essay.

    _____

    _____

5. Why does the author object to believers who try to challenge his non-belief?

    _____

    _____

6. How does the death of the author's mother change him?

    _____

    _____

7. Why does the author give a lesser value to science and religion than to spirituality?

    _____

    _____

8. To support his belief in spirituality, why does Bissoondath give the example of his uncle in paragraph 14?

    _____

    _____

9. Bissoondath "soared with lightness" during the traditional Hindu ceremony and mentions the "healing power of ritual." How do such words contradict his strong opinions about religion? Explain your answer

    _____

    _____

WRITING TOPICS

Write about one of the following topics. Remember to explore, develop, and revise and edit your work.

1. Bissoondath went to a traditional Hindu ceremony. All human cultures have special ceremonies, festivals, and holidays. For example, Canadians may celebrate Valentine's Day, Victoria Day, Thanksgiving Day, birthdays, anniversaries, and marriages. Compare and contrast two special events that people celebrate.

2. Present an opposing point of view to the one presented in this essay. Defend the belief in religion. You can use yourself and others as examples.

READING 18

Medicating Ourselves

Robyn Sarah

Robyn Sarah is a Montreal-based poet and author. She has contributed essays and reviews to the *Globe and Mail*, the *Montreal Gazette*, the *National Post*, and *Books in Canada*, and her poetry and other writings have been widely published and anthologized.

1   It is hard to pick up a magazine these days without finding an article attacking or defending some pharmaceutical remedy for syndromes of mood or behaviour. These drugs are in vogue because they have shown themselves spectacularly effective for a range of conditions, though their exact workings are not well understood and their long-term effects are not known. Yet for all the noise we continue to hear about, say, Ritalin—for children with attention deficit disorders and related learning or behaviour problems, or Prozac and the new family of antidepressants prescribed to the stressed and distressed of all ages—the real debate on pharmaceuticals has yet to begin.

2   The enormous strides science has made in understanding brain chemistry have precipitated a revolution no less significant than the "cyber-revolution" now transforming our lives. The biochemical model has brought relief to many suffering individuals and families, removing devastating symptoms and lifting blame from parents whose contorted responses to a child's **anomalous** behaviour were once mistaken for its cause. But the very effectiveness of corrective pharmacology engenders an insidious imperative: we can, therefore we must. The realization that we can chemically fine-tune personalities—that we may be able to "fix" what were once believed innate flaws of character—has staggering implications for our understanding of morality, our standards for acceptable behaviour, our mental pain threshold, and our expectations of self and others.

anomalous: unusual

3   The medication debate should not be a matter of "whether or not," but of where to stop. Mental illness is real and can be life-threatening. But when is something truly a disorder, and when are we **pathologizing** human difference, natural human cycles and processes? How do we decide what needs fixing, and who should decide? These are not simple matters.

pathologizing: making a disease of

4   During my own school years, the boy who today would be prescribed Ritalin used to spend a lot of time standing in the hall outside the classroom. His "bad boy" reputation dogged him year to year and became part of his self-image. He learned to wheel-and-deal his way out of trouble by a combination

subterfuge: evasion
pariah: outcast

of charm and **subterfuge**; he learned to affect a rakish persona to mask what anger he might feel about his **pariah** status. But in spite of his often superior intelligence, anything else he learned in school was hit-and-miss. Such bad boys rarely lasted beyond the second year of high school.

5   Defenders of Ritalin point out that in making it possible for such a child to focus and sustain attention, to complete tasks and take satisfaction from them, the stimulant breaks a cycle of disruptive behaviour, punishment, anger, and acting out. Begun early, Ritalin can prevent the battering of self-esteem such children undergo in school; introduced later, it allows a child to rebuild self-esteem. These are powerful arguments for a drug that, when it works, can effect what seems a miraculous transformation in a "problem child," giving him a new lease on life in a system that used to chew him up and spit him out.

6   But Ritalin is not a benign drug, and many are alarmed at the frequency and casualness with which it is prescribed (often at the school's prompting) for a disorder that has no conclusive medical diagnosis. Some argue that children who may simply be high-spirited, less compliant, or more physically energetic than the norm are being "drugged" for the convenience of teachers and smooth classroom functioning. Others wonder if the frequency of **ADD** and **ADHD** diagnoses says more about the state of schools than it does about the state of children. Do our schools give children enough physical exercise, enough structure and discipline, or enough real challenge? A proliferation of troublemakers can be an indication of something wrong in the classroom—witness any class with an inexperienced substitute teacher. Pills to modify the behaviour of "disturbers" may restore order—at the cost of masking the true problem.

ADD: Attention Deficit
Disorder

ADHD: Attention Deficit
Hyperactivity Disorder

7   Something similar may be going on as diagnoses of depression and other disorders proliferate, especially among groups in the throes of life change (adolescent, mid-life, or geriatric). Just as physical pain is our body's way of alerting us to a problem, psychic pain can be a response to our changed position in the world. Psychic pain might indicate that we should reorient ourselves by reassessing and rebuilding our primary relationships. For instance, if I swallow a pill to conceal my existential problems—an "equanimity" pill—I may be easier to live with, but I may also be masking the need for some fundamental work to be done, some exercise of the spirit. Giving a boost to my brain chemistry might help me do this work, but it is just as likely to take away the urgency to do it.

8   I am myself no stranger to depression, but in eschewing the chemical solution, I have begun to sense I am swimming against the tide. For a while, I felt all the worse because so many of my peers, with lives no less complicated than mine, seemed to be handling mid-life pressures better than I was. Slowly it emerged that several had taken antidepressants at some point "to get over a rough spot." Some are still taking them.

9   The arguments are seductive. Why make things harder for ourselves, and why inflict our angst on others, when there is an alternative? One father I know, the stay-at-home parent of small children, told me he put himself back on Prozac (originally prescribed for migraines) because under stress he tended to be irritable, and things were more stressful with a new baby in the house. His irritability was not something he wanted to inflict on his children. Who could fault him for such a decision?

10   If we can really smooth our rough edges by popping a pill, why not make life pleasanter for our loved ones and associates by popping a pill? If a pill

can make saints of us all, where is the virtue in resisting this pill? But the effect may be to mask how many people would otherwise be doing "badly," which not only induces the unmedicated to bash themselves for their human frailties, but blinds us all to societal ills that may explain why so many of us get depressed.

11   The new pharmaceutical culture could stigmatize the unmedicated. It could make us all less tolerant of our frailties and those of others. It could keep us reconciled to the values that have put us in the pressure cooker to begin with: the worship of youth and success, the pursuit of comfort and expediency, and a model of wellness based on uninterrupted productivity.

12   Shall we lose the sense of what it is to be unique, struggling, evolving souls in the world, and instead use designer drugs to make ourselves smooth-functioning cogs of an unexamined societal machine? Aldous Huxley predicted it in 1932, in his dystopian novel *Brave New World*. Remember the drug *soma*? It has "the advantages of Christianity and alcohol; none of their defects [. . .]. Anyone can be virtuous now. You can carry half your morality around in a bottle." Huxley's book, on the high school reading list a generation ago, enjoys that same place today. But I am beginning to think the satire may have been lost on us. Perhaps it was too late for the message even when he wrote it. With our complicity, his vision gets closer every day.

COMPREHENSION AND CRITICAL THINKING

1.   In paragraph 7, what does *proliferate* mean? _____

2.   In paragraph 11, define the word *stigmatize*. _____

3.   In your own words, restate the thesis statement.

      _____

      _____

4.   In which paragraph(s) does the author acknowledge an opposing viewpoint?

      _____

5.   What strategies does the author use to support her argument? There is more than one answer.
      a. fact
      b. anecdote
      c. quotations from informed sources
      d. statistics
      e. logical consequences

      For each type of support that you have identified, underline a sentence from the text.

6.   Using your own words, list at least four of the author's main arguments.

      _____

      _____

      _____

      _____

7. The author suggests some causes of overmedicating in our culture. What are they?

   _____

   _____

8. What are some of the effects of using medication to modify behaviour problems?

   _____

   _____

9. How does the author conclude her essay?
   a. suggestion
   b. prediction
   c. call to action

10. Why does the author quote Aldous Huxley in her concluding paragraph?

    _____

    _____

WRITING TOPICS

Write about one of the following topics. Remember to explore, develop, and revise and edit your work.

1. Argue for the use of mood-altering drugs.
2. Argue that vaccinations should or should not be mandatory. You will have to do some research and support your points with the opinions of experts.

APPENDIX I
THE BASIC PARTS OF A SENTENCE

Parts of Speech	Definition	Some Examples
Noun	Names a person, place, or thing.	*singular:* woman, horse, person *plural:* women, horses, people
Verb	Expresses an action or state of being.	*action:* look, make, touch, smile *linking:* is, was, are, become
Adjective	Adds information about the noun.	small, pretty, red, soft
Adverb	Adds information about the verb, adjective, or other adverb; expresses time, place, and frequency.	quickly, sweetly, sometimes, far, usually, never
Pronoun	Replaces one or more nouns.	he, she, it, us, ours, themselves
Preposition	Shows a relationship between words (source, direction, location, etc.).	at, to, for, from, behind, above
Determiner	Identifies or determines if a noun is specific or general.	a, an, the this, that, these, those any, all, each, every, many, some
Conjunction	Coordinating conjunction: Connects two ideas of equal importance. Subordinating conjunction: Connects two ideas when one idea is subordinate (or inferior) to the other idea.	but, or, yet, so, for, and, nor although, because, even though, unless, until, when
Conjunctive adverb	Shows a relationship between two ideas. It may appear at the beginning of a sentence, or it may join two sentences.	also, consequently, finally, however, furthermore, moreover, therefore, thus
Interjection	Is added to a sentence to convey emotion.	hey, yikes, ouch, wow

APPENDIX 2
IRREGULAR VERB LIST

Base Form	Simple Past	Past Participle	Base Form	Simple Past	Past Participle
arise	arose	arisen	feed	fed	fed
be	was, were	been	feel	felt	felt
bear	bore	borne/born	fight	fought	fought
beat	beat	beat/beaten	find	found	found
become	became	become	flee	fled	fled
begin	began	begun	fly	flew	flown
bend	bent	bent	forbid	forbade	forbidden
bet	bet	bet	forget	forgot	forgotten
bind	bound	bound	forgive	forgave	forgiven
bite	bit	bitten	forsake	forsook	forsaken
bleed	bled	bled	freeze	froze	frozen
blow	blew	blown	get	got	got, gotten
breed	bred	bred	give	gave	given
break	broke	broken	go	went	gone
bring	brought	brought	grind	ground	ground
build	built	built	grow	grew	grown
burst	burst	burst	hang[1]	hung	hung
buy	bought	bought	have	had	had
catch	caught	caught	hear	heard	heard
choose	chose	chosen	hide	hid	hidden
cling	clung	clung	hit	hit	hit
come	came	come	hold	held	held
cost	cost	cost	hurt	hurt	hurt
creep	crept	crept	keep	kept	kept
cut	cut	cut	kneel	knelt	knelt
deal	dealt	dealt	know	knew	known
dig	dug	dug	lay	laid	laid
do	did	done	lead	led	led
draw	drew	drawn	leave	left	left
drink	drank	drunk	lend	lent	lent
drive	drove	driven	let	let	let
eat	ate	eaten	lie[2]	lay	lain

[1] When *hang* means "to kill or die by hanging," then it is a regular verb: hang, hanged, hanged.

[2] Lie can mean "to rest in a flat position." When *lie* means "tell a false statement," then it is a regular verb: lie, lied, lied.

(continued)

Base Form	Simple Past	Past Participle	Base Form	Simple Past	Past Participle
fall	fell	fallen	light	lit	lit
lose	lost	lost	speak	spoke	spoken
make	made	made	speed	sped	sped
mean	meant	meant	spend	spent	spent
meet	met	met	spin	spun	spun
mistake	mistook	mistaken	split	split	split
pay	paid	paid	spread	spread	spread
put	put	put	spring	sprang	sprung
prove	proved	proved/proven	stand	stood	stood
quit	quit	quit	steal	stole	stolen
read	read	read	stick	stuck	stuck
rid	rid	rid	sting	stung	stung
ride	rode	ridden	stink	stank	stunk
ring	rang	rung	strike	struck	struck
rise	rose	risen	swear	swore	sworn
run	ran	run	sweep	swept	swept
say	said	said	swim	swam	swum
see	saw	seen	swing	swung	swung
sell	sold	sold	take	took	taken
send	sent	sent	teach	taught	taught
set	set	set	tear	tore	torn
shake	shook	shaken	tell	told	told
shine	shone	shone	think	thought	thought
shoot	shot	shot	throw	threw	thrown
show	showed	shown	thrust	thrust	thrust
shut	shut	shut	understand	understood	understood
shrink	shrank	shrunk	upset	upset	upset
shut	shut	shut	wake	woke	woken
sing	sang	sung	wear	wore	worn
sink	sank	sunk	weep	wept	wept
sit	sat	sat	win	won	won
sleep	slept	slept	wind	wound	wound
slide	slid	slid	withdraw	withdrew	withdrawn
slit	slit	slit	write	wrote	written

APPENDIX 3
VERB TENSES

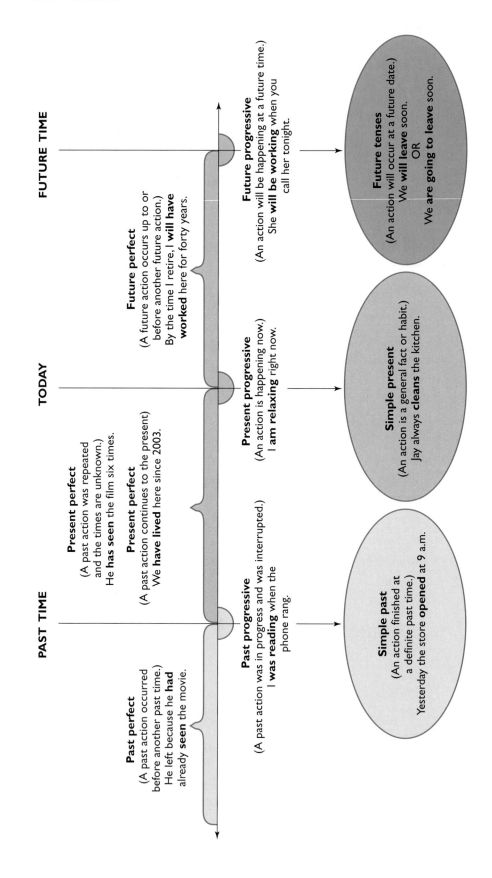

PAST TIME

Past perfect
(A past action occurred before another past time.)
He left because he **had** already **seen** the movie.

Past progressive
(A past action was in progress and was interrupted.)
I **was reading** when the phone rang.

Present perfect
(A past action was repeated and the times are unknown.)
He **has seen** the film six times.

Present perfect
(A past action continues to the present)
We **have lived** here since 2003.

TODAY

Present progressive
(An action is happening now.)
I **am relaxing** right now.

Future perfect
(A future action occurs up to or before another future action.)
By the time I retire, I **will have worked** here for forty years.

FUTURE TIME

Future progressive
(An action will be happening at a future time.)
She **will be working** when you call her tonight.

Simple past
(An action finished at a definite past time.)
Yesterday the store **opened** at 9 a.m.

Simple present
(An action is a general fact or habit.)
Jay always **cleans** the kitchen.

Future tenses
(An action will occur at a future date.)
We **will leave** soon.
OR
We **are going to leave** soon.

APPENDIX 4
COMBINING IDEAS IN SENTENCES

Making Compound Sentences

A.

B.

C.

Making Complex Sentences

D.

E.

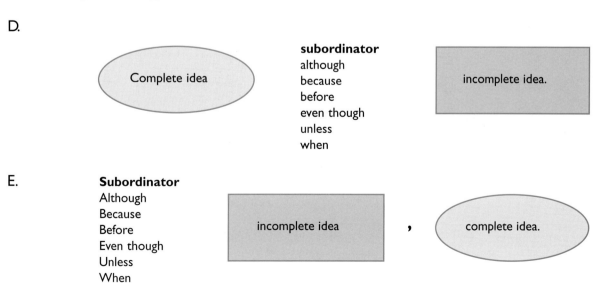

APPENDIX 5
SPELLING, GRAMMAR, AND VOCABULARY LOGS

In the first few pages of your writing portfolio or copybook, try keeping three "logs" to help you avoid repeating errors and improve your writing.

Spelling Log

The goal of keeping a spelling log is to stop repeating errors. Every time you misspell a word, record both the mistake and the correction in your spelling log. Then, before you hand in a writing assignment, consult the list of misspelled words.

EXAMPLE:

Incorrect	Correct
finaly	finally
responsable	responsible

Grammar Log

The goal of keeping a grammar log is to stop repeating errors in sentence structure, mechanics, and punctuation. Each time a writing assignment is returned to you, identify one or two repeated errors and add them to your grammar log. Next, consult the grammar log before you hand in new writing assignments in order to avoid making the same errors. For each type of grammar error, you could do the following:

1. Identify the assignment and write down the type of error.
2. In your own words, write a rule about the error.
3. Include an example from your writing assignment.

EXAMPLE: Cause and Effect Essay (Mar. 10) Fragment

Sentences must have a subject and verb and express a complete thought.

Also, an overbearing parent. That can cause a child to become controlling.

Vocabulary Log

A vocabulary log can provide you with interesting new terms to incorporate in your writing. As you use this book, you will learn new vocabulary. Keep a record of the most interesting and useful words and expressions. Write a synonym or definition next to each new word.

EXAMPLE: ubiquitous means widespread

Spelling Log

Grammar Log

Vocabulary Log

APPENDIX 6
READINGS LISTED BY RHETORICAL MODE

Argument

Cause and Effect

Classification

Comparison and Contrast

Definition

Description

Illustration

Narration

Process

Index

Credits

Literary Credits

Photo credits

Notes

Notes

Notes

Notes

Notes

Notes

Notes

Notes

Notes